ANNUAL EDITIONS

International Business

Seventeenth Edition

EDITOR

Fred H. Maidment
Western Connecticut State University

Dr. Fred Maidment is a Professor in the Department of Management of the Ancell School of Business at Western Connecticut State University in Danbury, Connecticut. He received his Bachelors from the Stern School of Business of New York University, his MBA from the Zicklin School of Business of the Baruch College of the City University of New York, and his Doctorate from the University of South Carolina. He also did post-graduate work at the Warrington College of Business of the University of Florida where he was a Resident Fellow. In addition to being the editor of Annual Editions: International Business, he is also the editor of Annual Editions: Management and Annual Editions: Human Resources. He and his wife reside in Connecticut and have four grown children, one granddaughter, and two grandsons.

The McGraw-Hill Companies

Mc Graw Hill   *Connect*
                Learn
                Succeed™

ANNUAL EDITIONS: INTERNATIONAL BUSINESS, SEVENTEENTH EDITION

1 2 3 4 5 6 7 8 9 0 QDB/QDB 1 0 9 8 7 6 5 4 3 2

ISBN 978-0-07-352875-5
MHID 0-07-352875-7
ISSN: 1091-1731 (Print)

Managing Editor: *Larry Loeppke*
Marketing Director: *Adam Kloza*
Marketing Manager: *Nathan Edwards*
Developmental Editor: *Dave Welsh*
Senior Project Manager: *Joyce Watters*
Buyer: *Nichole Birkenholz*
Cover Designer: *Studio Montage, St. Louis, MO*
Content Licensing Specialist: *DeAnna Dausener*
Media Project Manager: *Sridevi Palani*

Compositor: Laserwords Private Limited
Cover Images: © Colin Anderson/Blend Images LLC (inset), Steve Allen/Brand X Pictures (background)

Editors/Academic Advisory Board

Members of the Academic Advisory Board are instrumental in the final selection of articles for each edition of ANNUAL EDITIONS. Their review of articles for content, level, and appropriateness provides critical direction to the editor and staff. We think that you will find their careful consideration well reflected in this volume.

ANNUAL EDITIONS: International Business
17th Edition

EDITOR

Fred H. Maidment
Western Connecticut State University

ACADEMIC ADVISORY BOARD MEMBERS

Preface

In publishing ANNUAL EDITIONS we recognize the enormous role played by the magazines, newspapers, and journals of the public press in providing current, first-rate educational information in a broad spectrum of interest areas. Many of these articles are appropriate for students, researchers, and professionals seeking accurate, current material to help bridge the gap between principles and theories and the real world. These articles, however, become more useful for study when those of lasting value are carefully collected, organized, indexed, and reproduced in a low-cost format, which provides easy and permanent access when the material is needed. That is the role played by ANNUAL EDITIONS.

The theme of *Annual Editions: International Business Seventeenth Edition* is change. In September 2008, the global economy changed. It entered into the most severe economic recession since the Great Depression of the 1930s. Some people even labeled this period the "Great Recession." Actual unemployment in the United States reached levels that had not been seen since the last half of the Great Depression; the housing crisis was not just an American phenomenon, but a global one; and a small western country, Iceland, for all intents and purposes actually declared bankruptcy.

Governments the world over rushed to save their respective financial systems and the entire global economy was, for a time, in danger of collapsing. For now, the imminent danger that the world economy will collapse has passed, but the changes the economic crisis brought to the global economy and world trade have yet to be fully understood or realized.

The relative positions and importance of various national economies have changed. China has become much more important as have the economies of the rest of the developing world. In the United States, the debt the country has accumulated since the end of World War II is now beginning to impair the ability of the nation to grow and support the demands of its citizenry and its obligations. In Japan and Europe, the economic ramifications of population decline and stagnation are beginning to be realized as more people retire and fewer workers enter the workforce to take their place and support the social contract that provides many of the social services including medical and retirement benefits for an ageing population. While these problems are also present in the United States, they are much greater in Europe and Japan than in the United States.

The world is changing, and the financial crisis of 2008 was the first trumpet alerting the world to the changes occurring in the global economy. These changes, like any great societal change, will not come overnight. But they are coming. September 2008 was only the first of many financial, political, technological, and social changes that await the global economy in the future, the "Arab Spring" and the European debt crisis being only the most recent of others that are sure to follow.

The over 40 articles that have been chosen for *Annual Editions: International Business, Seventeenth Edition,* represent an outstanding cross-section of current articles in the field. This volume addresses the various component parts of international business including financial management, international trade theory, international marketing, foreign direct investment, the global corporation, as well as others. Articles have been chosen from leading business magazines such as *Business Week, Forbes,* and *The Journal of Business Strategy* to provide a wide sample of the latest thinking in the field of international business.

Annual Editions: International Business, Seventeenth Edition contains a number of features designed to be useful for people interested in international business. These features include a Table of Contents with abstracts that summarize each article using bold, italicized key ideas and a Topic Guide to locate articles on specific subjects. The volume is organized into five units, each dealing with specific interrelated topics in international business. Every unit begins with an overview that provides background for the reader to place the selection in the context of the larger issues concerning international business. Important topics are emphasized and key points that address major themes are presented.

With this seventeenth edition of *Annual Editions: International Business,* it is hoped that more will follow addressing these important issues. We believe that the collection is the most complete and useful compilation of current material available to the international business student that is possible in a printed edition. We would like to have your response to this volume, for we are interested in your opinions and recommendations. Please take a few minutes to complete and return the postage-paid Article Rating Form at the back of the volume. Any book can be improved and we need your help to continue to improve *Annual Editions: International Business.*

Fred Maidment

Fred Maidment
Editor

The Annual Editions Series

VOLUMES AVAILABLE

Adolescent Psychology

Aging

American Foreign Policy

American Government

Anthropology

Archaeology

Assessment and Evaluation

Business Ethics

Child Growth and Development

Comparative Politics

Criminal Justice

Developing World

Drugs, Society, and Behavior

Dying, Death, and Bereavement

Early Childhood Education

Economics

Educating Children with Exceptionalities

Education

Educational Psychology

Entrepreneurship

Environment

The Family

Gender

Geography

Global Issues

Health

Homeland Security

Human Development

Human Resources

Human Sexualities

International Business

Management

Marketing

Mass Media

Microbiology

Multicultural Education

Nursing

Nutrition

Physical Anthropology

Psychology

Race and Ethnic Relations

Social Problems

Sociology

State and Local Government

Sustainability

Technologies, Social Media, and Society

United States History, Volume 1

United States History, Volume 2

Urban Society

Violence and Terrorism

Western Civilization, Volume 1

Western Civilization, Volume 2

World History, Volume 1

World History, Volume 2

World Politics

Contents

UNIT 1
Overview of International Business

Part A. Introduction to International Business: The World Has Changed

Part B. International Trade Theory: Evolving Ideas on Trade and the Economy

The concepts in bold italics are developed in the article. For further expansion, please refer to the Topic Guide.

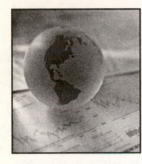

UNIT 2
International Finance

The concepts in bold italics are developed in the article. For further expansion, please refer to the Topic Guide.

UNIT 3
International Organizations and Operations

The concepts in bold italics are developed in the article. For further expansion, please refer to the Topic Guide.

The concepts in bold italics are developed in the article. For further expansion, please refer to the Topic Guide.

UNIT 4
Issues in International Business

The concepts in bold italics are developed in the article. For further expansion, please refer to the Topic Guide.

UNIT 5
The Future and International Business

The concepts in bold italics are developed in the article. For further expansion, please refer to the Topic Guide.

Correlation Guide

The *Annual Editions* series provides students with convenient, inexpensive access to current, carefully selected articles from the public press. **Annual Editions: International Business, 17/e** is an easy-to-use reader that presents articles on important topics such as *international trade policy, financial markets and exchanges, the monetary system,* and many more. For more information on *Annual Editions* and other *McGraw-Hill Contemporary Learning Series* titles, visit www.mhhe.com/cls.

This convenient guide matches the units in **Annual Editions: International Business, 17/e** with the corresponding chapters in four of our best-selling McGraw-Hill International Business textbooks by Hill, Ball/Geringer/Minor/McNett, and Geringer/Minor/McNett.

Annual Editions: International Business, 17/e	International Business: Competing in the Global Marketplace, 9/e by Hill	Global Business Today, 8/e by Hill	MP International Business with CESIM Global Challenge Simulation Access Card, 13/e by Ball/Geringer/Minor/McNett	M: International Business, by Geringer/Minor/McNett
Unit 1: Overview of International Business	**Chapter 1:** Globalization **Chapter 6:** International Trade Theory	**Chapter 1:** Globalization **Chapter 5:** International Trade Theory	**Chapter 1:** The Rapid Change of International Business	**Chapter 1:** The Rapid Change of International Business
Unit 2: International Finance	**Chapter 9:** Regional Economic Integration **Chapter 10:** The Foreign Exchange Market **Chapter 12:** The Global Capital Market	**Chapter 2:** National Differences in Political Economy **Chapter 7:** Foreign Direct Investment **Chapter 10:** The International Monetary System	**Chapter 2:** International Trade and Foreign Direct Investment **Chapter 8:** Understanding the International Monetary System and Financial Forces **Chapter 12:** Assessing and Analyzing Markets **Chapter 15:** Marketing Internationally	**Chapter 2:** Foreign Direct Investment: Theory and Evidence **Chapter 8:** Financial Forces **Chapter 17:** Financial Management
Unit 3: International Organizations and Operations	**Chapter 2:** National Differences in Political Economy **Chapter 4:** Differences in Culture **Chapter 6:** International Trade Theory **Chapter 7:** The Political Economy of International Trade **Chapter 8:** Foreign Direct Investment **Chapter 9:** Regional Economic Integration **Chapter 15:** Entry Strategy and Strategic Alliances **Chapter 16:** Exporting, Importing, and Countertrade **Chapter 17:** Production, Outsourcing, and Logistics	**Chapter 3:** National Differences in Culture **Chapter 5:** International Trade Theory **Chapter 6:** The Political Economy of International Trade **Chapter 7:** Foreign Direct Investment **Chapter 8:** Regional Economic Integration **Chapter 11:** The Strategy of International Business **Chapter 12:** Entering Foreign Markets **Chapter 13:** Exporting, Importing, and Countertrade **Chapter 14:** Global Production, Outsourcing, and Logistics	**Chapter 3:** International Institutions from an International Business Perspective **Chapter 6:** Political and Trade Forces **Chapter 10:** Organizational Design and Control **Chapter 11:** Global Leadership Issues and Practices **Chapter 12:** Assessing and Analyzing Markets **Chapter 13:** Entry Modes **Chapter 14:** Export and Import Practices **Chapter 15:** Marketing Internationally **Chapter 16:** Global Operations and Supply Chain Management **Chapter 17:** Managing Human Resources in an International Context	**Chapter 3:** The Dynamics of International Institutions **Chapter 6:** Political Forces **Chapter 7:** Legal Forces **Chapter 8:** Financial Forces **Chapter 9:** Labor Forces **Chapter 11:** Organizational Design and Control **Chapter 12:** Assessing and Analyzing Markets **Chapter 13:** Entry Modes, Export and Import Practices **Chapter 14:** Marketing Internationally **Chapter 15:** Global Operations and Supply Chain Management **Chapter 16:** Human Resource Management **Chapter 17:** Financial Management
Unit 4: Issues in International Business	**Chapter 8:** Foreign Direct Investment **Chapter 12:** The Global Capital Market **Chapter 16:** Exporting, Importing, and Countertrade **Chapter 17:** Production, Outsourcing, and Logistics **Chapter 18:** Global Marketing and R&D **Chapter 19:** Global Human Resource Management **Chapter 20:** Accounting and Finance in the International Business	**Chapter 7:** Foreign Direct Investment **Chapter 14:** Global Production, Outsourcing, and Logistics **Chapter 15:** Global Marketing and R&D **Chapter 16:** Global Human Resource Management	**Chapter 1:** The Rapid Change of International Business **Chapter 5:** Natural Resources and Environmental Sustainability **Chapter 6:** Political and Trade Forces **Chapter 9:** International Competitive Strategy **Chapter 11:** Global Leadership Issues and Practices **Chapter 17:** Managing Human Resources in an International Context	**Chapter 1:** The Rapid Change of International Business **Chapter 5:** Natural Resources and Environmental Sustainability **Chapter 6:** Political Forces **Chapter 10:** International Competitive Strategy **Chapter 16:** Human Resource Management
Unit 5: The Future and International Business	**Chapter 1:** Globalization	**Chapter 1:** Globalization	**Chapter 1:** The Rapid Change of International Business	**Chapter 1:** The Rapid Change of International Business

Topic Guide

This topic guide suggests how the selections in this book relate to the subjects covered in your course. You may want to use the topics listed on these pages to search the Web more easily.

On the following pages a number of websites have been gathered specifically for this book. They are arranged to reflect the units of this Annual Editions reader. You can link to these sites by going to www.mhhe.com/cls

All the articles that relate to each topic are listed below the bold-faced term.

Accounting
8. International Financial Regulation after the Crisis
10. Why a Second Bretton Woods Won't Work
11. The Balance of Payments: Office for National Statistics
12. The Next 80 Years
13. Internationalizing Business
15. Preparing for Significant, Multi-Year Changes
16. The Case for Global Accounting
28. Keynote Panel Session 1: Whose Income Is It? How Business Is Caught in the Global Competition and Controversy for Tax Revenues
33. Corporate Social Responsibility Reporting

Consumer behavior
1. World War II to 2011: Changes and Challenges in the Global Economy
20. Increasing Your Share of a Culturally Diverse Audience
21. General Mills' Global Sweet Spot
22. Expanding Opportunity at the Base of the Pyramid
23. Hailun Piano and the Quest for Quality
27. Explaining High Oil Prices
32. How Civil Society Can Help: Sweatshop Workers as Globalization's Consequence
37. The New Population Bomb: The Four Megatrends That Will Change the World

Corporate culture
5. A Bretton Woods for Innovation
14. Engaging China: Strategies for the Small Internationalizing Firm
15. Preparing for Significant, Multi-Year Changes
16. The Case for Global Accounting
19. NanoTech Firm Takes Passage to India
20. Increasing Your Share of a Culturally Diverse Audience
22. Expanding Opportunity at the Base of the Pyramid
23. Hailun Piano and the Quest for Quality
24. Distant Dilemmas
32. How Civil Society Can Help: Sweatshop Workers as Globalization's Consequence
33. Map Room: Global Graft
35. Current Mission Statement Emphasis: Be Ethical and Go Global
36. Corporate Social Responsibility: Pros and Cons

Developing countries
1. World War II to 2011: Changes and Challenges in the Global Economy
2. China Must Carry the World
3. Terra Instabilis: From the Arab Spring to the Great Recession to the Eurozone Crisis and Chinese Inflation: Are We Headed toward a New World Disorder?
4. The Theory of Competitive Advantage: Why It Is Wrong
5. A Bretton Woods for Innovation
6. Globalization with a Human Face
9. Solutions and Pitfalls
10. Why a Second Bretton Woods Won't Work
14. Engaging China: Strategies for the Small Internationalizing Firm
18. Going Global: The Risks and Rewards of China's New International Expansion
19. NanoTech Firm Takes Passage to India
20. Increasing Your Share of a Culturally Diverse Audience
22. Expanding Opportunity at the Base of the Pyramid
23. Hailun Piano and the Quest for Quality
25. The Impact of Globalization on Income and Employment. The Downside of Integrating Markets
26. Learn the Landscape: When Managing Benefits Globally, Government-Provided Services, National Mandates and Cultural Expectations Come into Play
27. Explaining High Oil Prices

30. Foreign Aid, Capitalist Style
31. Emerging Challenges: Emerging Markets Must Adapt to the New Global Reality by Building on Their Economic Success
32. How Civil Society Can Help: Sweatshop Workers as Globalization's Consequence
33. Map Room: Global Graft
34. Deadly Business in Moscow
36. Corporate Social Responsibility: Pros and Cons
37. The New Population Bomb: The Four Megatrends That Will Change the World
38. The Man Who Named the Future
39. The Future of History: Can Liberal Democracy Survive the Decline of the Middle Class?

Economic organizations
1. World War II to 2011: Changes and Challenges in the Global Economy
3. Terra Instabilis: From the Arab Spring to the Great Recession to the Eurozone Crisis and Chinese Inflation: Are We Headed toward a New World Disorder?
4. The Theory of Competitive Advantage: Why It Is Wrong
5. A Bretton Woods for Innovation
6. Globalization with a Human Face
8. International Financial Regulation after the Crisis
9. Solutions and Pitfalls
10. Why a Second Bretton Woods Won't Work
12. The Next 80 Years
13. Internationalizing Business
16. The Case for Global Accounting
17. The Work Left Undone: Perspectives on Small Business Opportunities in International Trade
18. Going Global: The Risks and Rewards of China's New International Expansion
19. NanoTech Firm Takes Passage to India
25. The Impact of Globalization on Income and Employment. The Downside of Integrating Markets
27. Explaining High Oil Prices
28. Keynote Panel Session 1: Whose Income Is It? How Business Is Caught in the Global Competition and Controversy for Tax Revenues
30. Foreign Aid Capitalist Style
31. Emerging Challenges: Emerging Markets Must Adapt to the New Global Reality by Building on Their Economic Success
32. How Civil Society Can Help: Sweatshop Workers as Globalization's Consequence
33. Map Room: Global Graft
35. Current Mission Statement Emphasis: Be Ethical and Go Global
36. Corporate Social Responsibility: Pros and Cons
37. The New Population Bomb: The Four Megatrends That Will Change the World
39. The Future of History: Can Liberal Democracy Survive the Decline of the Middle Class?
41. Finding a Job in the 21st Century

Ethics and international business
6. Globalization with a Human Face
7. The Global Debt Bomb
9. Solutions and Pitfalls
12. The Next 80 Years
14. Engaging China: Strategies for the Small Internationalizing Firm
16. The Case for Global Accounting
18. Going Global: The Risks and Rewards of China's New International Expansion
19. NanoTech Firm Takes Passage to India
23. Hailun Piano and the Quest for Quality
24. Distant Dilemmas
25. The Impact of Globalization on Income and Employment. The Downside of Integrating Markets

Global business strategy

Global Corporations

Global marketing

Globalization

Internet References

The following Internet sites have been selected to support the articles found in this reader. These sites were available at the time of publication. However, because websites often change their structure and content, the information listed may no longer be available. We invite you to visit www.mhhe.com/cls for easy access to these sites.

Annual Editions: International Business

General Sources

American Bar Association
www.abanet.org

The U.S. association for attorneys.

Business Week
www.businessweek.com

The online edition of Business Week includes information on the latest business news.

Chamber of Commerce, World Network
www.worldchamber.com

This site of the World Chamber Network and industry describes itself as "the world's oldest and largest business network." Access a global index of Chambers of Commerce Y Industry and Chambers of International Business, as well as information on "Strategic Alliance Partners," such as G-7.

International Business Times
http://ibtimes.com

"The mission of the International Business Times is to empower readers by bringing clarity and simplicity to global markets."

International Law Institute
www.ili.org

This site of the International Law Institute contains valuable research tools and links to Web resources regarding international law.

WashLaw
www.washlaw.edu

This site from the Washburn University School of Law Library reference desk can direct you to primary documents related to GATT and other information about the agreement. It also reproduces world constitutions and the text of NAFTA and other major treaties.

World Trade Centers Association (WTCA)
www.wtca.org

WTCS Online presents this site as a news and information service. Members can access the Dun & Bradstreet Exporters Encyclopedia and other valuable sources, and guests to the site can also gain entry to interesting trade-related information.

UNIT 1: Overview of International Business

Globalization
www.mtholyoke.edu/acad/global/index.html

This website contains a collection of scholarly papers dealing with the topic of globalization that can be of interest to the reader.

Information Institute: Law About . . . Pages
www.law.cornell.edu/topics/index.html

Explore this site's searchable index to learn about myriad international legal subjects. Organized by topic, it provides useful summaries with links to key primary source material and off-net references.

International Business Times
http://ibtimes.com

"The mission of the International Business Times is to empower readers by bringing clarity and simplicity to global markets."

The United Nations
www.un.org

The website of the United Nations.

UNIT 2: International Finance

American Finance Association
www.afajof.org/default.asp

The online site of the Journal of Finance, starting with articles and abstracts from February 1998 to the present.

Economist on the Internet (Resources)
www.rfe.org

International economic organizations such as the World Bank, the International Monetary Fund, the Organization for Economic Cooperation and Development are discussed here.

Financial Times (The)
www.ft.com

The website of the Financial Times of London. A financial newspaper dealing with business news from a non-American perspective.

Foreign Direct Investment Is on the Rise around the World
www.neweconomyindex.org

FDI data are a clear indicator of the trend toward globalization, as this report demonstrates.

Institute of International Bankers (IIB)
www.iib.org

Examine this site for information on the Institute of International Bankers (IIB), IIB events and publications in order to become familiar with trends in international banking. The site also features regulatory compliance issues relating to the year 2000 date change.

International Monetary Fund (IMF)
www.imf.org

The International Monetary Fund was founded by the Bretton Woods Agreement at the end of World War II and is designed to help and assist the global economy and to bring stability to the international marketplace.

Lex Mercatoria: International Trade Law Monitor
www.lexmercatoria.net

Access a number or resources related to international trade from this site, including data on the European Union and the International Monetary Fund. Among it many links, it addresses such topics as Principles of International Commercial Contracts and UN Arbitration Laws.

North American Free Trade Association (NAFTA)
www.nafta-sec-alena.org

NAFTA's stated objective is "to provide accurate and timely information to U.S. Exporters experiencing market assess barriers in Canada or Mexico."

Resources for Economist on the Internet
www.rfe.org

This site and its links are essential reading for those interested in learning about the Organization for Economic Cooperation and Development, the World Bank, the International Monetary Fund, and other important international organizations.

Internet References

World Bank
www.worldbank.org

Like its sister organization, the IMF, the World Bank was also founded as a result of the Bretton Woods Agreement. It is often the lender of last resort when countries are in financial difficulty and need funds.

World Trade Organization
www.wto.org

The World Trade Organization is the successor to the GATT agreements and is the organization that handles trade disputes between nations, often involving tariffs and quotas.

UNIT 3: International Organizations and Operations

CIA home page
www.cia.gov

The CIA covers news and events inside the intelligence community from the war on terror to all aspects of intelligence.

European Union
www.europa.eu

The website of the European Union.

Harvard Business School
www.hbs.edu

Harvard Business School's website provides useful links to library and research resources relating to the *Harvard Business Review* and to information regarding executive education opportunities.

International Business Resources on the WWW
http://globaledge.msu.edu/ibrd/ibrd.asp

Michigan State University's Center for International Business Education and Research provides this site that allows a keyword search and points you to a great deal of trade information and leads, government resources, and related periodicals. It also provides general and specific country and regional information.

International Labor Organization
www.ilo.org

ILO's home page leads to links that describe the goals of the organization and summarizes international labor standards and human rights. The site's official UN website locator can point you to many other useful resources.

Organization for Economic Cooperation and Development
www.oecd.org

The Organization for Economic Cooperation and Development has many reports and statistics available regarding international trade and development.

Outsourcing Center
www.outsourcingcenter.com

An Internet portal on methods for creating competitive advantages. The Outsourcing Center is part of the Everest Group.

Sales and Marketing Executive International (SME)
www.smei.org

Visit this home page of the worldwide association SME. Through the "Digital Resource Mall," you can access research and useful articles on sales and management. You can even listen in an marketing leaders discuss their latest strategies and ideas.

United States Department of State
www.state.gov/www/policy.html

Information on economic, social, political, legal, and global conditions is provided by the United States Department of State. There are extensive links for global issues and regional affairs.

United States Trade Representative (USTR)
www.ustr.gov

The home page of the U.S. Trade Representative provides links to many other U.S. government resources of value to those interested in international business. It notes important trade-related speeches and agreements and describes the mission of USTR.

UNIT 4: Issues in International Business

China.org
www.china.org

The official website of China.

CIVICUS
http://civicus.org

Civicus is a World Alliance for Citizen Participation. It is an international alliance of members and partners that constitutes an influential network of organizations at the local, national and international levels.

Downsizing of America
www.nytimes.com/specials/downsize/glance.html

A complete seven-week series on downsizing in America is available on the web by *The New York Times* where it originally appeared.

Green Peace
www.greenpeace.org/usa

Green Peace is a conservation organization that believes in direct action in protecting the environment and endangered species. It has been particularly successful in drawing the world's attention to the practice of whaling.

The Development Gateway
www.developmentgateway.org

The Development Gateway is an interactive portal for information and knowledge sharing on sustainable development and poverty reduction around the world. It includes analysis of business opportunities.

The Economic Times
www.theeconomictimes.com

An online publication focusing on business in India.

UNIT 5: The Future and International Business

Commission on the Future of the Worker-Management Relations
www.dol.gov

The report was issued by the U.S. Federal Commission on the Future of Worker-Management relations. Issues addressed include enhanced productivity and changes in collective bargaining.

The Economist
www.theeconomist.com

The Economist is a news publication that deals with global events both inside and outside the United States. It gives extensive coverage to events outside North American.

The Futurist
www.wfs.org/futurist.htm

A publication of the World Future Society, *The Futurist,* is a magazine devoted to analyzing the likelihood of future events.

UNIT 1

Overview of International Business

Unit Selections

Learning Outcomes

After reading this Unit, you will be able to:

- Explain if you think the recent changes have made the world global marketplace different than in the past.

- Describe how the role of China is changing in the global marketplace.

- The theory of comparative advantage has always been the basis of global trade. Explain if you think it still applies.

- Explain how innovation can be channeled to benefit all of the population of the earth while at the same time protecting and rewarding the innovators.

Student Website
www.mhhe.com/cls

Internet References

Globalization
www.mtholyoke.edu/acad/global/index.html

Information Institute About Law . . . pages
www.law.cornell.edu/topics/index.html

International Business Times
http://ibtimes.com

The United Nations
www.un.org

The world has changed. In October 2008 the financial markets in the United States and the rest of the world suffered the most significant reversal since the crash of the Great Depression of 1929, and what some have called the "Great Recession" began.

This collapse in the financial markets affected all of the economics of the world. Everywhere, at least the growth in the gross domestic product (GDP) declined from where it had been the year before: Banks failed; insurance companies failed; corporations could not get financing for their operations. Commerce on both the domestic and global levels started to come to a halt. It was a financial and economic crisis of epic proportions.

In the United States, the government came to the rescue of the private sector with the TARP funds designed to rescue the banks and to shore up their balance sheets so that they could weather the financial storm that, in many cases, they had brought upon themselves. If the U.S. Treasury had failed to do this, there would have been many more failures of financial institutions in the United States that most certainly would have led to the failure of financial institutions all over the world. A financial panic on that scale would certainly have made the recession much worse, and what other consequences may have been produced by such massive global failures of financial institutions could only be imagined. The failure of Lehman Brothers was only a small taste of the kinds of consequences that could be brought on by a massive global financial failure.

But, this brush with catastrophe has brought many changes. The giant financial institutions that were considered to be too big to be allowed to fail and were therefore rescued in the financial bailout are being examined. Should an organization be allowed to grow to the point where it is so big and so important to the economy that it cannot be allowed to fail no matter how poorly run it may be? Is the management of that organization then given a license by society to operate with impunity in the marketplace, free of the discipline of the market because it is too important to the society and too big to fail? Is the current understanding of the economic environment, sometimes called neo-liberalism, really valid in light of recent events? These questions are addressed in "World War II to 2011: Changes and Challenges in the Global Economy" and "Terra Instabilis: From the Arab Spring to the Great Recession to the European Crisis and Chinese Inflation. Are We Headed Toward a New World Disorder?"

One of the facts that emerged from the "Great Recession" is the ascendance of China as an important global economic power. China has become a great creditor nation, holding much of the debt of the United States. It is one of the faster-growing economies in the world and was one of the first economies to come out of the recession caused by the financial crisis of 2008, while the developed world of Europe, Japan, and the United States are not expected to truly come out of the recession for a few more years. China has a middle class of between 300 and 450 million, about the same size as the middle class of Europe. It is now the largest market for automobiles in the world. It also is the largest market for cell phones with more cell phone users than there are people in the United States. Its economy continues to outpace the growth of every industrialized country. The "Great Recession" has made China now a pole in what was once a tri-polar economic world consisting of the United States, Europe, and Japan. In the new "quad-polar" global economy, "China Must Carry the World" out of the global economic recession. It is a new role for the Chinese and one that they must

learn to use not only to their benefit, but to the benefit of the global economy. Taking the role of one of the major economies of the world carries with it certain responsibilities. It is simply no longer in the interests of China to ignore the trading concerns of other countries whether they are large or small. Intellectual property rights, something that has been an issue with China for some years, are now really important, and the Chinese government must take them seriously. Counterfeit goods must be curtailed and contracts must be enforced. The Chinese economy may not be fully mature, but it is now large enough so that it must take on the role of a leading economic power because it is one, and that role carries with it certain privileges and responsibilities.

For centuries, economist believed that the rationale for international trade was the law of comparative advantage. The law of comparative advantage can be explained most simply as one country has the ability to make lots of product "X" but little of product "Y." Another country has the ability to make lots of product "Y" but little of product "X." Each has a comparative advantage in a product. The two countries should trade "X" for "Y" and "Y" for "X" respectively to maximize their benefits so that their citizens get the most Xs and Ys.

This may sound fine in theory, but in practice it does not necessarily work out that way. Cost structures in the various countries may be different. Price purchase parity may be different (in country A, a potato may cost $.25; in country B, only $.05). Given the nature of the global economy and the ability access global workforces, today it is much easier to offshore work to much lower cost venues than was the case 20 years ago. There will always be winners and losers in any economic equation, but now many of those losers would seem to be in the developed world as organizations seek to cut their costs in a hyper-competitive global economy. There would seem to be few winners in the developing world, especially among those in low skilled positions.

Global trade has always been viewed as an opportunity, and so it is. But it also has costs that are frequently ignored by society. However, now, with the "Great Recession" some aspects of global trade are starting to be questioned. Questioning is healthy, and nothing should be taken for granted or etched in stone, so rethinking some of the benefits of free trade is probably a good thing. The issue is still open, and it is important that when they do rethink free trade, they develop the right answers.

World War II to 2011: Changes and Challenges in the Global Economy

Robert Hormats and Ariel M. Ratner

1. The Emergence of Women

Today, I was at a celebration that Secretary Clinton and First Lady Michelle Obama held for the 100th anniversary of World Women's Day. I mention this because it was very impressive to see women leaders from all over the world there, and all of them had interesting things to say. Prior to this, I was talking to Secretary Clinton about World Women's Day, and I told her that I was going to give a speech to NABE. We then discussed the emerging role of women in transforming economics—a point that I have also addressed in previous speeches. When I was at Goldman Sachs, the firm published a report that quoted the Chinese saying that women hold up half the world. It is certainly true that women make up at least half the world—and in some countries a lot more than that.

Think back on the American economy over the last hundred years and look at the major changes. A hundred years ago, the economic role of women was confined to very few areas. One of the most significant changes in American law and society that has enhanced opportunity and productivity over this century is the change in the economic status of women. There has been a growing and more significant role for women in the American economy, albeit that this development has not been perfect and still has a way to go. Much of the contribution of women remains unpaid or underpaid, despite its vital role in America's success.

When you look at developing countries—particularly the Arab world, but many other parts of the world as well—one of the reasons some countries are not living up to their full potential—and this was described by a number of the women honorees at today's anniversary celebration—is that they do not give women the chance to participate fully, or even at all, in their economy. As a result, they are depriving themselves of half of their human capital, of half of their economic potential. It is increasingly clear, when you look at economies around the world and determine how likely they are to achieve progress over the next 5, 10, 15 years, that if they do not allow women the opportunity to participate fully in their economies, those economies are going to underperform dramatically. For strong economic performance, it is necessary to give women the education, opportunity, and the rights they need, as well as other reforms.

One of many lessons from what is going on in North Africa and other parts of the Arab world is that liberation has to include liberation of women. It has to include women's rights and women's opportunities. If these countries are really going to be democracies and economies in which participation is meaningful, that participation has to include men and women, equally and fully.

As far as American foreign policy is concerned, ensuring equal opportunities and upward mobility for women is very important for Secretary Clinton. It is also very important for me, and I think it is going to be increasingly important for all economies that want to grow in the future—in the Arab world in particular. Perhaps that will be one of the lessons from the people in Liberation Square in Egypt. They were not only men. Women were just as participatory, just as enthusiastic, and just as expectant that their rights will be provided to them as the men were. So, changes in opportunities for women are something we ought to keep a very close eye on because they will, to a large degree, determine the political and economic future of many countries.

2. The Emergence of the Global Economic and Financial System

The second topic that I want to touch on is the historic point at which we stand today in the global economy. When you look at the world right after World War II, there were no global financial institutions dedicated to economic growth and financial stability. One the many reasons for World War I and for World War II—particularly for World War II—is that there were no global effective economic institutions. There was no equivalent to the International Monetary Fund for financial stabilization. There was no World Bank to help developing countries: many of today's developing countries were colonies at that point. And there was certainly no World Trade Organization (WTO) or General Agreement on Tariffs and Trade (GATT) or universal trading rules. If a country wanted to be protectionist, there was no international set of enforceable rules to constrain it from doing so. If a country wanted to do irresponsible things, it did them. The United States as well as others did such things in very destructive ways.

After World War II, however, there was an understanding by President Truman, Secretary Marshall, Secretary Acheson, and many others on the American side and people like Jean Monnet, Robert Schuman, and others on the European side that if we were going to pull the world back together, we would have to have effective global institutions. Together, they built the institutions of international economic and financial cooperation that we see today. These have served the world very well for over six decades—from the aftermath of World War II until the present time.

What we face now, however, is a very different kind of world compared with the world we faced in the 1940s and 1950s. The big difference is that today we have countries participating in the global economy that were not participants 30, 40, or 50 years ago. Also, we have a huge number of individuals in those countries that were not part of the global mass of international consumers or producers. They were behind the Iron Curtain or the Bamboo Curtain, living in very rigid, state-controlled economies, with little real economic opportunity.

Now, we face a different world. We face a world with a number of rapidly emerging economies that are major players in global finance, trade, technology, and many other areas as well. So we need to find ways of ensuring that we find a place in this system that was developed and nurtured after World War II for these emerging economies to play a role. They benefited enormously from this system. Now, it is just as important that they assume greater responsibilities for that system.

An important characteristic of this post–WWII world compared with that before the war is that the economic and financial system became rules-based and market-oriented. Now one of our goals—one of our challenges—is to bring emerging economies into the global system in a constructive, participatory way where they not only gain benefits, which they have been achieving, but also assume responsibilities for making the system work well, which they have not been doing sufficiently.

The changes that have occurred in emerging economics are not just in their economic power, but also in the way that they affect how the international economic and financial system works. That is to say, if you were to look at the world 30 or 40 years ago, how did capital flows go? For the most part, capital flowed from industrialized to developing countries. Now, some developing and emerging economies, such as China and some other countries in East Asia and the Middle East, are major exporters of capital. And the United States is now a major importer of capital. So the nature of the financial system has changed.

We also see that the average debt leverage of a large, emerging economy today as a portion of GDP is roughly half that of the large industrialized countries. So these countries have not levered themselves up to the same degree as have the United States, Japan, and many countries in Europe.

3. The Re-emergence of State-Owned and State-Supported Enterprises

For a while after World War II, states played a major role in economic systems in most parts of the world. Then, the world went through a period of massive privatization, where the role of the state diminished. Now, we see the role of the state rising again, creating a 21st-century kind of challenge.

One of the things we are trying to better understand is whether the world is moving toward a more state-oriented economic model whether it is sustainable and what its implications are. By state-oriented, I mean state-owned enterprises, state-supported enterprises, or enterprises that enjoy favorable benefits from the state, such as preferential banking lies or immunity from anti-monopoly laws. There are a whole range of things that the OECD has categorized as being state-supported measures. In addition, you also have companies that are owned by friends and relatives of government officials that benefit from crony capitalism.

Many state-owned enterprises are in the oil industry, and many are in various areas of high technology, as well as more general areas of manufacturing, finance, and commerce. This type of situation exists in many parts of the world. Increasingly, private-sector enterprises are competing with state enterprises. In many cases, governments provide an enormous amount of support for those enterprises by using funds that they have accumulated as a result of foreign trade surpluses, by providing special benefits with respect to regulatory latitude, or by giving special export subsidies or import protection for these companies. The prospect of the state continuing to play a substantial role in some countries is likely to persist for some time.

So, we must decide how we work with such countries to create a level playing field where state-owned enterprises do not distort trade or international competition vis-à-vis private enterprises that do not enjoy the kind of preferences or the kind of financial support, special legal support, or advantages that some of these state enterprises or state-supported enterprises enjoy? This is becoming a major challenge because this notion of state-directed capitalism or state capitalism has become quite appealing to certain countries, in part because it seems to work very well in China.

There are a number of negatives, however, for the countries that adopt this model. State-supported capitalism is not as advantageous as it seems. And I think one of the things we need to do is to explain to governments and individuals that this model has serious Haws. First of all, most emerging economies that favor model must recognize that they are competing with countries that have much deeper pockets, like China. That is an unenviable prospect for developing countries with fewer resources.

Second, to the extent that governments provide preferential flows of capital to certain privileged entities—entities that they own or that friends of the leaders own—that makes it harder for entrepreneurial start-up companies to get the resources, regulatory benefits, land, or other kinds of support that they need to thrive. This will hinder economic growth and job creation. This is yet another reason that this state-supported model, which again, looks attractive for the moment, may not be.

Among others, the French formerly had a dirigiste model. The Japanese, too, had a model where the state played a greater role. But these countries and others have come to realize that state control caused—and in some cases continues to cause—major distortions.

Thus, in protecting American interests and in helping other countries to develop their own potential, we face a long process of trying to work out a set of common rules that produce "competitive neutrality" so that government assistance to state-owned or state-supported enterprises does not distort competition vis-à-vis companies that are not owned or assisted by the state.

4. The Internet and the Free Flow of Information

Another 21st-century challenge that was never envisioned by the people who started the GATT, the World Bank, and the IMF is the Internet. Secretary Clinton [2011] has recently given an Internet freedom speech, and I am going to give a speech tonight on very much the same thing [Hormats 2011]. The role of the Internet is really quite dramatic, and if there is one thing we have learned—if we did not know it already—it is that the Internet is something that governments—however they try—cannot control over the long term. And if they try to control it to limit access to one kind of information, they cause major distortions in other areas.

If you try to limit the Internet's ability to transmit political ideas, you also—because it is one Internet; one entity, and one infrastructure—limit the ability of your own citizens to get access to market information, to get information about developments in the global economy, and to exchange ideas on research and development across borders. Therefore, the notion of Internet freedom and the liberty of people to communicate with one another, and to exchange ideas within their own countries and across borders, is one of the very interesting new challenges we face in the 21st century. Franklin Roosevelt during World War II famously talked about the "Four Freedoms."[1] We are now looking at yet one more freedom and that is the freedom to connect.

By "connect," I mean to be able to exchange ideas, exchange information, and exchange views. Connecting presents opportunities for people not just to get new ideas about, and learn more about, what is going on in the world; for many people, it is absolutely critical to their jobs and their livelihoods. You can see this in developing countries where more and more people resourcefully use telephones, PDAs, and other devices to get information on when to plant and harvest crops, weather forecasts, and markets.

How do we keep the Internet open and accessible for the flow of ideas, the flow of financial information, and the flow of economic information? This is enormously challenging for most countries to figure out. For the United States, it is not a major issue, because we have had the notion of freedom of press, freedom of communication, and freedom of exchange of ideas since our founding and long before. For many countries, such freedom is not in their DNA; and therefore moving in that direction has posed a major challenge.

5. The Diffusion of Opportunity and Innovation

We also need to look at one more great challenge that relates to this 21st century: the desire of more and more young people, who are connected to the rest of the world, to achieve economic and political opportunity—to be enfranchised, both economically and politically. We are seeing this in the Middle East, and we are going to see it in other countries as well. This is a movement that has begun to grow and expand to a lot of countries.

Our goal in many countries has shifted to provide ways of supporting entrepreneurs, innovators, small businesses, and other entities that create opportunities for people to get jobs. This is an important American goal because it is quite clear that people who do not see an opportunity for upward mobility have little hope in their lives. Their frustration becomes a cause of instability in many parts of the world. Therefore, in rethinking our approach to foreign assistance, one of the things we do in the State Department is energetically sponsor programs to support entrepreneurs around the world. Also, we try to connect entrepreneurs in the United States with those in other countries. Together, they create viral networks of communication.

The interesting point about this is that if you look at one of the areas that has been so important to the United States—which is innovation—more and more we are seeing that innovation is not done by any one company. It is done by a researcher at Johns Hopkins, Harvard, Caltech or Stanford working with his or her counterparts in Oxford, Moscow, Beijing, Singapore, Tel Aviv, or Bangalore. Increasingly, scholarly works and research on new drugs, new sources of energy, and new technologies are done in a much more active way by collaborative efforts across borders. These engage not just people in developed countries but people in developed and developing countries working together and in developing countries with one another. The result is that the whole innovative cycle in the world has shifted from Thomas Edison working in his lab to create an incandescent light bulb, or Henry Ford developing a car in his garage, to more and more people using the Internet in more and more countries around the world. It is really changing and accelerating the innovative process and utilizing the best talent from around the world.

6. Globalization as an Opportunity and as a Threat

Let me conclude on one issue that relates to American policy and how American policy needs to evolve in this very difficult and challenging environment. We now see a lot of people who see globalization as a threat—as something that has been disadvantageous to Americans: either a threat to their jobs or a threat to stability.

There are people who are concerned about new trade agreements and resist them because of the additional competition that expanded trade produces. There are people who are concerned about more immigration, when in fact one of the reasons the American economy has done so well is that we have enabled the best and the brightest to go to school here and to establish companies or work in entrepreneurial companies in Silicon Valley and many other parts of the United States.

The fact is that we can see globalization either as an opportunity or as a threat, and one of the great challenges for the world over the next several years is going to be how we harvest the benefits of globalization while mitigating the challenges and the disruptive elements that come from the increased competition that emerges from globalization. We are going to have to do both. We cannot deceive ourselves into thinking that globalization does not mean disadvantages or challenges for people who find it difficult to adjust to international competition. Yet, for most companies and for most workers, the opportunity for future growth in jobs, incomes, and opportunity lies in tapping rapidly growing foreign markets, particularly in an environment where consumer demand in this country, for the time being, is going to be relatively modest. A U.S. recovery notwithstanding, the growth in consumer demand and demand for infrastructure around the world—particularly in most emerging economies—far exceeds what we now see and will see in the United States. So, we need to be very clear: in the 21st-century world, expanding trade is essential to increasing American jobs.

I see a real historic challenge for the United States today. One choice is that we can decide that we want to, in effect, retreat from the world economy or at least take only tentatively internationalist positions. This implies imposing protectionist measures or refraining from participating proactively in international trade agreements, thereby trying to shelter ourselves from the competitive challenges of the global economy and sheltering ourselves from various people who want to come to the United States to create jobs, create companies, or go to school here.

The other choice is that we can regard internationalization or globalization as an enormous opportunity: an opportunity for identifying and taking advantage of new markets and bright minds around the world—an opportunity for attracting investment from countries that have accumulated a lot of capital and are looking to diversifying their investments, just as we do with our own portfolios. Diversification is natural for countries that develop large amounts of reserves.

Do we want to try to maintain our openness to the best and the brightest from around the world, who want to go to school here, who want to come here to start companies, who want to come to work in American companies, as we have done in the past? Do we take advantage of these networks of international research that are increasing in terms of intensity and in terms of the quality of cross-border research? Or do we try to avoid this for fear that we are losing too many opportunities by partnering with other regions of the world?

These are the kinds of challenges that I think the United States faces today. This last challenge is international in the sense that it affects our ability to compete in the world, but it is domestic in terms of the kinds of policies that we need to pursue. What do we do when other countries do not play by the rules? One important issue here is piracy of intellectual property. Also, there are countries like China that have policies that force the transfer of technology or of innovation from American companies to domestic companies as a precondition for doing business there. There are a number of countries that give special preferences to their companies when it comes to government procurement.

All those things are compelling issues. And they are all issues where the United States has to take a tough position on behalf of its companies, particularly protection of intellectual property because intellectual property is so critical to the future of American companies. So is ensuring a level playing field regarding state-supported enterprises.

Most of our companies do not thrive because they are low-wage companies. They thrive because they have innovative ideas and creative talent and come up with new ideas and communicate them. All these things are important reasons for us to take very strong positions in international negotiations to be sure that the rules are fair and that intellectual property is protected, as well as undertaking a wide range of other actions to defend our economic interests. This is being done by the State Department and other U.S. government agencies as well.

But no matter how well we do in protecting American interests, the key point from a competitiveness point of view is what we do at home: in terms of education; of developing new sources of clean energy so that we do not need to be as vulnerable to disruptions in other parts of the world, and in updating our antiquated infrastructure. While China, India, Brazil, and many other countries are building modern infrastructure, American infrastructure has, in many cases, deteriorated or at best simply not kept up.

How do we maintain an R&D environment that enables us to develop new ideas and keep this culture of innovation going? The answer depends largely, of course, on the private sector; but it also depends, as we have seen in the past, on institutions like the Defense Advanced Research Projects Agency. Now the Department of Energy has its own Advanced Research Projects Agency playing a proactive role in supporting early-stage energy research and innovation.

So in the end, my worry—or at least my worry that I can do something about—is not so much that China and India and others are becoming more competitive. That was inevitable. These countries for decades in the 19th and 20th centuries had not undertaken major reforms. China started its reforms in 1979; India in the early 1990s. Those reforms were bound to produce dramatic results, given the talent these countries have. Along with South Korea, Singapore, Malaysia, and many others, these countries were bound to increase their competitive capabilities and technical skills and become more important financially and commercially. This was a change in the world economy that many predicted—although probably few could imagine how dramatically it would occur. The direction, if not the speed, was fairly evident.

The key point now is not to wring our hands over the fact that other countries are more competitive or in some cases are not playing by the rules that we think they should play by. We should of course focus on getting them to play by the rules, take tough action if they do not, and work hard to convince them that playing by the rules is in their long-term interest. But no matter how successful we are in conducting our international economic policy in terms of protecting trade rights and international rights in other areas, we will not be able to provide the benefits for our children and our grandchildren and maintain a strong national economy unless we deal with the fundamental issues that the President talked about in the State of the Union speech: to make sure that what we are doing at home strengthens our economy—particularly the environment for entrepreneurial, creative business—and enables business to grow, come up with new ideas, and hire new people. That depends on education, infrastructure, energy availability, and a sound long-term fiscal policy.

We have to focus a lot more on these things today: the president mentioned that we are in a Sputnik moment, but I would even go beyond that. Sputnik was sent up by the Soviet Union, now we are seeing Sputnik-like developments from all over the world. There are Sputniks from China, India, Singapore, South Korea, Finland, Malaysia, and many other countries. Such countries are all doing very innovative things and developing new technologies and competitive products. We are seeing Sputniks go up every day, every week, and every month posing new competitive challenges for the United States.

The key for the United States today is to identify the kinds of things we need to do at home, with a sense of vision about our own future and how to make ourselves a more competitive economy. Most importantly, we must ensure that the companies that operate here, our workers, and the students who are expecting a better life when they get out of school all have the opportunities to thrive in this much more competitive world. We must focus on being a desirable location for doing business, for upward mobility, for research, and for education. That, to me, is the big challenge.

The Chinese plan. They have five-year plans. A number of other countries are thinking long term, too. We should not and will not engage in China-like planning. But we have to think about what we need to do now to make our companies, students, workers, and research labs more competitive in the global economy, not just today but over the next 5, 10, or 15 years. It is an enormous challenge. It requires vision; it requires leadership; it requires bipartisanship. And it requires a critical mass of national understanding that we are faced with a challenge that we have not faced before in our history. And we are going to have to meet it.

Questions and Answers (edited)

Q: The U.S. economy came into this year with considerable momentum, and Europe at the start of the year was also working on trying to resolve a sovereign debt crisis. Then suddenly in February, we had these sweeping geopolitical events—disruptions that probably are on a scale that we have not seen since the fall of the Soviet Union. I wonder if you can give us your perspective on how long the uncertainty may continue about these events and what impact they are going to have on the United States and the global economy for the foreseeable future.

Dr. Hormats: I think that given the nature of the uncertainty, predicting when these events would end would be virtually impossible because we are now in a process where political change has accelerated at a very rapid rate. There has been regime change in some of these countries, but what the new regimes are going to look like remains to be seen.

The question of the impact on U.S. policy is interesting. There are a number of preliminary conclusions that one can come to, one of which concerns a point I mentioned. That is, we have gone through several energy events in the past 40 years, such as 1973 and 1974, when we had the initial oil embargo against the United States and the Netherlands. Similar disruptions and consequent energy price increases occurred in 1979 and then in the first Gulf War. The current unrest in North Africa and the Middle East is one more reminder that we are vulnerable to disruptions in oil supply or extraordinary price disruptions that come from the concern about supply, even if the supply is really not disrupted very much. We have seen this in the current environment, where there are market concerns or concerns that people have that have tended to push the market up. Looking at this history over the past 40 years, we have really not taken as seriously as we must the need for a robust national energy policy that reduces our dependence on imported oil and hydrocarbons in general.

The second point is that—I think I touched on this earlier—our assistance to countries really needs to involve what one can call support for inclusive growth. That is. we must ensure that when we provide assistance, or when we provide advice, or when the World Bank or other institutions do it, more and more people are included in the benefits of that assistance and advice and of economic growth. That is particularly true when it comes to younger people in many, if not most, of these countries.

Look at Egypt. It has the world's second-largest percentage of college-educated young people who are unemployed. Number one is the Philippines. There are a lot of disenfranchised youth in such countries. One of the things we need to do is to focus our foreign-assistance programs on ways of helping these countries to enfranchise these people, to give them opportunities in the political as well as in the economic area. The broader point is that we have to recognize that when you get into these periods of major change, it is hard to know when they will end or what the final conclusion will look like.

There is this famous statement by Zhou Enlai, who some 30 years ago was asked what the implications of the French Revolution were. He said, "Well, it is too soon to tell." And I think that is the answer I would give here: It is too soon to tell. It tends to be the case that when you have these revolutions or these major outflowings of public disenchantment with the current regimes, they can lead in a variety of directions. I'll give you an example from the last 25 years. I had an opportunity to meet with Eduard Shevardnadze, who was the foreign minister under Mikhail Gorbachev when the Soviet Union dissolved into Russia and a number of independent republics. At the time, you had this outflowing of support of freedom throughout Eastern and Central Europe. I asked him about this, and he said that he did not anticipate that there would be this massive democratic movement. They assumed that there would be a lot of little Gorbachevs and that in most of the countries of Central and Eastern Europe the power of the state would still be in the hands of relatively few people. What happened was that you had almost all the leaders of Eastern Europe swept aside very quickly. This proves that even for someone who was pretty close to what was going on, it was impossible to predict. I asked Lech Walesa once, "Could you predict what was going to happen in Poland when you started Solidarity?" He answered that there was no way he could have predicted the outcome, and this is a guy who was very close to it.

Therefore, I just find it very difficult to make a prediction about what is going to happen. I do, however, think that from an American point of view, staying engaged and working with the forces of positive change is where we have to be—not so much that we will have enormous influence over them, but that what influence we do have will be constructive.

Q: My question is why the State Department and our intelligence services were caught off guard, without any contingency plans whatsoever over these events. And what is being done now to maybe not be that surprised when the next hot spot erupts?

Dr. Hormats: I am not in the intelligence part of the State Department, but I think there were people who understood that there had to be change in many of these countries. However, I do not think that very many who are experts in this area—either in the State Department or in academia—anticipated that such far-reaching change would come so quickly or that it would come the way it did. Many academicians who were following the situation understood that there was discontent in some of these countries and understood that there were pressures building up, but very few people really anticipated this.

What do we do now? It is really the same answer: stay in touch with the forces who are advocating constructive change and make sure that we have very active engagement. Our ambassadors who are in the region are meeting with various governmental and nongovernmental groups to stay in touch with developments, but there are no miracle answers. It is an ongoing set of engagements with people who are involved in these movements and who are involved in the desire for greater change and greater participation in the system. Our challenge is: How do we help them to get this in a constructive fashion?

Q: Thinking about the Doha trade talks, it seems to me that one of the main reasons those did not go further was that some of the emerging markets wanted the EU and the United States to give up some of their agricultural subsidies. I am wondering if you can envision the advanced economies in general, and especially the United States, giving up on some of these explicit and implicit farm subsidies in order to achieve growth in exports.

Dr. Hormats: We are in the negotiations now. They have been going on for quite some time. What we are prepared to give in that area depends in part on what we are likely to get in a variety of other areas, so I do not think we are really at the point where we are putting new offers on the table. But let me make a few observations because I think you have asked a very important question: What happens to the Doha Round? Everyone knows if that you are going to get something, you have to make offers, and we have been having a series of negotiations on what our specific offers are and what we hope to get in return.

The bigger issue for the ability to conclude the negotiations relates at least tangentially to a point that I made earlier. That is, when these negotiations started, China, India, and Brazil were not major commercial powers. They were trading countries, but they did not have the kind of commercial power that they have today. What has happened is that many of these countries still, to a degree, see themselves—or at least project themselves in their conversations with us—as emerging or developing economies, despite their new-found commercial and financial power; but they still have large numbers of low-income people. Therefore, economic development is one of their top priorities. This has made them very cautious, and in some cases unwilling, to move toward greater openness.

In the United States, being able to make progress on the trade negotiations—and particularly to get these things through the American Congress—is virtually impossible without having much more substantial offers of openness by the big three emerging economies —China, India, and Brazil. I would include Russia, too; but it is not in the WTO and therefore not part of the Doha Round. Our hope is that they join the WTO, because we want them in a system of rules and obligations. With those countries that are in, we want to make sure that they open their markets to a far greater degree than they have been willing to do so far, because their markets are so important to American companies.

Our job in the State Department is to support American companies and American workers, and we cannot have the kind of export growth that the President wants, which is a doubling over five years to create or support two million jobs, until we have greater access to the markets of these large emerging economies. It is just arithmetic, and so far it is proving very difficult to get them to agree to much further opening.

Even beyond American exports—and of course, that is our major priority—if you are a small, developing country, it is important for you that the Chinese, the Brazilians, and the Indians further open their markets. For countries with smaller domestic markets, it is even more important than it is for the United States that they get access to these large, emerging, fast-growing economies. Therefore, we have been making the argument in the G20 and the G8 that large emerging economies have to open up further if there is to be a negotiation that is credible, that has any chance of getting through the American Congress, and that provides benefits to some of these smaller economics. Balancing these interests is the major hang-up in the negotiation at this point.

Q: In your prepared remarks, you discussed the increased role of state-supported enterprises in many countries. What is the U.S. response to this?

Dr. Hormats: What we can encourage countries to do is to make sure that the provisions of state ownership and support do not distort international competition or distort international trade. In other words, we need rules that limit the degree to which, by virtue of being owned by the state or supported by the state, firms have competitive benefits or competitive advantages over companies that are not owned or supported by the state, such as those of the United States and many other parts of the world. This notion is called competitive neutrality, and it means you do not have exemption from antimonopoly rules; you do not have preferential access to capital; you do not have exemption from certain regulations. You do not have—for instance, if you are a bank or insurance company—government indemnity that enables you to borrow money more cheaply than a privately owned insurance company or bank. In many countries, that government support, or at least government backup, enables companies or financial institutions to get money more cheaply, which gives them a competitive advantage.

While we cannot tell countries whether they can have state participation in their economy or not, we prefer that they move toward a private-sector model. But if they choose state ownership or support, we want to make sure that there are rules and disciplines that avoid their firms being given a major competitive advantage due to state support—in financing, for example,

Also, we look at trade rules that deal with dumping, subsidies, and what we call "Special 301" violations of intellectual-property rules.[2] These trade rules are hard to enforce when, for example, a company has been given free land by the government or antitrust immunity, or when the bank that is owned by the government indirectly has been told to give a company money at 2 percent, when the market rate is 6 or 7 percent. You can, in some cases, go after some of these using traditional countervailing duty rules under the WTO. But in some cases, the problems are much more complex because many of these unfair arrangements are opaque.

How, for instance, do you judge what to do if you want to invest in a country when the host government says that you can only invest if you transfer a certain amount of technology to a domestic company or agree to a certain portion of procurement from a domestic company? That gives that domestic company an enormous competitive advantage and can, in many cases, be highly detrimental to the foreign investor. How do you measure that type of intervention? How do you quantify it? In many cases, it is opaque. In many cases, there is no paper trail: it is sort of subtly inferred from the negotiation that you have to do it. In other cases, it may not directly violate WTO rules that limit certain distortive practices. China, for instance, has not signed the Government Procurement Agreement of the WTO.

We are trying to figure out how to formulate new 21st-century rules. In the 20th century, there were very clear distinctions: tariff barriers and nontariff barriers. Now, there is a variety of creative means of protection, which we would call mercantilism or an aspect of "industrial policy" or the French would call dirigisme. Developing international rules, norms, and disciplines is much harder than it used to be because in many cases violations are opaque.

Another problem is that American companies are not going to go to the United States government and say: "Look what we are up against here." After all, they want to do business in these countries, and they are willing to shave off a little here and there in order to do it. So, we have some very complicated challenges before us to make sure there is a level playing field and that even if there is a growing role for the state in economies, there will be rules and obligations and disciplines to prevent state support from distorting global markets. This is a very big challenge for American companies that do not have these advantages. We are going to be working on this in our bilateral talks with many of these countries in the Trans-Pacific Partnership that is being negotiated in the OECD and in the WTO.

References

Clinton, Hillary Rodham. 2011. Internet Rights and Wrongs: Choices & Challenges in a Networked World, Remarks at George Washington University, Washington, DC. February 15, www.state.govlsecretaryl/rm/2011/02/156619.htm.

Hormats, Robert D. 2011. Keynote Address, Center for Democracy and Technology Annual Dinner, March 8, http://usoecd .usmission.gov/hormats-cdt-remarks2.html.

Roosevelt, Franklin D. 1941. The Four Freedoms, from The State of the Union, Address to Congress. Congressional Record, 87 Part I, www.avwnortonxom/coIiegc/history/raiph/ workbook7ralprs36b.htm.

Notes

1. The "Four Freedoms" are freedom of speech and expression, freedom of every person to worship God in his own way, freedom from want, and freedom from fear [Roosevelt 1941].
2. Section 301 of the Trade Act of 1974, as amended, requires that the United States Trade Representative must report annually on the actions of countries that deny adequate protection of U.S. property rights or deny access to markets that rely on such protection.

Source

Hormats, Robert, and Ariel M. Ratner. "World War II to 2011: changes and challenges in the global economy." *Business Economics* 46.3 (2011): 144+. *General Reference Center GOLD*. Web. 20 Dec. 2011.

Critical Thinking

1. How has the economy changed since the end of World War II?
2. What was the role of the United States in that change?
3. What is likely to be the role of the United States in the future?

ROBERT HORMATS was sworn in as Under Secretary of State for Economic, Energy and Agricultural Affairs on September 23, 2009. He was formerly vice chairman of Goldman Sachs (International), having joined Goldman Sachs in 1982. He served as Assistant Secretary of State for Economic and Business Affairs from 1981 to 1982, Ambassador and Deputy U.S. Trade Representative from 1979 to 1981, and Senior Deputy Assistant Secretary for Economic and Business Affairs at the Department of State from 1977 to 1979. He also served as a senior staff member for International Economic Affairs on the National Security Council from 1969 to 1977. He was a recipient of the French Legion of Honor in 1982 and the Arthur Fleming Award in 1974. Hormats has been a visiting lecturer at Princeton University and served on the Board of Visitors of the Fletcher School of Law and Diplomacy and the Dean's Council of the John F. Kennedy School of Government at Harvard University. He is also a member of the Council on Foreign Relations. He earned a B.A. with a concentration in economics and political science from Tufts University. He earned an MA and a PhD in International Economics from the Fletcher School of Law and Diplomacy. **ARIEL M. RATNER** serves as speechwriter and advisor to the Under Secretary of State for Economic, Energy and Agricultural Affairs, Robert Hormats. A Political Appointee in the Obama Administration, Ratner previously served as Congressional Liaison in the Bureau of Near Eastern Affairs at the Department of State. Before joining the Obama Administration, Ratner had a career in both journalism and American politics and is a veteran of the Obama for America campaign. He earned a BA in History from Stanford University and a Master's in Public Policy from the John F. Kennedy School of Government at Harvard University.

China Must Carry the World

ANDREW B. BUSCH

In December, the Chinese had a 30-year anniversary of an event that changed the nation. In 1978, Deng Xiaoping and his "capitalist roaders" managed to gain political control from the Maoists and embarked on a path of economic reform. The powerful black cat-white cat principle—it doesn't matter what kind as long as it catches mice—embodied what was sorely needed in a nation that ranked No. 175 in the annual income statistics.

The concept allowed individuals to make production decisions instead of the state. This unleashed the productive and creative energies of the private sector that were tethered during the previous 29 years of the Great Leap Forward and Cultural Revolution. The miracle that occurred has been stunning and reaffirms how critical economic liberty is to increasing growth.

Essentially, a middle class of 200 million people was created since 1990. To put this in perspective, this middle class is larger than the entire working population of the United States. During a 30-year period, China has grown by nearly double digits and is now the fourth-largest world economy (No. 2, if you use purchasing power parity). More important, it is the third-largest trading nation and runs the largest trade surplus with the United States. It also holds the largest U.S. dollar reserves of any nation, which are more than $2 trillion.

As an exclamation point, China hosted the Olympics last summer and wowed the world with its opening ceremonies that were a technological extravaganza. Without question, China's economic transformation is unparalleled and not likely to ever be repeated in our lifetime.

However, there are risks. The retrofitting of a capitalist economic system onto a communist/socialist political system may be inherently unstable. One system asks for individual decision making, risk taking and entrepreneurship; the other system asks the individuals to turn over decision making to a central body. With China, this is a great experiment, and so far, it has been extremely successful. (To be honest, the United States' capitalist economic system and representative government do not function very well together at times, either.)

The retrofitting of a capitalist economic system onto a communist/socialist political system may be inherently unstable.

A Challenge for China

Last year for SFO magazine, I interviewed the head of Eurasia, Ian Bremmer, and asked him about the risks for China. He said, "The longer-term issues are a greater concern. If the growing wealth gaps between the coast and the country's interior, between urban and rural Chinese, between those with connections and those without them get wider, we may see a backlash in the form of greater social instability. The confiscation of land for development projects without much compensation, the risk of public health crises and environmental catastrophes fuel the fire. So far, the party has managed to open China's economy without surrendering its monopoly on the country's political power. There is no guarantee they can pull that off indefinitely."

This strain increases when the structure is challenged by an unforeseen crisis like the current global recession.

For the first time in 30 years, Chinese political leaders are faced with a challenge to their economic reform from outside their country—and that is going to test the economic leadership. During the height of the U.S. credit crisis in the fall, Chinese exports shrank 2 percent, imports collapsed 18 percent and power generation fell 7 percent. The World Bank and other forecasters are now predicting Chinese GDP to shrink to 7.5 percent for 2009, which is a level that could bring "a reactive situation of mass-scale social turmoil" according to a senior party researcher. It's estimated that China needs to grow at 8 percent per year just to keep employment steady for the 7 million members of its workforce that join each year.

The Economist states, "Indeed, demonstrations and protests, always common in China, are proliferating, as laid-off factory-workers join dispossessed farmers, environmental campaigners and victims of police harassment in taking to the streets." Although this is an extreme view, 2009 is also the 20th anniversary of the Tiananmen Square uprising, or the June Fourth Incident as the Chinese call it. As an example of more aggressive and public action occurring, the Financial Times reported in December: "More than 300 Chinese intellectuals have called for the creation of a new democracy movement in a sign of growing dissatisfaction with the Chinese Communist party's strategy of encouraging economic reform without meaningful political liberalisation."

Perhaps the greatest challenge comes from the United States. The U.S. has had a credit-nuclear bomb explode with the failure of Lehman Brothers as the detonator. The ensuing shock waves have extracted credit from an economy that has been basing itself on credit to grow. What does this mean for a $14 trillion economy? Does it drop to $12 trillion or even $10 trillion from credit demand destruction before it stabilizes?

The U.S. has had a credit-nuclear bomb explode with the failure of Lehman Brothers as the detonator.

The U.S. consumer is also likely to cut back on spending from the mounting job losses that are occurring and are predicted to extend throughout 2009. Already 12 months old, the U.S. recession is forecasted to extend well into this year. As the top destination for Chinese exports, the United States recession is going to severely crimp Chinese economic growth. From the trade and current account data, the Chinese dependence on the U.S. consumer is strong.

Picking up the Slack

The Chinese leaders are not simply going to ignore what is happening. They have already announced an extremely large stimulus program of 4 trillion yuan ($600 billion) and indicated that they want to spur domestic demand to help pick up the slack from the drop in exports. Chinese consumers are increasing their spending, and domestic retail sales continue to be a bright spot. Some experts predict that BRIC (Brazil, Russia, India and China) consumers will be the stabilizing force for the global economy.

The problem is that these countries are much smaller in their contribution to global consumption: The United States, Japan and Europe account for 68 percent, while BRIC only represents 10 percent. The scale of the increase in domestic consumption by China would need to be enormous. Peking University Professor of Finance, Michael Pettis writes, "A decline in U.S. consumption equal to 5 percent of U.S. GDP, for example (which is a low estimate), would require an increase in Chinese consumption equal to 17 percent of Chinese GDP—or a nearly 40 percent growth in consumption. This is clearly unlikely."

There are two more major risks with China as the global economy remains in recession: deflation and trade wars. Think of the Chinese economy like an oil rig. You have a massive piece of productive capabilities that needs to be run by several crews of workers going around the clock to pump oil out of the ground. If the price of crude goes down below your operating costs, you don't shut down the rig. Why? The shut-down costs are extremely high with unemployment benefits, lost ability to

generate revenue to pay for debts and the cost of moth-balling the rig someplace. This means you continue to run the rig even as you lose money in the hope of keeping the operation going until the market turns around.

This is the dilemma facing Chinese business leaders and the government—with a twist. They will keep producing goods as the goals of businesses and the government are intently focused on keeping workers employed at all costs. This means that potentially the Chinese keep producing goods when the world's demand does not exist to absorb them. Instead of global production dropping to meet lower levels of global demand, output remains at elevated levels putting downward pressure on prices.

This also means that there is potential for producers from other nations to lose market share to the Chinese. Without serious government subsidies, how can foreign private-sector manufacturers keep producing goods with prices dropping and supply remaining unchanged? This could create a serious trade backlash against the Chinese as nations take actions to limit the amount of Chinese exports entering their economies.

A Democratic administration has come to power in Washington that is unlikely to be as tolerant of China's trade or currency policies. The textile quota agreement between the United States and China signed in 2005 is up for renewal soon, and that will be a test case for the rest of the world.

China's extraordinary economic growth during the past 30 years is truly a modern miracle that is unlikely to be repeated any time soon. The country has managed to balance economic growth with the challenges of one-party political rule. This delicate balance is under duress with a global recession putting pressure on growth and employment. This will challenge the Chinese leadership to act aggressively and to find creative solutions.

Thirty years ago, Deng began the economic reform and described it as "crossing the river by feeling for the stones." Now, the economic rocks are slippery and the current is strong. The world needs China to stay upright, or we will all get wet.

Critical Thinking

1. What is China's new role in the global economy?
2. What must the leaders of China do to assume that role?
3. How is China's new position in the world economy likely to affect the rest of the world?

ANDREW B. BUSCH is a keynote speaker, author of *World Event Trading* and CNBC contributor and guest host of "Man Vs. Market." He also writes the daily financial/political newsletter The Busch Update. He can be reached at his website AndrewBusch.com

---

Terra Instabilis

From the Arab Spring and the Great Recession to the Eurozone Crisis and Chinese Inflation: Are We Headed toward a New World Disorder?

JON HARRISON

In 1848 Europe was convulsed by revolution, the so-called "springtime of the peoples." In 1968 unrest swept through most of the developed world, from Prague to Paris, from Berkeley to Mexico City. These revolutionary outbreaks were once-in-a-century events brought on by political discontents.

Now, a new revolutionary storm, almost worldwide in scope, appears to be brewing. Its origins, outwardly political, are in fact traceable to economic and social disparities that have been building up over the past five or six decades. To address these disparities in a constructive manner will be a difficult if not impossible task. Political reform by itself is a relatively simple matter, given a modicum of goodwill. Broadening the franchise can be achieved through legislation. Free and fair elections can be guaranteed by admitting international observers who have access to the world media. Major economic and social reforms, on the other hand, require changes in both behavior and outcome at all levels of a society. Such reform almost never occurs without violence. And all too often violence results in nothing save the accession of new oppressors to power.

The so-called Arab Spring, playing out over a vast area stretching from Morocco to the Persian Gulf, appears, on its face, to be a political phenomenon. It's true that the cry in the Arab street is for liberation from corrupt and despotic governments. But a closer look reveals a more nuanced and distressing picture.

The narrative being presented to Western publics by their governments and media alike is one of Arab peoples yearning for free institutions similar to those in the West. But this goal motivates only a small minority of the protestors, mainly young people from middle-class families. These young people often speak Western languages and accept, to a large degree, Western political and social values. As such, they become the focus for the Western media in telling an apparently straightforward story that's easy for Western publics to understand. But this narrative is, at best, a sideshow to the real play of events in the Arab world.

The revolution that began in Tunisia in December 2010 is above all the consequence of economic distress and despair. Unemployment and soaring food prices, not political liberalization per se, are the motivating forces behind the mass protests, violence, and bloodshed we continue to witness. A massive youth bulge exists throughout the Arab world, and governments have shown no capacity to address the problems that come with it. In truth, the economic record of Arab regimes since independence has been largely one of stagnation. Even in oil-rich countries the economy remains in the hands of elites who have shown little inclination to foster individual initiative and entrepreneurship among the citizenry. Now these elites find themselves riding a tiger, as economic pain has provoked the masses to revolutionary violence.

Egypt, the most important and advanced nation in the Arab world, has so far escaped without major bloodshed, thanks in part to U.S. pressure that helped to force out the dictator there. But for Egypt all the big challenges remain—establishing a working democracy, eradicating corruption, and providing enough work and bread to keep the great mass of the people (40 percent of whom live on less than two dollars a day) content, or at least quiet. The history of modern Egypt provides no indication that the country will master these challenges. On the contrary, there is every reason to believe that at some point in the future a more radical revolutionary outbreak will occur, leading either to the establishment of an Islamic state, or a return to military rule, with the latter possibly degenerating, as before, into despotism.

Far too little reporting has been done on the real strength and goals of the Islamic Brotherhood in Egypt. When in February 2011 the virulently anti-American and anti-Israeli cleric Sheik Yusuf al-Qaradawi addressed an adoring crowd estimated at 1 million strong in Tahrir Square, Cairo, *The New York Times* gave it passing mention, while cable and network news ignored the occasion almost completely. The possibility of a radical outcome in Egypt should not be discounted, while elsewhere in the region the rise of radicalism is perhaps even more likely. Simply put, when large numbers of young men are without work, without prospects for marriage, and without any outlet for their social and political grievances, violence occurs and the fabric of society begins to disintegrate. At that point religious fanaticism comes to the fore, and the "solutions" it offers find new adherents. Witness Iran in the early 1980s.

Although Europe does not face the challenge of a youth bulge, there as well we're beginning to see a breakdown in social cohesion caused by economic distress. The protests over budget cuts in Britain that began last year and the riots this past summer are merely the overture to a crisis that is spreading across the continent. The revelation that Greece is an economic basket case, and that its citizens' standard of living must inevitably decline, has led to violence in the streets of Athens. Similar violence has occurred in Spain, where unemployment stands at over 20 percent.

The Eurozone crisis is not amenable to any solution based on a one-currency political economy. Germany and the other northern states are simply too productive; Greece and the rest of the South can't keep up. Bailouts and austerity programs kick the can down the road, but won't resolve the problem. Greece and probably the Iberian countries will suffer bankruptcy in one form or another, and will eventually have to detach themselves, or be detached, from the rest of the Eurozone. The German taxpayer will not subsidize southern Europe indefinitely, and the Greeks, Spaniards, and Portuguese won't starve to keep the euro afloat. Yet obvious as this conclusion appears to be, there is tremendous resistance to acknowledging its reality. The international financial ramifications are of course potentially enormous, especially as *no one* is sure just what exposure the major European banks have to Greek, Spanish, Portuguese, and Italian debt. The derivatives crisis of 2008 nearly brought down the U.S. economy, and might possibly have destroyed capitalism itself. That danger was averted by the great bank bailout, otherwise known as the Troubled Asset Relief Program (TARP), which was imposed on the U.S. Congress by the Treasury in October 2008. A similar crisis may be building in Europe today. In 2010 the EU bailed out its southern economies to the tune of 750 million euros (equivalent to about $1 trillion). To believe that the printing press will once again save capitalism from the abyss is the height of optimism. To believe that it can do so indefinitely is absurd.

In any case, a decline in the standard of living throughout much of Europe, which is clearly in the cards, would be unprecedented in the post-World War II era, and will undoubtedly provoke a combination of violence and malaise, a phenomenon we are already witnessing on a small scale. If conditions worsen, is a return to the 1930s possible? History doesn't literally repeat itself: one cannot envision Europe once again under the shadow of the swastika. But a breakdown of the liberal order in Europe would create a moral and intellectual vacuum. It's hard to predict precisely what would follow from this. The more severe the economic decline, the more likely it is that radical solutions will find favor with those who are suffering. Such at least is the evidence of history.

Clearly, both Europe and the Middle East are in crisis. But they're not alone. If we look eastward to China, we see economic and social problems building there as well. Here the difficulty is not, as in the Arab world, stagnation and the stifling of any initiative generated from below. Nor is it a case of deep regional disparities in wealth and productivity, as in Europe. The dangers China faces are those that occur when rapid growth threatens to overwhelm a still-developing political economy.

The Chinese economy has been growing at a double-digit pace for years. Such a boom breeds inflation, as new wealth chases goods and services, causing prices to spiral. In an attempt to stem inflation, China's central bank raised interest rates five times between late 2010 and the summer of 2011. Further increases are expected. In addition, the Chinese have raised bank reserve requirements, an action that drains money from the economy and puts a brake on any tendencies toward speculative excess. Despite these moves, inflation in China has been running as high as 6 percent *per annum,* with food prices increasing even more rapidly. Chinese officials have described this as a potential threat to social stability. This is not alarmism. The 1989 Tiananmen Square uprising is remembered in the West as a failed attempt to achieve democracy. In fact, Tiananmen was as much, if not more, about rising food prices as it was about any desire for political pluralism.

Protests on a small scale are happening in China today. Major unrest could occur again if inflationary pressures persist, particularly if the price of necessities like food and fuel exceeds the ability of the average citizen to pay. Centrifugal forces, long dormant in China, might then reappear. Unrest among the Muslim Uighurs in Xinjiang, and among the Tibetans, could flare up and spread to the Han Chinese homeland. Whether the current Chinese regime is nimble enough to manage such a crisis without severe repressive measures is very much in doubt. Nor is it certain that repression will work in this age of interconnectedness and social networking; the example of the Arab uprisings must give pause to every government and ruling class.

Looking further eastward from China, we come to the United States. The world's sole superpower is in deep trouble. Here the problems are fiscal and economic, but also political and attitudinal. The fiscal issues are palpable and well understood in political and financial circles. (The average citizen is another matter: polling data indicates, for example, that a plurality of Americans believe that ending foreign aid would bring the federal budget into balance.) The Federal debt is now approximately equal to GDP. Federal budget deficits running into the hundreds of billions of dollars annually are projected to continue for years, perhaps decades. Entitlement spending, particularly for Medicare, is out of control. Defense spending, currently about $700 billion per annum (but with ancillary costs included probably more like $1 trillion or more), continues to eat up enormous financial resources at a time when no major military threat to the U.S. exists. And yet, no *serious* effort is being made by the political class to deal with these problems that will eventually bankrupt the nation.

It would seem that the U.S. economy, rich and productive as it once was, is in deep decline. Structural unemployment is likely here to stay: companies can't find enough highly skilled workers to fill openings, even with unemployment high, while at the same time low-skill jobs have disappeared overseas. The official unemployment rate of around 9 percent will probably come down over time, but the real unemployment-underemployment rate (including those who have given up looking for work and those part-time workers who would like to be working full-time), currently about 17 percent, will almost certainly remain in double digits indefinitely. Add to this the tremendous amount of debt that exists at all levels of government and among households, and it appears unlikely that the U.S. will be able to grow its way back to financial health and a broad-based prosperity. Economic disparity between classes has been increasing in America since the early 1970s. Commodity prices—oil, metals, food—*must,* despite market fluctuations, trend higher, given the demands imposed by a growing world population and the economic dynamism of countries like China, India, and Brazil. In retrospect, we can see that the boom times of the 1980s and '90s in the U.S. were debt-fueled and lacked substance—they were, in other words, fundamentally different from the real, solid economic expansions that came before. The last of these true expansions began during the Second World War and ended in the early 1970s.

Sluggish growth, high unemployment, and increasing income disparity playing out against the background of a mounting fiscal crisis means, surely, that a perfect economic storm is brewing—a storm unlike anything seen in America since the 1930s. Add to this the fact that emerging economies unburdened by anything like the fiscal drag the U.S. suffers from are competing with us for both resources and markets, and you have, it would seem, a recipe for economic—and therefore social and political—disaster.

The economic dilemmas America now faces are politically driven. That is to say, past political choices—to run up massive deficits, to encourage consumption over investment, to impose a free trade regime on a playing field tilted against the United States—have landed the country in its current economic situation. These choices were made not by a well-informed electorate, but by political leaders acting at the behest of powerful constituencies, i.e., the interests that finance political campaigns and maintain the great lobbying firms on K Street. Solutions to the problems that have been created by the U.S. political system will come, if at all, from that same system. Should we expect this sort of self-correction? Given the record of the past, skepticism on this point seems more than justified.

Consider the two major political parties. The Democratic Party of today responds to interest groups like the trial lawyers and the unions, but its leaders no longer have any real connection to average Americans. Instead, they turn a blind eye to the vital need for fiscal reform; one could hardly be blamed for suspecting that, in their hearts, they subscribe to Keynes' dictum that "in the long run we are all dead." But Keynes had no children. In reality, when we are gone, our children and grandchildren will be left with an almost inconceivable amount of debt.

The Republican Party wants to solve the fiscal crisis by "reforming" key components of the welfare state such as Medicare and Social Security. Its conception as regards the former amounts to abolition, despite the fact that very few Americans of retirement age can afford private health insurance. Indeed, Medicare was created in large part because elderly Americans simply could not obtain private insurance. But Republican austerity plans are bound to fail in any case. The elderly, who

would be most affected by cuts in entitlements, not only constitute a very large voting bloc, but go to the polls in big numbers. In American terms, austerity is a cul-de-sac.

Both parties adhere slavishly to the current free trade regime, which has devastated U.S. manufacturing and turned a considerable portion of the working class into a new *lumpenproletariat.* And both parties continue to support foreign and defense policies that reflect not present-day realties, but those of the 1940–1990 period, when the existential threats of Nazism and Communism existed. No such threats exist today, yet we spend almost as much on defense as the rest of the world combined, maintain bases in some 130 countries, and pay 75 percent of the cost of the NATO alliance, even though the European economy is larger than our own. Like other empires before us, we have become overextended both militarily and fiscally. Bankruptcy stares us in the face, while our politicians sleepwalk through history.

Throughout the Northern Hemisphere nations and aggregates of nation-states face seemingly irresolvable contradictions in political economy. There are, in fact, remedies at hand, should we choose to apply them. These range from simple reforms such as restricting speculation in vital commodities like food and oil to companies that actually take delivery of such products, to a global effort to reduce the human population. (Current projections give a world population of about 10 billion in 2100, which would place terrific strains on the oceans, arable land, fresh water supplies, and mineral resources.) But there are no really powerful constituencies in support of such initiatives. The political will simply doesn't exist in Washington, Brussels, or Beijing. (Granted, Beijing has imposed strict population control on its own people. But there is no impetus from China or anywhere else for a global, enlightened, voluntary campaign to restrict population.) Nor should we expect widespread popular demands for remedies of this kind. Population control, for example, is anathema to billions of religious believers around the world. Yet it is a great mistake to believe, as many people do, that the Green Revolution has proved Malthus wrong. Resources *are* finite; even the earth's great bounty has limits. An ever-expanding human population will encounter these limits at some point. And then the human population will shrink whether we will it or not.

It has been made clear for some decades that the era of Western world domination, a period that lasted, roughly, from 1800 to 2000 C.E., is coming to an end. Even more important perhaps is the fact that the post-World War II architecture built up under the aegis of the Pax Americana—NATO, the European Union, and global economic organizations like the World Bank, the International Monetary Fund, and the World Trade Organization—appears to be headed for dissolution. The bases for the stability and relative prosperity of the postwar era are crumbling. A crack-up is probably coming that will make 1848 and 1968 look like child's play. A future of booming birth rates among the world's poorest inhabitants, of increasing income disparity between rich and poor, of cutthroat competition for scarce resources, and of political weakness and social confusion will lead, eventually, to violence. "Resource wars" between states (over water, for example) may occur, or states may use war as a means of deflecting internal discontent outwards. But the greatest danger is perhaps violence within states, with the desperate masses striking out against the ruling class and the state apparatus. The state in turn, if it chooses to fight (and most states do), would then unleash its full power upon its own citizens, as happened in China in 1989; as is happening in Syria now. States in disarray rarely roll over and die; the Soviet experience stands almost alone in history. Moreover, in an era lacking a relatively benign hegemon (and we are almost certainly entering such an era, as the United States' economic decline brings with it a retreat from global responsibilities), violence both within and between states inevitably increases. The period 1914–1945 is instructive; so too is the epoch of Rome's decline.

We cannot know the future. But it seems clear that economic and social distress is increasing worldwide. At the same time the political and economic dispensations that have prevailed since World War II are failing, with no clear alternatives in sight. Thus the world is made a tinderbox.

Critical Thinking

1. How has the Arab Spring changed the Middle East?
2. What are some of the things that are happening in Europe that make it less stable?
3. What does Chinese inflation mean to the rest of the world?

JON HARRISON is a contributing editor for *Liberty*, a journal about politics and culture. His writing has also appeared in *Antiwar.com*, *Rational Review*, the *International Business Times*, *VermontTiger.com*, and other publications. He currently lives in Vermont.

From *The Humanist*, vol. 71, no. 6, December 2011, pp. 25–29. Copyright © 2011 by Jon Harrison. Reprinted by permission of the author.

The Theory of Comparative Advantage

Why It Is Wrong

The theory of comparative advantage, invented by the British economist David Ricardo in 1817, is the core of the case for free trade. All the myriad things we are told about why free trade is good for us are boiled down to hard economics and weighed against the costs by this single theory and its modern ramifications. If this theory is true, then no matter how high the costs of free trade, we can rely upon the fact that somewhere else in our economy we are reaping benefits that exceed them. If it is false, we cannot.

IAN FLETCHER

Absolute vs. Comparative Advantage

To understand comparative advantage, it is best to start with its simpler cousin absolute advantage. The concept of absolute advantage simply says that if some foreign nation is a more efficient producer of some product than we are, then free trade will cause us to import that product from them, and that this is good for both nations. It is good for us because we get the product for less money than it would have cost us to make it ourselves. It is good for the foreign nation because it gets a market for its goods. And it is good for the world economy as a whole because it causes production to come from the most efficient producer, maximizing world output.

Absolute advantage is thus a set of fairly obvious ideas. It is, in fact, the theory of international trade most people instinctively hold, without recourse to formal economics, and thus it explains a large part of public opinion on the subject.

It sounds like a reassuringly direct application of basic capitalist principles. It is the theory of trade Adam Smith himself believed in.

It is also false. Under free trade, America observably imports products of which we are the most efficient producer—which makes absolutely no sense by the standard of absolute advantage. This causes complaints like conservative commentator Patrick Buchanan's:

"Ricardo's theory . . . demands that more efficient producers in advanced countries give up industries to less efficient producers in less advanced nations . . . Are Chinese factories more efficient than U.S. factories? Of course not."

Buchanan is correct: this is *precisely* what Ricardo's theory demands. It not only predicts that less efficient producers will sometimes win (observably true) but argues that this is good for us (the controversy). This is why we must analyze trade in terms of not absolute but *comparative* advantage. If we do not, we will never obtain a theory that accurately describes what happens in international trade, which is a prerequisite for evaluating whether what happens is beneficial.

Boiled down to its essence, the theory of comparative advantage simply says this:

Nations trade for the same reasons people do.

And the whole theory can be cracked open with one simple question:

Why don't pro football players mow their own lawns?

Why should this even be a question? Because the average footballer can almost certainly mow his lawn more efficiently than the average professional lawn mower. The average footballer is, after all, presumably stronger and more agile than the mediocre workforce attracted to a badly paid job like mowing lawns. (If we wanted to quantify his efficiency, we could measure it in acres per hour.) Efficiency, also known as productivity, is always a matter of *how much output we get* from a given quantity of inputs, be these inputs hours of labor, pounds of flour, kilowatts of electricity, or whatever. Because the footballer is more efficient, in economic language he has absolute advantage at mowing lawns. Yet nobody finds it strange that he would "import" lawn-mowing services from a less efficient "producer." Why? Obviously, because he has *better things to do with his time*.

This is the key to the whole thing. The theory of comparative advantage says that it is advantageous for America to import some goods simply in order to free up our workforce to produce more-valuable goods instead. We, as a nation, have better things to do with our time than produce these less valuable goods. And, just as with the football player and the lawn mower, it does not matter whether *we* are more efficient at producing them, or the country we import them from is. As a result, it is sometimes advantageous for us to import goods from less efficient nations.

This logic does not only apply to our time, that is, our man-hours of labor, either. It *also* applies to our land, capital, technology, and every other finite resource used to produce goods. So the theory of comparative advantage says that if we could produce something more valuable with the resources we currently use to produce some product, then we should import that product, free up those resources, and produce that more valuable thing instead.

Economists call the resources we use to produce products "factors of production." They call whatever we *give up* producing, in order to produce something else, our "opportunity cost." The opposite of opportunity cost is direct cost, so while the direct cost of mowing a lawn is the hours of labor it takes, plus the gasoline, wear-and-tear on the machine, et cetera, the opportunity cost is the value of whatever else these things could have been doing instead.

Direct cost is a simple matter of efficiency, and is the same regardless of whatever else is going on in the world. Opportunity cost is a lot more complicated, because it depends on what opportunities exist for using factors of production. Other things being equal, direct cost and opportunity cost go up and down together because if the time required to mow a lawn doubles, then twice as much time cannot be spent doing something else. As a result, high efficiency tends to generate both low direct cost and low opportunity cost. If someone is such a skilled mower that they can mow the whole lawn in fifteen minutes, then their opportunity cost of doing so will be low because there is not much else they can do in fifteen minutes.

The opportunity cost of producing something is always the *next most valuable thing* we could have produced instead. If either bread or rolls can be made from dough, and we choose to make bread, then rolls are our opportunity cost. If we choose to make rolls, then bread is. And if rolls are worth more than bread, then we will incur a larger opportunity cost by making bread. It follows that the smaller the opportunity cost we incur, the less opportunity we are wasting, so the better we are exploiting the opportunities we have. Therefore our best move is always to *minimize our opportunity cost*.

This is where trade comes in. Trade enables us to "import" bread (buy it in a store) so we can stop baking our own and bake rolls instead. In fact, trade enables us to do this for all the things we would otherwise have to make for ourselves. So

if we have complete freedom to trade, we can systematically shrug off all our least valuable tasks and reallocate our time to our most valuable ones. Similarly, nations can systematically shrink their least valuable industries and expand their most valuable ones. This benefits these nations and under global free trade, with every nation doing this, it benefits the entire world. The world economy and every nation in it become as productive as they can possibly be.

Here is a real-world example: if America devoted millions of workers to making cheap plastic toys (we don't; China does) then these workers could not produce anything else. In America, we (it is hoped) have more-productive jobs for them to do, even if American industry could hypothetically grind out more plastic toys per man-hour of labor and ton of plastic than the Chinese. So we are better off leaving this work to China and having our own workers do more-productive work instead.

This all implies that under free trade, production of every product will automatically migrate to the nation that can produce it at the lowest opportunity cost— the nation that *wastes the least opportunity* by being in that line of business.

The theory of comparative advantage thus sees international trade as a vast interlocking system of tradeoffs, in which nations use the ability to import and export to shed opportunity costs and reshuffle their factors of production to their most valuable uses. And (supposedly) this all happens automatically, because if the owners of some factor of production find a more valuable use for it, they will find it profitable to move it to that use. The natural drive for profit will steer all factors of production to their most valuable uses, and opportunities will never be wasted.

It follows (supposedly) that any policy other than free trade just traps nations producing less-valuable output than they could have produced. It saddles them with higher opportunity costs—more opportunities thrown away—than they would otherwise incur. In fact, when imports drive a nation out of an industry, this must actually be good for that nation, as it means the nation must be allocating its factors of production to producing something more valuable instead. If it were not doing this, the logic of profit would never have driven its factors out of their former uses. In the language of the theory, the nation's "revealed comparative advantage" must lie elsewhere, and it will now be better off producing according to this newly revealed comparative advantage.

Quantifying Comparative Advantage

Let's quantify comparative advantage with an imaginary example. Suppose an acre of land in Canada can produce either one

16

unit of wheat or two units of corn. And suppose an acre in the U.S. can produce either three units of wheat or four units of corn. The U.S. then has absolute advantage in both wheat (three units vs. one) and corn (four units vs. two). But we are twice as productive in corn and thrice as productive in wheat, so we have *comparative* advantage in wheat.

Importing Canadian corn would obviously enable us to switch some of our corn-producing land to wheat production and grow more wheat, while importing Canadian wheat would enable us to switch some of our wheat-producing land to corn production and grow more corn. Would either of these be winning moves? Let's do some arithmetic.

Every three units of wheat we import will free up one acre of our land because we will no longer need to grow those three units ourselves. We can then grow four units of corn on that acre. But selling us that wheat will force Canada to take three acres out of corn production to grow it, so it will cost Canada $3 \times 2 = 6$ units of corn. Canadians obviously will not want to do this unless we *pay* them at least six units of corn. But this means we would have to pay six units to get four. So no deal.

What about importing Canadian corn? Every four units of corn we import will free up one acre of our land, on which we can grow three units of wheat. Selling us those four units will force Canada to take $4/2 = 2$ acres out of wheat production, costing Canada $2 \times 1 = 2$ units of wheat. So we can pay the Canadians what it cost them to give us the corn (two units of wheat) and still come out ahead, by $3 - 2 = 1$ unit of wheat. So importing Canadian corn makes economic sense. And not only do we come out ahead, but because the world now contains one more unit of wheat, it is a good move for the world economy as a whole, too.

The fundamental question here is whether America is better off producing corn, or wheat we can exchange for corn. Every nation faces this choice for every product, just as every individual must decide whether to bake his own bread or earn money at a job so he can buy bread in a store (and whether to mow his own lawn or earn money playing football so he can hire someone else to mow it). The entire theory of comparative advantage is just endless ramifications of this basic logic.

The above scenario all works in reverse on the Canadian side, so it benefits Canada too. Free traders generalize this into the proposition that free trade benefits *every* trading partner and applies to every product and factor of production. As the late Paul Samuelson of MIT explains it, using China as the trading partner:

Yes, good jobs may be lost here in the short run. But still total U.S. net national product must, by the economic laws of comparative advantage, be raised in the long run (and in China, too). The gains of the winners from free trade, properly measured, work out to exceed the losses of the losers.

Low Opportunity Costs Equals Poor Nation

Note that the opportunity cost of producing a product can vary from one nation to another even if the two nations' *direct* costs for producing the product are the same. This is because they can face different alternative uses for the factors of production involved. So having a low opportunity cost for producing a product can just as easily be a matter of having poor alternative uses for factors of production as having great efficiency at producing the product itself.

This is where underdeveloped nations come in: their opportunity costs are low because they do not have a lot of other things they can do with their workers. The visible form this takes is cheap labor, because their economies offer workers few alternatives to dollar-an-hour factor work. As Jorge Castaneda, Mexico's former Secretary of Foreign Affairs and a critic of the North American Free Trade Agreement (NAFTA), explains it:

The case of the auto industry, especially the Ford-Mazda plant in Hermosillo, Mexico, illustrates a well-known paradox. The plant manufactures vehicles at a productivity rate and quality comparable or higher than the Ford plants in Dearborn or Rouge, and slightly below those of Mazda in Hiroshima. Nevertheless, the wage of the Mexican worker with equal productivity is between twenty and twenty-five times less than that of the U.S. worker.

The plants in the U.S. and Japan are surrounded by advanced economies containing many other industries able to pay high wages. So these plants must match these wages or find no takers. The plant in Mexico, on the other hand, is surrounded by a primitive developing economy, so it only needs to compete with low-paid jobs, many of them in peasant agriculture. As a result, the productivity of any one job does not determine its wage. Economy-wide productivity does. This is why it is good to work in a developed economy even if the job you yourself do, such as sweeping floors, is no more productive than the jobs people do in developing countries.

If wages, which are paid in domestic currency, do not accurately reflect differences in opportunity costs between nations, then exchange rates will (in theory) adjust until they do. So if a nation has high productivity in most of its internationally traded industries, this will push up the value of its currency, pricing it out of its lowest-productivity industries. But this is a good thing, because it can then export goods from higher-productivity industries instead. This will mean less work for the same amount of exports, which is why advanced nations rarely compete in primitive industries, or want to. In 1960, when Taiwan had a per capita income of $154, sixty-seven percent of its exports were raw or processed agricultural goods. By 1993, when Taiwan had a per capita income of $11,000, ninety-six percent of its exports were manufactured goods. Taiwan today is hopelessly uncompetitive in products it used to export such as tea, sugar, and rice. Foreign competition drove it out of these industries and destroyed millions of jobs. Taiwan does not mind one bit.

What the Theory Does Not Say

The theory of comparative advantage is sometimes misunderstood as implying that a nation's best move is to have as much comparative advantage as it can get—ideally, *comparative* advantage in every industry. This is actually impossible by definition. If America had superior productivity, therefore lower direct costs, and therefore absolute advantage, in every industry, we would still have a greater margin of superiority in some industries and a lesser margin in others. So we would have comparative advantage where our margin was greatest and comparative disadvantage where it was smallest. This pattern of comparative advantage and disadvantage would determine our imports and exports, and we would still be losing jobs to foreign nations in our *relatively* worse industries and gaining them in our *relatively* better ones, despite having absolute advantage in them all.

So what is the significance of absolute advantage, if it *does* not determine who makes what? It does determine relative wages. If the U.S. were exactly ten percent more productive than Canada in all industries, then Americans would have real wages exactly ten percent higher. But because there would be no *relative* differences in productivity between industries, there would be no differences in opportunity costs, neither country would have comparative advantage or disadvantage in anything, and there would be no reason for trade between them. There would be no corn-for-wheat swaps that were winning moves.

All potential swaps would cost exactly as much as they were worth, so there would be no point. (And under free trade, none would take place, as the free market is not stupid and would not push goods back and forth across national borders without reason.)

Conversely, the theory of comparative advantage says that whenever nations do have different relative productivities, mutual gains from trade *must* occur. This is why free traders believe that their theory proves free trade is always good for every nation, no matter how poor or how rich. Rich nations would not be bled dry by the cheap labor of poor nations, and poor nations would not be crushed by the industrial sophistication of rich ones. These things simply cannot happen, because the fundamental logic of comparative advantage guarantees that only mutually beneficial exchanges will ever take place. Everyone will always be better off. It follows that trade conflicts between nations are always misguided and due solely to their failure to understand why free trade is always good for them.

The theory of comparative advantage is thus a wonderfully optimistic construct, and one can certainly see why it would be so appealing. Not only does it appear to explain the complex web of international trade at a single stroke, but it also tells us what to do and guarantees that the result will be the best outcome we could possibly have obtained.

It is actually rather a pity that the theory is not true.

The Theory's Seven Dubious Assumptions

The flaws of the theory of comparative advantage consist of a number of dubious assumptions it makes. To wit:

Assumption 1: Trade Is Sustainable.

This problem divides into two parts: unsustainable imports and exports.

When America does not cover the value of its imports with the value of its exports, it must make up the difference by either selling assets or assuming debts. If either is happening, America is either gradually being sold off to foreigners or gradually sinking into debt to them. Xenophobia is not necessary for this to be a bad thing, only bookkeeping: we are poorer simply because we own less and owe more. Our net worth is lower.

And this situation is unsustainable. We have only so many existing assets we can sell off, and can afford to service only so much debt. By contrast, we can produce goods indefinitely. So deficit trade, it it goes on year after year, must eventually be curtailed—which will mean reducing our consumption one day. We get a decadent consumption binge today and pay the price tomorrow, but because the free-market economics does not traffic in concepts like "decadent," it does not see anything wrong. We wanted consumption and that is what we got, so it is efficient.

The implied solution is to tax exports. And that is not free trade.

Now consider unsustainable exports. This usually means a nation that is exporting nonrenewable natural resources. The same long vs. short term dynamics will apply, only in reverse. A nation that *exports* too much will maximize its short-term living standard at the expense of its long-term prosperity. But free market economics—which means free trade—will again perversely report that this is "efficient."

The oil-rich nations of the Persian Gulf are the most obvious example, and it is no accident that OPEC was the single most formidable disruptor of free trade in the entire post–WWII era. But other nations with large land masses, such as Canada, Australia, Russia, and Brazil, also depend upon natural resource exports to a degree that is unhealthy in the long run. Even the United States, whose Midwestern agricultural exports rely upon the giant Ogallala Aquifer, a depleting accumulation of water from glacial times, is not exempt from this problem.

The implied solution is to tax or otherwise to restrict nonrenewable exports. And that is also not free trade.

Assumption 2: There Are Not Externalities.

An externality is a missing price tag. More precisely, it is the economists' term for when the price of a product does not reflect its true economic value. The classic *negative* externality is environmental damage, which reduces the economic value of natural resources without raising the price of the product that harmed them. The classic *positive* externality is technological spillover, where one company's inventing a product enables others to copy or build upon it, generating wealth that the original company does not capture. The theory of comparative advantage, like all theories of free-market economics, is driven by prices, so if prices are wrong due to positive or negative externalities, it will recommend bad policies.

For example, goods from a nation with lax pollution standards will be too cheap. As a result, its trading partners will import too much of them. And the exporting nation will import too much of them, overconcentrating its economy in industries that are not really as profitable as they seem, due to ignoring pollution damage. Free trade not only permits problems such as these, but positively encourages them, as skimping on pollution control is an easy way to grab a cost advantage.

Positive externalities are also a problem. For example, if an industry generates technological spillovers for the rest of the economy, then free trade can let that industry be wiped out by foreign competition because the economy ignored its hidden value.

Some industries spawn new technologies, fertilize improvements in other industries, and drive economy-wide technological advance; losing these industries means losing all the industries that would have flowed from them in the future.

These problems are the tip of an even larger iceberg known as GDP-GPI divergence. Negative externalities and related problems mean that increases in GDP can easily coincide with *decreases* in the so-called Genuine Progress Indicator or GPI. GPI includes things like resource depletion, environmental pollution, unpaid labor like housework, and unpaid goods like leisure time, thus providing a better metric of material well-being than raw GDP. This implies that even if free trade were optimal from a GDP point of view (it is not), it could still be a bad idea economically.

Assumption 3: Factors of Production Move Easily between Industries.

As noted, the theory of comparative advantage is about reshuffling factors of production from less-valuable to more-valuable uses. But this assumes that the factors of production used to produce one product can switch to producing another. Because if they cannot, then imports will not push a nation's economy into industries better suited to its comparative advantage. Imports will just kill off its existing industries and leave nothing in their place.

Although this problem actually applies to all factors of production, we usually hear of it with regard to labor and real estate because people and buildings are the least *mobile* factors of production. (Thus the unemployment line and the shuttered factories are the classic visual images of trade problems.) When workers cannot move between industries—usually because they do not have the right skills or do not live in the right place—shifts in an economy's comparative advantage will not move them into an industry with lower opportunity costs, but into unemployment.

Sometimes the difficulty of reallocating workers shows up as outright unemployment. This happens in nations with rigid employment laws and high *de facto* minimum wages due to employer-paid taxes, as in Western Europe.

But in the United States, because of our relatively low minimum wage and hire-and-fire labor laws, this problem tends to take the form of *under* employment. This is a decline in the quality rather than quantity of jobs. So U.S. $28 an hour ex-autoworkers go work at the video rental store for eight dollars an hour. Or they are forced into part-time employment.

In the Third World, decline in the quality of jobs often takes the form of workers pushed out of the formal sector of the economy entirely and into casual labor of one kind or another, where they have few rights, pensions, or other benefits. Mexico, for example, has over forty percent of its workers in the informal sector.

This all implies that low unemployment, on its own, does not prove that free trade has been a success. The human cost is obvious, but what is less obvious is the purely economic cost of writing off investments in human capital when skills that cost money to acquire are never used again.

This kind of cost is most visible in places such as Moscow in the 1990s, when one saw physics PhDs driving taxis and the like, but America is not exempt.

There is also a risk for the economy as a whole when free trade puts factors of production out of action. As Nobel Laureate James Tobin of Yale puts it, "It takes a heap of Harberger triangles to fill an Okun gap." Harberger triangles represent the benefits of free trade on the standard graphs used to quantify them. The Okun gap is the difference between the GDP our economy would have, if it were running at full output, and the GDP it does have, due to some of its factors of production lying idle. Tobin's point is simply that the benefits of free trade are quantitatively small, compared to the cost of not running our economy at full capacity due to imports.

Assumption 4: Trade Does Not Raise Income Inequality.

When the theory of comparative advantage promises gains from free trade, these gains are only promised to the economy as a whole, not to any particular individuals or groups thereof. So it is entirely possible that even if the economy as a whole gets bigger thanks to freer trade, many (or even most) of the people in it may lose income. This is not a trivial problem: it has been estimated that freeing up trade reshuffles five dollars of income between different groups of people domestically for every one dollar of net gain it brings to the economy as a whole.

Free trade squeezes the wages of ordinary Americans largely because it expands the world's effective supply of labor, which can move from rice paddy to factory overnight, faster than its supply of capital, which takes decades to accumulate at prevailing savings rates. As a result, free trade strengthens the bargaining position of capital relative to labor. This is especially true when combined with growing global capital mobility and the entry into capitalism of large formerly socialist nations such as India and China. As a result, people who draw most of their income from returns on capital (the rich) gain, while people who get most of their income from labor (the rest of us) lose.

The underlying mechanism of this analysis has long been part of mainstream economics in the form of the so-called Stolper-Samuelson theorem. This theorem says that freer trade raises returns to the abundant input to production (in America, capital) and lowers returns to the scarce one (in America, labor).

Because America has more capital per person, and fewer workers per dollar of capital, than the rest of the world, free trade tends to hurt American workers.

Free trade also affects different kinds of labor income differently. The impact of free trade on a worker in the U.S. is basically a function of how easy it is to substitute a cheaper foreign worker by importing the product the American produces.

For extremely skilled jobs, like investment banking, it may be easy to substitute a foreigner, but foreign labor (some yuppie in London) is just as expensive as American labor, so there is no impact on American wages. For jobs that cannot be performed remotely, such as waiting tables, it is impossible to substitute a foreign worker, so again there is no direct impact. The occupations that suffer most are those whose products are easily tradable and can be produced by cheap labor abroad. This is why unskilled manufacturing jobs were the first to get hurt in the U.S.: there is a huge pool of labor abroad capable of doing this work, and manufactured goods can be packed up and shipped around the globe. Because low-paid workers are concentrated in these occupations, free trade hurts them more.

There is another problem. Suppose that opening up a nation to freer trade means that it starts exporting more airplanes and importing more clothes than before. (This is roughly the situation the U.S. has been in.) Because the nation gets to expand an industry better suited to its comparative advantage and contract one less suited, it becomes more productive, and its GDP goes up, just like the theory says. So far, so good. But here is the rub: suppose that a million dollars' worth of clothes production requires one white-collar worker and nine blue-collar workers, while a million dollars of airplane production requires three white-collar workers and seven blue-collar workers. This means that for every million dollars' change in what gets produced, there is a demand for two more white-collar workers and two fewer blue-collar workers. Because demand for white-collar workers goes up and demand for blue-collar workers goes down, the wages of white-collar workers will go up and those of blue-collar workers will go down. But most workers are blue-collar workers—so free trade has lowered wages for most workers in the economy!

It follows from the above problems that free trade, even if it performs as free traders say in other respects (it does not), could still leave most Americans with lower incomes. And even if it expands our economy overall, it could still increase poverty. Taking an approximate mean of available estimates, we can attribute perhaps twenty-five percent of America's three-decade rise in income inequality to freer trade. It was estimated in 2006 that the increase in inequality due to freer trade cost the average household earning the median income more than $2,000.

Assumption 5: Capital Is Not Internationally Mobile.

Despite the wide scope of its implications, the theory of comparative advantage is, at bottom, a very narrow theory. It is *only* about the best uses to which nations can put their factors of production. We have certain cards in hand, so to speak, the other players have certain cards, and the theory tells us the best way to play the hand we have been dealt. Or more precisely, it tells us to let the free market play our hand *for us,* so market forces can drive all our factors to their best uses in our economy.

Unfortunately, this all relies upon the impossibility of these same market forces driving these factors right *out* of our economy. If that happens, all bets are off about driving these factors to their most productive use *in* our economy. Their most productive use may well be in another country, and if they are internationally mobile, then free trade will cause them to migrate there. This will benefit the world economy as a whole, and the nation they migrate to, but it will not necessarily benefit us.

This problem actually applies to all factors of production. But because land and other fixed resources cannot migrate, labor is legally constrained in migrating, and people usually do not try to stop technology or raw materials from migrating, the crux of the problem is capital. Capital mobility replaces comparative advantage, which applies when capital is forced to choose between alternative uses within a single national economy, with our old friend absolute advantage. And absolute advantage contains no guarantees whatsoever about the results being good for *both* trading partners. The win-win guarantee is purely an effect of the world economy being yoked to comparative advantage and dies with it.

Absolute advantage is really the natural order of things in capitalism, and comparative advantage is a special case caused by the existence of national borders that factors of production cannot cross. Indeed, that is basically what a nation is, from the point of view of economics: a part of the world with political barriers to the entry and exit of factors of production.

This forces national economies to interact indirectly, by exchanging goods and services *made from* those factors, which places comparative advantage in control. Without these barriers, nations would simply be regions of a single economy, which is why absolute advantage governs economic relations *within* nations. In 1950, Michigan had absolute advantage in automobiles and Alabama in cotton. But by 2000, automobile plants were closing in Michigan and opening in Alabama. This benefited Alabama, but it did not necessarily benefit Michigan.

(It only would have if Michigan had been transitioning to a higher-value industry than automobiles. Helicopters?) The same scenario is possible for entire nations if capital is internationally mobile.

Capital immobility does not have to be absolute to put comparative advantage in control, but it has to be significant and as it melts away, trade shifts from a guarantee of win-win relations to a possibility of win-lose relations. David Ricardo, who was wiser than many of his own modern-day followers, knew this perfectly well. As he put it:

The difference in this respect, between a single country and many, is easily accounted for, considering the difficulty with which capital moves from one country to another, to seek a more profitable employment, and the activity with which it invariably passes from one province to another of the same country.

Ricardo then elaborated, using his favorite example of the trade in English cloth for Portuguese wine and cutting right to the heart of present-day concerns:

It would undoubtedly be advantageous to the capitalists of England, and to the consumers in both countries, that under such circumstances the wine and the cloth should both be made in Portugal, and therefore that the capital and labor of England employed in making cloth should be removed to Portugal for that purpose.

But he does not say that it would be advantageous to the workers of England! This is precisely the problem Americans experience today: when imports replace goods produced here, capitalists like the higher profits and consumers like the lower prices—but workers *do not* like the lost jobs. Given that consumers and workers are ultimately the same people, this means they may lose more as workers than they gain as consumers. And there is no theorem in economics which guarantees that their gains will exceed their losses. Things can go either way, which means that free trade is sometimes a losing move for them.

Assumption 6: Short-Term Efficiency Causes Long-Term Growth.

The theory of comparative advantage is a case of what economists call static analysis. That is, it looks at the facts of a single instant in time and determines the best response to those facts at that instant. This is not an intrinsically invalid way of doing economics—balancing ones checkbook is an exercise in static analysis—but it is vulnerable to a key problem: *it says nothing about dynamic facts.* That is, it says nothing about how today's facts may change tomorrow. More importantly, it says nothing about how one might cause them to change in one's favor.

Imagine a photograph of a rock thrown up in the air. It is an accurate representation of the position of the rock at the instant it was taken. But one cannot tell, from the photograph alone, whether the rock is rising or falling. The only way to know *that* is either to have a series of photographs, or add the information contained in the laws of physics to the information contained in the photograph.

The problem here is that even if the theory of comparative advantage tells us our best move today, given our productivities and opportunity costs in various industries, it *does not* tell us the best way to raise those productivities tomorrow. That, however, is the essence of economic growth, and in the long run much more important than squeezing every last drop of advantage from the productivities we have today. Economic growth, that is, is ultimately less about *using* one's factors of production than about transforming them—into more productive factors tomorrow. The difference between poor nations and rich ones mainly consists in the problem of turning from Burkina Faso into South Korea; it does not consist in being the most efficient possible Burkina Faso forever. The theory of comparative advantage is not so much wrong about long-term growth as simply silent.

> **Analogously, it is a valid application of personal comparative advantage for someone with secretarial skills to work as a secretary and someone with banking skills to work as a banker. In the short run, it is efficient for them both, as it results in both being better paid than if they tried to swap roles. (They would both be fired for inability to do their jobs and earn zero.)**

But the path to personal success does not consist in being the best possible secretary forever; it consists in upgrading one's skills to better-paid occupations, like banker. And there is very little about being the best possible secretary that tells one how to do this.

Ricardo's own favorite example, the trade in English textiles for Portuguese wine, is very revealing here, though not in a way he would have liked. In Ricardo's day, textiles were produced in England with the then-state-of-the-art technology like steam engines. The textile industry thus nurtured a sophisticated machine tool industry to make the parts for these engines, which drove forward the general technological capabilities of the British economy and helped it break into related industries like locomotives and steamships. Wine, on the other hand, was made by methods that had not changed in centuries (and have only begun to change since about 1960, by the way). So for hundreds of years, wine production contributed

no technological advances to the Portuguese economy, no drivers of growth, no opportunities to raise economy-wide productivity.

And its own productivity remained static: it did the same thing over and over again, year after year, decade after decade, century after century, because this was where Portugal's immediate comparative advantage lay. It may have been Portugal's best move in the short run, but it was a dead end in the long run.

> **Today, the theory of comparative advantage is similarly dangerous to poor and undeveloped nations because they tend, like Portugal, to have comparative advantage in industries that are economic dead ends. So despite being nominally free, free trade tends to lock them in place.**

Assumption 7: Trade Does Not Induce Adverse Productivity Growth Abroad.

As previously noted, our gains from free trade derive from the difference between *our* opportunity costs for producing products and the opportunity costs of our trading partners. This opens up a paradoxical but very real way for free trade to backfire. When we trade with a foreign nation, this will generally build up that nation's industries, i.e., raise its productivity in them. Now it would be nice to assume that this productivity growth in our trading partners can only reduce their direct costs, therefore reduce their opportunity costs, and therefore increase our gains from trading with them. Our foreign suppliers will just become ever more efficient at supplying the things we want, and we will get even cheaper foreign goods in exchange for our own exports, right?

Wrong. As we saw in our initial discussion of absolute vs. comparative advantage, while productivity (output per unit of input) does determine direct costs, it does not on its own determine opportunity costs. The alternative uses of factors of production do. As a result, productivity growth in some industries can actually raise our trading partners' opportunity costs in other industries, by increasing what they give up producing in one industry in order to produce in another. If the number of rolls they can make from a pound of dough somehow goes up (rolls get fluffier?), this will make it more expensive for them to bake bread instead. So they may cease to supply us with such cheap bread! It sounds odd, but the logic is inescapable.

Consider our present trade with China. Despite all the problems this trade causes us, we do get compensation in the form of some very cheap goods, thanks mainly to China's very cheap labor. The same goes for other poor countries we import from. But labor is cheap in poor countries because it has poor alternative employment opportunities. What if these opportunities improve? Then this labor may cease to be so cheap, and our supply of cheap goods may dry up.

This is actually what happened in Japan from the 1960s to the 1980s, as Japan's economy transitioned from primitive to sophisticated manufacturing, and the cheap merchandise readers over forty will remember (the same things stamped "Made in China" today, only less ubiquitous) disappeared from America's stores. Did this reduce the pressure of cheap Japanese labor on American workers? Indeed. But it also deprived us of some very cheap goods we used to get. (And it is not like Japan stopped pressing us, either, as it moved upmarket and started competing in more sophisticated industries.) The same thing happened with Western Europe as its economy recovered from WWII from 1945 to about 1960, and cheap European goods disappeared from our stores. Remember when BMWs were cheap little cars and Italian shoes were affordable?

It is as if our football player woke up one morning and found that his lawn man had quietly saved his pennies from mowing lawns and opened a garden shop. No more cheap lawn mowing for him! (Maybe it was a bad idea to hire him so often.)

Now this is where things get slippery and non-economists tend to get lost. Because, as we saw earlier, gains from trade do not derive from absolute but comparative advantage, these gains can be killed off *without* our trading partners getting anywhere near our own productivity levels. So the above problem does not merely consist in our trading partners catching up to us in industrial sophistication. But if their *relative* tradeoffs for producing different goods cease to differ from ours, then our gains from trading with them will vanish. If Canada's wheat vs. corn tradeoff is two units per acre vs. three and ours is four vs. six, all bets are off. Because both nations now face the same tradeoff ratio between producing one grain and the others, all possible trades will cost Canada exactly as much as they benefit the U.S. leaving no profit, no motivation to trade, and no gain from doing so. And if free trade helped raise Canada's productivity to this point, *then trade deprived us of benefits we used to get.*

It is worth retracing the logic here until it makes sense, as this really is the way the economics works. Most of the time, this problem has low visibility because it consists in the silent change of invisible ratios between the productivities of industries here and abroad. Few people worry about it because it has no easily understood face like cheap foreign labor. But it definitely does mean that free trade can "foul its own nest"

and kill off the benefits of trade over time. Even within the most strictly orthodox Ricardian view, only the existence of gains from free trade is guaranteed. It is not guaranteed that changes induced by free trade will make these gains grow, rather than shrink. So free trade can do billions of dollars worth of damage even if Ricardo were right about everything else (he was not).

This problem is actually even more significant than explained here because it is also the foundation of an even more radical critique of free trade based on so-called multiple-equilibrium analysis. This concerns the nightmare scenario that *really* haunts Americans: the idea that free trade can help other nations catch up with us in industrial sophistication, driving us out of our own most important industries. Unfortunately, this type of analysis is beyond the scope of this essay because it is outside the Ricardian framework, though it is worth knowing that it exists.

Conclusion: Trade Yes, Free Trade No

Given that the theory of comparative advantage has all of the above-described flaws, how much validity does it really have? Answer: some. Asking what industries a nation has comparative advantage in helps illuminate what kind of economy it has. And insofar as the theory's assumptions do hold to some extent, some of the time, it can give us some valid policy recommendations. *Fairly open trade, most of the time, is a good thing.* But the theory was never intended to be by its own inventor, and its innate logic will not support its being, a blank check that justifies 100 percent free trade with 100 percent of the world 100 percent of the time. It only justifies free trade insofar as its assumptions hold true, and they largely do not.

Source

Adapted from *Free Trade Doesn't Work: What Should Replace It and Why*, by Ian Fletcher (USBIC, 2010), www.freetradedoesntwork.com.

Critical Thinking

1. What is the theory of comparative advantage?
2. Why wouldn't the theory of comparative advantage work in the modern world?
3. Are some people hurt by the developments in global trade?

IAN FLETCHER is an Adjunct Fellow with the U.S. Business & Industry Council.

From *Social Policy*, Spring 2011, pp. 37–46. Copyright © 2011 by Ian Fletcher. Reprinted by permission of the author.

A Bretton Woods for Innovation

STEPHEN EZELL

Sixty-seven years ago, representatives from 44 nations convened in the small resort town of Bretton Woods, New Hampshire to make financial arrangements for the post-World War II economy. The meetings spawned the International Monetary Fund, the World Bank, and the General Agreement on Tariffs and Trade—the precursor to the World Trade Organization. While these institutions worked well for half a century, now that the commodity-based manufacturing system has evolved into a knowledge and innovation economy, the strains on the Bretton Woods system have become clear.

As countries increasingly recognize that innovation drives long-run economic growth, a fierce race for an innovation advantage has emerged. During the past decade alone, over three dozen countries have created national innovation agencies and strategies. Going forward, the challenge will be to balance countries' pursuit of the highest possible standard of living for their citizens in a way that promotes, rather than distorts, global innovation.

We need a new international framework that sets clear parameters for what constitutes fair and unfair innovation competition, creating new institutions (and updating old ones) that maximize innovation.

The Good, The Bad, The Ugly

Countries' focus on innovation as the route to economic growth creates both opportunities and risks. They can apply their innovation policies in ways that are: "Good," benefiting the country and the world simultaneously; "Ugly," benefiting the country at the expense of other nations; "Bad," appearing to be good for the country, but actually failing to benefit either the country or the world; or "Self-destructive," failing to benefit the country while benefiting the rest of the world.

"Good" innovation policies include increasing investments in scientific research; offering research and development tax credits; welcoming highly skilled immigrants; providing strong science, technology, engineering, and math education; and deploying advanced information and communications technologies. Countries' "Good" innovation policies are positive for the entire world—as discoveries, inventions, and innovations made in one nation ultimately spill over to the benefit of citizens worldwide, even as they drive economic growth in the originating nation. For example, the United States initially profited the most from creating the Internet (enormous economic growth was generated by start-up "dot-coms"), but now the Internet's benefits flow to billions around the world.

Countries' "Ugly" policies include intellectual property theft or forced technology transfers as a condition of market access (designed to promote innovation in one nation to the detriment of others). China's government forces many multinational companies to share their technologies with state-owned enterprises in order to operate in the country. To compete in China's high-speed rail market, for example, foreign multinational locomotive manufacturers like Japan's Kawasaki or Germany's Siemens had to offer their latest designs and produce 70 percent of each system locally. As a result, China's state-owned locomotive manufacturers, CSR and CNR, acquired key technologies and manufacturing know-how. Now they not only dominate China's market but compete internationally against the same multinationals that supplied them with the knowledge and skills in the first place.

"Bad" policies are strategies like import substitution industrialization that a country believes will help it, but in fact do more harm than good to the country's economy. For every dollar of tariffs that India imposed on imported information technology products (in its effort to spur creation of an indigenous information industry) it suffered an economic loss of $1.30 because its firms and citizens had to use inferior technologies. Back in the days of Indira Gandhi's rule, news bureaus seeking to bring the first American PCs into New Delhi found them impounded, and their executives told they should buy an Indian product—a gargantuan contraption with vacuum tubes that took up a large room.

Finally, "Self-destructive" innovation policies, such as the United States' unwelcoming posture toward highly skilled immigrants, hurt a country while actually benefiting competitors.

Sadly, there is disturbing evidence that the global economic system is increasingly distorted, as a growing number of countries embrace what might be called innovation mercantilism. These approaches are based on the view that achieving economic growth through technology exports is preferable to raising domestic productivity through genuine innovation. Such nations—and China is only the most prominent—are not so much focused on innovation as on the manipulation of currency, government procurement, technology standards, intellectual property rights, and non-tariff barriers to gain an unfair advantage favoring their own technology exports in international trade. China's currency manipulation, Brazil's neglect for foreign intellectual property holders' rights, and the European Union's tariffs and restrictions on information technology imports are all forms of innovation mercantilism.

Such practices impose large costs on the global economy, while retarding global innovation and productivity. For example, by stealing intellectual property, countries reduce revenues that could have been invested in innovation. Indeed, in 2007, intellectual property theft reduced global trade by 5 to 7 percent, according to the World Customs Organization. Likewise, the OECD says that complying with country-specific technical standards adds 10 percent to the cost of an imported product.

To be sure, there is nothing wrong with countries engaging in aggressive innovation and economic competition—so long as they are competing according to the rules established by the global community. In fact, when a country competes intensely, within the rules of the system, it benefits both itself and the rest of the world. That's because fair competition forces countries to implement the right policies to support science and technology, the right tax credits to encourage research and development, and the right education policies to train the next generation. So when France offers an R&D tax credit six times more generous than the United States', or Denmark creates innovation vouchers to help small businesses, or countries increase their investments in science and technology, they make tough, fair moves that force other countries to raise their games by enacting "good" policies of their own. The problem occurs when countries start to use "ugly" policies. Such strategies create incentives to cheat, and the whole system fails as everyone fights for a slice of an ever shrinking pie.

Failing Institutions

Unfortunately, the international economic system is governed by institutions rooted in a past era. Regrettably, the Bretton Woods framework was not designed to maximize innovation. So far, the international order has failed to produce a sustainable globalization system largely because it's organized to deal with finances and the flow of goods across borders, not with innovation. Not only are the three major international economic organizations—the IMF, World Bank, and WTO—ill-equipped to take on new forms of unfair or counterproductive behavior but also, by sins of omission and commission, they perpetuate the problems. These institutions do little to promote innovation policies and even less to pressure countries to play fair. There's no one refereeing the global innovation competition.

There's no one refereeing the global innovation competition.

Established after World War II, the IMF was charged with overseeing the international monetary system—the exchange rates and payments that enable countries and their citizens to buy goods and services from one another. The new entity was designed to ensure exchange rate stability and encourage member countries to eliminate trade restrictions. Unfortunately, the IMF has proven unwilling or unable to take serious action on its most important charge—curtailing the rampant currency manipulation that continues unabated in countries such as China.

As for the World Bank, not only does it do almost nothing to pressure innovation mercantilists to shape up, it often unwittingly abets them by failing to differentiate between legitimate policies and mercantilist policies. To see why, it is important to recognize that the World Bank isn't really the "world's" bank. It's a collection of country desks (for example, the China desk and the India desk). The Bank's development professionals appear to be evaluated primarily on their response to one question—did they support projects that spurred economic growth in the countries for which they are responsible? If they can get China or India to export more earth movers, routers, biotech products, or airplanes to the rest of the world, they get rewarded. It doesn't matter if the result is fewer American or European workers making earth movers, routers, biotech products, or airplanes.

Like the other two bodies, the WTO has largely abdicated its role in fighting innovation mercantilism. Instead, it adjudicates disputes and views what is systemic as merely occasional infractions of trade provisions that should be handled on a case-by-case basis.

Why do these international organizations either sit on the sidelines or actively support nations engaged in innovation mercantilism? It's because sustainable global innovation is either not their mission or not thought to be important. For the WTO, expanded trade flow is all that matters. For the World Bank and the IMF, two priorities stand out—responding to individual national economic fiscal crises and ensuring robust international capital and trade flows. Neither asks if these are the results of deeply dysfunctional mercantilist policies.

New Frameworks

It's time to create an international innovation policy framework that will spur a robust global innovation economy. First, it must recognize that the central task of global economic policy should be to encourage nations to boost innovation and domestic productivity, instead of focusing on export-led growth. The second step is to revamp the mission of existing international bodies not only to support sustainable global innovation but also to fight against innovation mercantilism. This means stronger enforcement by global bodies like the WTO against mercantilist strategies. Third, international development organizations need to reformulate foreign aid policies as carrot-and-stick tools to prod countries toward the right kinds of innovation policies.

Finally, we need more capable international institutions that support global science and innovation. Now more than ever, the benefits of research flow globally. Nations that invest in science and research are not just helping themselves, but the entire world.

Now more than ever, the benefits of research flow globally.

But many countries invest too little in R&D, free-riding off investments in leading countries like the United States, Germany, and Japan. The worldwide benefits of pharmaceuticals allow governments to receive new drug developments without having to pay the associated costs of researching that drug. Britain free rides by only allowing a return on domestic capital and investment. Pharmaceutical companies cannot take into account the cost of American or other foreign R&D when determining the price to sell in the U.K.

Moreover, there is less focus on global challenges. We see this particularly in research that could produce non-carbon energy sources or address pandemic diseases. In part, this is because in hot high-tech fields like biotechnology, patent races develop with competing nations perceiving a winner-take-all situation where they believe value can be appropriated from knowledge only by those who first create it. As David Hart, professor of science and technology policy at George Mason University, and Dieter Ernst, senior fellow at the East-West Center, note, "the result is duplication of effort, imprudent crash programs, and even outright fraud."

Leading nations should therefore establish a Global Science and Innovation Foundation. GSIF's mission would be to fund scientific research around the globe on key challenges and in particular support internationally collaborative research. For any nation to be eligible to receive funds, it would have to commit 0.1 percent of its GDP in funding and be certified by the IMF as a nation not engaged in innovation mercantilism. Such an agency would be as committed to implementing a Bretton Woods for innovation as the IMF has been to implementing the goals of the original post-World War II fiscal conference.

It's time for the world to move beyond seeing the pursuit of economic growth through innovation as a zero-sum game, where one country's loss is another's gain. The goal, instead, should be to embrace mutual global prosperity as the ideal—indeed, a multiplier—of any investment. A new approach is needed, one grounded in the ideas that markets drive global trade; that countries should adhere to their trade agreements; that genuine innovation drives economic growth; and that constructive competition forces countries to ratchet up their game by putting in place "good" innovation policies. New institutions will have to be created—and old ones updated—to realize this vision.

Critical Thinking

1. Do you think innovation needs to be globally coordinated?
2. Why are patents important?
3. Why should patents be respected globally?

STEPHEN EZELL is a senior analyst with the Information Technology and Innovation Foundation (ITIF). He is the co-author with Dr. Robert D. Atkinson, the foundation's founder and president, of the forthcoming book *The Global Race for Innovation Advantage, and Why the United States Is Falling Behind* (Yale, 2012).

Globalization with a Human Face

Jagdish Bhagwati on the trouble with protectionism, how to deal with climate change, and why NAFTA was bad for free trade.

SHIKHA DALMIA

Free trade is never more necessary—or vulnerable—than in times of economic distress. The current global downturn is no exception. Protectionist barriers have shot up all over the world, including the United States. Earlier this year, Congress killed a pilot program allowing Mexican trucks to transport goods across America and included "Buy America" provisions in the stimulus bill banning foreign steel and iron from infrastructure projects funded by the legislation. More disturbingly, President Barack Obama, after chiding the Congress for flirting with protectionism, initiated his own ill-advised affair by imposing a 35 percent tariff on cheap Chinese tires.

If the world manages to avoid an all-out trade war of the kind that helped trigger the Great Depression after the U.S. imposed the Smoot-Hawley tariffs in 1930, it will be in no small part due to the efforts of one man: Jagdish N. Bhagwati, an ebullient and irreverent 76-year-old professor of economics at Columbia University. Bhagwati has done more than perhaps any other person alive to advance the cause of unfettered global trade.

A native of India, Bhagwati immigrated to the United States in the late '60s after a brief stint on the Indian Planning Commission, where he learned first-hand the insanity of an economic approach that tried to modernize a country by cutting it off from world trade. Since then, he has devoted his efforts, both in academia and in the popular press, to showing that there is no better way of improving the lot of both advanced countries and the developing world than through free trade. His path-breaking contributions to trade theory have put him on the short list for a Nobel Prize in economics.

Though a dogged trade advocate, Bhagwati is anything but dogmatic. He is a free spirit who draws intellectual inspiration from many disparate ideological camps. A self-avowed liberal, he is also something of a Gandhian social progressive, though Gandhi himself supported economic autarky. Bhagwati works with numerous Third World NGOs on a host of human rights issues. Yet he has no problem taking on these groups—or his famous student, Nobel laureate Paul Krugman—when they question the benefits of trade. In fact, he devoted his 2004 magnum opus, *In Defense of Globalization,* to a point-by-point rebuttal of these critics. Although he doesn't vote Republican because he dislikes the party's nationalistic jingoism, he readily declares that Democrats pose a far bigger threat to international exchange than Republicans.

This summer Shikha Dalmia, a senior analyst at the Reason Foundation, interviewed Bhagwati in his New York office.

reason: You have been on the short list for a Nobel Prize in economics for your contribution to trade theory. Could you explain what your main contribution is?

Jagdish Bhagwati: My breakthrough in trade theory was very simple, as all breakthroughs are. Back in the 1950s, when the case for free trade was widely regarded as less compelling analytically than today, protectionists had one very powerful argument on their side. They noted that a country necessarily benefits from free trade only when markets are perfect—that is to say, only when market prices reflect true social costs can we expect these prices to guide allocation correctly. Take pollution. Say your production process makes you spew things into the air and water but you do not have to pay for this pollution. Then the social cost of harming others is not being taken into account by you and hence your production costs are less than the "correct" social costs.

So you could take two points of view. The time-honored view was that when there is such "market failure," or what might be better called a "missing market," the case for free trade was compromised and any form of protectionism was justified. I argued that if you had a market failure, fix that, and you are back to perfect markets and the legitimacy of free trade. So, for example, you can have a polluter-pay principle on the environment. If you do that, then there's no damaging spillover which has not been taken into account.

The proper policy response then is not to abandon free trade but rather to fix the market failure and then to embrace free trade. This was a revolutionary thought. For 200 years, serious economists had abandoned free trade in the presence of market failures of one kind or another.

27

reason: *In Defense of Globalization* was addressed to non-academic critics of free trade and globalization who claim that globalization does not have a human face. What was your argument?

Bhagwati: When I was in Seattle in 1999, when everything went haywire as far as trying to get a new round of trade negotiations, I realized that the young people who were agitating, and some of the older folks also, were not interested in whether trade was good for national income and prosperity. They were claiming that globalization has an adverse impact on a whole lot of social issues—gender equity issues, environmental issues, the effects of globalization on the polity and democratic rights. In short, to use the fetching phrase, they were concerned that economic globalization lacked a human face.

My book addressed precisely such issues. I found that, contrary to the fears of the critics, most social agendas were advanced rather than handicapped by globalization. Globalization, I concluded, *had* a human face.

Take women's issues, for example: If you look at what happens to the gender gap on pay inequality, it turns out that you can make a perfectly solid argument that in fact it's narrowed rather than widened as a result of international trade. The reason is very simple: If a man is paid twice as much as a woman, when they are both equally competent, that is inefficient. So when you are engaged in international competition, you're really not going to be able to indulge your prejudice in this way. This will lead to more demand for women and less for men, bringing pressure to bear on their relative wages in the direction of greater pay equality.

Two brilliant young women, Sandra Black and Elizabeth Brainerd, did their dissertation at Harvard on this hypothesis. They found that in two decades in internationally traded industries in the United States, the gender wage gap narrowed faster than in non-traded industries. Trade had thus been good for an important social objective, not a drag on it.

reason: You still hear the argument—President Obama made it during his campaign—that we want fair trade, not free trade.

Bhagwati: In the United States the phrase "fair trade" holds a lot of sway, because fairness is an important issue here. In the United States it's the equality of opportunity, not of outcome, that matters. We have a fairness-oriented culture. The Europeans, who are actually more stratified—they're more into equality of outcome. The social mobility of people is much less, so they want the state to intervene and redistribute. They're more into justice and we're more into fairness.

So if you want to be a protectionist in the U.S., you've got to say that these Japanese or these Indians are trading unfairly. People will much more readily give you protection if they think the other guy is a wicked unfair trader.

President Obama hasn't really understood the case for free trade because I don't think he's been too interested in trade. His background is as an activist working with the poor people, so he hasn't thought about these issues. So he ends up listening to other people, and a lot of people who are protectionist are around him, particularly the unions, who are afraid of international competition. But they dress up the fair trade argument in altruism, that they're doing it to raise the labor standards and wages of workers in India and Brazil and so on and so forth, when in fact, they're doing it to protect their own workers from competition. The president doesn't seem to realize that this is something which other people, whom you pretend you're trying to help, actually see as a naked, cynical ploy.

Instead of pandering to union fear, Obama has got to engage them. You have got to help these doubting Thomases confront their fears. He's got to say that trade with the poor countries is actually helping, not hurting, you. The unions' main fear is that unskilled jobs are disappearing. They see these jobs being taken up elsewhere where the labor is cheap. But they can't hold onto these jobs anyway. What they get in return from trade are cheap products that they need as consumers. So free trade moderates the downward pressure on their real wages.

Big portions of the wages of poor workers go toward low quality textiles, for instance. That is well-established. But if you look at the structure of protectionism, if you go and buy something from Anne Klein that's going to be expensive, but it carries no tariff at all because these high-end designers compete on variety. Tariffs matter where the competition is on prices. So the low-quality items which poor people buy end up carrying higher tariffs than high-end items that rich people buy.

reason: So free trade's harm to union workers as producers is minimal, but the harm to them as consumers would be very great if we didn't have free trade?

Bhagwati: Yes. So what President Obama has to do is basically change the ethos in this country so that it understands that the United States has profited enormously from free trade. Free trade has rescued India and China from poverty, yes. But the U.S. working class has also profited from international trade.

He's got to make an eloquent case like that. He's got to see that this is something that needs as much attention and as much of his eloquence as the speech he made on race after he got into trouble over his pastor.

But then to move the case of free trade forward, the Obama administration has to show global leadership, because the U.S. is the biggest trading country. He has got to make sure that the stimulus package and everything that he does is completely consistent with openness. I think he's got to understand this is not something he can keep postponing and postponing.

When President Clinton came in the first year, he was into Japan bashing and he hadn't made up his mind on whether he wanted trade or not, because he had advisors on both sides. So his first year was extremely tentative. Then he made up his mind and was fiercely pro-trade after that. President Bush, the junior, he too gave into steel tariffs when he first came in, but after the first year, when he found his feet, he was very pro-trade.

28

President Obama doesn't have that luxury because the weaknesses are showing in the way the stimulus is being designed and played out. So someone has to tell him very clearly that he doesn't have the luxury of most presidents, which is to use a first year to find your feet on trade. He's got to be out there and he's got to provide the leadership. He's got to bring in the people who waiver and dither, the AFL-CIO, the Democrats who are indebted to the AFL-CIO, and say: "Look, you're wrong. Here, let's have a debate." There are lots of Democratic economists who'd be able to engage these guys in a proper debate.

reason: In recent years, the opposition to free trade hasn't just come from left-wing unions, but also people on the right who fear that outsourcing will cause the U.S. to lose its economic edge as it imports high-value-added products and exports low-value-added ones. How do you respond to that?

Bhagwati: It's an irrelevant argument. To say that the United States should be exporting high-value items rather than low-value items is itself a fallacy. But America's great comparative advantage lies in innovation. For someone like me who has come from India it is very obvious that this country is full of innovators. When I was a student I read about Britain's Industrial Revolution. And it was powered by all kinds of people, inventing the spinning jenny and so on. They were like little Americans, you know, thinking of new ways of doing things and making a buck. Almost every other American I know is thinking about something, some way to do something. We are a highly inventive people, and technology therefore is our driving force. It's not savings and investments which are driving our productivity. It's technology and innovation and immigrants like me—not me in particular—lots of people who come here and by the second generation go through the mill and become Colin Powell or Orlando Patterson at Harvard.

Almost every other American I know is thinking about something, some way to do something. We are a highly inventive people, and technology therefore is our driving force. It's not savings and investments which are driving our productivity. It's technology and innovation and immigrants.

Nobody can compete with us in the long run, in my view, because these are not advantages which people in traditional societies can reproduce. So we're always going to be doing high value. We'll lose the high value we generate to others quickly because now technology diffuses very fast. But then we'll have new ideas, new technologies.

reason: Which side poses the bigger threat to free trade, conservatives on sovereignty, neo-mercantilist grounds, or liberals on equity and environmental grounds?

Bhagwati: In the U.S., I think the Democrats are the biggest threat to free trade. I don't see the right-wing threat to globalization in terms of sovereignty as being a major one, frankly.

Conservatives are principled people, so they have Edmund Burke type of reservations about continuous change and so on. But they are not people who are going to undermine the rule of law when it comes to trade. Even their arguments against immigration are rule-of-law arguments. Anti-globalization noises saying we've lost our sovereignty and so on and so forth, it's not going to get very far in the U.S. system.

The threat from the left, on the other hand, is much more serious because they oppose free trade on equity grounds. I love America. I have settled in it. But there is a tendency, particularly on the part of the Democrats, to become totally self-righteous on everything and this is the way it has to be and if you disagree, then you're a Republican. I mean, that's the way they argue it. It's unbelievable. They don't want to argue the merits of the case.

The threat from the left . . . is much more serious because they oppose free trade on equity grounds. . . . There is a tendency, particularly on the part of the Democrats, to become totally self-righteous on everything. . . . They don't want to argue the merits of the case.

---

reason: Why do you think Republicans are better on free trade than Democrats?

Bhagwati: Both the last Bush and Ronald Reagan believed in America. They thought that their own people could win. That made them more prone to accept international competition and trade.

They carried that attitude over into politics, of course. For instance, President Reagan won the Cold War by pushing Gorbachev to the limit. But he was lucky. President Bush went into Iraq with the same attitude, and that was unfortunate.

But since they both believed that Americans would win, they were good on international trade, although maybe for the wrong reasons. Democrats don't believe that America can remain number one, and hence they cannot bring themselves to be completely in favor of open markets.

reason: You are a big believer in multilateral trade agreements over bilateral trade agreements. What's wrong with bilateral trade agreements?

Bhagwati: Free trade agreements and protectionism are two sides of the same coin. When I have free trade just with you, I'm freeing trade with you but I handicap those who are not members of our free trade area. They have to keep paying the duties to get into our markets. So that becomes a de facto way of increasing protection against outsiders. Multilateral free trade would be a closer thing to pure free trade.

Free trade agreements and protectionism are two sides of the same coin. When I have free trade just with you, I'm freeing trade with you but I handicap those who are not members of our free trade area. They have to keep paying the duties to get into our markets.

But there are two additional worries about bilateral trade agreements: One, we don't just have two or three free trade agreements. Today there are close to 500, and every week there's another new one being constructed. As a result, you're getting all kinds of special tariffs, rules of origin, and other things multiplying in the system, something which I've called the spaghetti bowl. Exporters rightly get upset by the large numbers of tariffs they face depending on where you're coming from.

Two, how do you enforce these agreements in a globalized world? It's very chaotic. Parts are coming from everywhere. For a country to have to then decide which product is my partner country's product rather than an outside country's product becomes completely arbitrary. A car produced in Canada with Japanese steel and German chemicals, where 80 or 90 percent of the parts may come from elsewhere—is that a Canadian car or is it really something else? Does it qualify for the zero tariff under the North American Free Trade Agreement or not?

reason: Was NAFTA a mistake?

Bhagwati: I think in retrospect, yes. It's not a slam dunk argument because it did bring in Mexico. Otherwise, they were talking about CAFTA which included just Canada and the U.S. But when you brought in Mexico, it made it a much bigger thing.

President Clinton was carrying on the multilateral negotiations in tandem with NAFTA. But NAFTA created worries on the part of the unions here, because this is a poor country and they were worried that Mexican competition would really hurt their wages. So even though the multilateral talks would've gone through without any difficulty, President Clinton ended up having to fight very hard for NAFTA, which survived by a very narrow majority. In order to win NAFTA, he had to give in on things like labor standards and so on. That's when all these social things became part of trade deals. From there, it never looked back.

So in retrospect, I would say, because of the concessions they had to make, Clinton started us down a road which really has been counterproductive.

There is another thing to worry about. When you look at a trade agreement like NAFTA, it's about that thick (*holds his hands about two feet apart*). When I debate people like Lori Wallach of Public Citizen, she arrives with a lot of books, and among them is this NAFTA treaty she carries for effect. I hope she gets a hernia from doing this often enough, because it looks pretty heavy to me. I wouldn't be carrying it around. Anyway, she shows this book and asks, "Is this free trade?" And mad as

she is, she's right to raise that issue. You should be able to say maybe in 10 pages that in these sectors we are going to liberalize and so on. But nine-tenths of what's in these agreements are things which have nothing to do with trade. Labor standards, environmental standards, intellectual property rights. If I were Jane Fonda, in order to sell more workout tapes, I could put into the agreement a clause that the president of Mexico has to do his exercise to my tapes. And it would go in, because ours is a lobbying culture and nobody really would know that it's there. Because who opens these things except the lobbyists?

So many developing countries are now waking up to the fact that they're being sold a bill of goods in the form of trade agreements.

reason: Do you think a global externality problem like global warming poses a fundamental threat to free trade?

Bhagwati: I think it depends on the way you do it. First, you've got to decide whether there is a problem of an externality. I have doubts about these scientists who claim to have a consensus on global warming because, you know, Freeman Dyson, a great scientific figure, says these guys are really low-level scientists and I'm told by many that they, in fact, are. And if they reach a consensus, I don't care. I mean, that's the consensus of incompetents.

But so long as only the scientists were talking about global warming, nobody paid the slightest attention. Remember, not a single senator voted for the Kyoto resolution back in the '90s. Even Al Gore and Clinton had to walk away from Kyoto. But then the polar bears were threatened, the glaciers began to melt, and then that great French film about the penguins, which touched all our hearts came out. So these were three whammies. Even if you live in Peoria you will understand, wrongly maybe, that global warming is a problem. I tell all my students: If they think of something like that for free trade, please let me know.

What countries like India and China are saying is that if the CO_2 was accumulating and it's going to create a disaster, then that took a lot of time to establish. So they want the West to bear primary responsibility for the damage it has caused in the past. If America applies some kind of a carbon tax and it says that if India and China don't impose a similar tax, it's going to use what is called border tax adjustment, then that is protectionism. And there's no reason why Indians and Chinese have to accept this. Just as America was not willing to accept it when it didn't sign onto Kyoto and Europe started threatening a countervailing duty on American exports. But everybody reacted to that talk and said this is a cockeyed thing to do. Peter Mandelson, who was the EU Commissioner, said it was very unwise because the United States will retaliate.

It's ironic that we are now using exactly that kind of threat on India and China. But America's fuel tax is so much lower than that of most other countries, except the Middle East. So India and China are going to hit us because we had a low gas tax for a long time. And all hell would break loose. India and China are big guys. They can get legal [World Trade Organization] retaliation against the U.S. Or India could take away contracts from Boeing and give them to Air France. It can have nuclear reactors go to France rather than to G.E. Caterpillar would be shut out.

So I suggest a different way. If in our own U.S. system you're going to get your companies to clean up under the Superfund Act, that's a tort principle which we accept. Then we ought to be willing to pay in some form to other poor countries for the past damages. The West has completely ignored this suggestion so far. It has provided maybe a few million dollars in assistance to Third World countries for this purpose. But if the West seriously starts contributing to this fund, Third World countries could get anywhere from $150 million to $1 billion to mitigate global warming.

reason: This is a political non-starter, you know.

Bhagwati: Yes. But the president actually has made some remarks about border tax adjustments not being such a good idea. He's got to do more than that. He's got to say this is a crazy thing to do. He's still very cool—he needs to lose his temper once in a while. Because it's too important. The U.S. is one of the biggest trading nations in the world. We want the rule of law. We don't want retaliation, which would be massive. India and China are not Zaire or Zimbabwe. They're not little countries you can push around. We don't want to unleash that kind of trade war, because it would be very hard to control, I'm afraid.

Critical Thinking

1. Is climate change real?
2. Why is free trade important?
3. What do you see as the future for regional trade associations?

From *Reason* Magazine and Reason.com, December 2009, pp. 28, 30–34. Copyright © 2009 by Reason Foundation, 3415 S. Sepulveda Blvd., Suite 400, Los Angeles, CA 90034. www.reason.com.

UNIT 2

International Finance

Unit Selections

Learning Outcomes

After reading this Unit, you will be able to:

- Express your thoughts about the national debt, what you think about the debt in other countries, and what you think about private debt.

- Explain whether you think there should be international financial regulation.

- Describe what you think China's role will be.

- List and explain the challenges that are likely to come in the future.

- Explain what you think some of the solutions might be to the European debt crisis.

- Describe how you think corporations will respond to those challenges.

Student Website
www.mhhe.com/cls

Internet References

American Finance Association
www.afajof.org/default.asp

Economist on the Internet (Resources)
www.rfe.org

Financial Times (The)
www.ft.com

Foreign Direct Investment Is on the Rise around the World
www.neweconomyindex.org

Institute of International Bankers (IIB)
www.iib.org

International Monetary Fund (IMF)
www.imf.org

Lex Mercatoria: International Trade Law Monitor
www.Lexmercatoria.net

North American Free Trade Association (NAFTA)
www.nafta-sec-alena.org

Resources for Economists on the Internet
www.rfe.org

World Bank
www.worldbank.org

World Trade Organization
www.wto.org

In October 2008, the international financial markets came crashing down and all the aspects of global business changed for the foreseeable future. It was not only Wall Street in the United States that experienced the crisis, but the financial markets of London, Japan, and the rest of the world that spun out of control. Financial institutions that were thought to be solid and secure were suddenly found to be insolvent; corporations whose stock resided in the most conservative portfolios suddenly revealed themselves to be mere shadows of their corporate images; and the financial system began to collapse like a house of cards before the autumn winds.

Governments, corporations, central bankers, financial institutions, and global organizations scrambled first to stop the slide into what everyone feared would be the coming of the next Great Depression and then to find a way out of what has become what some have called the "Great Depression." "The Global Debt Bomb," "The Next 80 Years" and "International Financial Regulation after the Crisis" all deal with what is likely to happen, now, after the crisis and beyond. What will the GDP be in places like China, India, Indonesia, and the United States?—the four largest economies in the world in terms of population. How much and how well will Europe and Japan grow in this crisis? It is going to take time for the financial markets to recover from the shocks that occurred in 2008, and it is going to take longer for other sectors of the economy to rebound from the shocks that shook the global markets in the fall of 2008. However, evidence suggests that the developing world will take longer where the people had more to lose, and lost it. In the developing world, however, people had less to lose, so when they lost it, it did not matter as much. As a result, people in the developing world have less to make up than people in the developed world because they were not as exposed to the risks that the financial markets had created through their irresponsible behavior. Developing countries are now growing while the developed world remains bogged down in a deep, prolonged recession.

For the global economy to successfully recover from the current recession, individuals need to reconsider their role in the global economy. What no one could anticipate were the actions that governments would take and the way that would cause global confidence to disintegrate. The system of world trade, including the financial system of world trade and the way the government regulatory agencies interact with the marketplace, needs to be evaluated. There are agencies such as the International Monetary Fund (IMF) and the World Bank that are designed to address some of these issues. "Preparing for Significant Multi-Year Challenges" will be a key to success in the future for any person. The conditions that brought on the financial crisis and global economic recession will require more than just a single solution. The solutions will also require political will on the part of the global community that might not yet be present as the current crisis may not be dire enough. It may take a truly terrible economic collapse to provide the political will to institute the necessary reforms to prevent a global economic meltdown from happening. The success that institutions have currently experienced in avoiding that kind of disaster is unlikely to lead to the necessary changes to reform the global economic system. There are "Solutions and Pitfalls" that are awaiting any attempt to right the global economy. One pitfall is the current

© Photographer's Choice/Getty Images

European debt crisis for which a solution must be found. There are both short-and long-term solutions for this crisis, but the crisis could be easily expanded should the wrong decisions be made and implemented. Obviously, that should be avoided.

Despite the upheavals of the global marketplace and the problems of the international financial markets, global business and global trade continue to move on. While perhaps not at the rate prior to the autumn 2008 crash, investments are still made, goods are still transported and sold, and people continue to invest in the future.

China represents an alluring market for investment by large and small firms. One of the first economies to come out of the recession, China represents a unique opportunity for direct foreign investment. Most of the very large companies are already there, but opportunities remain for small organizations to participate in the largest market in the world. "Engaging China: Strategies for the Small Internationalizing Firm" offers some interesting approaches for the small multinational corporation to enter the Chinese market through direct foreign investment. While these companies may have lost the "first mover" advantage to their larger cousins, they have the advantage of learning from the mistakes the big multinationals made in going into the Chinese market earlier on.

Changes are also afoot in the way that financial results are going to be reported. The Securities and Exchange Commission (SEC) is going to require American firms doing business outside the country to start reporting their results using the International Financial Reporting Standards (IFRS) instead of FASB in 2011. This is certain to result in some very different reporting from what would have been previously reported under the old standards. It is true that reporting under IFRS standards will put the U.S. firms more in line with the rest of the international community in reporting their financial results, but in the short term, this is bound to lead to some confusion on the part of investors, especially during a time of economic uncertainty.

The financial markets continue to be a focus of uncertainty for many involved in international trade. The worldwide interconnection of the financial markets was made more than evident during the crisis and has been reaffirmed by the continuing inability of the developed countries to bring themselves out of the morass. Until the financial crisis is resolved, whether it starts in the United States, Europe, China, or Japan, world trade will continue to lag, and this will affect the growth of economies around the world.

The Global Debt Bomb

Spending our Way out of Worldwide Recession Will Take Years to Pay Back—and Create a Lot of Pain.

DANIEL FISHER

Kyle bass has bet the house against Japan—his own house, that is. The Dallas hedge fund manager (no relation to the famous Bass family of Fort Worth) is so convinced the Japanese government's profligate spending will drive the nation to the brink of default that he financed his home with a five-year loan denominated in yen, which he hopes will be cheaper to pay back than dollars. Through his hedge fund, Hayman Advisors, Bass has also bought $6 million worth of securities that will jump in value if interest rates on ten-year Japanese government bonds, currently a minuscule 1.3%, rise to something more like ten-year Treasuries in the U.S. (a recent 3.4%). A former Bear Stearns trader, Bass turned $110 million into $700 million by betting against subprime debt in 2006. "Japan is the most asymmetric opportunity I have ever seen," he says, "way better than subprime."

Bass could be wrong on Japan. The island nation (and the world's second-largest economy) has defied skeptics for so long that experienced traders call betting against it "the widowmaker." But he may be right on the bigger picture. If 2008 was the year of the subprime meltdown, 2010, he thinks, will be the year entire nations start going broke.

The world has issued so much debt in the past two years fighting the Great Recession that paying it all back is going to be hell—for Americans, along with everybody else. Taxes will have to rise around the globe, hobbling job growth and economic recovery. Traders like Bass could make a lot of money betting against sovereign debt the way they shorted subprime loans at the peak of the housing bubble.

National governments will issue an estimated $4.5 trillion in debt this year, almost triple the average for mature economies over the preceding five years. The U.S. has allowed the total federal debt (including debt held by government agencies, like the Social Security fund) to balloon by 50% since 2006 to $12.3 trillion. The pain of repayment is not yet being felt, because interest rates are so low—close to 0% on short-term Treasury bills. Someday those rates are going to rise. Then the taxpayer will have the devil to pay.

Whether or not you believe the spending spree was morally justified, you have to be concerned about the prospect of a dismal, debt-burdened fiscal future. More debt weighs heavily on GDP, says Carmen Reinhart, a University of Maryland economist. The coauthor, with Harvard professor Kenneth Rogoff, of *This Time It's Different: Eight Centuries of Financial Folly* (Princeton, 2009), Reinhart has found that a 90% ratio of government debt to GDP is a tipping point in economic growth. Beyond that, developed economies have growth rates two percentage points lower, on average, than economies that have not yet crossed the line. (The danger point is lower in emerging markets.) "It's not a linear process," she says. "You increase it over and beyond a high threshold, and boom!" The U.S. government-debt-to-GDP ratio is 84%.

We've been through this scenario before. It's especially ugly because we get hit by inflation, too. In the years immediately after World War II inflation surged past 6%, while economic growth flagged and the government-debt-to-GDP level exceeded 90%, note Reinhart and Rogoff. The country worked that ratio down over the next half-century. Now the ratio is shooting up again.

America is a nation of spendthrifts, addicted to easy credit and dependent on the kindness of savers overseas to keep us comfortable. Our retail industry hangs on credit cards and our real estate on 95% financing and the tax rewards for mortgage interest. The personal savings rate has climbed from negative 0.4% in 2006 to a positive 4.5% rate now, but that is still a pathetic figure for a

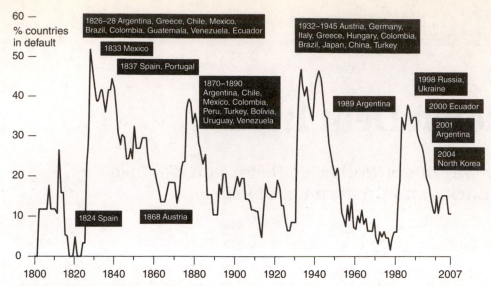

The Stumble Cycle   Sovereign defaults—when a country stops paying its bills—go in waves, often following global financial crises, wars or the boom-bust cycles of commodities. Some countries, like Spain and Austria, mend their ways; others, like Argentina, are repeat offenders.

Sources: Standard & Poor's; Kenneth Rogoff, Harvard; Carmen Reinhart, U. Maryland.

Graph: David Lada for Forbes Magazine

nation whose government is un-saving all that and more with its deficit budget. Politicians on this continent are good at compassion, whether trying to help people stay in their overpriced homes or offering health care to millions of those without it. They are not so adept at nurturing growth.

If the GDP doesn't expand at "normal" rates of 3% to 5% coming out of this recession, wrestling down the debt will be very tough, indeed—perhaps impossible without drastic cuts in spending and higher tax rates on many fronts. The Congressional Budget Office currently projects the fiscal deficit will decline from 10% of GDP next year to around 4.4% from 2013 to 2015. But that assumes economic expansion of at least 4%, not the 2% predicted in the study by Reinhart and Rogoff. You see the vicious cycle here: Debt depresses growth, and then low growth makes paying down the debt an impossible task.

U.S. corporate income tax receipts were down 55% in the year ended Sept. 30, 2009 to $138 billion. It may be a long while before these tax collections get back to where they were. As corporate profits recover, factory utilization will be up and inflation will be close behind. At that point the 0% yield on Treasury bills will be history. Rolling over the national debt will become a lot more expensive. Higher rates on Treasuries will work their way through the debt market, driving up the cost of money for homeowners, businesses and already struggling state and local governments.

"The economy over the last six months has been on a sugar high," says Benn Steil, senior fellow at the Council on Foreign Relations and author of *Money, Markets and Sovereignty* (Yale, 2009), a survey of the relationship between money and the state. If Congress and the Obama Administration don't trim deficits, he says, "we will get to the point where credit is much more expensive in the U.S. than it ever has been in the past."

Most states are already having trouble paying their bills and, of course, don't have printing presses with which to finance their debts. They are turning to Washington for help and may succeed in putting some of their liabilities on the federal balance sheet. With growing off-balance-sheet obligations, notably unfunded pension liabilities, the states will be competing for years with the federal government for scarce taxpayer dollars.

"U.S. states are like emerging markets," says Reinhart. "They spend a lot during the boom years and then are forced to retrench during the down years." Cutting expenses sounds good theoretically, but look at California: Students (and faculty) are up in arms over proposed tuition increases and cutbacks at the state's once prestigious university system; state employees are mounting a fierce legal battle against furloughs and other wage concessions.

Mainstream credit analysts are worried. The U.S. has been able to sell vast amounts of debt because the Treasury market, with $500 billion a day in turnover, is

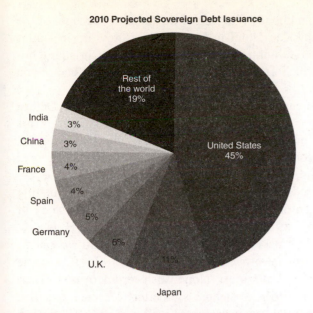

2010 Projected Sovereign Debt Issuance

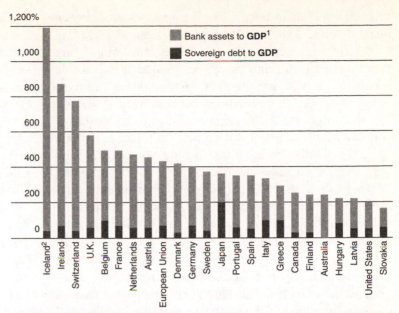

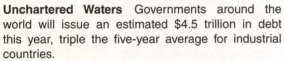

Unchartered Waters Governments around the world will issue an estimated $4.5 trillion in debt this year, triple the five-year average for industrial countries.

Sources: IMF World Economic Outlook and other various public sources, including news media and respective government data; Hayman Advisors estimates.

It's the Total Debt, Stupid Private banking assets tend to become public problems in a crisis. By that measure European countries are far worse off than the U.S.

[1]Assets for five largest banks. [2]Iceland data represent pre-financial-crisis conditions.
Source: Hayman Advisors.

Graph: David Lada for Forbes Magazine

considered safe and dwarfs all other debt markets. But Brian Coulton, head of global economics at Fitch Ratings in London, warns that once rock-solid economies like the U.S. and the U.K. could join shakier nations like Japan and Ireland in losing their AAA ratings if they don't get their bad habits under control. "While AAAs can borrow in the short term, very high and rising government debt-to-GDP ratios are ultimately not consistent with AAA status," Coulton says.

A FORBES survey of sovereign credit, taking into account trends in spending and revenue, economic freedom and the price of the debt insurance, a.k.a. credit default swaps, ranks the U.S. number 35 in a class of 85, below Germany, the Netherlands and China. The CDS market is priced to imply a 3.1% chance of default over five years on Treasury debt. Other countries are likely to hit the debt wall sooner, and with greater impact. The U.K., for example, is 38 on the list, two notches above Slovenia. One culprit is much higher levels of private banking debt that could land on the British government balance sheet à la Fannie Mae and Freddie Mac in the U.S. The sovereign debt of the U.K., plus the assets of its five largest banks, exceeds 500% of GDP, compared with 200% in the U.S. Even closer to the edge is Ireland. Sovereign debt is at 41% of GDP. But total banking-system assets are another 800% of GDP *(see graph)*. If those assets sour, the government will almost certainly step in

to protect the banking system, as Iceland was forced to do in 2008. Iceland's currency and stock market collapsed soon thereafter, and its president recently blocked a law to repay $5 billion-plus to British and Dutch investors. That move puts at risk a pending bailout package for Iceland from the International Monetary Fund and its application to join the European Union.

Most investors seem to believe, as the late Citibank chairman Walter Wriston put it, that "countries don't go bust." The opposite is true. "There was a massive default wave in 1980s and 1990s," says Reinhart. Investors may not have paid much attention since the defaults were mostly in emerging market countries like Guatemala and Romania. But the deadbeats included current investor favorites like Brazil, which defaulted in 1983, went through a bout of hyperinflation in 1990 and effectively defaulted again, for the same reason, in 2000. Reinhart and Rogoff show that, on average, nations add 86% to their debt loads within three years of a credit crisis. At the same time, government revenue falls an average of 2% in the second year after the onset of the troubles.

The combination can be fatal for investors holding bonds issued by financially shaky countries like Argentina or Greece, which sell a lot of their debt outside their own borders (as does the U.S.—45% of all publicly held debt). As a nation's finances deteriorate, foreign investors sell their bonds, putting upward pressure on interest rates. That usually sets off a spiral including a deteriorating currency, which, if the bonds are denominated in foreign currencies, makes it impossible for the country to pay its debt. Greece doesn't have to worry about this last syndrome, because it uses the euro. But that might make things worse since it can't print its way out of its financial difficulties. "It's like entering a prize fight with one hand tied behind your back," Bass says. Argentina takes a different tack. Still struggling in the wake of its 2002 default on foreign-held debt, its president recently tried, and failed, to seize central-bank dollar deposits (and cashier her central banker) in order to repay overseas debt.

Even if countries don't stiff creditors outright, they can sometimes accomplish the same thing through inflation. Reinhart and Rogoff found this to be the case in roughly one-third of the countries they tracked that had currency depreciation rates above 15% a year, following the 1980–81 recession. Of course, this works only for debt denominated in the home currency and only if investors are taken by surprise. If they see inflation and devaluation coming, they price it into the interest they collect.

Making money on sovereign defaults isn't as easy as picking off subprime mortgages. Credit default swaps on potential basket cases like Dubai, Greece and Ukraine have doubled and tripled in price over the past 12 months as their debt loads grew. To buy insurance against a default in Greece over the next five years costs 3.4% a year.

How about Switzerland—once considered an impregnable money center? Credit default swaps on Swiss debt cost 46 basis points (0.46% a year), compared with 33 for the U.S. The Swiss government is not itself deeply in hock, but it may have to bail out its private banks in the manner of Iceland or Uncle Sam. Swiss private-bank debt is seven times GDP. The U.S. isn't a disinterested bystander: The Swiss central bank borrowed $40 billion from the Federal Reserve under a little-known swaps program last year to remove bad assets denominated in dollars from private banks. The Fed considers the transaction low risk because the Swiss promise to repay in dollars. But it signals how losses on private loans—in this case, U.S. subprime mortgages—can cycle back into a problem for the Swiss government. As hedge fund operator Bass notes, a 10% hit on Swiss banking assets would represent 80% of its 2008 GDP of $488 billion and 400% of annual government revenue. "You can invest a very small portion of capital, so if you're wrong it costs very little," says Bass. "If you're right it can pay hundreds of percent."

Shorting countries comes naturally to Bass, 40, who has spent most of his career investigating overvalued

stocks and bonds. The son of the onetime manager of the Fountainbleau Hotel in Miami, Bass grew up in Dallas and won a diving scholarship from Texas Christian University in Fort Worth, where he studied real estate and finance.

He spent most of the 1990s at Bear Stearns in Dallas, attracting a group of well-heeled clients who took his advice on shorting stocks like Delgratia Mining Corp. of Vancouver, B.C., which plunged after a highly touted gold find in Nevada turned out to be a hoax.

Around that time Bass learned the danger of betting too much on his own research. He shorted the stock of RadiSys, a telecom technology maker in Hillsboro, Ore., after he called the company's recently departed chief financial officer at home and was told of possible financial irregularities. (None was ever uncovered.) Bass was forced to take steep losses after Carlton Lutz, then an influential stock promoter, called RadiSys "the son of Intel" in his newsletter and the stock doubled. (More recently the company lost $58 million on revenue of $320 million in the 12 months ended Sept. 30.) "Even when you do great investigative work and you understand the accounting, it doesn't matter if you know everything," Bass says. "You can still lose a fortune."

Last spring Bass lost $110 million buying credit default swaps on Portugal, Ireland, Italy and Greece. He may have been right but too early. He is holding on.

His biggest potential score is in Japan. Government debt has soared to 190% of GDP from 50% in the mid-1990s, hitting an estimated $10 trillion in 2009. But because interest rates are so low, the government paid only 2.6% of GDP to service its debt in 2008, less than the U.S. at 2.9%.

Yet low rates mask a growing problem for Japan. The government took in $500 billion in taxes last year, plus another $100 billion in other revenue that included money borrowed by a government investment program. But the Tokyo feds spent $980 billion, including $100 billion-plus on interest and $190 billion or so it transferred to regional and municipal governments. That left a $360 billion hole it could plug only by writing more IOUs, on top of the debt it must roll over each year as bonds mature.

Today Japan can borrow all it wants from its own citizens. Over the decades they have dutifully (if mechanically) piled up a $7.7 trillion cache of savings they keep mostly in low-yielding bank deposits. Those savings equal two-thirds of the total household wealth of Germany, France and the U.K. combined, says John Richards, North American head of strategy at RBS, who spent the early 1990s in Japan trying to build a channel for selling Japanese government bonds overseas (the country still sells but 6% of its debt to foreigners). "You

Debt Weight Scorecard

Free-spending America isn't quite a banana republic yet. But in a FORBES ranking of sovereign debt the U.S. comes out number 35, one rung below Estonia, on a global list of 85.

How do the 50 U.S. states stack up against one another? Have a look at the best and worst below. We considered a dozen or so factors, including unfunded pension liabilities, changes in tax revenue, debt as a percentage of GDP, debt per capita, growth expectations for employment and the state economy, net migrations and a moocher ratio that compares government employees, pension burdens and Medicaid enrollees to private-sector employment. Utah finished first overall thanks to AAA ratings from both Moody's and S&P, as well as a debt per capita of only $447. Bringing up the rear is Illinois, which lagged several high-tax, debt-burdened states in the Northeast. More people left the Prairie State than took up residence over the past five years, and its unfunded pension obligations are fifth highest in the country.

—Kurt Badenhausen

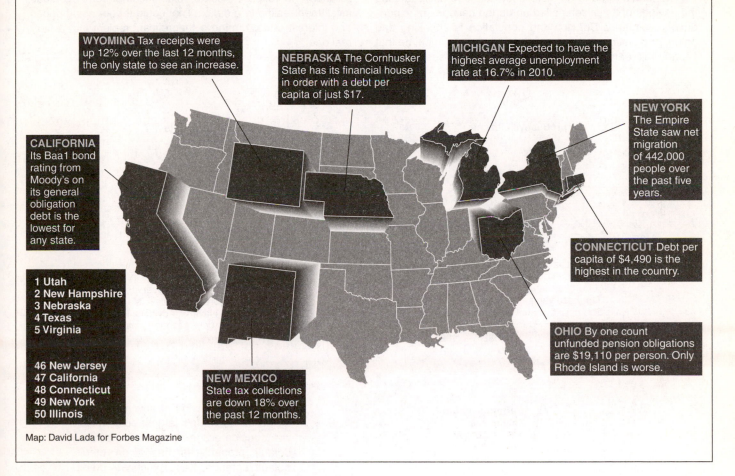

WYOMING Tax receipts were up 12% over the last 12 months, the only state to see an increase.

NEBRASKA The Cornhusker State has its financial house in order with a debt per capita of just $17.

MICHIGAN Expected to have the highest average unemployment rate at 16.7% in 2010.

NEW YORK The Empire State saw net migration of 442,000 people over the past five years.

CALIFORNIA Its Baa1 bond rating from Moody's on its general obligation debt is the lowest for any state.

1 Utah
2 New Hampshire
3 Nebraska
4 Texas
5 Virginia

46 New Jersey
47 California
48 Connecticut
49 New York
50 Illinois

CONNECTICUT Debt per capita of $4,490 is the highest in the country.

OHIO By one count unfunded pension obligations are $19,110 per person. Only Rhode Island is worse.

NEW MEXICO State tax collections are down 18% over the past 12 months.

Map: David Lada for Forbes Magazine

---

ask how would Japan turn into a sovereign debt crisis and you can't find the trigger," Richards says. "Shorting the yen because you think there's going to be a rollover crisis makes no sense at all."

The trigger could be demographics. Japan's population is aging quickly. Today 22% of Japanese are 65 or older; in 20 years it will rise to 30% or so (compared with a current 13% of Americans and 20% in 2030). At the same time Japan's total population peaked at 128 million in 2004 and has settled into long-term decline.

The combination means Japan's government pension fund has become a net seller of government bonds, while the nation's savings rate has plunged from 18.4% in 1982 to 3.3% today. When that drops to zero, Japan will be forced to look overseas for financing—and risks exposing itself to international rates.

JPMorgan Chase analyst Masaaki Kanno in Tokyo says that Japanese bonds are in a bubble that could pop in the next three to five years, as savings rates drop. Even if the government can somehow keep borrowing at a 1.4% interest rate, he says, interest expense will rise to roughly $200 billion by 2019, or 45% of government revenue, unless it pushes through a big increase in the national value-added tax.

But those rates are unlikely to hold. For years the government has been able to replace bonds paying as much as 7% interest with steadily lower-rate debt. The favorable rollovers ended in 2007, leaving the government much more vulnerable if it has to sell debt overseas,

Setting Sun
With an Aging Population and Ballooning Debt, Japan Soon May Have Trouble Financing Itself

It's a measure of Japan's mounting fiscal problems that its finance minister, Hirohisa Fujii, resigned in early January because of exhaustion. Nobody can come up with an elegant way out of Japan's dilemma.

The island nation has historically financed itself, tapping the savings of its citizens piled up during decades of export-driven prosperity. But now the population is shrinking and aging, and savings rates have plunged at the same time that Japan's left-leaning Hatoyama administration is spending like never before. The chart below shows what's likely to happen next: Debt per working citizen will surge as growing fiscal deficits are spread across a shrinking population.

The crunch may come soon after Japan's current account balance—net export income, plus income from overseas investment—slips to a deficit. That could trigger rising prices and interest rates, turning a theoretical problem into a very real one.

—D.F.

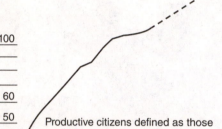

Debt per productive citizen

$200 thou

Productive citizens defined as those aged 15–64. Figures converted using current exchange rate of 91.25 Japanese yen per U.S. dollar.
Source: Hayman Advisors.

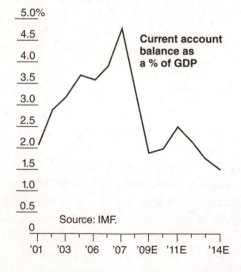

Current account balance as a % of GDP

Source: IMF.

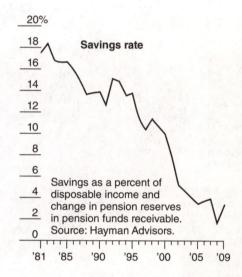

Savings rate

20%

Savings as a percent of disposable income and change in pension reserves in pension funds receivable.
Source: Hayman Advisors.

Credit Crunch

To compile a ranking of soveregin debt for 85 of the world's largest economies, we considered, among other factors, default probabilities based on credit default spreads, trade balances, credit agency ratings and debt as apercentage of GDP.

Best	Worst
1 Qatar	81 Serbia
2 Hong Kong	82 Argentina
3 China	83 Venezuela
4 Luxembourg	84 Pakistan
5 Singapore	85 Ukraine

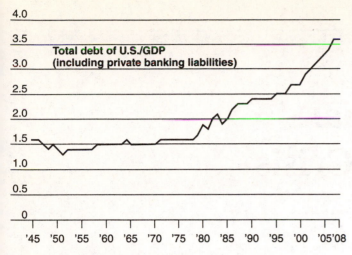

The Leverage Factor Total U.S. debt, including banking liabilities, has soared relative to economic growth over the past 20 years.

Source: Federal Reserve.

where ten-year rates are two to three percentage points higher than Japan's. If rates rise past 3%—the scenario Bass is betting on—interest expense will exceed total government revenue by 2019.

The process will accelerate if the yen falls and interest rates rise, prompting Japanese savers to pull their money from low-yielding bank accounts, which, in turn, are invested in government bonds. "That will be the beginning of a vicious cycle," Kanno says, when "consumers will realize what is happening" and shift their money to more attractive investments overseas. Bass thinks the crisis will come sooner. For $6 million he has secured options on $12 billion in ten-year government bonds that will pay $125 million if Japanese rates rise to 4%.

"The good news is the wolf's at the door in Japan and that we in the U.S. have front row seats to see what's going to happen," he says. "I hope we learn something from it."

Critical Thinking

1. How much debt will there be after coming out of the recession?
2. Is this debt manageable?
3. Who is going to pay for this debt?
4. How is this debt going to be paid?

International Financial Regulation after the Crisis

BARRY EICHENGREEN

What was once almost quaintly referred to in the United States as the Subprime Crisis eventually came to be known, in America and abroad, as the Great Global Credit Crisis of 2008–2009. The change in terminology is itself indicative of the international spread of the crisis. It reflects how, in the end, no country was immune to the global reach of financial instability.

Now that the worst effects are past, officials have begun drawing lessons and formulating policy responses. The United States has focused on strengthening mortgage underwriting standards, moving transactions in derivative financial instruments onto organized exchanges, and curbing proprietary trading by depository institutions insured by the Federal Deposit Insurance Corporation (FDIC). The United Kingdom has emphasized the perverse incentives created by bonus-based compensation of financial executives and sought to reform executive pay. France and Germany have singled out the risks created by lightly regulated hedge funds and private equity firms. Officials in other countries have prioritized still other issues. On what should take precedence there is little agreement.

Herein lies the problem: to be effective, regulation of financial markets and institutions must be coordinated across countries. Most big banks operate in more than one country, affording them the opportunity to relocate their operations and employees. When the United Kingdom moved to tax bankers' bonuses, the bankers in question threatened to move to Geneva. When the European Union began to contemplate strict regulation of hedge funds, fund managers proposed moving their operations to New York. When the EU then mooted the possibility of prohibiting residents from investing in hedge funds and private equity firms regardless of where they were located, the U.S. Treasury complained that such measures unfairly discriminated against the U.S. financial services industry and violated international treaties like the General Agreement on Trade in Services.

Not only is disagreement among national regulators over priorities and strategies a source of potential conflict, but it threatens to vitiate their efforts to make the world a safer financial place. In a financially integrated world, many regulatory restrictions are impossible to effectively enforce purely at the national level. Whatever the regulatory response—taxing bank size, bank bonuses, or specific bank activities—limiting evasion requires a significant degree of international cooperation.

The above examples are specific instances of the general phenomenon known as *regulatory arbitrage*. When restrictive regulation raises the cost of doing business (as it is designed to do when business activities have social costs), businessmen have an incentive to relocate to more permissive jurisdictions, frustrating regulators' efforts and raising the costs to society of the business activity in question. In the United States, regulatory arbitrage may mean shifting an activity between affiliated firms that are subject to different regulations and overseen by different regulators—from a bank to an affiliated insurance company or a structured investment vehicle (SIV), for example. Regulatory arbitrage can also mean shifting high-risk activities from a country with more stringent regulation to another where regulation is more permissive. To limit this behavior, international cooperation in establishing a common regulatory standard is the obvious way forward.

While the case for cooperation is straightforward in principle, the mobility of finance creates a temptation for regulators to undercut one another in practice. Competition for business may create a race to the bottom. Competing jurisdictions, seeking to attract footloose financial firms, have an incentive to offer more permissive regulation or lax enforcement. More than one country has launched "Big Bang" reforms, liberalizing burdensome regulation and, sometimes, weakening enforcement in an effort to enhance its attractions to internationally mobile financial firms. To address this problem, competing countries might enter into an international agreement that requires consenting parties not to undercut one another's regulatory efforts.[1]

A further argument for international cooperation is that individual countries, making decisions in isolation, lack adequate incentive to engage in rigorous supervision and regulation of domestic financial firms and markets. While doing so is costly, the benefits accrue not just to the individual country but also to its neighbors. The virulence of financial "contagion"—the speed and extent to which instability can spread, infecting the financial systems of other countries—such as that which was evident in the aftermaths of the Bear Steams, American International Group, and Lehman Brothers crises in March and September 2008, illustrates the point. In these episodes, inadequate supervision and regulation in the United States spawned a crisis that engulfed the entire world. As Thomas Mayer, chief economist of Deutsche Bank, put it, "In this day and age, a bank run spreads around the world, not around the block."[2]

The implications for regulation are direct. If a government invests in regulation, some of the benefits may accrue to other countries, giving the initiating country inadequate incentive to invest. The problem is not unlike that of residents of a fire zone. It is in the self-interest of each resident to clear the underbrush around his home in order to enhance his own safety. But the individual homeowner may not consider the additional benefits, from a social point of view, of his brush-clearing exercise; he may not see that doing so also enhances the safety of his neighbors. In the urban context, municipal regulation requires everyone to clear additional brush. In the context of global finance, the solution rests on international standards and coordination of financial regulation.

Finally, cooperation could create a viable alternative to the uncontrolled bankruptcy of troubled financial institutions on the one hand and emergency rescues on the other. Emergency rescues are criticized on both equity and efficiency grounds. To the extent that a rescue is financed by taxpayer money, present or future, it is rightly seen as unfair. Moreover, because banks know they will receive assistance in the event that the bets they make go bad, they have an incentive to place bigger and riskier bets. Regular recourse to rescues creates moral hazard, which has social costs.

But the alternative—allowing a big bank to declare bankruptcy—is not tenable if doing so threatens the stability of the financial system. The troubled institution will have borrowed from other financial institutions. It will have other contracts outstanding, many of which will be frozen when bankruptcy is filed and an automatic stay is imposed. A stay may therefore cause liquidity problems—and worse—for the bank's counterparties, forcing them to call in their own loans in order to raise funds. Asset prices may collapse in a fire sale, and the liquidity crisis may cascade through the financial system. Lack of attention to third-party effects in Chapter 7 and Chapter 11 bankruptcy proceedings coupled with the slow pace of court proceedings render these problems especially pervasive and this approach to resolution particularly problematic in the case of financial firms.[3]

In the United States, the FDIC can step in, seize, and ring-fence the operations of a bank to which it extends deposit-insurance coverage. It can pay off a bank's obligations to its counterparties. But the FDIC lacks this authority with regard to the big, complex bank holding companies that pose the most serious threat to systemic stability. Insurance companies and other large nonbank intermediaries are also beyond its jurisdiction.

The Dodd-Frank financial reform bill adopted in Summer 2010 gives federal regulators new authority to seize and break up large troubled financial firms. What it fails to recognize, unfortunately, is that most large financial companies—the presumed targets of these procedures—operate internationally. A case in point is Lehman Brothers, which had consequential operations in the United Kingdom as well as in the United States. The conflicting claims of creditors in the two jurisdictions, together with differences in resolution regimes, created serious difficulties for courts and regulators seeking to limit the systemic consequences of the institution's failure in 2008.

Establishing an orderly resolution regime as an alternative to bailouts is desirable. But meaningful progress will require, at a minimum, that provisions adopted at the national level be coordinated internationally. And if cooperation proves inadequate, regulators will have to contemplate creating a supranational resolution authority.

Not everyone is convinced, however, by the case for international regulatory coordination. Regulatory oversight, to be effective, must be tailored to local needs. National financial structures and systems differ, requiring differences in the structure and application of regulation. In some countries, financial systems are predominantly bank-based. In others, the United States and the United Kingdom being prominent examples, the securitization of financial claims is more extensive. In these countries, the growth of securities markets has led to "disintermediation"—the displacement of bank borrowing and lending to securities markets. Financial systems must be regulated differently according to whether they are dominated by banks or securities markets. Further differences include whether the state owns a stake in the country's leading financial institutions; whether Internet banking is prevalent; and whether the country is predominantly Islamic, as Islamic banking prohibits the payment of interest, requiring lending to be structured in other ways. All these are reasons why one-size-fits-all regulation, which is what tends to come out of international agreements, is undesirable.

An additional danger is that international coordination may lead to lowest-common-denominator regulation. Agreements on matters such as minimally adequate capital ratios for internationally active banks, to be effective, must be accepted by all countries with consequential banking systems. As a result, agreements tend to be by consensus. For all concerned countries to agree, any provision that one country finds objectionable must be removed from the agreement or, at the least, watered down. The result is a weak and ineffectual agreement. As a case in point, critics of international agreements point to the Basel Accord for Capital Adequacy for Internationally Active Banks. The Basel Accord is designed to ensure that banks have buffers to cope with adverse circumstances, but it has not prevented bank capital from falling to near zero and bank solvency from being threatened in each of our recent financial crises.

Part of the problem may be that international agreements negotiated in far-distant places like Basel are prone to be captured by the regulated. Banks with a preference for relatively permissive regulation have the resources and expertise to influence the Basel Committee on Banking Supervision. This is not so for the man or woman in the street concerned that regulation should be sufficiently stringent to protect his or her interest. This is another reason that international agreements may lead to weak and ineffectual rules.

Finally, some argue that regulatory diversity is desirable for the same reasons that biodiversity is desirable. Efforts at international coordination, whereby governments converge on a single set of standards, may in fact leave the global financial system more exposed. The standards in question may turn out to be poorly designed and inappropriately targeted. If they are designed to contain one set of risks and a different set materializes, the fact that all jurisdictions have adapted their regulatory policies in the same way may only contribute to financial instability. From this standpoint, given the possibility of diverse shocks to global financial markets, the presence of diverse regulation may enhance the stability of the financial ecosystem.

There is something to these arguments—which is precisely why there is a debate about the efficacy of internationally coordinated reform. Yet, even conceding these points, the case for cooperation is overwhelming. For one, the implications of differences in financial structure should not be overstated. Despite variance across national systems, over time there has been a strong tendency toward convergence. Furthermore, countries with bank-based financial systems and those with market-based systems can adopt the same approach to regulation of their banks and securities markets; the consequential difference would be to which set of regulations they devote the bulk of their enforcement effort.

Second, the fear that agreement by consensus leads to lowest-common-denominator regulation should not preclude cooperation. Rather, countries most concerned with risks to financial stability should move ahead with coordinated reforms and apply sanctions that discourage their financial institutions from doing business with the countries that lag behind. They should similarly prohibit financial firms chartered in less regulated jurisdictions from entering their markets.

Finally, if nonfinancial interests are inadequately represented in international negotiations, then the appropriate response is not to abandon those negotiations but to open them up to additional stakeholders.

Historically, the most prominent international institution concerned with regulatory reform has been the Basel Committee on Banking Supervision, which is made up of representatives of central banks and other banking supervisors. The Basel Committee meets on the premises of the Bank for International Settlements in Basel, Switzerland, a minimum of four times a year. When it was founded in 1974, only the United States, Canada, Japan, and seven European countries were represented. Membership has since expanded to twenty-seven countries, including the emerging markets of Latin America and Asia.

While the Basel Committee has traditionally focused on ensuring that banks have enough capital to weather shocks, over time it has also considered a variety of other stability-related issues, including, most recently, liquidity risk. Its signature achievement is the Basel Accord for Capital Adequacy for Internationally Active Banks, as virtually all large banks today are internationally active.

Unfortunately, the Basel Accord, and especially the updated version, Basel II, published in 2004 and adopted by a growing list of countries subsequently, are now understood to be seriously flawed. Basel II allowed banks to hold less capital against assets that received investment-grade ratings from commercial credit rating agencies. Because ratings are revised upward in good times and downward in bad times, this practice was strongly procyclical. It encouraged even more lending when lending was booming and more retrenchment when financial institutions were retrenching. It ignored the conflicts of interest to which the rating agencies were subject. It also allowed banks to use their own internal models—later shown to be problematic—to evaluate the risk of losses and the amount of capital that had to be held against those risks. It bought into the bankers' arguments that they could safely reduce their own funds held in reserve (so-called Tier 1 capital) to little more than 2 percent of bank assets.

Some of these problems issue from the Basel Committee's origins and their influence on its remit. The Committee was created in 1974 in response to problems with a major cross-border *bank* (Germany's Herstatt Bank); the focus of the Basel Committee on Banking Supervision, therefore, is on *banking* supervision. Once upon a time, the perimeters of the banking and financial systems were roughly coincident because banks were the dominant providers of financial services. But with the growth of securities markets and nonbank financial firms, this is no longer the case.

As a result, the Basel Committee set capital adequacy standards for commercial banks; meanwhile, in countries such as the United States, it was not just the large commercial banks (and commercial bank holding companies) that posed potential risks. Once upon a time, investment banks like Lehman Brothers invested only their own partners' capital, but more recently, they began leveraging their operations with borrowed funds. Broker dealers like Bear Stearns that booked and cleared the trades of others increasingly engaged in proprietary trading, using an even higher ratio of borrowed money to own capital than was typical of investment banks. Insurance companies like the American International Group (AIG) were overseen only by state insurance commissioners—to the extent that they were overseen at all, Markets in structured derivative securities were often entirely unregulated. The members of the Basel Committee were aware of these gaps, but awareness does not equate to the capacity to act.

Early recognition of these problems led to the 1999 formation of a second body, the Financial Stability Board (FSB: originally named the Financial Stability Forum). The FSB, which is supported by a small secretariat also housed at the Bank for International Settlements, has a mandate to assess vulnerabilities affecting the entire financial system and to oversee action to address them. It seeks to monitor market activity, highlight regulatory developments, and identify systemic risks. Some two dozen countries are represented. Members include not just central banks and other regulators but also financial standard-setting bodies like the International Association of Insurance Supervisors and the International Organization of Securities Regulators. The FSB has created committees concerned with a range of issues that potentially pose risks to financial stability, including international capital flows, hedge funds, and offshore financial centers. Its deliberations, when agreement is reached, result in a set of recommendations and a published report.

The FSB's mandate to monitor the global financial system as an integrated whole constitutes an important step forward. The Board's limitation is that it is essentially a talk shop: a place to exchange information and pontificate on what is desirable, after which regulators are free to go home and do more or less as they please. Like the Pope, the FSB has no army. It has even less sanctioning power.

Its members are aware of this problem. Indeed, one need only consult the FSB's antiseptically titled January 2010 report, "Framework for Strengthening Adherence to International Financial Standards." This report succeeds in identifying only three mechanisms for ensuring adherence to its standards: leading by example on the part of member jurisdictions, peer review, and a vaguely specified "toolbox of measures" (specific tools presumably being too sensitive for the lid on the box to be lifted). It seems unlikely that the FSB entertains any illusion that these limp instruments will get national regulators to sit up and listen.

Then there is the Group of 20 (G20), which, recognizing the emergence of a more multipolar world, has assumed the role of steering committee for the world economy (a role played previously by the Group of 7 and Group of 10 advanced countries). Its twenty members include advanced countries and emerging markets alike, as well as the European Union. At recent meetings, it has also included a twenty-first member, Spain, a large country that was inexplicably excluded when the G20 was formed but whose attendance was insisted upon by the European Commission, and a twenty-second. The Netherlands, a member of previous groupings that insisted on inviting itself. The G20 is a mechanism to ensure that not just regulators but leaders (finance ministers and prime ministers, who presumably give marching orders to the regulators) buy into the process of policy reform. Following its biannual meetings of heads of state and government, it issues communiqués that include commitments on financial reform. At its June 2010 summit in Toronto, for example, leaders committed to phasing in higher capital standards for banks. Similar to the FSB, the G20 forms working groups to investigate financial problems and offer recommendations.

But the G20 has a legitimacy problem: it was formed in response to an earlier crisis in the late 1990s, essentially in ad hoc fashion. (The equally ad hoc participation of Spain and The Netherlands, whether desirable or not, is indicative of this fact.) No one appointed this particular set of countries to make decisions for the world. Nothing ensures that their recommendations will be respectfully received and acted upon by countries represented in their deliberations.

A final institution concerned with financial stability is the International Monetary Fund (IMF). The IMF has a written constitution, the Articles of Agreement, to which its members are bound. It organizes countries into constituencies, each of which is represented by a member of its Executive Board, ensuring that all 180-plus national members have voice: it therefore does not suffer from the same kind of legitimacy deficit as the G20. It publishes a Global Financial Stability Report designed to provide a synthetic assessment of risks to the international system. In conjunction with the FSB, it conducts early-warning exercises designed to anticipate financial problems. Together with the World Bank, its sister organization, it conducts regular financial-sector assessments intended to provide outside reviews of the financial strength and regulatory practices of its members. In the course of this review it recommends adherence to international best-practice standards. Countries that borrow from the Fund are subject to an enforcement mechanism; the IMF can deny disbursement of the next quarterly installment of its loan to countries it judges to have made inadequate progress in fixing economic and financial problems.

But the IMF possesses no such power over other countries. Illustrative of this limitation is the fact that countries must agree before a potentially embarrassing assessment of their financial sectors can be conducted. Shortly before the Subprime Crisis, the IMF and World Bank reportedly approached the U.S. government to request an assessment and were refused.

E vidently, there is no dearth of studies and no shortage of committees, boards, and organizations concerned with international aspects of regulatory reform. There is, however, a shortage of consequences for countries whose regulatory policies are not adequate. The question is how to address this problem.

One option would be to create a new body, a World Financial Organization (WFO), membership in which would create concrete obligations whose violation would have significant consequences. In the same way that the World Trade Organization (WTO) establishes principles for trade policy (such as nondiscrimination, reciprocity, transparency, binding and enforceable commitments) without prescribing outcomes, the WFO would establish principles for prudential supervision and regulation (capital and liquidity requirements, limits on portfolio concentrations, adequacy of risk measurement systems and internal controls) without attempting to prescribe the structure of regulation in detail.

But once the WFO defined obligations for its members, the latter would be obliged to meet them. Membership could be made mandatory for all countries seeking freedom of access to foreign markets for their investors and domestically chartered financial institutions. The WFO could appoint independent panels of experts to determine whether countries were in compliance with their obligations. In cases of noncompliance, other members would be within their rights to restrict the ability of financial institutions chartered in the offending country to do business in their markets. Not only would this measure protect members from the negative consequences of inadequate regulation abroad, but doing so would provide a real incentive to comply.

Critics will undoubtedly object that governments, not least the U.S. government itself, will never allow an international organization to dictate their national financial policies. However, the WFO would not dictate; the specifics of implementation could be left to the individual country. Furthermore, the equivalent already exists for trade. The United States is among the countries that have signed WTO agreements with specific obligations. The WTO has the power to establish dispute settlement panels and determine whether national law complies with a country's WTO obligations. Violators have the choice of changing that legal provision or facing trade sanctions. If the United States and other countries accept this authority in the case of trade, one might ask, why shouldn't they accept it in the case of finance?

There is no reason why the Basel Committee, the FSB, the IMF, and the others should not continue their useful work studying regulatory problems, encouraging their correction, and promoting the international coordination and harmonization of regulatory initiatives. It has become clear, however, that more comprehensive, binding, and coordinated international regulation will be crucial to financial stability worldwide, now and in the future.

Notes

1. To be sure, some would assert that restrictions on financial firms and markets are excessive and that regulatory competition is desirable as a countervailing force. But their position is less tenable in the wake of the crisis.

2. Quoted in Mark Landler, "Europe Catches What's Ailing U.S. Financial Sector." *The New York Times,* October 1, 2008.

3. Chapter 7 and Chapter 13 are the provisions of the bankruptcy code under which the operations of an insolvent entity are liquidated and reorganized, respectively.

Critical Thinking

1. Should global financial regulation be coordinated?
2. How would that be done?
3. Who would be in charge of it?

Solutions and Pitfalls

The **European debt crisis** remains the key concern for global economic growth as well as financial markets. After much effort and hard cash thrown at it, the problem remains as intractable as ever. One key reason is that the long-term and the short-term aspects of the problem have not been separately addressed adequately.

Earlier last week, Klaus Regling, CEO of **European** Financial Stability Facility, and I were co-speakers at a conference in Thailand. When I was chatting with him before the conference, he complained that the financial markets were too focused on the short term. But my point was that we need to cross the short term before we reach the long term!

The **European debt** problem has returned as the key issue for the global economies and the financial markets in the new year, even as signs are spreading that the US economy is healing. The **European** problem has the potential to rock the US and Asia not only through trade and investment links, but also through financial-sector contagion. But after an unending series of summits, meetings, announcements and agreements, and even after much hard money has been thrown at the problem, the **European crisis** remains as difficult to solve as ever.

Short-Term Fixes

While there are several structural issues that need to be solved in the eurozone, the very survival of the currency union depends on finding successful financing for the indebted countries over the next few years. Although many short-term fixes have been proposed, each of them faces a challenge.

The idea of issuing Euro bonds, which will be a joint liability of all the eurozone countries, will be welcomed by the market. But stronger countries are wary of creating a permanent link between the fiscal positions of the different countries. Germany, with its strong credit rating, is staunchly opposed to it, as it fears that such a pooling of liabilities would dilute pressure for reforms in troubled countries. Even if strict fiscal rules were put in place, the idea evokes the fear of handing over a country's tax revenues to unknown and profligate strangers.

The other source of intermediate financing is the **European** Central Bank, which has an unlimited capacity to provide financing to troubled countries. Germans, however, believe that the central bank should not finance fiscal deficits directly (which is prohibited by the EU constitution anyway). They are also opposed to unlimited purchases by ECB of sovereign **debt** in the secondary market to bring down the yields (which is permitted). In their minds, direct financing by central banks of government **debt** raises the spectre of potential hyperinflation, irrespective of where actual inflation might be at the moment. For them, it is a sacred line that is best not crossed. They are also afraid that financial backstopping by the ECB will reduce the pressure for structural reforms.

The third possibility is for more loans from the stronger to the weaker countries. Having already announced loans of several billion euros—110 billion euros of EU/IMF loan for Greece (May 2010), 68 billion euros for Ireland (November 2010), 78 billion euros for Portugal (May 2011) and 109 billion euros for Greece (July 2011). Part of these bailout funds have been provided by EFSF, IMF and other official sources—the stronger countries may not have the financial wherewithal for more. Already, Standard & Poor's has cut the ratings of several eurozone countries, including France, in response to the deepening **crisis**.

The IMF has already provided funds to Greece, Ireland and Portugal. One advantage of getting the IMF involved is that it has the expertise and experience required to impose structural reforms and to supervise their implementation. But this idea runs up against limits on IMF's lending capacity. The Bundesbank is against the ECB routing its funds through the IMF. The other problem with IMF financing is that the IMF would have a preferred creditor status, thus subordinating private sector loans and potential imposing larger losses on them in the future.

The proposed solution for Greece includes a provision for write-downs of the sovereign **debt** held by private investors, including banks and others. While the net present value (NPV) of the private sector **debt** was to be written down by 21% in the previous round, the current plan envisages a haircut of 50% of the nominal value through a bond exchange and a potentially larger cut in the NPV. There are many issues to be resolved in this plan. Europe would like to keep the bond exchange "voluntary" in order to ensure that the credit default swaps would not be triggered. (It is not clear why this insistence on a "voluntary" exchange, since only about 4 billion euros of credit default swaps remain outstanding.) It still remains to be seen whether the 50% nominal haircut will gain a 100% acceptance. The last time, with a 21% NPV haircut, the acceptances inched close to 90%. Although Institute of International Finance, an association of banks, has said that the haircut would be accepted, we will know the actual acceptance level only when the exchange takes place later this quarter; many hedge funds and other investors are not members of IIF and may have no incentive to abide by the negotiations. As the ECB has purchased the bonds in the secondary market, just as many of the other holders have, how will Greece be able to foist losses on one set of bondholders but not on the other? Ultimately, it is not clear how the non-participating investors would be dealt with. One possibility is that a "collective action clause" might be bolted on to the non-participating bonds issued under Greek law (91% of the total), but such a coercive action would trigger the credit default swaps. If there is no such coercion, then why would any investor take a haircut voluntarily?

The **European** Financial Stability Facility (EFSF), a special purpose vehicle set up to raise funds for eurozone rescues, has a lending capacity of 440 billion euros, of which it has uncommitted amounts of about 250 billion euros. Although the **European** summit has raised the possibility of leveraging the EFSF to provide 1 trillion euros, it is doubtful whether the market would accept such leveraging. Leveraging EFSF through a "first loss insurance" idea would raise the risk of contagion from one distress to another, as every default would leave less in the kitty to cover the remaining outstanding insurance, generating doubts over the value of the remaining insurance. EFSF's ability to leverage and to raise resources would be further curtailed if another rating agency were to cut its top rating (following S&P, which recently cut EFSF to AA+ from AAA).

At one point, there was some talk about attracting large contributions for a bailout fund from China, India, Brazil and other emerging countries, but it is not clear why it would be in their interests to contribute. The only possible answer is that a collapse of the eurozone would lead to a severe shrinkage of their export markets and would also unleash powerful risk aversion that would damage the emerging economies. But this is just another way of saying "Europe is too big to fail"—not enough to persuade the emerging countries to part with hard cash. Even if they did, some of the emerging countries may seek a quid pro quo, which may not be acceptable to developed countries (such as China's desire to be recognised by Europe as a market economy under WTO rules).

Long-Term Repairs

Quite apart from the immediate financing needs, the eurozone needs to address the structural issues that have given rise to the current set of problems. Underlying the **crisis** is the fact that the countries making up the union differ widely in terms of language, culture and economic structure. Hence, their currency union depends to some extent on the calculations by the different countries on the costs and benefits of the union. It also depends on adherence to a set of rules with adequate supervision, even though that may sound like a mechanical rule-bound marriage that takes away the spontaneity.

A lack of fiscal discipline was not the only cause of the current **crisis** (Italy has a primary surplus; Ireland's troubles arose from a real-estate and banking **crisis**; Spain had low **debt** levels). The recent summit has proposed a "fiscal compact". All the countries would incorporate strict fiscal rules into their constitutions or legal systems. The rules would include a limit on the annual "structural" deficit of 0.5% of GDP, **debt**/GDP ratio of 60%, automatic consequences for exceeding 3% deficit, automatic sanctions and fines unless a qualified majority waives it, and **European** Court of Justice jurisdiction over the implementation of the 0.5% rule. An immediate question is whether all the countries would be able to obtain approvals from their respective parliaments and courts. But more importantly, a strict interpretation of the rules would remove the flexibility for counter-cyclical fiscal support; and if the rules provide for breaches in "extraordinary" circumstances, then there is likely to be interpretation problems, leading to market worries. It is also worth remembering that the current eurozone **crisis** started when Greece owned up to cooking its books to reflect a lower deficit. Ultimately, a rule is only as good as the intentions.

There is an element of truth in the argument that the southern **European** countries ran a current-account deficit, eagerly financed by northern **European** capital, until the lack of competitiveness caught up. In the absence of actual labour mobility, the southern countries face a mammoth task of improving their competitiveness. How are they to quickly restore competitiveness—through internal cost reductions through recession-producing austerity, or perhaps exit from the euro followed by a devaluation of their national currency? Equally, while Germans have been happy to prescribe austerity to the southerners, they also need to relax and start consuming more.

Separating the Two

One of the problems with the various approaches to solving the euro **crisis** has been the confusion between short-term and long-term solutions. For instance, France's and Germany's focus on the "fiscal compact" is laudable for its longer-term objective, but it cannot obviate the need to find financing solutions for the present needs. Of the two, it is the short-term financing that is proving to be more problematic, since it involves finding real money, as opposed to be more comfortable task of discussing long-term principles.

In a way, it may be argued that the real task before the eurozone is to raise the financial market confidence sufficiently such that sovereigns can refinance themselves from the market. The steps taken and the solutions discussed so far have singularly failed to boost market confidence, partly because the leaders have wrongly hoped that longer-term solutions would convince the markets to provide short-term financing.

Over the long term, the eurozone either needs to move towards closer fiscal integration (and being a fiscal transfer union), or it would have to face further near-death crises. In the meantime, it needs a funding mechanism that could be tapped from time to time. Unfortunately, none exists in a sufficient scale, and that is the reason for the market nervousness. Until that is addressed directly and forcefully, expect more turbulence.

The author is a credit strategist at Macquarie Asian Markets in Singapore. He is not a member of the research department. Views are personal.

Source

"Solutions and pitfalls." *Financial Express* 3 Feb. 2012. *General Reference Center GOLD*. Web. 23 Feb. 2012.

Critical Thinking

1. What can be done about the financial crisis in Europe?
2. What would be some short-term answers?
2. What were some of the mistakes that led to the financial crisis?

Why a Second Bretton Woods Won't Work

The world economy's dire situation can't be fixed with an international agreement.

BERNARD CONNOLLY

Does the world need a new Bretton Woods meeting, as David Smick suggested in the previous issue of *The International Economy*? Despite the Davos hyper-optimism, the world is in a dire state and certainly needs something. But a new global monetary system run by governments (not that this was what Smick was advocating) or, heaven forbid, NGOs and cabals of businessmen and bankers, might be the last thing it needs.

The "non-system" that has been in place for the past four decades has had a mixed record. The 1970s were pretty awful. But they were awful because of failures of policy, not failures of the "non-system." The ossification of many developed economies via government regulation, control, and intervention, substantial union power, high taxes, capital controls, and a rigid financial and industrial technostructure produced a decline in trend productivity. Preserving employment would have required real wages lower than otherwise. And loose monetary and fiscal policies in the final days of the Bretton Woods system, especially in the United States, sparked a commodity price boom that intensified the downward pressure—if employment were to be preserved—on real wages. But unions and governments attempted to resist that downward pressure and many central banks validated that resistance. NAIRUs rose sharply almost everywhere and there was widespread, prolonged, and substantial stagflation. That some countries—notably Germany and Switzerland—performed better than others in this period was largely because they ran monetary policies different from the international consensus. In Germany's case, it was not until the misconceived "coordination" of policies in the Bremen and Bonn summits of 1978 that the country was sucked into the kind of mess already suffered by many others. It is very hard to see, given the intellectual climate of the time and the widespread economic misconceptions and the misdirected political pressure, how some sort of global economic and monetary "system" would not have made things even worse. (At a regional level, the "system" represented by the European

"snake" simply could not hold together in those intellectual, economic, and political circumstances.)

In the 1980s and 1990s, the "non-system" worked very well. The dramatic changes in economic structure brought about by the tremendous, if not untarnished, efforts of Reagan and Thatcher (not forgetting, of course, the pioneering Roger Douglas in New Zealand) had worldwide demonstration effects. And, just as important, the heroic work of Michael Milken smashed the technostructure, facilitating the productivity revolution of the early 1990s. Globalization and financial liberalization spread capitalism to virtually all parts of the world, lifting hundreds of millions out of poverty. True, there were financial crises in this period, most of them in emerging markets and some of them very serious. But none derailed the march to greater prosperity—except in Japan. That country suffered from its acceptance of international "coordination" in the infamous Louvre Agreement (a certain Jean-Claude Trichet was a crucial player), which not only led very directly to the Wall Street crash of 1987 but also, much more damagingly, gave additional impetus to the final stages of the Japanese bubble. And, of course, the Exchange Rate Mechanism created instability and significant economic damage in Europe.

This was not an ideal world, even aside from the Louvre Agreement and the ERM. But at a global level, it was probably better than anything else the modern world has seen. (What about the final third of the nineteenth century? I'll come back to that.)

Why did things go so badly wrong from the mid-1990s? There were three main problem areas and a unifying intellectual mistake. First, U.S. Federal Reserve Chairman Alan Greenspan totally misread the policy implications of the productivity surge in the United States. Second, the monetary union in Europe magnified the faults of the ERM dramatically, with implications not only for its unfortunate members but also for economies such as Britain's with strong trade links with the union. Third, China's integration into the world economy, constrained by the weight of history—and initial poverty—took place in conditions that made its development almost inevitably "unstable, unbalanced, uncoordinated and unsustainable," as Premier Wen Jiabao famously put it in 2007 (showing, one might note, much more realism than western leaders at that time).

The thread running through all these episodes was a distortion of the key relationships in a capitalist economy: between the anticipated rate of return on investment, the *ex ante* real long(ish) rate of interest, and the subjective rate of households' time preference. And, as I argued in the Fall 2008 issue of *TIE,* a major source of these distortions was the triumph of a Bundesbank-style model of central banking emphasizing price stability. That triumph produced substantial income inequality (just as Dennis Robertson had worried in the 1920s that the Fed, in "going all out for price stability," as he put it, might be robbing workers). It also made bubbles and Ponzi games inevitable. The mechanism emphasized in the recent International Monetary Fund paper on "Inequality, Leverage and Crises" (Kumhof and Rancière, 2010) describes an effect of these developments rather than a cause. But it is a very dangerous effect, and one pointed to by none other than Karl Marx. (Is China perhaps the country now most at risk of unrest of the kind prophesied by Marx?)

The immediate question now is whether the world can recreate a bubble that will last as long as the 2003–07 bubble.

The immediate question now is whether the world can recreate a bubble that will last as long as the 2003–07 bubble. If it can, the world will simply find itself back in the totally unsustainable situation it was in 2007, but probably with a significantly weaker dollar than now and a shift in at least part of the burden of unsustainability away from the United States to someone else to be named later. The financial crisis that will bring this re-created bubble to an end might originate, this time, somewhere other than the United States. But another financial crisis would be an unavoidable result of the process. And accommodating commodity price increases in commodity-importing countries (rather than attempting to offset them through lower nominal wages—an attempt which would bring higher unemployment) would mean an even tighter and longer squeeze on real wages and potentially even greater—perhaps uncontrollable—political strains.

But the alternative is that worry about commodity-price inflation in either emerging markets or in mature economies, or an investment crash in China, aborts the bubble much sooner this time around. Risk asset markets would correct downwards and hopes of a sustained global recovery would be scuppered. Another "Austrian" liquidation crisis would be upon us. The political consequences of that, too, might be uncontrollable.

The world thus remains in a dire state. But it is hard to see how any feasible agreement among governments about an international "system" could really help improve things.

Certainly, a return to any kind of commodity standard would be fraught with danger. The final third of the nineteenth century, the heyday of the "classical" gold standard, is often held as a paragon of systemic virtue. But that period saw a very rapid retreat from free trade everywhere except Britain and its colonies. That retreat, along with colonialist exploitation by all the major powers, reflected a desire to maintain rates of return in the more mature economies at levels elevated enough for high global real rates of interest, induced by high rates of return in the "emerging markets" of the day, not to destroy employment. Income-distribution struggles became virulent and incipiently violent. One does not have to be a Marxist to see the strains created by a rigid global monetary system in the face of dynamically changing geographical patterns of comparative advantage and rates of return as being a major contributory factor in the slide into the First World War. Similar rigidities today would probably destroy not only capitalism but peace.

One can see these dangers all too clearly in the economic, financial, social, and political disaster that is European monetary union. In the world more broadly, the lesson of the experience both of "systems" and of the "non-system" is that in a globalized, dynamic economy, macroeconomic policies in individual countries must be tailored to suit their individual circumstances. The alternative must involve either devastating boom-busts or "coordination," not just of monetary policy and macroeconomic policy, but coordination of all policies in all areas that might impact the rate of return: industrial policy, trade, educational, labor market and incomes, social, demographic, cultural, religious—everything you can think of. "Coordination" is an excuse for proto-Marxists, or at least statists, corporatists, and market-phobes, to impose a centrally planned economy and an anti-democratic polity. This nightmare is now very visibly playing out in Europe, coordinated by the two arch market-phobes, the French and German governments. This has been a very predictable development (indeed I predicted it fifteen years ago in my book, *The Rotten Heart of Europe*) but it is no less alarming for that.

But even total central "coordination," horrendous as it would be, could not solve the existing problems created not by the "non-system" or even just by EMU, but by a failure of monetary policy understanding, most crucially in the second half of the 1990s, which has made the world as a whole an enormous Ponzi game. The academic macro-economics industry must bear a heavy burden of shared responsibility for this *trahison des clercs,* or treason of the intellectuals. At all events, the world now faces a dilemma. One route involves abandoning loose monetary policies and triggering a collapse and goodness knows what else. The other involves continuing those policies and having, sooner or later—and probably sooner, even in rich countries—to face the political and social consequences of further shifts in the distribution of wealth. Inequality will increase between financial market booms on one side and, on the other, real wages reduced by commodity price booms together with real returns to savings reduced by a secular downward trend in real rates of return, real interest rates, and—delusion of delusions—risk premiums.

Again, "coordination" can do nothing to resolve this dilemma, which, for want of a better term, one can perhaps christen "Austro-Robertsonian." A counter-example arguably can be found: the G-20 late in 2008 may have helped steer many countries towards providing fiscal support in conditions of a global collapse both in "animal spirits" and in the availability of private-sector finance. But it is only in extremely rare globally Keynesian conditions—as prevailed for six months or so after the Lehman bankruptcy—that coordination can potentially be helpful. In all other conditions, "coordination" means, in practice, doing something which is damaging in the aggregate in one country but helpful for a particular interest group in another country if that other country agrees in return to do something equally damaging for it in the aggregate but helpful to an interest group in the first country.

No set of macroeconomic policies going forward can avoid the dreadful dilemma between potential collapse and certain income-distribution calamities.

Of course, genuine international imbalances exist. The most immediately damaging is that between Germany and the peripheral countries of EMU. It is beyond doubt that the best way—though, given the unfortunate present existence of EMU, still highly disruptive—to resolve that imbalance would be through a return to a "non-system" of exchange rates in Europe. The bilateral issue between the United States and China has similarities. If China is not going to accept a need to make huge unrequited transfers to the United States every year, it must choose between much more flexibility in the renminbi and eventual massive U.S. default.

But while a resolution of some bilateral problems could help the world at the margin, there can be little optimism that international meetings, "coordination," or the erection of new international monetary systems could help. And the bigger problem is that the "non-system" required, for its benefits to be reaped, that monetary policy in all the major economies must be pursued appropriately. In fact, it has been pursued inappropriately, ever since the second half of the 1990s, in the United States, the euro area, and China (as I noted above, it was pursued highly inappropriately in Japan in the late 1980s precisely because of the attempt of the Louvre Agreement to

establish elements of a "system")—and, in consequence, virtually everywhere else. No set of macroeconomic policies going forward can avoid the dreadful dilemma between potential collapse and certain income-distribution calamities. Anything that might be implemented at the international level would simply be, in large measure, shuffling problems around between countries, at undoubtedly enormous cost in terms of the establishment of new international bureaucratic, unaccountable, and anti-democratic institutional structures—a global *nomenklatura,* in fact.

A capitalist system cannot work without capitalism.

What is instead needed is some way of allowing real interest rates to rise, bringing them into closer alignment with subjective rates of time preference, without producing a terrifying "liquidationist" collapse. The only way to do that is to create a worldwide rise in the rate of return, such that future income and (non-bubble) demand prospects validate *ex post,* so to speak, the volume of real fixed assets, at present reflecting expectations of future bubble conditions demand currently in place. That requires competition—in cutting tax rates, in reducing government interference and control, in stimulating initiative, in fostering globalization, and in restoring the spirit of free enterprise. In other words, it requires everything that current moves in Europe are designed to avoid or at least to distort. A capitalist system cannot work without capitalism. And attempts to create a global monetary and economic "system" are the enemy of capitalism—and of democracy, freedom, and political stability.

Critical Thinking

1. How has the world changed since the first Bretton Woods conference?
2. What were the conditions that allowed the first Bretton Woods conference to be a success?
3. Why don't those conditions exist today?
4. How have these conditions changed?

BERNARD CONNOLLY is Managing Director of Connolly Global Macro Advisers.

The Balance of Payments
Office for National Statistics

GRAEME CHAMBERLIN

The Balance of Payments records one nation's transactions with the rest of the world. This not only includes the conventional flows of goods and services that make up international trade, but also cross-border payments associated with the international ownership of financial assets and current transfers, including remittances by workers from one country to another. In fact, remittances have become increasingly important in recent decades as capital and labour becomes increasingly mobile and financial markets in different countries more strongly integrated. Therefore the means of production are becoming just as likely to move across borders as the actual goods and services produced.

The purpose of this article is to outline the main structure of the UK Balance of Payments so the reader can understand how international trade in goods, services and financial assets and cross-border income flows are recorded in the National Accounts.[1] In doing this the changing patterns over time are presented, along with a more recent analysis of how the current global economic downturn is being reflected in key parts of the Balance of Payments.

The Balance of Payments can effectively be broken down into two parts. The Current Account records international trade in goods and services, international income flows and current transfers. The Capital Account and Financial Account form the counter part to this, recording the changing pattern in the international ownership of assets. While the Financial Account records changes in the cross-border flows of assets, the International Investment Position measures the total stocks of foreign assets and liabilities held by a nation. Some features of this, in particular its relation to investment income, are also analysed in this article.

Current Account

The Current Account consists of four parts:

- Trade in goods
- Trade in services
- Net income flows
- Current transfers

Table 1 presents the UK Current Account for 2007. Although data for 2008 are available these have been significantly affected by the turmoil in the global financial markets and the world recession so are not the best to use for demonstration purposes.

The trade in goods balance is the difference between the value of goods exported and the value of goods imported. Hence, in 2007 a £220.9 billion credit to the Current Account resulted from goods exports and a £310.6 billion debit from imports giving an overall deficit of £89.8 billion. The trade in services is recorded in the same way, with credits to the Current Account reflecting services exports and debits services imports. In 2007, the UK ran an overall surplus of £44.8 billion on the balance of trade in services.

An often cited measure is the trade balance which is the overall balance in the trade in goods and services. In 2007 this would have been negative to the tune of £45.0 billion, as the deficit in goods trades outweighs the surplus in services trade. The trade balance though is not to be confused with the overall Current Account which consists of two further, but less well-known, items.

Table 1   UK Current Account in 2007

	£ billions		
	Credit	Debit	Balance
Goods trade	220.9	310.6	−89.8
Services trade	150.6	105.8	44.8
Net income flows	291.3	270.5	20.8
Current transfers	14.0	27.6	−13.5
Current Account (total)	676.8	714.6	−37.7

Source: ONS Balance of Payments.

Net income flows reflect international payments associated with the ownership of the factors of production (land, labour and capital).

Two types of income transactions are distinguished; compensation of employees which is paid to non-resident workers involved in the production process and investment income which is the return for providing financial assets and rent for natural resources.

In 2007, net compensation of employees debits (outflows) exceeded credits (inflows) by £734 million. However, this clearly accounts for only a small proportion of the total given UK net income was £20.8 billion in surplus in 2007.

The remainder of net income relates to investment income—these are the payments associated with the international ownership of financial assets such as interest payments and dividends. For example, if a UK citizen owned shares in a foreign company, then any dividends earned from this would be counted as a credit. Alternatively, if a UK company borrowed money from a foreign bank then any interest payments accrued would be recorded as a debit.

As financial markets around the world become increasingly integrated it is likely that residents (households, firms, financial institutions such as banks and pension funds, non-profit institutions and the public sector) in one country will seek to diversify their portfolios of financial assets to take advantage of higher returns overseas and reduce exposures to individual country risks. Therefore the ownership of foreign assets and foreigner's ownership of UK assets have grown rapidly and investment income flows are becoming a major determinant of the Current Account.

Current transfers are the final component of the Current Account. This records a miscellaneous set of net payments including workers remittances, social security, foreign aid and contributions to international organisations such as the European Union (EU). As Table 1 shows, these flows are small compared to other parts of the Current Account and in 2007 were in overall deficit of £13.5 billion.

Current Account—Some History

In sum the UK Current Account deficit was £37.7 billion or 2.7 per cent of Gross Domestic Product (GDP) in 2007. The longer-term history of the UK Current Account and its main components are presented in Table 2, and here it can be clearly seen that the overall UK Current Account has been predominately in deficit over the last 40 years.

The main factor behind the UK's persistent Current Account deficit has been the deficit on the balance of trade in goods. In fact, since 1946 this has been in deficit every year bar five. An average surplus was recorded between 1980–84 when UK goods trade was aided by

Table 2 The UK Current Account and Its Main Components

Year	Percentage of GDP (five year averages except later years)				
	Goods Trade	Services Trade	Net Income	Current Transfers	Current Account
1955–59	−0.4	0.4	0.8	0.0	0.9
1960–64	−0.9	0.1	0.9	−0.1	0.0
1965–69	−0.9	0.4	0.8	−0.2	0.0
1970–74	−2.1	1.2	0.9	−0.3	−0.3
1975–79	−2.0	2.2	−0.1	−0.6	−0.5
1980–84	0.1	1.8	−0.6	−0.5	0.7
1985–89	−3.1	1.8	−0.4	−0.7	−2.4
1990–94	−2.1	1.1	−0.4	−0.7	−2.1
1995–99	−2.1	1.7	0.2	−0.8	−1.0
2000–04	−4.2	1.9	1.2	−0.8	−2.0
2005	−5.5	2.1	1.7	−0.9	−2.6
2006	−5.8	2.6	0.7	−0.9	−3.3
2007	−6.4	3.2	1.5	−1.0	−2.7
2008	−6.4	3.8	1.9	−0.9	−1.7

Source: ONS Balance of Payments.

North Sea oil production and high oil prices, but since then the deficit has consistently grown as a proportion of GDP to 6.4 per cent in both 2007 and 2008.

As manufacturing goods make up the largest proportion of goods trade then the relative decline in UK manufacturing output might suggest why this deficit has grown over the last two decades. The emergence of low cost producers in emerging markets have meant that the bulk of UK manufacturing including automobiles, clothing and footwear, consumer electronics and materials processing have seen its global market share fall. However, the UK has managed to increase its export share in smaller higher technology manufactures such as medical and pharmaceuticals, communications equipment, office machinery and computers.

On the other hand exports of services have exceeded imports every year since 1951 except two, and surpluses as a proportion of GDP have grown continuously since EU membership in 1973. This is consistent with the changing composition of UK output, with the largest surpluses in financial and business services—and is evidence that structural change in the UK economy has followed its comparative advantage in international trade.[2]

Net income has been more erratic over the years reflecting the inherent volatility in financial markets. It was last negative as recently as 1999 due to the impact of the Asian financial crisis, but during the last decade has generally made a positive contribution to the Current Account.

In comparison current transfers have made a negative contribution to the Current Account but the deficit has been fairly stable as a proportion of GDP over the last 30 years. The typical deficit reflects net contributions to the EU and the cost of foreign aid.

Capital and Financial Accounts

So what does it mean if the UK ran a Current Account deficit of £37.7 billion in 2007? Basically it states that foreigners are adding to their stock of UK assets by a sum of £37.7 billion more than UK residents are adding to their stock of foreign assets—or that the UK is essentially increasing its net liabilities to the rest of the world by this amount.

The Capital and Financial Accounts records the counterparts to the Current Account, which are the offsetting changes in the ownership of financial assets as implied by the Current Account surplus or deficit. In fact, Table 3 shows that in 2007 both UK residents have added to their stock of foreign assets and foreign residents have added to their stock of UK assets by over £1,000 billion (£1 trillion)—but the key is that foreigners have added to their stock of assets by somewhat (£37.7 billion) more.

In Table 3, the credit column refers to money spent by foreign residents on UK assets and the debit column to money spent by UK residents on foreign assets.

The Capital Account consists of several miscellaneous items such as land purchases and sales associated with embassies, the transfers of migrants, EU regional development fund payments and so on. It is small relative to the Financial Account, and in 2007 credits exceeded debits by £2.6 billion.

The Financial Account has been broken down according to the main types of assets.

Direct investments refer to the purchase by the residents of one country of a significant part of an enterprise in another country. This not only consists of factories or production units but larger shareholdings (in excess of 10 per cent of total equity) which is considered to give the owner influence over the management of the enterprise and the set level of dividends.

The purchase of British Airports Association (BAA) by the Spanish company Ferrovial and British Energy Group by Electricite de France (EDF) are examples of direct investment credits in the Financial Account. Likewise, the purchase of the German telecoms firm Mannesmann by Vodafone and Atlantic Richfield by BP Amoco would be examples of significant direct investment debits. Major (in excess of £5 billion) direct investment acquisitions of foreign companies by UK companies and vice-versa during the last ten years are recorded in Table 4.

Portfolio investments relate to the smaller purchases of equity (less than 10 per cent of the total) and also debt securities.

Other investments in the main refer to financial intermediation services. For example, a deposit made by a UK local authority in an Icelandic bank would have been scored as a debit. Alternatively a loan from a foreign bank to a UK household would be classified as a credit.

The sums recorded in both the debit and credit columns in the other investment category are huge, representing around 70 per cent of UK Gross Domestic Product. This is because the UK financial system is highly integrated with the rest of the world's financial markets and plays a large intermediary role between them.

For example, a UK bank may receive £1 billion in deposits from a German pension fund that it then lends to US firms. In this case both the credit and debit columns of the other investment category will increase by £1 billion. Alternatively, the UK bank may decide to lend the £1 billion to a UK firm that purchases a majority shareholding in a foreign company. In this case the debit column in the other investment category and the credit column in the direct investment category will both increase by £1 billion. Because these types of intermediary transactions are so commonplace it is easy to understand how the size of credits and debits in the Financial Account may be a large proportion of GDP but the difference between them is relatively small. This is demonstrated in Figure 1, where both foreign assets and liabilities (holdings of

Table 3 UK Capital and Financial Accounts in 2007

	£ billions		
	Credit	**Debit**	**Balance**
Capital Account	4.6	2.0	2.6
Financial Account			
Direct investment	98.2	136.1	−38.0
Portfolio investment	203.3	92.0	111.3
Other investment	725.9	767.5	−41.6
Total	1027.4	995.7	31.7
Balancing item			3.4
Grand total			37.7

Source: ONS Balance of Payments.

Table 4 Major Direct Investment Acquisitions by/of UK Companies in the Last Decade by Value

Outwards Acquisitions of Foreign Companies

£113.0 billion: Mannesmann AG by Vodafone (2000 Q1)

£37.5 billion: Airtouch by Vodafone (1999 Q2)

£32.6 billion: Amoco Corp by British Petroleum (BP) (1998 Q4)

£21.0 billion: Zeneca PLC by Astra AB (1999 Q2)

£18.5 billion: Alcan Inc by Rio Tinto (2007 Q4)

£18.0 billion: Atlantic Richfield by BP Amoco (2000 Q2)

£9.3 billion: Altadis SA by Imperial Tobacco Group (2008 Q1)

£9.1 billion: Household International by HSBC (2003 Q1)

£7.7 billion: MedImmune Inc by AstraZeneca (2007 Q3)

£6.6 billion: Credit Commerciale de France by HSBC (2000 Q3)

£5.8 billion: Charter 1 by Royal Bank of Scotland (RBS) (2004 Q3)

£5.5 billion: Hutchison Essar by Vodafone Group (2007 Q2)

£5.0 billion: Innovene Inc by Ineos Group (2005 Q4)

Inward acquisitions of UK companies

£23.5 billion: Orange PLC by France Telecom (2000 Q3)

£19.5 billion: Orange PLC by Mannesmann AG (1999 Q4)

£17.7 billion: O2 by Telefonica (2006 Q1)

£12.5 billion: British Energy by Electricite de France (EDF) (2009 Q1)

£11.0 billion: Alliance Boots PLC by AB Acquisitions Ltd

£10.1 billion: British Airports Association (BAA) by Ferrovial (2006 Q2)

£9.0 billion: Abbey National by Banco Santander (2004 Q4)

£8.5 billion: Reuters Group by Thomson Corporation (2008 Q2)

£8.3 billion: Hanson PLC by Heidellberg Cement AG (2007 Q3)

£8.2 billion: BOC Group PLC by Linde AC (2006 Q3)

£8.1 billion: Imperial Chemical Industries by AKZO Nobel (2008 Q1)

£7.5 billion: Scottish & Newcastle by Sunrise Acquisitions Ltd (2008 Q2)

£6.7 billion: ASDA by Wal-Mart (1999 Q3)

£5.3 billion: Amersham PLC by General Electric Group (2004 Q2)

£5.2 billion: Powergen by E. on (2002 Q3)

Source: ONS Balance of Payments.

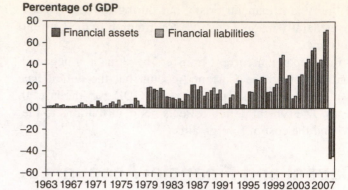

Percentage of GDP

Figure 1 Net acquisitions of financial assets and liabilities

Source: ONS Balance of Payments.

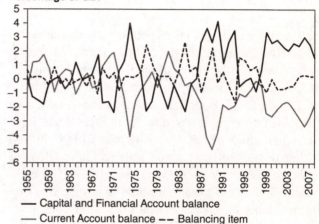

Percentage of GDP

— Capital and Financial Account balance
— Current Account balance — — Balancing item

Figure 2 Balancing the Balance of Payments

Source: ONS Balance of Payments.

Figure 2 shows the long-term history of the UK Current Account balance, the Capital and Financial Accounts balances, and the balancing item as a percentage of GDP. Clearly there is an offsetting relationship between the two main parts of the Balance of Payments, so the data behaves as expected. The balancing item exhibits some volatility but in recent years has been relatively minor.

International Investment Position

While the Financial Account records international flows in the acquisition and disposals of financial assets, the stock positions are presented in the International Investment Position (IIP). This is the difference in the value of foreign assets held by UK residents (UK's foreign assets) and UK assets held by foreign residents (UK's foreign liabilities). Therefore it is also referred to as the net-asset position.

Like Financial Account flows in Figure 1, the UK's stocks of foreign assets and liabilities have grown rapidly

UK assets by foreigners) have grown significantly as a proportion of GDP yet in each year differ by a relatively small amount.

The final element, which does not officially form part of the Capital or Financial Accounts is the balancing item. Although in theory the Capital and Financial Accounts should offset the Current Account, in practise it rarely does due to errors and omissions. The purpose of the balancing item is therefore reconcile the two sides of the Balance of Payments.

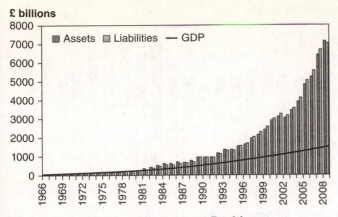

£ billions

Figure 3   **International Investment Position**
Source: ONS Balance of Payments.

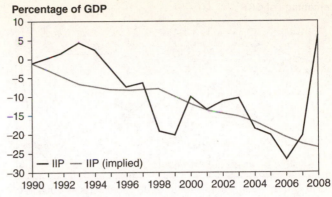

Percentage of GDP

Figure 4   **International Investment Position and the Current Account**
Source: ONS Balance of Payments.

and now far outstrip GDP. As Figure 3 shows, stocks of foreign assets and liabilities are near £7,000 billion (£7 trillion) or about 4 and half times GDP. This ratio is much higher than in most developed countries (for the US stocks of foreign assets and liabilities were around 100 per cent of GDP in 2005) and is a strong indication of the relative openness of the UK economy, and in particular its financial sector, to the rest of the world.

And like the balance on the Financial Account, in any one year the IIP or net asset position is relatively small given the size of the asset stocks, further indication of the intermediary role played by UK financial institutions in the global economy.

As the IIP and Financial Account are linked by a stock-flow relationship, in theory, there should also be a relationship between the IIP and the Current Account. The UK's persistent Current Account deficit over the last thirty years implies that the nation has been living beyond its means for a considerable period of time requiring offsetting surpluses on the Financial Account. Therefore, as this feeds through into asset stocks it would be expected that a long run decline in the IIP would result.

Figure 4 plots the actual UK IIP since 1990, and the IIP implied by the accumulation of Current Account deficits. Up until 2007 the IIP has generally behaved as expected, deteriorating in line with Current Account deficits. However, in 2008, the IIP jumped sharply into positive territory for the first time since 1994.

This can be explained by looking at what determines the actual dynamics of the IIP between time period (t) and (t-1):

$$IIP(t) = IIP(t-1) + Current\ Account(t) + asset\ revaluations(t)$$

where asset revaluations = price changes + exchange rate changes + other adjustments

That is changes in the net asset position do not just reflect Financial (Current) Account flows but also revaluations of those assets. Furthermore, revaluations of assets do not just reflect the volatility in equity and bond markets but also in exchange rates. Almost the entire jump in the UK IIP during 2008 can be accounted for by the depreciation of sterling.

As foreign assets are expressed in foreign currency, depreciation of sterling against that foreign currency means that the valuation of that asset in sterling terms increases. If UK liabilities (UK assets held by foreigners) are valued in sterling then there is no change following depreciation. But were they also valued in foreign currency then the sterling value of liabilities would also rise following depreciation. However this is generally not the case. The majority of UK foreign assets will be valued in foreign currency and the majority of UK assets held by foreigners will be valued in sterling so sterling depreciation improves the IIP and sterling appreciation deteriorates the IIP.

Given that the trade-weighted effective sterling exchange rate fell by about 25 per cent during 2008 and the stock of foreign assets held by UK residents amounts to 4 and a half times GDP then it is quite plausible to explain how such a large jump in the IIP was possible. The jump in the value of foreign assets can be seen in Figure 3 as well as in the IIP in Figure 4.

International Investment Position and Net Investment Income

Until last year (2008) the declining UK IIP was a curiosity in that net international investment income continued to be positive (see Figure 5)—suggesting that an increasingly negative net asset position was managing to create robust positive net investment income.[3] An explanation for the divergence in IIP and net investment income requires the

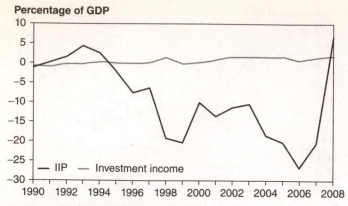

Percentage of GDP

Figure 5 International Investment Position and net investment income

Source: ONS Balance of Payments.

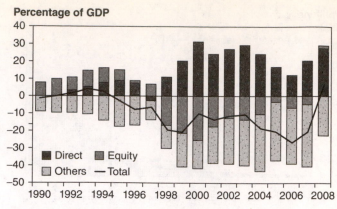

Percentage of GDP

Figure 7   IIP breakdown by asset type

Source: ONS Balance of Payments.

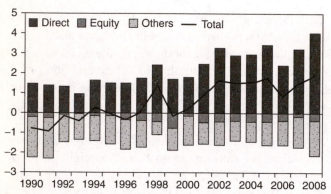

Figure 6   Breakdown of investment income by asset type

Source: ONS Balance of Payments.

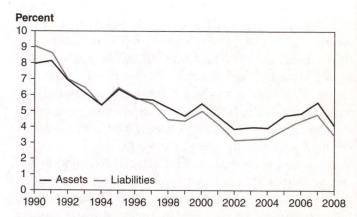

Percent

Figure 8   Rates of return on UK assets and liabilities

Source: ONS Balance of Payments.

data in Figure 5 to be broken down into the contributions by each type of asset.

Starting with net investment income, Figure 6 presents a breakdown by three main asset classes: direct investments, equity investments and other investments which are predominately interest bearing financial assets including debt securities. Surpluses on the investment income balance have clearly been driven from direct investment, while the other two asset classes make negative contributions.

Figure 7 presents the composition of the UK IIP according to the same asset categories. Although the aggregate IIP is generally in deficit, primarily due to the contribution of other investments, the UK has managed to sustain a robust surplus in direct investment assets.

For a negative IIP to generate a surplus in net investment income it must be the case that the UK's stock of foreign assets are generating higher returns than the stock of UK assets held by foreigners. This is confirmed in Figure 8. Rates of return[4] on the UK's foreign assets and liabilities have generally fallen since the early 1990s in line with

global interest rates, but since the mid 1990s the UK has enjoyed a distinct rate of return advantage. It is this that accounts for the positive investment income despite the overall negative position on the IIP.

Figure 9, by presenting rates of return for each asset class, ties together the trends in Figures 6, 7 and 8. There are a number of observations that can be made:

- Rates of return in direct investment can be volatile, reflecting the global economic cycle, but on the whole exceed those of other asset classes. This differential has grown in the last decade as the fall in global interest rates pushes down on income from other investments including debt securities which are predominately interest bearing.

- Direct investments, which include equity holdings of over 10 per cent of an enterprise, offer far higher rates of return than smaller equity investments (minority shareholdings). This implies that exercising some degree of control over

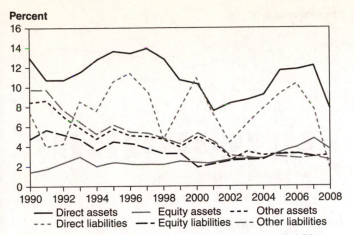

Percent

Direct assets — — — Equity assets - - - Other assets
- - - Direct liabilities — · — Equity liabilities — · — Other liabilities

Figure 9   Rates of return by types of asset and liability
Source: ONS Balance of Payments.

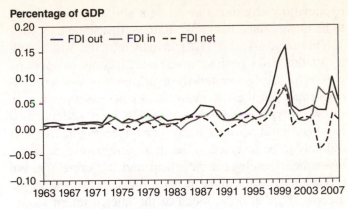

Percentage of GDP

— FDI out   — FDI in   - - FDI net

Figure 10   UK Foreign Direct Investment
Source: ONS Balance of Payments.

the enterprise including the power to influence dividend payments yields a superior return.

• Returns on UK held foreign direct investments have generally exceeded those of foreign direct investments into the UK, while there is little rate of return difference in equity and other assets.

Therefore the UK's rate of return advantage is down to two factors.

First, it has a strong net-asset position in higher yielding direct investments. In this respect, Nickell (2006) describes the UK IIP as similar to a successful venture capitalist by borrowing cheap interest bearing funds through its negative IIP in other investment assets and maintaining a surplus in its IIP of more lucrative direct investment assets.

Second, even within the direct investment category the UK has a rate of return advantage. In addition to the successful venture capitalist argument that the UK is just relatively good at picking profitable FDI opportunities three other explanations for this advantage have been suggested.

The US also enjoys a rate of return advantage in FDI, which Hausmann and Sturzenegger (2006) put down to exports of 'dark matter[5]'. These are the unseen intangibles (or knowledge capital) such as managerial expertise, organisational structure, brand names, IT systems, design and technical (R&D) capabilities that usually accompany direct investments and make it more successful. The same reasoning may also apply to the UK–that its direct investments abroad are supported by significant transfers of quality intangibles. This reasoning may also account for the rate of return advantage of direct investments over smaller equity investments.

Another explanation is that, for one reason or another, foreigners may be prepared to accept a relatively lower

rate of return on their direct investments in the UK. It might be considered as a price for accessing the large EU market allowing firms to benefit from economies of scale in production. The UK is also considered to be a less risky environment in which to do business than other economies, mainly due to the superior development of its legal and financial institutions. As a result, the risk premium and yields on inward FDI to the UK would be correspondingly lower.

It might also be the case that firms deliberately report lower profits on their UK operations to reduce tax liabilities of the UK. As the production process becomes more vertically integrated across borders it gives firms scope to move profits through transfer pricing (also known as toll processing). For example, if the UK was considered a relatively high tax country then companies would face an incentive to reduce their reported earnings in the UK. This could be achieved by raising the internal prices of the output produced downstream, or reducing the prices charged upstream, as either would squeeze the margins on UK operations relative to the parts of the production process undertaken in other countries.

Finally, the rate of return on UK direct investments abroad may be exaggerated by underestimating the value of these direct investments and hence the overall IIP. Most financial assets such as equity and debt securities are frequently traded so that they can be valued using established market prices. Direct investments though are large, unique and illiquid assets for which market prices do not exist and the actual value can differ significantly from book or historic values—making life difficult for statisticians. As a result an undervaluation of the value of direct investment abroad would lead to an overstatement of the rate of return. But it should also be acknowledged that the same argument could be applied to inward foreign direct investment, so this reasoning would require an explanation why direct investment abroad is more likely to be undervalued than inward direct investment.

This analysis also gives insight into the sustainability of the UK's positive investment income balance. As it is primarily generated through direct investment it is important that the UK maintains its net asset position in this asset type. And given that the UK's net asset position has been built up over many years (see Figure 10) it is unlikely to be reversed in the short term. However, direct investment earnings are cyclical and the current global recession appears to be putting downward pressure on income. Furthermore, much of the rate of return advantage enjoyed by the UK has resulted from falling global interest rates making it easier to fund its large negative IIP in other (predominately interest bearing) assets. So should global interest rates start to push upwards it would put downward pressure on UK net investment income.

Recent Trends in the UK Balance of Payments

In this final section more recent trends in the UK Balance of Payments are analysed. These are of special interest given the global nature of the current recession and financial crisis.

Figure 11 shows, as a percentage of GDP and on a quarterly basis, the main component parts of the UK Current Account. Most striking is that since the beginning of 2008 the UK Current Account deficit has grown, despite the balance of trade (goods and services) improving. Transfers have been very stable, so the deterioration over the last year has been primarily driven by falling net investment income.

In Figure 12 the exports and imports of goods are presented. As most of the balance on goods trade is determined by manufactures (semi and finished goods) then both exports and imports have fallen quickly as a result

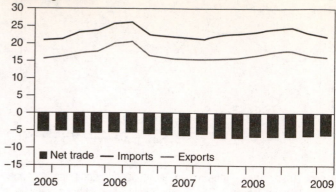

Percentage of GDP

Figure 12   Trade in goods
Source: ONS Balance of Payments.

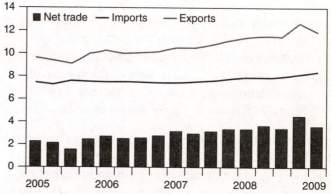

Percentage of GDP

Figure 13   Trade in services
Source: ONS Balance of Payments.

of the global economic downturn being concentrated in the manufacturing sector. However, because UK imports have fallen faster than exports the overall goods deficit has narrowed in recent quarters.

Services trade though has been relatively robust through the recession. In fact, as Figure 13 shows, there has been no notable downturn as a proportion of GDP and the overall UK balance has improved. One area that appears to have been doing well is the financial sector, ironically as a result of the global financial crisis.

Financial sector output consists of two main parts. First there are activities for which fee and commission income is earned, and as expected, this has fallen in line with business activity in the global recession. These are direct outputs, known as Financial Intermediation Services Directly Measured (FISDM). However, much of the output of the financial services sector is not charged for directly, such as current account services. Here incomes are usually made by a spread between deposit (savings) and credit (lending) rates—this output is known as Financial Intermediation Services Indirectly Measured

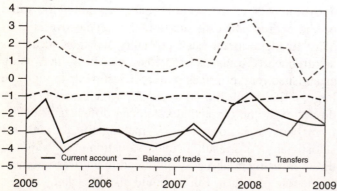

Percentage of GDP

Figure 11   Current Account
Source: ONS Balance of payments.

Percentage of GDP

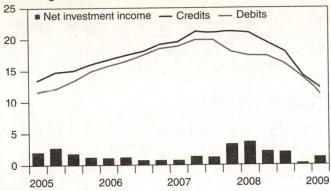

Figure 14   Net investment income
Source: ONS Balance of Payments.

Percentage of GDP

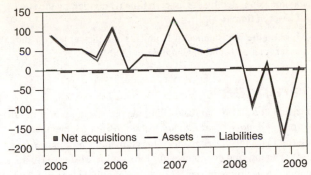

Figure 15   Financial Account transactions
Source: ONS Balance of Payments.

(FISIM). One of the consequences of the financial crisis is that these spreads have widened. Central banks around the world have been aggressive in cutting interest rates which have been passed on quickly into deposit rates. But lending rates have come down less quickly, and for many consumer loans they have actually not come down at all or gone up—a reflection of the banking sectors updated view on risk and their desire to cut back on some lending. Given that the deposit base hasn't changed that much this has led to a large jump in calculated FISIM output in the last year. And because the UK financial services sector is large and operates on a global scale it is likely that FISIM exports will have increased as well.

Net investment income though, despite continuing to make a positive contribution to the Current Account, has fallen sharply in recent quarters. Although it must also be acknowledged that net income had been particularly strong in 2007, so much of the reversal may just be trend correcting. Strong investment income was the main factor closing the Current Account in early 2008, and has been the main factor in the widening deficit thereafter.

Given the UK's strong net asset position in direct investment, most of the deterioration can be traced to this asset class. Earnings on direct investment abroad, and on foreign earnings on direct investments in the UK have fallen, mostly likely as a consequence of the global recession and credit crunch on company profits. Particularly affected are the earnings of financial corporations. As direct investment in the UK from overseas are highly concentrated in the banking sector it explains why income flows out of the UK have fallen faster than flows to the UK in recent years.

As explained already, Capital and Financial Account transactions are the mirror of Current Account transactions. Hence the deterioration in the Current Account would be associated with a growing surplus on the Capital and Financial Accounts as the UK reduces its net-asset position vis-à-vis the rest of the world.

However, it is still worth looking at because while the balance may actually be quite small, there have been very large recent movements in the flows of financial assets. This is shown quite clearly in Figure 1, where the UK's cross-border accumulation of financial assets and liabilities was massively negative in 2008.

The quarterly figures underline the recent volatility in financial markets (see Figure 15). The striking feature which is also picked up in Figure 1 are the periods of large disinvestment–where UK residents cut back on their stocks of foreign assets and foreign residents on their stocks of UK assets. This could be to reduce more 'risky' holdings of foreign assets or simply to repatriate assets to cover domestic losses and shore up balance sheets. For example, securities have been one of the financial asset classes most affected by the fallout from the US sub-prime mortgage market and the credit crunch and much of the volatility in the UK Financial Account has resulted from disinvestments in these assets. In the past, net disinvestment in equities has frequently coincided with financial shocks—for example the UK's exit from the Exchange Rate Mechanism in 1992, the Asian financial crisis in 1997 and the collapse in equity markets in 2002. The most recent crisis though is more unique in that disinvestment has happened across a broad range of asset classes, not just the more volatile ones.

Notes

1. Much of this article follows and updates the analysis in Nickell (2006).

2. Chamberlin (2008) provides further evidence on the shifting composition of UK output and trade including its implications for the terms of trade.

3. Similar analysis and background on the UK International Investment Position can be found in Nickell (2006) and Whitaker (2006).

4. The rate of return on an asset in time (t) is calculated as the income generated by the asset in time (t) divided by the stock of asset in time (t-1).

5. More on the US Balance of Payments and the subject of 'dark matter' can be found in Chamberlin (2009).

References

Chamberlin G (2008) 'Command GDP: the purchasing power of UK output', *Economic and Labour Market Review* (September).

Chamberlin G (2009) 'Dark matter. Does it matter?' in Linda Yueh (ed) 'The law and economics of globalisation', Edward Elgar.

Hausmann R and Sturzenegger F (2006) 'Global imbalances or bad accounting? The missing dark matter in the wealth of nations', Centre for International Development, Harvard University, *Working Paper* no. 124, January.

Nickell S (2006) 'The current account and all that', *Bank of England Quarterly Bulletin* Summer.

Whitaker S (2006) 'The UK international investment position', *Bank of England Quarterly Bulletin* 2006 Q3.

Critical Thinking

1. What is the balance of payments?
2. Why is the balance of payments important?
3. What are some of the important pieces of the balance of payments?
4. How does the balance of payments work?

From *Economic and Labour Market Review,* vol. 3, no. 9, published by Palgrave Macmillan, September 2009, pp. 44–51. Source: Office for National Statistics. Crown Copyright material is reproduced with the permission of the Office of Public Sector Information (OPSI). www.palgrave-journals.com.

The Next 80 Years

We asked leading financial executives and business leaders how the next 80 years of global finance will evolve. Some offered cautious prognoses, others predicted fundamental, sweeping change and one scenario was simply out of this world.

ELLEN M. HEFFES

Any conversation about the future financial executive and the profession must consider the changing regulatory landscape and the up-and-coming talent pool. Like a major league ball club, organizations of all types require a pool of qualified individuals from which to draft and develop their future stars.

Gone are the days that a company's outside auditors would serve as the primary training ground for such talent, as more than half of all current accounting grads do not initially work for a CPA firm, according to the AICPA. As to the future financial and regulatory environment, GAAP as we know it is coming under increasing pressure both from abroad (IFRS vs. GAAP) and domestically (private vs. public GAAP).

Toss into this mix the seemingly endless quest for tax reform at the federal level and it is easy to see how volatile the atmosphere is becoming for the future. Facing this, will the future financial executive become more of a technocrat over time, enforcing rules and statutes primarily, or will the environment become more business development-oriented, reversing the trend of the last few decades of ever more complex rules setting and regulation, with the result that once again the CFO becomes an equal member of the management team? One can only hope.

Tim Anglim, president and founder,
YesCFO, FEI member

Given all the changes in the accounting profession and the business world over the past 80 years, it would be presumptuous for me to predict the next 80. But I'm virtually certain that having enough cash will continue to be the lifeblood of any successful corporation and that the debits and credits will still have to balance each other.

Denny Beresford, professor University of Georgia,
former Financial Accounting Standards Board chairman,
FEI 2006 Hall of Fame inductee

The primary responsibility for today's financial executive is to drive intrinsic value. Finance executives partner with the CEO and COO as their companies' senior strategists to achieve success. I don't see this role changing much, but the competencies required to perform effectively in this role will evolve.

In the future, the CFO will need to focus externally more so than internally and create and leverage connections and drive change outside their organizations as well as inside to create value. As a result, strategic thinking, creative vision and the ability to "connect the dots" will be much more important to the financial executive of the future.

George Boyadjis, CPA, FHFMA, executive director,
Corporate Real Estate Services, CresaPartners,
FEI member, current FEI chairman

Financial executives are ultimately stewards of growth for their organizations. Smart, quality growth is ever more reliant on sound financial management, which underpins the strategy of any organization. At Grant Thornton, we look forward to close, rewarding relationships with these business leaders for decades to come.

Stephen Chipman, CEO, Grant Thornton LLP,
FEI Strategic Partner

In the short term (five years), getting comfortable with data and core processes operating in a cloud environment. Days of having all data stored/managed/locked down internally will be gone and procedures for security will need to adapt. Given the increasing role of government, I'd expect financial executives will need to be more directly involved in shaping public policy, without the often high-cost middleman of lobbyists or other interpreters guiding their view.

Countries with aging demographics will need to find ways for financial executives to contribute in some fashion beyond the traditional boundaries of retirement and pay-by-the-drink consulting. Possibly some form of knowledge bank creation and toolset. Finance recruitment and training will need to focus more heavily on emerging economies, particularly in the southern hemisphere.

Kevin Cunningham, vice president,
Sun Solar LLC, FEI member

The financial executive will need to continue to evolve into a business leader with global experience and a global perspective. More than any other executive in a corporation, the financial executive will need to be multifaceted to help deliver returns to the shareholders.

J. Scott Di Valerio, CFO, Coinstar Inc., FEI member,
Financial Executive Editorial Advisory Board

Financial executives will remain ever critical to business success and work in an ever-increasing global economy with ever-increasing government and professional regulation.

Alexis Dow, CPA, FEI member, former FEI chairman

Over the next 80 years, information technology may exert an increasingly powerful influence on financial executives. Computers and the Internet have already changed many aspects of financial management, but the relentless creativity of IT developers means the process may accelerate and be less expensive than today. Sooner than we think, software could permit "continuous monitoring" that allows management to track and improve performance in real time, and "continuous auditing" could enhance auditors' reviews and analyses, down to the transaction level on a real-time basis.

Management's intensified performance monitoring and improvement activities may promote more consistent and positive earnings, internal auditors' more regular, thorough and complete reviews may enhance controls and compliance and independent auditors' issuance of more efficient and frequent audit reports may provide assurance at speeds consistent with the rapid pace of the high-tech 21st century marketplace.

Joe Echevarria, CEO, Deloitte LLP,
FEI Strategic Partner

I have two questions: Will CFOs, members of senior management and their boards increase their use of cash flow-based information (receipts and disbursements, etc.) to monitor their business operations in the face of the ongoing complexity of accounting statements, which can result in changes in financial outcomes independent of any changes in operations?

And, will management and boards begin to "price" their senior management positions—that is, figure out what a position in the company is worth at that point in time, and then find the best available person who will accept that price, as opposed

to finding the best available person in the marketplace and paying that individual whatever the market requires?

H. Stephen Grace, chairman, H.S. Grace & Co.,
FEI member, former FEI chairman

Financial executives will continue to evolve into a more strategic and operational role, as internal business advisers and risk mitigation experts. From supporting critical analysis in the development of corporate strategies, to making better decisions in the execution of actions consistent with goals and objectives, supplementing intuition with facts. I foresee corporate financial executives devoting an ever-decreasing proportion of their time reporting the results and monitoring dashboard performance indicators and more time devoted to making a real difference in the results they report and monitor.

Included is proactive risk analysis and assessment, best practice implementation, optimized resource allocation, prioritization of initiatives and alternatives, compliance efforts, cost reduction and data mining.

The future will reward well-rounded training and preparation for financial executives, so that they are able to add real value to the business operations, operating environment and related analytics, while keeping up with the changing financial reporting standards.

Allen Greene, CEO, SmartPros Ltd.,
FEI Strategic Partner

An important trend I see is that financial reporting, tax policy and compliance will become more and more inextricably connected with corporate responsibility and there will be even more demand for increased transparency with closer engagement with government and regulatory bodies to drive a closer connection with shareholders and the capital markets.

The "green" movement and the growing importance of emerging territories as new markets for multinational corporations will only increase this trend.

In other words, corporations will need to be more fully engaged in territories in which they do business in ways they never have before—it will no longer merely be about complying with accounting standards and tax laws and paying taxes and completing financial reports.

Scott Gruchot, vice president and general manager–corporate
CCH, a Wolters Kluwer business,
FEI Strategic Partner

There will be some things that are very much the same and some that we can't even envision now. We could ask some key questions: Will reporting be globally consistent and comparable? My guess is that it will. Will the content change? I'd say "yes," in certain degrees I think it will have changed. Also, the use of technology is going to allow for more and more easily obtainable content. Reporting more nonfinancial information and relating that to the financial information, more information on sustainability and environmental impacts, all seem to be trends that continue to grow in demand and importance.

Will there still be the basic financial statements or will it be replaced by just electronic data that you can plug into your model and create your own build-to-suit financial statements? I believe there still will be a core set of financial statements and there will be the ability to plug in data to your models. Some of these mentioned here will occur well before 80 years.

Robert H. Herz, former Financial
Accounting Standards Board chairman

Since long before FEI was founded, financial information has been expensive, hard to get and difficult to interpret. This created a need for accountants and financial executives and professional organizations to support them. Music, movies, newspapers and books used to be expensive and hard to get, too. Digital technology reduced the cost and disrupted employment and long-established business models.

There is no reason to believe that financial information is immune from the technologies that caused dramatic changes in other types of information. The universal labeling of financial information with XBRL promises to commoditize financial information just as MP3 technology did with music. Digital music provided a universal standard for recorded music that made it easily accessible from anywhere.

It will certainly be more expensive, complicated and difficult to digitize financial information. But it will happen.

Joe Howell, founder and managing director, WebFilings,
FEI Strategic Partner

The most significant driver for finance and the CFO in the future will be continued globalization. Finance leaders will have to have experience and be comfortable with other cultures, be able to understand and react to distant markets and customers, recognize new and different competitors and build and manage very diverse work forces. In essence, finance leaders will have to become truly global leaders themselves. Aiding them will be much more timely, deep and useful information. Finance leaders will be getting updates on the key variables that drive their firm's value virtually instantaneously. Then, using their global perspective and information flow, they will be in the necessary position to impact the firm's global strategy and value-creating performance.

Robert A. Howell, professor, Tuck School of Business, Dartmouth,
FEI member, Financial Executive Editorial Advisory Board

The past 80 years have taught us a single valuable lesson: That despite our hunger to ascertain the "new normal" at each turn in the road, the persistency of that is fleeting. Therefore, just

as the human species owes much of its success to its ability to adapt to changing environmental conditions much better than other species (unlike Neanderthals, who couldn't adapt and perished), so, too, the successful financial executive will be one that is able to commit to a path and yet remain nimble and alert enough to adapt when the path is no longer optimal.

Stewart D. Lawrence, FSA, senior vice president,
National Retirement practice leader, Sibson Consulting,
FEI member, Financial Executive Editorial Advisory Board

When most of us look back at the last 80 years, I am sure we conclude that this period of history had more changes than any other. Looking ahead to the next 80, I believe the conclusion will be the same. This tells me that the most important thing in any period is not the amount of change but the reaction to the change by the individuals involved.

Based on this conclusion, I believe the adaptation of financial executives over the past 80 years has been remarkable. Looking ahead, I see nothing to indicate that the financial executives of the next 80 years will not continue to learn, to adapt and to contribute as well as those who met the challenges of the past. I feel some regret that I will not be there to participate in this wonderful future, but I wish my successors well in those exciting times ahead.

Ulyesse LeGrange, retired senior vice president and CFO,
Exxon USA, FEI 2010 Hall of Fame inductee

It's been several decades since I played a direct and active role as a financial executive. However, I continue to stay closely abreast of the activities and contributions of today's financial community. I anticipate that tomorrow's financial leaders will be much closer to operations of an enterprise and will be considered the co-leader along with the CEO in responding to issues related to globalization, corporate mobility, information technology and ethical conduct. Governance and control will be significantly more important and play an extremely vital role in tomorrow's enterprises.

In short: you ain't seen nothin' yet!

Robert W. Moore, former FEI president and CEO,
FEI member, FEI 2006 Hall of Fame inductee

Technology gains will change business as we know it today. The data to information to insight cycle will accelerate to literally "real-time" across the globe. Data and information management will enable real-time, automated decision-making and risk management. For example standard taxonomies and XBRL will permit one version of electronic data to meet each country's reporting requirements for securities, tax, environmental and bank regulators.

Compliance enforcement will be virtually instantaneous, removing significant uncertainties and workload. Cross-border information-sharing will evolve to become the norm to ensure governments get their fair share of a multinational's taxes. These trends will drive enormous productivity improvements for both industry and governments that will completely change the nature of how finance and tax people do their jobs. Time currently spent on data management and reporting will instead be spent on analysis, decision-making, business strategy, sustainability and how to produce things better, cheaper and faster.

Bob Norton, chief income tax officer,
Vertex Inc., FEI member,
Financial Executive Editorial Advisory Board

When FEI was founded, the CFO of the day was the quintessential historian of the corporation, keeping detailed accounts on past activities, establishing solid personal relationships with the town's bankers, and providing essential insight to management on investment decisions . . . revered, trusted, competent, conservative and under-appreciated. He found comfort and benefit in conversing with other FEI chapter members and attending FEI programs. In those 80 years, nothing has changed except what used to take weeks to complete now must be finished in minutes. Mistakes lead to subpoenas, regulatory requirements are ever-changing and irrational, advice is judged with the benefit of hindsight and the rewards of an FEI membership are more important than ever.

William U. Parfet, chairman & CEO, MPI Research,
FEI member, former FEI chairman

There are three conflicting pressures bearing on the profession, which are more likely to intensify than abate over the medium term: first is the desire for the financial function, and the CFO specifically, to provide strategic support to the business, the CEO and the board. This need has been growing for at least the last 20 or 30 years, and is often the first qualification mentioned by a CEO when looking to fill a CFO slot.

Second is the increasing complexity of financial statements and financial reporting. The "rule book" is growing at an alarming pace, despite the occasional initiatives at streamlining (none of which has made any material progress in lessening complexity). FASB is working hard to promulgate more and more direction in response to accounting issues that have arisen and that will arise. At the same time, they are coping with the desire to conform U.S. GAAP to IFRS, while the political and regulatory will to do that is questionable at best, but the inevitable outcome of these efforts is additional complexity.

The third pressure is the need for increasing efficiency. With technology enabling real-time communication around the world and transaction processing speeds that are advancing at impressive rates, all competitors need to find the lowest possible cost of doing business, because others are. This means being open to novel ways of fulfilling the financial role, and ultimately may mean outsourcing large chunks of it to the lowest-cost labor markets, and surrounding the work with enormously more effective and complex control structures. Cutting

the finance budget isn't the answer to all business needs, but finance can and must play its part.

David B. Rickard, former executive vice president, CFO
and chief administrative officer, CVS Caremark Corp.,
FEI 2011 Hall of Fame inductee

My fervent hope is that in the next 80 years we will undo the damage being done by ever more suffocating government regulation. Every mistake or crime has been followed by a colossal new regulation, which punishes everyone and decreases the competitiveness of U.S. companies.

Bryan Roub, retired CFO of Harris Corp.,
FEI member, former FEI chairman

CFOs need to fully understand the business and be able to communicate financial results with others (within and outside the organization) in an honest and unbiased manner. Understanding the balance between managing risks and going too far needs to be clearly stated to those in management. The best CFOs would be the moral force on decision-making. They also need to understand the global marketplace and how it applies to their organization and participate in the major decision-making to be considered successful.

The next 80 years will be challenging and competitive forces will make change a byword of daily demands. Those who can adapt to changes in the marketplace while keeping their moral compass in the right direction will succeed.

Jack Ruffle, former vice chairman and director,
J.P. Morgan & Co. Inc.,
FEI member, FEI 2008 Hall of Fame inductee

I have often wondered what the role of the regulators will be in our future as financial executives. The SEC has seen some significant changes since its inception and the role that it plays in our daily lives as public company financial executives.

I believe that the information demand will exceed the capabilities of the regulatory agencies to provide the potential "real-time" performance visibility of public companies. In the age of social media and the immediate information sharing as we move forward into the future, will the demands for real-time visibility to a company's performance be in the best interest of the company, regulators and investors?

It took the SEC what seemed like years to develop electronic filings and to accelerate deadlines for reporting in the last decade of changes. I can't imagine the burden that it will feel when the demands of more frequent (more than quarterly and annual reporting) financial performance reporting in our "instant information age" are placed on the public companies by their investors.

Katherine L. Scherping, CPA,
FEI member, Financial Executive Editorial Advisory Board

I see a revolutionary change of the role of finance and the role of the finance executive in organizations. The functions that the traditional finance organization handles today—treasury, accounting, AP and AR, statutory compliance, internal audit—will be completely automated as companies adopt systems with artificial intelligence that are self-learning and can organically adapt to the unique characteristics of a particular business. The traditional static between systems that require human intervention will be replaced by a umbilical integration of applications—such as HR, CRM, ERP, BI platforms that will seamlessly exchange data and reduce the coding, mapping, formatting and reporting that now take up an inordinate amount of time.

The finance executive of the future will be a strategic partner—playing a critical role in the development and the maintenance of revenue generation opportunities, understanding customer profitability metrics and drive conversation around future positioning of the industry in general and their organizations in particular. The distinction between accounting, strategic planning and financial analysis will blur and merge into a single role. The finance executive will also be a communicator—interpreting data for the benefit of his/her peers internally and for lenders, investors and the regulatory community externally.

Technology will evolve to being a utility and will eliminate any first-mover advantages. All applications will be cloud-based and can be bolted onto any current system. The emergence of utility computing will purge all legacy systems and will drive technology adoption across all kinds of businesses globally. Information will be a commodity and the management of information will become a key competitive attribute for the finance function. Technology will be the tool, but knowledge will reign supreme.

Mahesh Shetty, COO and CFO, Encore Enterprises Inc., FEI member, member of FEI's Committee on Finance and Technology

The next 80 years will be a logical extension of the past 80 years. Financial executives will be expected to do more with less. Technology will provide the ways and means to do so.

William M. Sinnett, senior director, Research, Financial Executives Research Foundation (FERF)

The last 80 years have seen great changes within the financial community and within the profession. I believe we should expect no less in the coming 80 years. There are several trends and factors that will have long-term implications and effects: The changing/shifting demographics are transforming the global workforce. The big demographic shifts are the ones around gender, ethnicity, religion, sexual orientation and age. To navigate these, we will need to make sure that we help teams maximize the incredible diversity of perspectives that will be brought to bear in innovating and in navigating challenges. Diverse teams are rarely mediocre. They are either really good or really bad. And we need them to be really good.

There are also some unknowns—for instance, while we continue a trend toward globalization where people, business and capital move almost seamlessly across borders, regulation and laws are still national and can create uneven and inconsistent oversight across global markets.

Right now the goal of global regulatory harmonization seems illusive, but information is free-flowing across markets and that information is critical to well-functioning capital markets. If investors and other capital market participants are better equipped to find out about national differences that should cause them to interpret the information differently and incorporate those differences into their investment decisions, it could make for a more dynamic and high-performing global capital market.

James S. Turley, chairman and chief executive officer, Ernst & Young

Financial specialists have been around for at least 600 years—since the heyday of Venice trading in the 15th Century. Nevertheless, looking presciently into the future for another 80 years is beyond our grasp. It is possible, however, to emphasize those traits that have made Finance valuable over the centuries and predict that they will also be needed in the future.

First, they are objectivity and integrity. Finance executives deal with numbers, and numbers don't lie, or shouldn't lie. Tell it like it is, good or bad. Second, there is the need to understand the business. Numbers only make sense if they are correctly used in interpreting, measuring and valuing the business and its successes and failures.

Third, if computer and mathematical models produce numbers too complex to fully understand, there is probably something wrong with them. Business doesn't need to be that complicated. I would be surprised if these basic tenets were not to stand the test of time.

Karl M. von der Heyden, former vice chairman and CFO, PepsiCo Inc., FEI 2010 Hall of Fame inductee

Critical Thinking

1. How has the role of the Chief Financial Officer (CFO) changed?
2. How is that role likely to change in the future?
3. Why is evolving of the role of the CFO important?

Internationalizing Business

Marydee Ojala

Globalization isn't merely an abstract concept in today's business environment. It's a deeply embedded way of life. Products made in one country are sold in many others. Components of products are sourced from a variety of countries and suppliers are frequently not located in the same country as the manufacturer. I'm fascinated, when I look at clothing labels, to see the variety of countries represented. Mergers and acquisitions routinely cross national borders. Particularly for larger companies, multinational is assumed to be the case. Even smaller companies, however, are increasingly participating in a globalized economy.

When smaller companies are looking for companies with which to partner—as a supplier or co-marketer—it helps to know the financial status and stability of the company. One source for public, listed companies, is local stock exchanges. These bourses can also provide valuable information on the economic and business climate of the country in which they are located.

> **These bourses can also provide valuable information on the economic and business climate of the country in which they are located.**

Companies can list on multiple stock exchanges. In fact, they may list on a stock exchange different from the nation in which they have their headquarters. Take Yandex (www.yandex.com), for example. It's a Russian search engine company that first incorporated in The Netherlands, and then went for an IPO in the U.S. It's now listed on the NASDAQ (www.nasdaq.com). Companies can also list on multiple stock exchanges. News Corporation (www.newscorp.com) lists on the NASDAQ, the Australian Stock Exchange (www.asx.com.au), and the London Stock Exchange (www.londonstockexchange.co.uk).

Worldwide Stock Exchanges

There are a number of different sources to guide you to websites of stock exchanges worldwide. The World Stock Exchanges (www.world-stock-exchanges.net) provides a list of world stock exchanges, securities commissions, and other regulatory agencies, along with stock market resources. The list includes links to stock and commodity exchanges worldwide, including those dealing in futures, options, and derivatives. It identifies the top three as the New York (www.nyse.com), Tokyo (www.tfx.co.jp), and London stock exchanges.

World Stock Exchanges has a very comprehensive list of exchanges, sometimes representing countries so small you're surprised they can support a stock exchange. The site not only lists stock exchanges but also commodity exchanges, such as the European Energy Exchange (www.eex.com), the Buenos Aires Grain Exchange (www.bolcereales.com.ar), and the Chinese Gold & Silver Exchange Society (www.cgse.com.hk/en).

The wiki for investors, WikInvest, also has a list of global stock exchanges (www.wikinvest.com/wiki/List_of_Stock_Exchanges). This wiki exists as a grassroots project, with the typical open wiki philosophy that individuals can add information. In the case of this wiki, it is individual investors who contribute. The site has ads to keep it "free and independent." It also says it licenses data to other companies, such as Forbes.com, NPR.org, USAToday.com, and some brokerage companies.

Not to be outdone, and possibly in its attempt to remain a player in the web search engine arena, Yahoo! Finance has its own list of stock exchanges (http://finance.yahoo.com/exchanges). Keep in mind that, although Bing now powers the main Yahoo! search, the finance portal remains separate. Yahoo! Finance does not list as many exchanges as World Stock Exchange, but does reveal the delay time for reporting data and the name of the data provider. For the latter, the options are Interactive Data Real-Time Services, Telekurs, or Direct from Exchange.

Noted British internet researcher and trainer, Karen Blakeman, also keeps a list of stock exchanges at the website for her company, RBA Information Services, but it hasn't been updated in about a year (www.rba.co.uk/sources/stocks.htm).

Although business customs and legal situations vary depending on where in the world you are, one thing remains constant: It's easier to find companies that list on exchanges than it is to find those that are privately held.

Stock Exchange History

As I was thinking about international business, an article in the KLM in-flight magazine, *Holland Herald,* October 2011 ("Big Ideas from a Small Country," by Jane Szita; http://holland-herald

.com/2011/10/big-ideas-from-a-small-country), reminded me that some aspects of internalization aren't as new as we like to think. She notes that the Dutch East India Company, founded in 1602, was the world's first multinational. It not only did business globally, but also issued shares, which started the idea of stock markets and share trading.

It took another 190 years for the New York Stock Exchange to emerge. On May 17, 1792, stockbrokers who had been trading shares under a buttonwood tree on Wall Street, created the Buttonwood Agreement, which established the New York Stock & Exchange Board. The Exchange gained a constitution in 1817 and changed its name to simply New York Stock Exchange in 1863.

Internationalizing Stock Exchanges

When most people think about stock exchanges, they assume that they have a national orientation. The lists mentioned above are generally arranged by country. However, stock exchanges have become just as susceptible to global mergers and acquisitions forays as other industries and companies. They even indulge in hostile takeovers. The New York Stock Exchange (www.nyse.com) bought the French exchange Euronext, itself the result of a merger of stock exchanges in Amsterdam, Brussels, and Paris, and is now NYSE Euronext. The market activity data on its website is supplied by NYSE Euronext Data.

Stock exchanges have become just as susceptible to global mergers and acquisitions forays as other industries and companies.

The U.S.-based NASDAQ (www.nasdaqomx.com) bought OMX in 2007. OMX originated in Sweden but quickly acquired stock exchanges in Finland, Estonia, Latvia, Lithuania, Denmark, Iceland, and Armenia before being acquired by NASDAQ. The London Stock Exchange (LSE) acquired Borsa Italiana the same year, 2007. An attempt by LSE to take over the Toronto Stock Exchange (www.tmx.com) was thwarted in June 2011.

On the Singapore Stock Exchange (www.sgx.com), 40% of the listed companies are headquartered outside of Singapore, mainly in China, Japan, and India. It also announced its intent to acquire the Australian Securities Exchange (www.asx.com.au). This deal fell apart earlier this year.

As I write this column, in October 2011, the EU is holding hearings concerning the proposed acquisition of NYSE Euronext by Deutsche Börse (http://deutsche-boerse.com/dbag/dispatch/en/kir/gdb_navigation/home). On its website, Deutsche Börse prominently features some of its nonfinancial, non-regulatory activities, particularly its art collection. The photographic collection comprises over 800 photographs taken by some 80 international artists and is on display in Eschborn, near Frankfurt and Luxembourg.

Changes in Exchanges

International consolidation of stock exchanges can be seen as reflecting the increasing globalization of business in general. It can also be interpreted as a natural response to stock exchanges morphing into for-profit, public traded, listed companies. Whether the future holds a truly global capital market or whether nationalism will triumph is an open question. Searching the economic, business, financial, and political literature reveals no consensus of opinion—not concerning what will happen nor what the overall effect would be. What is acknowledged is the increasing trend away from locking away financial activity in national silos. The regulatory, legal, and behavioral boundaries that separated global stock exchanges are dissolving. At the same time, however, nationalism lingers as a strong counter-balance.

Despite the recent stock exchange M&A activity, countries like the notion of having their own exchanges. Therefore, although many of the Nordic and Baltic country exchanges are part of NASDAQ OMX, they retain the names of the original cities of origin (Copenhagen Stock Exchange, Stockholm Stock Exchange, Riga Stock Exchange, etc.). Typically, the older URL will redirect to NASDAQ OMX NORDIC. For Copenhagen, www.cse.dk redirects to www.nasdaqomxnordic.com/nordic/Nordic.aspx.

On the NASDAQ OMX NORDIC website, you will see a running ticker at the top, below which are lists of the most active stocks and market indexes. Also near the top are tabs for shares, indexes, bonds, options and futures, exchange traded funds, funds, and news. Lists of advancers, decliners, and new listings appear on the main page. A "thermometer" shows at a glance how the markets are doing—rising share prices show in green, neutral in blue, and falling prices in red.

Information at Exchange Websites

Independent stock exchanges have different website designs but all display similar information. You will generally see charts and graphs depicting market activity for the day. Lists of companies appear, categorized in ways that make sense to investors and for which the exchange has data. These reflect performance, for the most part. Some exchanges also include news about listed companies and news about the economy, business climate, and political events that could affect the markets.

Some exchange websites provide data not only on their equities markets but also for commodities. This depends upon whether the exchange trades commodities, which is more common in smaller countries that can't support a separate exchange for commodities. Another option is to show currency exchange rates.

The Irish Stock Exchange (www.ise.ie) is typical with its list of most traded companies, a daily chart of the market, and latest announcements from listed companies. It also shows equity index series, bond index series, and ISEQ exchange traded funds. Tabs at the top of the page lead you to prices, indices, and statistics.

South Korea's KRX (http://eng.krx.co.kr), which says on its website, in both Korean and English, that it wants to be a world-class premium exchange, has tabs to take you to information about stocks, derivatives, equity products, and bonds. It presents data on its main page for both most active trading in terms of volume and of price changes for individual company shares, along with several KRX indices and a market schedule for upcoming investing events. It also provides a chart of stock trading by institutions, foreigners, and individuals. Foreigners, obviously, are those who aren't South Korean.

Although the stock exchange in Cairo was closed for two months during the Egyptian revolution that began January 25, 2011, the site for the Egyptian Stock Exchange (www.egyptse.com) is now very robust. You can view it in either Arabic or English. It has a running ticker at the top, and tabs for members, listing, products and services, trading, market activity, international relations, and investor education. On its main page are displays for market summary, various indices, traded stocks statistics, and the latest news of interest to investors.

It may surprise you to realize that even small countries have stock exchanges. They may have few companies listing on them, restricted hours for trading, and a low volume of trading, but it's a point of pride for some to participate in global capital markets. Still, the ability to maintain a stable market may be beyond the reach of these countries. Sudan, for example, has a website for its Khartoum Stock Exchange (www.kse.com.sd) but it's updated infrequently. Trading hours are only 1 hour per day, Sunday through Thursday.

Slightly over 300 companies list on the Nepal Stock Exchange (www.nepalstock.com/listedcompany.php), many of them commercial and development banks. The website provides a wide range of data on the companies listed in Nepal and on the NEPSE Index. The primary language of the website is English, although the occasional Hindi press release shows up.

News on the Markets

Stock exchanges, in addition to facilitating the buying and selling of financial instruments and regulating markets, publish an astonishing amount of data. Unless there is a specific market, country, or company that interests you, the better bet could be the business press.

The Wall Street Journal Online (http://online.wsj.com) collects much of the data gathered by the exchanges and reprints this. At one time, the data was published in the printed version of *The Wall Street Journal*, but this migrated to the electronic version years ago. This makes sense, as it is much more current online than it would ever be in print. The Financial Times also publishes extensive international business and company data at its website (www.ft.com/intl/markets).

There are, of course, the other usual suspects—the finance portals of Yahoo!, Google, and Bing and sites that exist to stimulate the quantitative minds of the investing public. I'm thinking CNNMoney (http://money.cnn.com), which isn't always as global as I'd like, and other sites such as Trader Planet (www.traderplanet.com) and iStock Analyst (www.istockanalyst.com).

Knowing the ins and outs of international markets becomes increasingly important as businesses venture out into the global market and physical distances cease to be barriers.

Critical Thinking

1. Why do people the world over insist on investing?
2. Where are the largest stock exchanges?
3. Are there some stock exchanges in remote areas?

MARYDEE OJALA (marydee@xmission.com) edits *ONLINE: Exploring Technology & Resources for Information Professionals.*

Engaging China: Strategies for the Small Internationalizing Firm

Rolf D. Cremer and Bala Ramasamy

Foreign Investments in China: Large or Small?

Despite concerns of an over-heating economy, increasing operational costs, dominance in important world markets, and widening income gaps within China, the Chinese economy continues to grow relentlessly. In 2007, China's real gross domestic product (GDP) grew by more than 10 percent—again. The continuing expansion is due in large part also to its international economic relations. China's foreign trade volume surpassed US$1.1 trillion in 2004, replacing Japan as the third largest trading nation after the USA and Germany. In 2003, China overtook the USA as the most popular destination for foreign direct investment (FDI), with inflows of $53 billion. In 2006, FDI inflow increased further to US$70 billion. There are more than half a million foreign enterprises active in China. The US-China Business Council (n.d.) reports indicate that since 1990 foreign multinationals like P&G, YUM!, AIG, Alcatel, Carrefour, Motorola, Nestle, Siemens, and Volkswagen are generating higher profits from their China ventures.

It is not surprising then that companies from around the globe—big and small—are considering China ventures seriously. However, the chances of making mistakes and failing in China are daunting. Cases of messy joint ventures, negotiations that have gone bad, fierce price competition, intellectual property rights (IPR) problems and betrayals, or market promises that never existed are also part of the business reality in China.

Nevertheless, after 30 years of reforms, the Chinese economy is fast approaching normalcy. Membership in the WTO, the presence and influence of many multinationals, as well as many important reforms and adjustments in the legal system, have made China much more predictable today than in the past. Mechem in 2004 claimed that predictability, more than anything else, has made it possible for even smaller firms to consider their China dream (Mechem, 2004).

While literature on the internationalization of small firms has proliferated, most research on how to do business in China tends to be biased towards larger multinationals. This is perhaps due to the attention that these multinationals receive in the media or simply because 400 of the *Fortune* 500 companies are already in China. The result of this is a lack of attention in the literature regarding the specific situation of smaller firms. Consider the data in Table I. The average value of projects contracted in 2003 is a mere US$1.3 million. The average size of investment is not much different between a joint venture and a wholly owned enterprise. With more than 40,000 relatively small projects, one could imagine that most projects involve relatively small firms.

This suggests that there is a problem: Most of the firms and/or investments entering the Chinese market are, in fact, small. On the other hand, many proposed strategies for doing business in China are derived from studying multinationals. For instance, Wong and Maher's (1997) study that appeared in the *Business Horizons* in 1997 was based on two major US multinationals. Reports on doing business in China by consultancy firms like McKinsey (see for example, Woetzel (2004) and Chen and Penhirin (2004)) are based on fast-moving consumer goods giants like Procter and Gamble. Although many of these strategies may be workable for companies whatever their size, smaller firms are different in terms of availability of resources, capabilities and core competencies, as well as how they are perceived by the Chinese market and authorities.

In this paper, we focus on those smaller firms planning to expand their operations to China, either for trade or for investment purposes. The definition of small and medium-sized companies (SMEs) varies across countries. In the European Union (EU), SMEs are those firms with fewer than 250 employees, but in the USA these include firms with fewer than 500 employees. On the other hand, Waste Management New Zealand—a company listed among the top 200 New Zealand firms—employs only

Table I FDI in China, By Type, 2003

	No. of projects	Contracted value (billion US$)	Used value (billion US$)	Average contracted value (million US$)	Average used value (million US$)
Total FDI	41,081	115.1	53.5	2.8	1.3
Joint ventures	12,521	25.5	15.4	2.0	1.2
Wholly owned	26,943	81.6	33.4	3.0	1.2

Source: National Bureau of Statistics of China (2004)

870 employees and contractors. Given these variations, for the current study, we define small firms as those that do not have strong core competencies embedded in technology, marketing networks or brand names; and those firms that have limited accessibility to resources, be they financial or managerial. In this study, we identify some core strategies and mindsets that are required by such firms for successful engagements in China.

The Study
The Small Internationalizing Firm

Figure 1 provides a visual of our research focus and its ensuing strategies. The size-time matrix distinguishes four main fields. The two fields on the left refer to firms that entered China in the early stages of the reform era. They comprise large multinationals like Volkswagen and Philips, who obtained early mover advantages in the 1980s and 1990s.

There were also smaller enterprises that entered the Chinese market when it opened up to the outside world. We call these firms explorers. A large number of companies from greater China (particularly Hong Kong and Macau) belong in this bottom left field.

After 15 to 20 years of reform, however, China, and especially the coastal regions, no longer offer any early mover advantages. Firms that have ventured into China more recently fall in the fields on the right of Figure 1.

Large multinationals are still making their moves into China. For instance, Ford and several Japanese and Korean multinationals could fall into this category. But they are latecomers. This does not necessarily imply an earlier mistake, as the example of Daimler-Chrysler shows a long tradition of targeting maturing markets for their luxury brand. Our research, however, focuses on the firms in the bottom right field, representing small and medium-sized late movers. This field comprises three types of players that we group together and call small internationalizing firms (SIFs).

1. The first category of SIFs comprises small multinationals. While these are multinationals in that they operate in more than one country, they typically do not possess the kind of resources or intangible assets (e.g., brand names) of their larger counterparts. These firms exist everywhere, obviously, but in some countries like New Zealand, Australia, Canada, and for newly industrializing economies like Korea and Singapore, they are the dominant class of internationalizing firms.

2. The second category of SIFs comprises professional service providers and includes, for example, legal, advertising, public relations, design, accounting and consultancy firms. As with other internationalizing service firms (Li and Guisinger, 1992), their primary reason for setting up operations in China is usually to extend support services to their clients who have moved to China, and only secondly to expand their market to other foreign subsidiaries as well as to domestic enterprises.

3. The final category of SIFs comprises single entrepreneurs. They are no different from the explorers in the early stage of China's reform era. One could argue that they are not really international firms, but rather a form of business migrant venturing into China with an idea and a great deal of confidence that they will be able to carve out a small piece of the action.

For the purpose of this research, we have chosen New Zealand companies as our population. New Zealand was the first nation to reach an agreement on China's accession to the WTO as well as the first developed country to start negotiations for a free trade agreement (FTA) with China. In 2003, China became New Zealand's fourth largest trading partner, overtaking the UK, historically the most important trading partner. Between 1990 and 2006, bilateral trade between the two countries grew at an average annual rate of 98.5 percent, compared to 9.1 and 5.1 percent for Australia and the USA respectively.

By global standards, New Zealand's foreign direct investment into China is small. Up to the end of December 2003, the stock of New Zealand's contractual investment in China amounted to US$812 million in 819 projects,

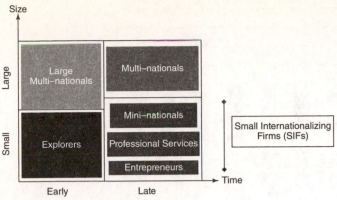

Figure 1 The size-time matrix.

with actual investment of US$405 million. One of New Zealand's largest investments in China was Lion Nathan's US$280 million investment in a brewery in Suzhou and a purchase of another brewery in Wuxi. Apart from the Lion Nathan investment, the size of investment projects is typically small, in terms of visibility, relative size and extent of resource commitment to the China business. Hence, New Zealand's firms are suitable for the purposes of this study.

Research Methods: Questionnaire and Focus Group Discussion

We followed a two-pronged methodology. The first stage involved mailing a questionnaire to the 200 largest companies in New Zealand as listed in the *New Zealand Management* magazine. Comprising 29 questions in five sections, the questionnaire solicited information on the current state of business activities in China, the strategies employed, obstacles faced in China and expected assistance from the authorities. The purpose of the questionnaire was to gauge the views regarding the China engagement from an overseas located headquarter perspective. Questionnaires were sent out to 191 of the 200 companies. In nine cases, the postal and email addresses were incorrect or unavailable. A total of 50 companies responded (26 percent); 40 of the returned questionnaires were relevant. Responses from ten companies were excluded as they had no past, present or planned engagement with China. The responses of the survey participants were analyzed and relevant issues were drawn out for the second stage of the research process.

The second part of the study was designed to seek in-depth views of the opportunities and challenges faced by New Zealand businesses at "ground zero." The primary purpose of this part was to identify experience-based key success factors for SIFs, proven in the day-to-day struggle for survival and success. A secondary purpose was to draw out a comparison on China, on the Chinese and on doing business in China between decision makers based at overseas headquarters and managers actually based in China. A questionnaire-based study among New Zealand businesses in China was not statistically feasible as the number of known companies was too small to produce meaningful quantitative results. As an alternative, a focus group approach was used. The advantage of a focus group discussion is that it can capture perceptions on a specific area of interest in a permissive, non-threatening environment.

Four focus group discussions were organized—two each in Beijing and Shanghai. The members were drawn from an incomplete list of NZ companies complied by NZ Consulates General in China. The discussions involved 14 companies in total, with representatives from all three categories of SIFs explained above—small multinationals, professional services providers and single entrepreneurs. They also represented various industries including agriculture (forestry), manufacturing and services. There was an average of six participants per discussion, allowing for in-depth discussion. The discussions revolved around five issues: core competencies of New Zealand businesses in China, mode of entry, challenges faced by New Zealand firms in China, the Chinese consumer market and role of government assistance.

Strategies for Success in China
Manager Characteristics and Vision

In a 1990 seminal article in the *Harvard Business Review,* Prahalad and Hamel (1990) wrote that "only if the company is conceived of as a hierarchy of core competencies, core products, and market-focused business units will it be fit to fight." For many large multinationals, the core competency might lie in their technology know-how and IPR, in the range of their distribution networks, or in their brand names. Still, even multinationals state time and again that their key concern in China, with its dominance of relationship-based business practices as opposed to the transaction-based business practices of the West, is talent management, i.e. the recruitment, development and retention of key personnel.

Our findings suggest that SIFs do not normally possess the advantages typical of multinationals. This in turn means that the remaining factor—the skills of their leading people—becomes even more critical; in particular, the individual traits of the manager and the personal relationships they have with business people in China. When asked what core competencies New Zealand firms have in China, our respondents in both Shanghai and Beijing were unanimous and had this to say:

> New Zealand people are quite a likeable people and the Chinese tend to respond to the New Zealanders' personality a little better than to an American or European.

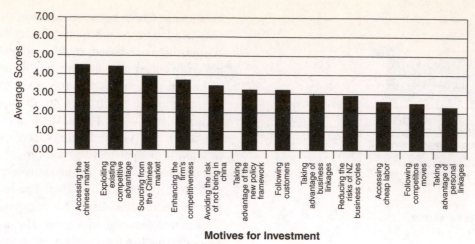

Figure 2   Investment motives in China.

We're not so steeped into tradition and formal ways [. . .] we are willing to give anything a try, we can be innovative. We're often very adaptable, we just get on and get the job done. Others may be more inhibitive.

When you say you're a New Zealander [. . .] the reaction is very visual, very noticeable.

It is important to note that these interpersonal relational skills are of little impact, unless they are brought actively into play. The selection of the right people to open markets in China thus is critical for small multinationals. Virtues like sincerity, caring, open-mindedness and adaptability may be more forthcoming among executives who come from smaller and lesser-known countries like New Zealand. Further, the perception that the Chinese have of such countries is a bonus. For instance, the perception that New Zealand is clean, agriculture-based and neutral in its international relations helps build initial relationships with the Chinese.

It must be emphasized that inter-personal relational skills are necessary, but not a sufficient condition for success in China. Indeed, a core competency based on individual traits alone has limitations if not combined with a visionary mindset. Relying on a pool of likeable but small-minded people might not take a company far in China. Consider, for instance, the following comment from a discussant from Beijing:

> [In my Timaru coffee shop] I had ten people there, or three, or sometimes 20. In Zhenjiang, I have 3,500 customers every lunch.

Kedia and Mukherji (1999), in the *Journal of World Business,* state that managers need to have a growth mindset from the outset, even before leaving their local shores. This global mindset is aptly described by Rhinesmith (1993) as "a way of being rather than a set of skills. It is

an orientation of the world that allows one to see certain things that others do not." SIFs that originate from market bases that are small, like New Zealand or Singapore, need to visualize the enormous magnitude of the China market and have the confidence that this is within their capabilities, although the size of their operation may be several times the size they are used to at home.

Business Focus

At an estimated 0.87 percent growth annually, China's population grows by about 11.2 million people a year. It is not surprising that rapid economic growth and penetration into the China market have been listed as important motivations for investing in China by surveys done by consulting firms like PriceWaterhouseCoopers (2004). Market-related factors are also seen to be the more important reasons in our survey of New Zealand businesses (see Figure 2). However, the size of the market may prove to be elusive for small multinationals. Studwell (2003), in *The China Dream,* for instance, describes the limited success experienced by firms attracted to China's billion customers. Zeng and Williamson (2003) explain that the number of local enterprises competing in markets ranging from beer to computers has increased competition to unprofitable levels. Still, China has in recent years become the hotbed for fast-moving consumer goods companies, attracting world-renowned brand names.

[. . .] the number of local enterprises competing in markets ranging from beer to computers has increased competition to unprofitable levels. Still, China has in recent years become the hotbed for fast-moving consumer goods companies, attracting world-renowned brand names.

How then does an SIF avoid the cutthroat competition of the mass-product markets yet still take advantage of the size of China? Our findings suggest that to survive and profit in China, small multinationals must steer clear from large mass markets and focus on small niche markets.

Sheth and Sisodia (2002) discovered that in mature markets, three big companies dominate, with the remaining players concentrated in niche markets. Niche markets may be small but the scope of being small in China is obviously relative. One focus group discussant in the carpet industry stated:

[. . .] in New Zealand, 1000 square meters is a big order, but in China this might involve 2 million square meters per order for a new hotel [. . .] In 2002, we sold nearly 700,000 square meters.

Targeting niche markets has been recommended when markets are globalized or when competition becomes excessive. In a Business Sector Round Table discussion organized by the International Trade Council in Brussels in May 2001, successful exporters from least-developed countries were those who were able to find:

[. . .] niche products for niche markets, moving up the value chain through processing and design, responding to the ever rising demand from consumers for higher quality standards; entering brand new markets like services' or shortening the distribution chain to capture a greater share of the value.

Dalgic and Leeuw (1994) characterize niche markets as those that have:

- sufficient size and are potentially profitable;
- no real competitors or have been overlooked by other players;
- growth potential;
- the necessary purchasing ability;
- a need for special treatment;
- customer goodwill; and
- opportunities for a company to exercise its superior competence.

Craig and Douglas (1997) advise smaller multinationals to identify niches that are not large enough to attract other Western firms or those which require customization of product or services. They highlight the ability of a firm to leverage its core competency within the niche market through a positive association with the country of origin. Our focus group discussants in the wool carpet and fitness industries confirm that niche markets can be secured using the country of origin as an advantage (in our case, New Zealand). Niche markets also exist in the manufacturing sector. A focus group discussant in Shanghai represented Scott Technology, a Dunedin-based firm that specializes

exclusively in the design and manufacture of large-scale automation systems for the major domestic appliance industries of the world. Scott Technologies is one of four firms producing such systems worldwide.

SIFs should therefore identify their specific position in the relevant emerging international, multi-firm supply chain and concentrate their resources in developing a niche for themselves in this position. A related question is, how does an SIF develop a niche in a consumer market which is overzealous on brand names and international recognition? The China market is a demanding one where brand names of international repute not only compete with their global competitors, but also with local brand names and counterfeiters. Our findings on the niche market strategy suggest focusing on the industrial/commercial buyer who may provide small multinationals with the answer to the question posed above. A business to business (B2B) focus also provides the following advantages:

- A smaller number of potential buyers who buy in bulk. This could reduce the amount of resources required for marketing purposes, such as advertising.
- Less price competition as industrial buyers may be willing to pay for quality. Industrial buyers are professionals who are paid to make the right buying decision. Hence, quality and after-sales service would be considered more seriously than the impulse buying behavior of consumers.
- Smaller quantity purchase, but an emphasis on custom-made product/service. Note, however, that small is relative, but could be within the capabilities of smaller multinationals.
- Personal relationship is critical and small multinationals may excel in their relationship compared to their larger counterparts.

The fourth advantage listed above requires further elaboration as it relates to other dimensions described in this study. Bell and Zacharilla (2003) state that B2B buying decisions are influenced by three factors: reputation, referrals and references. Faced with scarce resources allocated by the head office, small multinationals need to work on their relationships with Chinese businesses and through them acquire greater contacts, i.e. develop *guanxi* with a few businesses and expand the network base over time.

A discussant in the Beijing focus group explained how B2B relationships work for the SIF:

[. . .] There are two ways of doing business in China. First, if you are selling goods like toothpaste or toothbrushes or products that everyone uses—especially if you are one of those large American

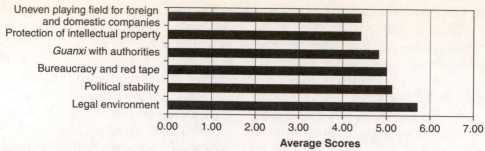

Figure 3 Legal and political challenges in China.

companies—you give it free for about two years and then you use large billboards and spend a lot on advertisements. This is the American way, the big guys in the business can do this. But for small companies, the best way is to join the relevant associations. For example, we are a member of the tourism and hotels association, the American Chamber of Commerce in China, the Australian Chamber of Commerce (but they were too small) and you know people and they know the product that you deal with [. . .] and they will contact you if they need anything. I have had business with seven embassies in Beijing.

Developing Guanxi (Networks)

An important factor that contributes to the success of business in China is *guanxi* or connections. Fan (2002) describes *guanxi* as a potential solution to the obstacles faced when entering and operating in China, where individuals can be more powerful than the legal system. It is considered the lifeblood of the Chinese community, without which nothing gets done. In a survey carried out by PriceWaterhouseCoopers, building *guanxi* with local and provincial governments was ranked as the second greatest legal challenge faced by multinationals operating in China. Similarly, in our survey of New Zealand businesses, *guanxi* also appeared to be an important challenge (see Figure 3).

"[. . .] building *guanxi* with local and provincial governments was ranked as the second greatest legal challenge faced by multinationals operating in China."

Even after a quarter century of reforms, the role, authority and influence of government and government officials continue to play an important role in China. Gordon and Li (1991) state that as a result of economic reforms, the decentralization of decision-making has moved to the level of the local or provincial government. Their role is not expected to diminish either as most developing countries that have long adhered to market economy principles continue to place senior government officials on a pedestal. Media reports of ministers and mayors opening business premises, cutting ribbons, digging the first dirt and other photo opportunities are common in many developing Asian economies. In a study on Singaporean investments in China, Yeung (2000) states that it is imperative for foreign firms to collaborate with local officials and party cadres to facilitate business operations.

Thus, SIFs in China, in particular, need to take heed of the governmental relationships in business. A company like GM or Toyota might have a direct route into the mayor's office of a Chinese city, but this may not be the case for small multinationals. *Guanxi* is helpful, but for new multinationals the right *guanxi* may not be forthcoming. It is in this context that the assistance of home governments is useful.

What type of assistance are New Zealand businesses expecting from their home government? Our headquarters survey reveals that respondents are primarily looking for information assistance regarding the workings of business in China. Among the list of options provided, they ranked advice on legal matters and information on local business partners at the top of their priority list. Within the context of our study, the role of the New Zealand government in providing such information becomes imperative if it seeks to strengthen the economic relationship with China. Similarly, informal discussion with experienced people in China-related affairs is also considered important. The list of assistance, as shown in Figure 4, clearly shows the need for general information. More specific information like accounting and M&A advice seems less important.

Discussants in our focus groups were more pragmatic. They wanted physical government presence in China. For example, a discussant in Shanghai explained:

[. . .] for small businesses in China, if the government officials could assist you to meet the Vice Mayor or other officials, it helps. In my case, our

Figure 4   Assistance sought by New Zealand businesses.

single biggest problem is getting natural gas connected to the houses we're building. I really need to get this done [. . .] If someone like the Trade Commissioner invites me for lunch and I get to sit next to the head of the Gas Bureau, well [. . .]

In home countries, access to senior government officials like ministers, ambassadors or trade officials can be easier in smaller countries like New Zealand. In China, the level of protocol and bureaucracy may hinder the contact between the SIF and government officials. However, apart from size, the position of government officials of home countries is equivalent to those of the host country. For instance, the mayor of Ashburton (population: 15,800) might have a better chance of meeting the mayor of Xiamen (population: 1.24 million) than a senior executive based in China. Thus senior officials of embassies in Beijing, Shanghai and Guangzhou have a critical role to play as facilitators of business in China. It is well worth the investment for governments to allocate more resources to these embassies if they wish to see more businesses engaging China.

Inter-governmental *guanxi* is important, but relying on this alone may be unwise. SIFs need to build their own *guanxi* for sustainable success in China. These firms might have overlooked an important resource in their own home country to develop *guanxi*—the thousands of Chinese tourists and students who visit every year. As overseas education and travel is still a luxury good, those who can afford such travels are likely to be "someone" in China, or know someone in China's business or political hierarchy. In New Zealand, for example, 56.8 percent of foreign students for the academic year 2003/2004 were from China. There were also more than 84,000 tourists from China who visited New Zealand in the year ending March 2005.

Chinese students, in particular are excellent resources as they can help businesses by sharing the *guanxi* that

they and their family might have. Additionally, these foreign-trained students can also make up the managerial talent that China lacks.

As explained earlier, the image of the country serves as a comparative advantage for small multinationals and it is beneficial for policy makers to provide the right impression to Chinese tourists who visit. While the physical environment of New Zealand speaks for itself, the human touch exemplified through good manners, due diligence, patience and goodwill—virtues important in the Chinese culture—can be instrumental in building the foundations needed to support the complex web of relationships required to be successful in China.

SIFs from smaller economies can also enhance their political and economic clout by promoting relationships with selected cities in China. We find, for example, that "well-managed sister-city relationships can play an important role in international trade and investment, which in turn can provide the development of cultural and social ties with a lasting economically viable foundation."

Finally, another approach for developing *guanxi* is to promote what we refer to as the "reverse Colombo Plan." The well-known Colombo Plan was initiated by the developed countries of the British Commonwealth in 1950 with a view to highlight the needs and requirement of the poorer members of the organization. The primary purpose of the plan was to develop human resources in the region. The plan's most successful activity was the aid given to bright young scholars of developing countries to pursue their studies in institutions of higher learning in the more developed nations like the UK, Australia and New Zealand. The reverse Colombo Plan refers to the idea of sending open-minded young executives to China with the intention of studying in some of the good universities there. China boasts several universities with international reputations, including Beijing University and Fudan University. These universities have joint programs with top business schools from the USA and Europe. Living in China for a period of one-to-two years, learning in China with equally bright Chinese scholars, familiarizing themselves with the culture and language all contribute to both the understanding and appreciating the Chinese culture as well as developing *guanxi* among future business leaders of China. While this may be a long-term strategy, such is the nature of *guanxi* and the learning of culture. Given the opportunities in China, such long-term investments may provide the SIFs with the competitive edge to succeed in China.

Conclusion

China's economic growth continues to mesmerize international firms the world over. Unabated GDP growth has surpassed 9 percent for nine consecutive quarters since the end of 2003. In the first three quarters of 2005, exports grew 31.3 percent despite a revaluation of the *renminbi*. No doubt, an increasingly affluent market and a perceived abundance of natural and human resources continue to attract firms into China. Today, no firm can truly claim to be international if it does not have some form of Chinese connection. We do not aver that China is a bed of roses. Even after 27 years of economic reforms, a weak rule of law and corruption continue to be major issues, as attested by Ahlstrom *et al.* (2002). Perhaps it is due to, rather than despite of, poor governance in China that direct investment is more popular than other forms of investment, e.g. portfolio investment. Li in 2005, explained that direct engagement with China is necessary although it seems more "time consuming, complicated and illiquid, thus exposing investors to greater risks" (Li, 2005).

Unabated GDP growth has surpassed 9 percent for nine consecutive quarters since the end of 2003.

The purpose of this paper is to equip managers with several strategic mindsets that would strengthen their respective core competency. Our main focus is on SIFs, multinationals that are small by global standards with limited access to resources and core competencies, particularly those originating from small countries. We believe that these firms need to have strategies that may be different from their larger counterparts, due to their size, capabilities and core competencies.

Our findings, based on both the questionnaires and the focus group discussions, reveal three inter-related dimensions that characterize successful SIFs. These dimensions are visualized in Figure 5. At the heart of success—and

Figure 5   Key dimensions of success.

also of failure—of SIFs in China lies a human factor embedded in the respective business leader, regardless of whether this leader is on the ground in China or primarily located overseas. More specifically, the core competency of the management of an SIF lies with the interpersonal relational skills, the personality and the vision of the leader(s). The second dimension for success relates to the operational strategies of the business in terms of its market focus. Faced with such a large and complicated market, the chances of an SIF being engulfed by the market are high. This is particularly true if an SIF undertakes marketing strategies akin to those of larger multinationals. We find that focusing on niche markets through a B2B approach increases the rate of success. Finally, the third dimension refers to the environment in which the SIF, or for that matter all business in China, operates. Particularly for a small firm, the web of connections or *guanxi*, determines its survival in China. Our findings highlight two approaches towards building *guanxi*, namely by capitalizing on home government networks as well as through Chinese students studying abroad. The latter approach can be considered a specific factor that creates the equivalent of an overseas-Chinese network.

We find that focusing on niche markets through a B2B approach increases the rate of success.

China will continue to attract foreign firms both large and small and it is unlikely that the opening of markets will be scaled back. The mindsets and strategic moves proposed in our study are relevant for any company entering China. The point we wish to make is that these strategic mindsets are particularly crucial for SIFs as they can decrease the risks in the China engagement and increase success rates.

References

Ahlstrom, D., Young, M. N. and Nair, A. (2002), "Deceptive managerial practices in China: strategies for foreign firms", *Business Horizons*, November-December, pp. 49–59.

Bell, R. and Zacharilla, L. (2003), *B2B without the BS: The Business to Business Sales and Marketing Manual*, Alan Anthony, New York, NY.

Chen, Y. and Penhirin, J. (2004), "Marketing to China's consumers", *McKinsey Quarterly*, April 11, special issue.

Craig, C. S. and Douglas, C. P. (1997), "Managing the transnational value chain—strategies for firms from emerging markets", *Journal of International Marketing*, Vol. 5 No. 3, pp. 71–84.

Dalgic, T. and Leeuw, M. (1994), "Niche marketing revisited: concept, applications and some European cases", *European Journal of Marketing*, Vol. 28 No. 4, pp. 39–55.

Fan, Y. (2002), "Questioning *guanxi*: definition, classification and implications", *International Business Review*, Vol. 11 No. 5, pp. 543–61.

Gordon, R. H. and Li, W. (1991), "Chinese enterprise behavior under the reform", *American Economic Review*, Vol. 81 No. 2, pp. 202–6.

Kedia, B. L. and Mukherji, A. (1999), "Global managers: developing a mindset for global competitiveness", *Journal of World Business*, Vol. 34 No. 3, pp. 230–51.

Li, J. and Guisinger, S. (1992), "The globalisation of service multinationals in the triad regions: Japan, Western Europe, and North America", *Journal of International Business Studies*, Vol. 23 No. 4, pp. 675–96.

Li, S. (2005), "Why a poor governance environment does not deter foreign direct investment: the case of China and its implications for investment protection", *Business Horizons*, Vol. 48 No. 4, pp. 297–302.

Mechem, R. M. (2004), "Strategies for investing in China", *The China Business Review*, September-October.

National Bureau of Statistics of China (2004), *China Statistical Yearbook, 2004*, China Statistics Press, Beijing.

Prahalad, C. K. and Hamel, G. (1990), "The core competence of the corporation", *Harvard Business Review*, May-June, pp. 79–91.

PriceWaterhouseCoopers (2004), *Doing Business in China*, PriceWaterhouseCoopers, Hong Kong.

Rhinesmith, S. H. (1993), *A Manager's Guide to Globalization: Six Keys to Success in a Changing World*, Irwin, New York, NY.

Sheth, J. and Sisodia, R. (2002), *The Rule of Three: Surviving and Thriving in Competitive Markets*, Free Press, New York, NY.

Studwell, J. (2003), *The China Dream: The Quest for the Last Great Untapped Market on Earth*, Grove Press, New York, NY.

US-China Business Council (n.d.), "Foreign direct investment in China", available at: www.uschina.org/statistics/fdi_cumulative .html

Woetzel, J. R. (2004), "A guide to doing business in China", *McKinsey Quarterly*, April 11, special issue.

Wong, Y. Y. and Maher, T. E. (1997), "New key success factors for China's growing market", *Business Horizons*, Vol. 40 No. 3, pp. 43–52.

Yeung, H. W. (2000), "Local politics and foreign ventures in China's transitional economy: the political economy of Singaporean investment in China", *Political Geography*, Vol. 19, pp. 808–40.

Zeng, M. and Williamson, P. J. (2003), "The hidden dragons", *Harvard Business Review*, Vol. 81 No. 10, pp. 104–12.

Further Reading

International Trade Forum (2001), "A new generation of LDC exporters emerges", No. 1, Brussels.

Ramasamy, B. and Cremer, R. D. (1998), "Cities, commerce and culture: the economic role of international sister city relationships", *Journal of the Asia Pacific Economy*, Vol. 3 No. 3, pp. 446–61.

Rolf D. Cremer is Dean of the China Europe International Business School and Professor of Economics. He works and lives in China. His research focuses on foreign direct investment, international trade and international business strategies involving China.

Bala Ramasamy is Professor of Economics at the China Europe International Business School. His research focuses on foreign direct investment, international trade and international business strategies involving China. Bala Ramasamy is the corresponding author and can be contacted at: bramasamy@ceibs.edu

Critical Thinking

1. What are some strategies for entering the Chinese market?

2. Why is it more difficult for a small firm to enter the Chinese market than a large one?

3. How can a small firm learn from the larger firms in entering the Chinese market?

ROLF D. CREMER is Dean and Professor of Economics and **BALA RAMASAMY** is Professor of Economics, both at the China Europe International Business School, Shanghai, China.

Preparing for Significant, Multi-Year Changes

Sean Torr

International Financial Reporting Standards are currently permitted or required in approximately 120 nations and reporting jurisdictions across the globe, according to the American Institute of Certified Public Accountants IFRS Resources (as of September). As such, IFRS has become a common language of accounting in the international business community.

In February 2010, the U.S. Securities and Exchange Commission issued a statement expressing the SEC's "strong commitment to a single set of global standards" and "the recognition that IFRS is best-positioned to be able to serve the role as that set of standards for the U.S. market."

In May 2011, the SEC issued a staff paper that outlined a possible method of incorporating IFRS into the U.S. financial reporting system and requested comments on the proposed framework. The proposed framework combines elements of convergence and endorsement and was characterized by the SEC as a "phased transition" approach.

Proposed Framework, Comments and Considerations

Under this framework, the Financial Accounting Standards Board and the International Accounting Standards Board will continue their current agenda to converge U.S. generally accepted accounting principles and IFRS. Upon completion of the current convergence agenda, FASB would continue to be involved in the process for developing IFRS and would "incorporate newly issued or amended IFRS into U.S. GAAP pursuant to an established endorsement protocol." This "would be accomplished over a period of several (e.g., five to seven) years."

FASB would "retain the authority to modify or add to the requirements of the IFRS incorporated into U.S. GAAP" when in the public interest and necessary for protection of investors. It was also noted in the staff paper that modifications to IFRS during their incorporation process into U.S. GAAP should be "rare and avoidable," and that the issuance by FASB of requirements that conflict with IFRS should only occur "in unusual circumstances."

The goal of incorporating IFRS into the U.S. financial reporting system "would be full alignment of U.S. GAAP and IFRS."

The SEC is currently analyzing comment letters received in response to the proposed framework outlined in the staff paper. In a keynote speech in June for the Society of Corporate Secretaries and Governance Professionals 65th Annual Conference, former SEC Commissioner Kathleen L. Casey indicated that "The commission is slated to make a decision on these questions [i.e. whether, and how, to incorporate IFRS into the U.S. financial reporting system for U.S. issuers] this year, and we can no longer kick the can down the road. I believe the choice is clear—the commission must decide to incorporate IFRS for U.S. issuers.

"In addition to the benefits of IFRS that I have already mentioned, the risks of not moving forward with IFRS for U.S. issuers are simply too great." she said.

Irrespective of the SEC's decisions on the timing and method of incorporation of IFRS into the U.S. financial reporting system, FASB and IASB continue to make progress on the convergence of U.S. GAAP and IFRS in certain "high-priority" accounting areas such as revenue recognition, leases, insurance contracts and financial instruments. Many of these convergence standards may result in significant accounting changes and long implementation lead times for certain companies.

Though the details of a possible approach of incorporating IFRS into the U.S. financial reporting system are yet to be finalized, companies are likely to be faced with a multi-year period over which many potentially significant new accounting pronouncements would need to be implemented.

To efficiently navigate through this period, companies should consider early planning and readiness activities to prepare for a multi-year effort. Such activities will allow sufficient time to make informed resourcing decisions and to minimize risk inherent in accounting change. Key elements of these planning and readiness activities might include:

- Developing an Overall Strategy

It will be important to develop an overall strategy related to the company's adoption of IFRS and implementation of convergence standards. Such a strategy may include the phasing in and prioritization of potential new standards, as well as considering when a company may wish to avail itself of an option to voluntarily adopt IFRS, if permitted by the SEC.

Should this option be permitted, companies may wish to develop an overall business case and cost/benefit analysis for determining whether and how to voluntarily adopt. This evaluation should balance the cost implications of a gradual but potentially extended transition with a more concentrated conversion effort, consider other in-flight finance and/or information technology initiatives with which such a conversion effort, might be aligned or synchronized, and comprehend the expectations and needs of investors and other constituents and consider various other factors (tax considerations, staffing, training, etc.).

• Prioritizing Issues, Developing Detailed Work Plans

Companies may want to perform assessment activities to identify issues with higher resource requirements and longer implementation lead times (leases, revenue recognition, development costs, share-based payments, fixed-asset componentization, etc.).

Based on the results of the assessment and prioritization of issues, organizations might consider building detailed implementation plans that will provide useful tools to operationalize the expected changes, estimate resources and establish accountability for responsible parties.

• Developing an IFRS and Convergence Roadmap

An IFRS and convergence roadmap can be used to facilitate coordination of resources and focus implementation over a multi-year period. Items of the roadmap may include:

• Key milestones to be achieved related to high priority issues;
• Points of coordination between strategic initiatives, including current/planned technology upgrades, finance transformation programs or other initiatives;
• Key dates for any system and process changes necessary to accommodate "dual reporting," either for particular convergence standards, statutory reporting or any consolidated transition requirements as ultimately determined by the SEC;
• Identification of key decision/approval points along the timeline (e.g., decision to voluntarily adopt IFRS or to early-adopt a particular standard, if permitted);
• Contingency plans to help facilitate a cost-effective implementation; and
• Milestones related to educating stakeholders, training employees and building awareness across the organization.

• Developing Accelerators and Solutions

Companies should consider utilizing tools or solutions to assist management in effectively implementing new standards or making informed accounting, system or other program decisions. Leveraging these tools may help management achieve cost efficiencies and focus on higher priority items. Examples may include:

• Tools to assist with data-gathering activities related to key proposed changes, such as techniques or routines to assist with capturing lease data in anticipation of the converged lease standard;
• Tools and resources from IFRS conversions in other countries where IFRS statutory reporting requirements currently exist;
• Project management tools and templates to promote efficiency, transparency of status reporting and accountability for project assignments; and

• Use of foreign country statutory reporting and tax databases to assist in understanding the detailed filing requirements by country, identification of countries where an IFRS requirement or opportunity exists and identification of tax planning and operational opportunities and risks.

• Developing a Project Management Infrastructure

A multifunctional project management structure, such as a Project Management Organization (PMO), can be used to efficiently leverage resources and skills and mitigate risks inherent in accounting changes.

The objectives of the PMO are to operationalize the IFRS and convergence work plans, communicate with key stakeholders and identify interdependencies with other company initiatives. The PMO may include resources representing key functions, including accounting, tax, information technology, treasury and human resources.

• Developing a Statutory Conversion Strategy

The increased use of IFRS as a replacement for various local GAAPs may provide opportunities to centralize and standardize statutory reporting for foreign subsidiaries and may promote efficiency in the use of internal and external resources. Companies might consider developing a statutory conversion strategy and roadmap to synchronize statutory reporting conversions and maximize efficiency by leveraging statutory reporting tools reusable for future statutory reporting conversions.

As companies consider the impact of IFRS and convergence, management should consider proactive steps now to efficiently and effectively navigate through this anticipated period of substantial accounting change. This includes commencing a planning effort to develop a roadmap and executable work plans, leveraging templates and solutions to maximize the cost effectiveness of the implementation and developing a strong project management structure and implementation team.

An early, thoughtful and pragmatic approach to IFRS and convergence planning and readiness will help minimize risk inherent in accounting change and facilitate a cost-efficient conversion process.

Source

Torr, Sean. "Preparing for significant multi-year changes." *Financial Executive* Nov. 2011: 14+. *General Reference Center GOLD*. Web. 22 Dec. 2011.

Critical Thinking

1. How will the International Financial Reporting Standards (IFRS) change accounting in the United States?
2. Will firms have to redo prior year results based upon IFRS?
3. What will this mean for investors in American corporations?

SEAN TORR (storr@deloitte.com) is a senior manager for Deloitte & Touche LLP.

The Case for Global Accounting

FLOYD NORRIS

For more than a decade, politicians and regulators around the world have claimed to want a common set of high-quality accounting standards that applied globally. The extent to which that rhetoric will become reality may soon become apparent.

Last week, the American government reaffirmed its commitment to common accounting rules, something that Timothy F. Geithner, the Treasury secretary, has argued was necessary for common global regulation of banks, among other things.

"China and the United States support the objective of a single set of high-quality global accounting standards," the two countries said in a joint statement after a meeting in Beijing.

The Securities and Exchange Commission, the American regulator responsible for deciding what accounting rules apply in the United States, was represented in the American delegation in Beijing, but has not stated what it will do.

The commission is expected to publish a report on the question of adopting international accounting standards within the next several weeks, but it is not clear if any action will follow. There has been some speculation that the current S.E.C. chairwoman, Mary L. Schapiro, will step down after the election and would be happy to leave that decision to her successor.

The issue of American adoption of International Financial Reporting Standards, known as I.F.R.S. to accountants, for years has provoked intense debate and anger within the accounting world. Those standards, written by the London-based International Accounting Standards Board, are used by companies in many countries around the world, including all the countries in the European Union.

Some Americans argue that accepting international standards would reduce the quality of American financial statements. But some in Europe say that the best hope for assuring that the international standards are uniformly followed around the globe would be having the S.E.C. involved in enforcing them.

Ideally, comparable accounting around the world would make markets more efficient by letting investors compare companies from different countries. But that would be true only if the standards were of high quality and applied in a consistent manner.

The S.E.C. promised it would make a decision on adopting I.F.R.S. by the end of last year, and then said that would be delayed a few months. Sir David Tweedie, the former chairman of the international board, said in an interview that many in Europe would be angry if the United States did not soon agree to use the international standards, although it would be acceptable for the Americans to set a fixed date for adoption that was several years out.

"If the U.S. delays this indefinitely, or starts having lots of exceptions, I think the global standards will be damaged," he said. "Other countries will do exactly the same thing."

In one sense, it is clear that there will not be a single set of standards around the globe. Already some countries have announced exceptions and carve-outs to the rules for their companies. And the United States is virtually certain not to abandon its own rules, known as U.S. GAAP for "generally accepted accounting principles."

But the hope among American advocates of international standards is that the S.E.C. will set a date by which it expects that virtually all international standards will be incorporated into U.S. GAAP. Since there are areas where the United States has standards that the international body does not, like accounting for regulated utilities, the Americans could continue to apply those standards. But there would be few, if any, areas where American standards contradicted international rules.

Others, including the Financial Accounting Standards Board, which sets American standards, have been pushing for slower action and for more latitude in differing from international rules. "I am in favor of some form of incorporation of international standards, but we do not have a compelling, urgent need to adopt I.F.R.S.," said Leslie F. Seidman, the chairwoman of the American board, in an interview. "We believe in the goal of minimizing differences and ultimately having a common set of standards."

Efforts have been under way for years to accomplish that through a process called convergence, in which the two boards deliberated together as they sought to adopt identical standards. But in a number of areas, they have been unable to reach agreement. That includes accounting for financial instruments, arguably the most important issue of the day.

At an accounting conference at Baruch College in New York last week, Ms. Seidman and her predecessor, Robert H. Herz, seemed to differ on how the decision should be made regarding which American standards should be replaced by international rules. They agreed that the American board should recommend to the S.E.C. whether each new international standard should be endorsed by the United States. Ms. Seidman said that the criterion the American board should use was whether a new standard was an improvement for American investors and companies. If not, American companies should not have to bear the expense of changing systems, even if the new rule was almost as good.

Mr. Herz, who now serves on the parent body of the Canadian agency that sets accounting rules, argued for a policy similar to the one adopted there, in which the international standard is accepted unless there is clear evidence that it is a bad standard or was adopted as a result of undue political interference.

Such interference has been present in both Europe and the United States. During and after the financial crisis, banks and politicians in both regions put heavy pressure on the boards to relax rules that forced the banks to report losses because the market values of some securities had collapsed, and both boards backtracked to some extent.

Twenty years ago, there was a de facto international accounting standard—American GAAP. While there were widely differing rules used in many countries, many major international companies chose to list their securities in the United States, and that meant either using the American rules or reconciling the statements to produce the same results as American rules would call for.

But with pressure growing, particularly in Europe, for an end to American domination, the S.E.C. and other international regulators agreed in the late 1990s to establish the international board under a parent board intended to preserve its independence. The first chairman of the parent body was Paul A. Volcker, a former chairman of the Federal Reserve. Arthur Levitt, then the S.E.C. chairman, promised that the United States would consider adopting what the board produced.

Then in 2008, the commission, headed by Christopher Cox, surprised many by agreeing to allow foreign companies using international rules to file financial statements without reconciling them to U.S. GAAP, as long as the companies used international standards as the international board had written them, rather than relying on exceptions approved by national bodies. The European Commission, at the request of French banks, had decided to allow the banks to ignore part of one rule, related to the valuation of derivatives.

At the time, S.E.C. officials said they were satisfied that the international rules were being consistently applied in countries that had adopted them.

It was never clear just how thorough a study had produced that opinion. But last year the S.E.C. staff studied the financial statements of 183 companies in 22 countries that used

international standards, and found considerable divergence. In some cases, the rules appeared not to have been followed. In others, required disclosures were not made. Variation in practice appeared to have been particularly prevalent among banks—the area in which international comparability may now be the most important. Many banks simply ignored rules requiring disclosure of how they estimated the fair value of securities.

Mr. Tweedie, the former chairman of the international board, said he feared that if the United States did not set a clear timetable for adoption of the standards, and make clear that exceptions to the standards would be rare, other countries, particularly in Asia, either would not adopt the standards or would allow substantial variations. He said some Europeans would demand that the four Americans on the 15-member international board be replaced by people from countries that had adopted the rules.

The International Accounting Standards Board, like its American counterpart, has no ability to enforce its rules. That is up to national regulators. In the United States, the S.E.C. is the ultimate arbiter of compliance with GAAP.

At the Baruch conference last week, James L. Kroeker, the chief accountant of the S.E.C., asked the audience of accountants, "Does anybody know of an entity that will provide global enforcement" of international standards? No hands were raised.

Mr. Tweedie thinks the S.E.C. can be that enforcer. Even for companies that do not register their securities in the United States, the commission could notice different interpretations or outright violations, he said. "The S.E.C. will take action," he said. "It will complain to other regulators," which could be embarrassed into forcing their companies to comply.

"This is why the U.S. is so critical," he said. "Arthur Levitt had the vision. The S.E.C. can complete it, or not."

Source

Norris, Floyd. "The Case For Global Accounting." *New York Times* 11 May 2012: B1(L). *General OneFile*. Web. 29 May 2012.

Critical Thinking

1. Do you think the United States should adopt the International Accounting Rules? Why or why not?

2. If they are adopted, how do you think the rules should be enforced?

3. If they are adopted, who is going to enforce them?

4. What would happen if the United States does not adopt the international rules and simply continues with GAAP?

UNIT 3

International Organizations and Operations

Unit Selections

Learning Outcomes

After reading this Unit, you will be able to:

- Describe the prospects for small businesses in the global marketplace.

- Explain what you think the impact will be of China's new expansion policies on the rest of the global marketplace.

- Describe your view of the use of outsourcing/off-shoring by small firms.

- Dealing with diverse audiences is going to be a major challenge in the future. Explain your view of the best way to do that.

- Describe how you see globalization impacting income and employment in the developed world.

- Explain how corporations are responding to the problem of taxation when it comes to reporting their income.

- A key to the success of many multinational firms is their supply chain. Describe the future evolution of the supply chain.

Student Website

www.mhhe.com/cls

Internet References

CIA Homepage
www.cia.gov

European Union
www.europa.eu

Harvard Business School
www.hbs.edu

International Business Resources on the WWW
www.globaledge.msu.edu

International Labor Organization
www.ilo.org

Organization for Economic Cooperation and Development
www.oecd.org

Outsourcing Center
www.outsourcingcenter.com

Sales and Marketing Executives International (SME)
www.smei.org

United States Department of State
www.state.gov/www/policy.html

United States Trade Representative (USTR)
www.ustr.gov

International organizations come in all shapes and sizes, from the large multinational corporation to the import/exporter who is doing business on a shoestring. While most people tend to focus on the larger companies, the small firm should not be overlooked. Well over half of the exports from the United States come from small businesses, not from multinational corporations. There are opportunities for these small companies in international trade, and the U.S. government is willing to help as seen in, "The Work Left Undone: Perspectives on Small Business Opportunities in International Trade."

When people think of large organizations, they tend to think of firms that are rooted in the developed countries, But, while that may have been the case 40 or 50 years ago, that is no longer the case today. Large companies can also be found with their roots in the developing world. Many of them are multinational in scope, while some of them are in markets that are so large that their international ventures have been very limited.

Global corporate strategy is a key to the success of global organizations, especially in an era of extreme economic uncertainty. Each company must develop a strategic plan that is unique to its particular strengths, weaknesses, opportunities, and the threats that its market and industry present. This applies to consumer goods, industrial goods, services, indeed to all of the types of businesses in the global marketplace. Multinational companies from the developing countries can aspire to being the leading company in a particular business. Tata Industries of India has pursued a strategy of growth that involves the purchase of divisions of other corporations that seem to be troubled and turning them around. While most organizations that use this approach to grow their business often engage in a kind of "slash-and-burn" strategy for the newly acquired division, Tata leaves most of the management and workers intact and tries to develop the newly acquired business into a profitable unit managed by people who know the business best. Companies from developed countries can also have a global strategy, even if they are small and essentially entrepreneurial in nature. In "NanoTech Firm Takes Passage to India," there is an excellent example of an essentially entrepreneurial, high-tech organization taking its manufacturing, testing, and marketing to the developing world before taking it to the developed world; going global before going domestic: an interesting and possibly growing trend.

An axiom of international business is to "Think global, but act local." But now, that is being challenged. There are really few global brands that this can be applied to. Thinking global may be an ideal situation, but the fact is that most markets are local. For a brand to be a success, it must be a part of the local culture, and few brands have been successful in achieving that status on a worldwide basis. Opportunities for achieving global brand status may lie at the base of the economic pyramid. There are four billion people who live on US$2.00 a day or less. This represents about half or so of the world's population. These people have needs for consumer goods just like everyone else, and they live in countries where the price purchase parity makes that US$2.00 a day goes much further than in the developed world. For example, a potato in the United States may cost twenty-five cents, but in a place where the average daily income is US$2.00 a day, that same potato may only cost five cents. "Expanding Opportunity

© Brand X Pictures/Jupiterimages

at the Base of the Pyramid" may be a way for companies to truly think local and establish themselves as global brands.

Another way to establish the global brand would be to take the opposite direction from the base of the pyramid, to go to the top of the pyramid. General Mills is doing this with its Häagen-Dazs brand of super-premium ice cream. Marketed in wealthy countries and wealthy pockets of developing countries throughout the world, Häagen-Dazs is becoming the ice cream of choice of people with extra money to spend on themselves for a super-premium product. It has placed itself at the absolute top of the pyramid among ice creams and, as a result, has become more than just an ice cream, but a symbol of status in many countries throughout the world. An extremely fine product, it is highly profitable and is, indeed, "General Mills' Global Sweet Spot."

Chinese companies face a particular problem when trying to market their goods outside the Middle Kingdom. Chinese products often have the reputation of being of lesser quality than goods produced elsewhere. This is because they generally cost less to produce, and there have been some unfortunate incidents involving the safety and quality of goods manufactured in China. However, this does not apply to all of the goods produced in China. Hailun Piano has been producing quality pianos at an affordable price for the export market for a number of years. Because of the tax laws in China, Hailun Piano, a privately held firm, was forced to produce products for the export market early on in its history, but is now selling in the domestic market in China because the Chinese recognize the superior quality over other pianos available in the Chinese market. But the people of Hailun Piano are not satisfied with being a contender in the world market for pianos, or the domestic market in China. What Hailun Piano wants is recognition as among the best pianos in the world as seen in "Hailun and the Quest for Quality."

Human resources offers another aspect of organization and operations of global business that is far more complicated than domestic operations. Dealing with corrupt foreign practices that may be common in other societies but completely illegal in the United States can present problems for American executives and the companies they represent. The Corrupt Foreign Practices Act defines illegal practices that in some countries are simply a part of doing business; American firms and their executives are sometimes caught doing them and have to pay a price.

Off-shoring has become very controversial. It is certain that companies will continue to do what is best for their stockholders, especially in a world of ruthless competition. That is going to mean cutting costs wherever possible, which often means off-shoring jobs. How governments and societies respond to this is going to determine how developed countries are going to prosper in the coming decades. There is really no way to stop this from happening, but societies can prepare themselves to deal with it so as to minimize the damage and to take advantage of the opportunities that will be available.

The question of off-shoring leads to a larger question of international operations and the cost of doing business. Right now, the global economy is in recession so the price of nearly everything is down. However, when the global economy recovers and the demand starts to climb, it is a virtual certainty that the price of nearly everything will start to climb, as discussed in "Explaining High Oil Prices." The cost of everything, everywhere will increase and businesses will be further challenged to keep their costs down as much as possible. Businesses will be looking to lower-cost venues with more enthusiasm than they do today, and governments, faced with the same increases in costs, will be looking for additional revenue sources. The situation leads to a conundrum outlined in, "Whose Income Is It? How Business Is Caught in the Global Competition and Controversy for Tax Revenue."

Businesses need to make money, and governments need tax revenue. The question is how to maximize both for each. Businesses do not like to pay taxes, but governments need to collect taxes so that they can provide the necessary services for businesses to be able to do business so that they can make a profit. The two are not mutually exclusive, but are dependent upon each other. But when do taxes become too burdensome for industry? When do other tax authorities offer more attractive tax codes for industry so as to attract industry to their location? What taxing authority has the right to tax profits, assets, and other aspects of the business, for how much and when? These are all questions that are going to become more important in the future as taxing authorities become more aggressive in their quest for additional funds to run their operations.

The Work Left Undone

Perspectives on Small Business Opportunities in International Trade

Matthew Carr

There's an old adage that "art imitates life." In the musical *Annie,* the red-haired orphan escapes from the diabolical Miss Hannigan in search of the parents that had left her on the doorstep of the Municipal Girls Orphanage years earlier, promising to return. While on the run and exploring the streets of New York City during the Great Depression, Annie not only finds her famous sidekick Sandy, but she also shares a meal (and a song) with a Hoovervile of individuals made homeless by the recent economic collapse. In classic musical logic, while hovering around the communal cauldron, the shanty town breaks into song, singing:

We'd like to thank you, Herbert Hoover/For really showing us the way/You dirty rat, you Bureaucrat, you/Made us what we are today . . .

Now, there's plenty of evidence to demonstrate that placing the blame for the stock market crash and the resulting depression solely on the shoulders of former President Herbert Hoover is short-sighted. During the Great Depression, just like in our modern crisis, greed, questionable corporate ethics and insufficient regulation were the ultimate villains. Nonetheless, the psychological need to single out a lone individual as the guilty party always trumps reality.

There are many parallels between *Annie*'s story and what is currently happening in the United States today. Unemployment has surged into double-digit territory and Americans from coast-to-coast are losing their homes. Animosity is brewing because President Barack Obama hasn't already delivered salvation, and bleak and weak economic indicators provide a steady chain of ammunition. And maybe some of that hostility is understandable as it would've been as difficult for Hoover to explain to the unemployed and homeless in *Annie*'s Hooverville that it wasn't his fault as it would for Obama or former President George W. Bush to do so today.

The world has just experienced one of the greatest eras of economic turmoil ever, maybe second only to the Great Depression. Not surprisingly, it has earned the moniker the "Great Recession," as global markets were held hostage for more than 20 months, more than twice as long as the average duration of a normal recession. And the world still isn't out of the woods yet.

Global trade, the one reliable ally through the sinking bog of the economic downturn, became shaky and has slowly returned over the last several months, ebbing and flowing as nations emerge and then recede back into uncertainty. The United States was buoyed from sinking into a depression by a surge in export activity, spurred on by the weakening dollar. Germany's first unsteady steps from the fog of recession in the second quarter have since been strengthened by export stimulus, while the rest of Europe continues to trail behind. Canada is now confident that recovery is imminent, despite its strong reliance on the United States, while emerging Asian markets continue to bud and blossom.

Many experts had predicted that a rebound would be in full swing at this point and that the third quarter for most of the world would be one of flourishing revived economies. In part, that is true. The United States continues to plod forward, regaining ground at a modest pace, but has slipped along the way due to a still-elusive consumer confidence. Germany and France have long since been free of recession and the rest of Western Europe is making progress. In all likelihood, the light at the end of the tunnel is drawing near, but the upticks in recovery have been nowhere near as steep as anticipated.

Many experts had predicted that a rebound would be in full swing at this point and that the third quarter for most of the world would be one of flourishing revived economies.

Unfortunately, recovery is not uniform and in business the meek aren't clearly destined to inherit anything.

Cut Down to Size

To strengthen the country's foundation and help speed recovery, the United States has made small businesses and small business exporting its top priority. The Obama Administration has worked with legislators and the Office of the United States Trade Representative (USTR) to clear any obstacles from the path of businesses looking to make the leap from Main Street to International Drive. The Small Business Administration (SBA) has partnered in the initiative and has revamped its size limitations on loans, while the U.S. Export-Import Bank (Ex-Im Bank) has been on a campaign to make sure every interested enterprise knows that it's there.

"As an economy, we have to really figure out how to get better tools for small businesses so that they can get the cash flow moving through their business and into other small businesses and throughout the entire ecosystem that's out there," said Jim Swift, CEO and president, Cortera, Inc. Swift is skeptical that the federal moves will have much impact, particularly those from the SBA. "It's helpful and maybe it gives that business the predictable cash to go and hire that person that they've been waiting to hire because they were unsure about things, but what it doesn't ensure is that that company is going to pay its suppliers who also need the money," he said.

There are obviously significant differences between small and larger companies. Larger enterprises are typically better suited to survive economic uncertainties because they have a broader pool of resources to lean on to steady their footing. That has been the onus behind trying to make more capital available to smaller businesses as the financial downturn lags on, exponentially increasing the impacts from a lack of credit and consumer confidence, and slow payments from debtors. Cortera tracks payment trends throughout the supply chain with its Supply Chain Index (SCI). Right now, commercial accounts receivable (A/R) debt more than 30 days past due is 50% higher than what was seen in September 2007 just prior to the official start of the recession. Overall, payments are also arriving 40% later than in September 2007, demonstrating the lingering effects of the crisis. "Everyone kind of hoarded cash for a while," said Swift.

Now, all eyes are on the returns from the holiday shopping season as a barometer for the economic climate. During the months leading up to the big winter retail rush, manufacturers, retailers and suppliers typically take on additional trade credit debt as they prepare for this season. This is usually represented in the SCI as an annual spike in late A/R from November to the end of the year, but in 2009, the spike in accounts days beyond terms (DBT) arrived in September, two months earlier than normal.

Swift thinks that the early arrival of the DBT uptick in October may be because U.S. companies are stretching out payments on that seasonal debt. Every fall and winter, companies dramatically slow down payments to suppliers as they try to manage their capital for the holidays. Under normal conditions, this slowdown happens in November or December and then quickly recedes after the New Year when companies—sitting on a cache of cash—begin paying off debts again. He said that it could also be that overall confidence in the economy's recovery has taken a severe blow.

The biggest problem continues to be the disparity between how large companies and small companies are paying. Late payments from larger companies have dwindled, but the situation seems to be exacerbated for smaller firms. "I'm kind of surprised we don't see a rebound in how fast small businesses are paying," said Swift. "It's still 28% or so higher than it was

at this point two years ago and they're not showing any signs that they're speeding up payments." He added, "It looks like it's taking longer for those companies to feel the effects of the economic rebound shake down to their business."

The return to normalcy also appears to be much more measured for smaller domestic firms as evidenced by the National Federation of Independent Business' (NFIB) Index of Small Business Optimism that found outlook inched upward only slightly in October. Since the second lowest reading ever in the index's history in March 2009, there has been a steady upward trend to a reading of 89.1. That's a significant benchmark because, during the recession from 1980–82, the NFIB's optimism index fell below 90 only once. Throughout this prolonged downturn, the index has been below 90 six times, reflecting the pure severity of the decline.

"Just because a business gets a loan, that business still has to be confident in the other parts of its operation and whether its customers will continue to pay and flow cash through. That's the key," said Swift. "The government, I don't think, can really do anything about it and shouldn't necessarily pretend that they can get businesses to get that cash flow moving. It's really up to the businesses themselves."

In the United States, the debate will continue about the effectiveness of the current strategies to nurture recovery. Nonetheless, there may finally be some success in pushing more American companies to diversify by getting them involved in international trade.

"I haven't seen any game-changing initiatives," said Iosh Green, CEO and president, Panjiva, Inc. of the current federal moves. "I think the economic forces are the key drivers here. Perhaps one of the legacies of this downturn could be a rise in entrepreneurship. People are out of jobs. They can't find somebody to give them a job, so they create a job for themselves. And that wouldn't surprise me at all if some of those jobs related to importing."

Profits of Doom

As the U.S. government urges more and more businesses to get involved in international trade, the World Trade Organization (WTO) warned all last year that global trade will be on the decline in 2010. Despite the fact that the weak dollar made U.S. goods and commodities like crude and gold more affordable on the international level, the mood has become more subdued in the global marketplace, particularly compared to brimming enthusiasm witnessed even just a handful of months ago. This makes it even more harrowing for small businesses either importing or exporting that are already at a disadvantage by having fewer resources than their large counterparts, let alone lacking the resources on the ground in emerging markets.

"I really encourage people to consider the multitude of risks," said Green. "People are very accustomed to thinking about financial risk: the risk that the company they are doing business with will go out of business. The reality is there are more than just financial risks that you need to worry about, particularly if you are doing business internationally."

Anybody involved in international trade already understands that it isn't a plug-and-go/turn-key endeavor. There are the many activities an overseas partner company can be engaged in to put a company's brand at risk, including capacity risk, pricing risk, currency risk, and political risk. "I think it's important that as people do business internationally, they do it with eyes wide open about the variety of risks and the ways to manage those risks," Green said.

According to Panjiva, Inc., from August to September 2009, the number of global manufacturers shipping to the United States slipped as international trade buckled. Then, in October, global trade regained steam and there was a slight uptick. Specifically, there was a 3% increase in the number of global manufacturers shipping to the U.S. market. At the same time, there was a 2% increase in the number of U.S. companies receiving waterborne shipments.

Of course, even during a global recession, any sort of panic in a major consuming economy like the United States can have significant impacts for distributors around the world. The great thing about international trade is that it's a two-way street. On one side, there was a sense of disappointment when the Department of Commerce announced that the U.S. trade deficit increased dramatically in September to $36.5 billion from August's $30.8 billion. On the other, those numbers included the effects of the media love affair with H1N1 and the predicted impending crisis the "swine flu" virus would create. "We had a hunch that given the swine flu scare, hand sanitizer shipments would be up significantly," said Green. "We looked into the data and, sure enough, there was a massive spike in shipments to the United States."

Spike is a relative term. During the three months ending in September, Panjiva discovered that shipments of waterborne hand sanitizer to the United States had increased 129% year-over-year. In the third quarter of 2009, there were 128 shipments destined for the U.S., compared to 56 such shipments in the third quarter of 2008. The cargo loads also represented a threefold increase when analyzed on a weight basis.

What these numbers also reveal is the wide range of opportunities that exist in the global market that make it attractive for small enterprises.

The Road Ahead

Since global trade hit bottom in February 2009, it has been recovering at a modest pace, in fits and starts. Import activity in the U.S. has recovered, although the absolute level of activity is still well below pre-recession numbers. Unfortunately, rebound is anticipated to be slow and there are few people who expect a great improvement any time soon.

"Some people were hoping to see one with the holiday season, but that didn't materialize," said Green. "My best guess at this point is that we'll continue to see a slow recovery. Obviously, any further macroeconomic shocks could change that dynamic."

Despite all the talk over the last year about trade shifting from China and more toward Central and South America, the change hasn't been enormous. Coface expects 2009 growth for China and India to come in at 8.5% and 6% respectively. For 2010, Coface reports that growth for China will remain strong, increasing to 10%, while India's growth will trend upward to 8%.

"People need to go beyond just thinking about countries," said Green. "Having a country orientation when you're thinking about where to buy products and where risks lie is really inappropriate. You need to think about the company level. You really need to dig in and understand what's going on with the companies you are interacting with and are considering interacting with because that's where the bulk of the risks lie."

In the business world, companies are constantly relying on the cash inflows from their customers to go out the back door.

Companies like Panjiva offer an array of informational services on international distributors and Green said his company feels that information is critical. "The way I look at it, it's not about any one business; it's about the interaction between the businesses," said Swift. "If you think of the economy as a whole, the more confident we are about things, the more money we spend. Knowing that we're going to get paid, we're going to get jobs, we're going to spend more and those people are then going to spend more and you really can't put your finger on it, but in a thriving economy everyone has confidence and the money flows freely. In the business world, companies are constantly relying on the cash inflows from their customers to go out the back door. The confidence is a huge factor in all of this."

Critical Thinking

1. What are some of the opportunities for small business in international trade?
2. How is the government helping?
3. What else could the government do?

From *Business Credit*, January 2010, pp. 40–43. Copyright © 2010 by Business Credit Magazine, the official publication of the National Association of Credit Management (NACM). Reprinted by permission.

Going Global
The Risks and Rewards of China's New International Expansion

Chi Lo

China has been expanding its economic power through overseas investment in recent years in order to secure supply of raw materials, energy, and other commodities for its economic development. Others are beginning to grasp how China is shaping the world with its huge appetite for energy and natural resources. However, what is less understood is the way China is itself being shaped by the world as it integrates with the global system.

The recent Middle East–North Africa turmoil shows that China's "going global" policy does not come at a low cost, as Beijing might have thought. In other words, the time for China to quietly reap economic benefits with limited risk exposure to the global markets is past. Even the need to ensure the welfare of Chinese citizens, whose outflow follows the overseas investment expansion, means that China cannot stay away from geopolitical risk anymore. As China becomes more involved in world affairs, the United States will need to rethink its China engagement strategy because America's superpower leverage has diminished significantly after the subprime crisis. And China knows that.

China's Great Investment Outflow

China's rapid economic growth has raised its confidence in looking outside its boundaries for investment opportunities. Increased competition and the drive to maximize profits have raised Chinese awareness of foreign market potentials. There is also a growing need to acquire raw materials from external sources. Hence, Chinese foreign investments have grown rapidly in recent years, though they are still small in absolute size, accounting for just about 1.5 percent of GDP. The subprime crisis will help speed up China's investment outflow trend in the coming years by lowering the cost of acquisition by Chinese companies, since global asset prices have dropped.

China's overseas direct investment is concentrated mainly in the developing countries, especially in Africa. In the 1980s, China's overseas direct investment was quite small and driven primarily by political rather than economic considerations.

Before 1985, only state-owned and local government-owned enterprises were allowed to invest overseas. Private enterprises were allowed to apply for overseas direct investment projects after 1985, when Chinese authorities started designing and developing the necessary procedures and policies. Under the investment liberalization program, there was a flow of investment to Hong Kong in the 1990s. But most of the projects went bad due to lack of investment know-how, ignorance about the rule of law in overseas markets, and corruption among Chinese officials and corporates.

The Asian financial crisis in 1997 prompted Chinese authorities to rethink their overseas direct investment strategy. The regional crisis changed the global economic landscape by highlighting the strength of the overseas markets. These markets were growing strongly at that time and acted as an "economic savior" for the Asian economies by absorbing Asia's excess capacity via imports. Seeing the great opportunity in foreign demand growth, China issued a directive in 1999 to develop direct investment abroad that would promote Chinese exports via processing trade investment. This directive signified a crucial shift of China's policy from promoting overseas investment to directing it.

In 2002, Chinese authorities started pushing the "going global" or "stepping out" strategy as part of the economic reform process and to promote global industry champions in the wake of its accession to the World Trade Organization. Then in 2004, the Chinese authorities made another change in their overseas direct investment policy. In addition to just approving overseas direct investment applications, they further defined explicitly their roles in supervising the projects and providing facilitation services. This prompted Chinese enterprises to go global aggressively. China has invested in over 170 countries and engaged in an extensive range of economic activities, including information technology, finance, retail, fish processing, and forestry. The bulk of these overseas investments are concentrated in a few areas, including Australia, Hong Kong, Macau, southeast Asia, Russia, and the United States.

China's overseas investment expansion in recent years has been seen as politically driven to secure raw materials and strategic resources to feed its industrialization process.

China's overseas investment expansion in recent years, especially after the subprime crisis, has been seen as politically driven to secure raw materials and strategic resources to feed its industrialization process. Indeed, China's direct investment in geographically and politically sensitive regions such as Africa and increasingly South America for the purpose of acquiring natural resources has raised international concerns about its aggressive procurement policy upsetting global economic and political balances. However, academic studies show that seeking markets and resources are not the only motives driving China's investment overseas. Other crucial motives include cost of production, agglomeration or herding behavior, and pressure to seek higher investment returns for the huge US$2.8 trillion (and growing) foreign exchange reserves.

What all this means is that China has been integrating into the global system deeper by the year as it expands its economic influence beyond its borders. While this "going global" strategy has delivered economic benefits, it also means that, due to the complex structure of China's investments, their full exposure to global risks is not readily visible until events eventually unfold. The Middle Eas–North Africa turmoil is a good example of the flip side of China's push for overseas investment.

greater price hike that we have seen so far were sustained for a year or longer, the impact on the developed world's growth would be significant.

However, history has also shown that the world economy could continue to grow even though oil prices soared. For example, in 2004–08 prices went from under US$30 per barrel to over US$100 due to a positive demand shock stemming from buoyant oil demand from Asia (notably China). The current situation is not as benign. The most recent oil price hikes come from a negative supply shock due to geopolitical crises in the Middle East–North Africa region, while the developed world is stuck with high unemployment and weak demand in its post-bubble adjustment process. Rising oil prices will eventually feed through to the consumer price index, albeit slowly, while pricing power will remain weak in the post-bubble adjustment process so that firms will not be able to pass on the full cost of oil price hikes to the consumers. Margins will be squeezed, and workers will not be able to secure higher wages on a sustained basis. As far as stagnant demand growth in the developed world is concerned, it would hurt Chinese exports as Europe and the United States together account for over 42 percent of China's total export market share.

However, the odds for this stagflation outcome are still low, as the Middle East–North Africa turmoil is expected to be a temporary event so that the oil supply disruption is also temporary. Recent events should keep the major central banks from tightening too early (or aggressively in the case of the ECB and possibly the Bank of England); even policy hawks would agree that tightening in the face of a geopolitical oil shock would only cause more damage to the fragile developed-world economy.

Risk of Inflation or Deflation, or Both

The economic disruption stemming from the Middle East–North Africa trouble comes mainly from the risks of both a sustained rise in oil prices pushing up global inflation, and geopolitical contagion to unaffected regions (including Asia) leading to a sharp rise in risk aversion. The former may lead to stagflation—a combination of stagnant growth and inflation—while the latter would have a negative impact on risk-taking.

Oil price hikes are inflationary due to the role of oil as the cost base for almost all production, directly or indirectly. Oil price hikes also affect inflationary expectations, which could feed wage inflation that adds to general price inflation. On the other hand, oil price hikes are also deflationary, as they erode buying power in other sectors. Econometric models suggest that a sustained US$10 per barrel rise in crude oil prices would cut global economic growth by 0.2 to 0.5 percentage points. This may not be a huge effect. But if the US$30 or

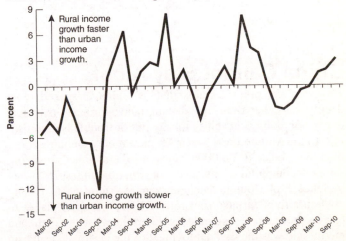

China's rural-urban income growth gap

Rural income growth faster than urban income growth.

Rural income growth slower than urban income growth.

Sources: CEIC, HFT (HK).

The Relevance Risk to China

The situation is different in Asia, where growth and the financial system have not been damaged much by the subprime crisis. Inflation is a real risk here. China is a prime example, with both headline inflation and inflationary expectations rising. The oil price hikes may put further upward pressure on China's consumer price index. Increases in oil prices will also have an indirect impact on other costs, including fertilizer, petrochemicals, transport, and other raw materials, feeding into rising inflationary expectations. Workers are demanding higher wages under these circumstances. We have seen double-digit wage increases recently, fueling fears of a wage-price spiral.

All this will lead to more fears of policy tightening and price controls, and hence downside risk for Chinese asset prices in the short term. There is also a chance of more price controls on basic food items, fertilizer, animal feed, and electrical power, as Beijing is worried about the potential social and political implications of surging food prices. A critical reason people in Tunisia, Egypt, and Libya took to the streets was soaring food prices eroding their standards of living.

Income growth for young and rural Chinese workers in recent years suggests that the odds for political contagion from Middle East–North Africa to China are small, though addressing income inequality is still a top policy priority in China. Most participants in the Middle East–North Africa unrest are educated but unemployed youth, who resent poverty and ever-rising income inequality. This means that steady growth will need to remain a priority for China for years to come, as demand growth creates jobs and income.

The double-digit rise in wage growth for migrant workers since 2010 is a move toward narrowing the income gap between lower-class and middle-class workers. This is also reflected by per capita rural income growth outpacing urban income growth recently (see figure). However, China does have an income inequality problem, driven partly by surging property prices. Beijing is addressing the problem by getting tough on property speculation and increasing housing supply by pushing forward massive social housing programs in the coming years. In a nutshell, all the cyclical and geopolitical risks that China is facing are still manageable.

China Cannot Stay Aloof

However, the point remains that as China is sucked more deeply into the affairs of distant lands through its global expansion policy, its ability to stay out of trouble is diminishing. In the Middle East–North Africa troubles, Beijing scrambled to evacuate its 35,000 Chinese workers in the Libyan oil, rail, telecommunications, and construction industries when violence broke out in late February. In addition to twenty civilian aircraft, it also sent four military transport planes to rescue thousands of stranded workers in what the mainland media said was the first deployment of the air force in such an operation. Some political analysts even argue that the Libyan

deployment marks a profound shift in China's security policy. It put China on par with the United States, the United Kingdom, and other advanced countries that can protect citizens far from home.

Beijing is worried about the potential social and political implications of surging food prices.

The question of how to protect Chinese citizens abroad goes well beyond Libya. There are 50,000 Chinese workers in Nigeria, 20,000–50,000 in Sudan, 40,000 in Zambia, 30,000 in Angola, 20,000 in Algeria, and tens of thousands more scattered throughout Africa. Chinese companies are now pushing into South America, another resource-rich region far from home. With all these commitments overseas, will Beijing feel compelled to try to shape the economic and political realities of the countries in which its companies operate? This is certainly food for thought for American policymakers.

From China's perspective, its overseas economic expansion comes at a cost of exposing the country to exogenous risks that Beijing might not have expected when the "going global" push began. If the Middle East- North Africa events proved anything, it is that the days of China keeping its head down are probably over, and with expanding clout overseas comes certain burdens.

Income growth for young and rural Chinese workers in recent years suggests that the odds for political contagion from Middle East–North Africa to China are small.

Food for Thought for the United States

For the United States, perhaps it is worth rethinking its engagement strategy towards China. America's current economic policy towards China is similar to earlier strategies under Bill Clinton and George W. Bush, when the United States was able to enforce its will effectively in bilateral meetings. This is not working now. During the Clinton/Bush years, U.S. military power was at its height; the country was experiencing its strongest-ever economic expansion; and U.S. information technology was changing the world's economic landscape. China then was still emerging from backwardness.

The U.S. position is now much weakened. Daunting issues on the fiscal, banking, and economic fronts need resolving. At the same time, China's economic ascent has raised eyebrows, with robust GDP growth lifting hundreds of millions out of poverty, its expanding role in global trade, and its growing diplomatic ties in Asia, Latin America, and Africa. Most importantly, it has amassed US$2.8 trillion (and growing) in foreign reserves, becoming a critical creditor to the United States.

China is unlikely to become a superpower anytime soon, but America's superpower leverage has diminished significantly, and China knows it. New times need new policies. A plausible way to make China play by the international rules would be to weave a web of multilateral arrangements into which China could fit and by which China would be bound. This is food for thought for the United States.

Critical Thinking

1. What are the risks to China in attempting to secure sources of supply for it economy?

2. As China becomes more involved in the global economy, what will be its additional responsibilities?

3. How can China continue to grow at the pace it has in the past?

CHI LO is CEO of HFT Investment Management (Hong Kong) Ltd., and author of *China After the Subprime Crisis: Opportunities in the New Economic Landscape* (Palgrave Macmillan, 2010).

From *The International Economy*, 25(2), Spring 2011, pp. 52–55. Copyright © 2011 by The International Economy. Reprinted by permission.

NanoTech Firm Takes Passage to India

PETER GWYNNE

A small high-tech company in New England is going global in an ambitious way. The firm, Nanobiosym, has started a collaboration with the governments of India and two Indian states on a public-private partnership that will give it and other Western companies a local presence on the subcontinent from which they can carry out R&D—as well as manufacturing and marketing their technologies.

The project is in its early phases. Nanobiosym does not want to reveal details of its discussions with potential corporate collaborators, although it is still prepared to welcome business partners from North America and Europe to the venture. However, the company's experience so far provides valuable insights into ways in which technology companies can gain a foothold in a country with a potentially large middle-class market that has begun to overturn a longstanding tradition of protectionism.

Physicist-physician Anita Goel, M.D., founded Nanobiosym, Inc. in Medford, Massachusetts in 2004, with the goal, she says, "of creating an environment in which physics, biology, and nanotechnology could be combined as a nexus." The company initially worked in R&D, earning contracts from the United States Department of Energy and other government agencies.

Genetic Fingerprints

One project developed proprietary nanochip technology capable of detecting the genetic fingerprints of any biological organism fast and accurately. The technology, called Gene-RADAR, has potential use in homeland security, by detecting pathogens in food, water and the air, for example.

Dr. Goel, who is Nanobiosym's chairman and CEO, created a subsidiary firm, Nanobiosym Diagnostics, to commercialize that and other advances. She realized that portable devices based on the Gene-RADAR technology had medical value in third-world nations. The devices could diagnose infections and other illnesses within a few minutes of receiving a drop of blood or saliva. "The technology takes the ability to diagnose disease outside the pathology lab and into handheld devices," she explains. "That would be a paradigm shift."

Equally important, Dr. Goel saw the need to continue research and development on the technology, as well as manufacturing and marketing the devices, in the developing world. She quickly identified India as the initial target. Why India? "It's an emerging market," Dr. Goel explains. "We have a technology platform. My vision is to bring it to emerging markets. India represented a place that would be a foothold to help drive down the costs of our products, especially as we scale up our technology to bring it into new markets in the developing world." Dr. Goel's heritage helped steer her toward India. Her parents had emigrated from there to the U.S. before she was born.

A Worldwide Stage

From the beginning, Dr. Goel wanted more than a conventional agreement in which a Western company sets up overseas manufacturing sites. For a start, she determined to work on a worldwide stage. "Our vision is more global," she says, "with India being a piece of that." Just as important, she aimed to use Nanobiosym's opportunity as the gateway for taking a burst of Western technology into India and other developing countries. "Initially, the Indian government said: 'Why don't you manufacture your products over here and create jobs over here?'" she recalls. "We have the vision of something bigger—a test bed ecosystem where cutting edge technologies can be introduced into emerging markets. There's a different science and art in bringing products into these markets than into the more developed markets of the West, for example."

The initial result of her negotiations is land for a 500-acre science park in Himachal Pradesh state, about two hours north of the Indian capital of New Delhi, along with the corporate-government institutional structure that will enable the project. The park, Dr. Goel says, "will harness the resources of the local environment and also bring in global players to create a bridge to the global economy. We have a broad vision of creating an ecosystem where companies from around the world can come together to bring emerging technologies into emerging markets. Many companies are approaching us to explore innovative partnership models, as well as ideas of how best to create a win-win symbiotic relationship with the local communities." India's western-most state of Gujarat has signed up to work on a similar project with Nanobiosym.

Global Showcase

The projects are in the early stages and remain open to participation. "We're looking for special kinds of partners—best-of-breed people who share our sense of global mission, Dr. Goel says. We're very open to companies, enterprises, and organizations that feel they have a niche in this ecosystem we're building. We're building a global consortium of all kinds of partners—manufacturing, R&D, education, and even entertainment. It's the idea of a global showcase in which we all learn from each other."

The agreements have come at an appropriate time. India's long-skeptical attitude toward overseas corporations has begun to mellow in recent years. Both the ruling Congress Party and the main opposition Bharatiya Janata Party have indicated that they welcome the presence of overseas corporations as well as the goods and services they produce. And at the beginning of 2005, the Indian Patent Office brought the country's patent act in line with the requirements of the World Trade Organization's Agreement on Trade Related Aspects of Intellectual Property. That change permitted the first local filings of product patents on compounds for use as drugs and other medications. "Traditionally they focused on outsourcing," Dr. Goel notes. "They seem now to be wanting to take a step toward innovation."

But change does not take root overnight. In a recent case, an Indian court upheld the patent office's decision to reject a patent application by Swiss pharmaceutical firm Novartis for its chronic myeloid leukemia drug Gleevec. Its contention: The drug represented only a small improvement to an existing drug. In addition, Indian bureaucracy has not entirely shed its reputation of being difficult and time-consuming to navigate.

Two Indias

In her negotiations, Dr. Goel has seen evidence of both changing attitudes and the old style of doing business. "There are two Indias," she says. "One seems to be very progressive, moving to the future, and high-tech friendly. The other is still living in the past and living up to its reputation. At every step—in government, corporations, and other institutions—you are dealing with both Indias."

How does Dr. Goel deal with the two? "There's no magic bullet," she says. "It's a process—not as deliberate as it may look. We had these products we wanted to bring into an emerging market. Our company is focused on innovation where

physics, medicine, and nanotechnology meet to develop new ways of attacking global problems. A series of events luckily happened that brought this unique opportunity about."

Some of those events came about by design. Last fall, for example, Dr. Goel brought Ratan Tata, chairman of India's giant Tata Group and perhaps India's best-known technology executive, to Nanobiosym's global advisory board. "I am inspired by his example, which provides us with a practical road map for bringing cutting-edge technologies into emerging global economies and extending our reach to broad markets at the bottom of the pyramid," Dr. Goel said. The appointment helped to seal the relationship with India. In addition, she worked with such organizations as the USA-India Chamber of Commerce. As to her Indian heritage: "It sometimes helps and sometimes hurts, depending perhaps on which India you are dealing with" she says.

Words of Advice

What advice does Dr. Goel have for technology-based corporations whose executives want to create a presence in India in particular and the developing world in general? "I would encourage companies, whether they are small, medium or large, to join us," she says. "We're building partnerships in a very collaborative way, including R&D, manufacturing, innovation, education, and even entertainment in an ecosystem that plays into the local economy. We are eco-friendly, green and fitting into the local markets. We're thinking in a global context. I'm sure that many companies interested in going global and bringing their technologies into those markets are thinking that way. In my opinion, they should be evolving beyond the idea of being perceived as Western companies exploiting local labor, into global enterprises seeking to address the needs of the local economies."

Critical Thinking

1. Why would a small company go to the developing world to develop its products?
2. Is this limited to only high-tech firms?
3. Besides India, where else might a high-tech firm go?

From *Research-Technology Management*, May–June 2009, pp. 7–8. Copyright © 2009 by Industrial Research Institute, Inc. Reprinted by permission.

Increasing Your Share of a Culturally Diverse Audience

How is diversity incorporated into your overall strategic plan to acquire a larger share of the market, attract new franchisees, deliver better service to customers and outperform your competitors?

Leah Smiley

In today's economic environment, global expansion is a business imperative. The Internet and technology makes this feat easier, but there are some things that organizations must know about culturally diverse audiences to be successful in acquiring a larger share of the global market.

For one, diversity, inclusion and multi-cultural competence are not the same terms as affirmative action or quotas. In the past, some people implemented affirmative action requirements as if they were in a fire sale. Their intentions were good, but the methods were bad. Fast forward 50 years and businesses recognize the value that diversity and inclusion brings to the table, particularly as it pertains to building market share and improving global competitive positioning.

Here are a few facts:

* The World Bank estimates that the global middle class is likely to grow from 430 million in 2000 to 1.2 billion in 2030. China and India will account for two-thirds of the expansion;
* According to the U.S. Census Bureau, the number of business start-ups (brick and mortar and others) by minorities and women outpaces start-ups by the majority population;
* According to a recent study by *Socio-Economic Trends,* in heterosexual households, females make 43 percent of the financial decisions versus 31 percent of joint decisions;
* According the U.S. Census Bureau, 1 in 5 Americans is considered disabled, and the number of disabled Americans will increase with the aging population; and
* The lesbian, gay, bisexual and transgender community's buying power is fast approaching $800 billion this year, according to research by Witeck-Combs Communications and Marketresearch.com. A recent study by Witeck-Combs/Harris Interactive also found a substantial majority (70 percent) of gay men and lesbians report that they have switched products or service providers because they found out the company had engaged in actions that are perceived as harmful to the LGBT community.

In this way, affirmative action is different from diversity. Affirmative action had nothing to do with customers, and it is a policy that only affects organizations operating in the United States. If we honestly look at the policy as a whole, it did achieve its purpose of including underrepresented groups in the workplace. And, those groups (women and minorities) do work hard to contribute to the bottom line. But diversity is different. Diversity has everything to do with competitive advantage and customers—including new markets, global business opportunities and new organizational strategies. It is the future of economic viability and sustainability.

Accordingly, if there is a gap between your corporate vision and your organization's growth, there are three easy steps that you can apply today to increase your share of the culturally diverse marketplace:

* Evaluate customer trends
* Implement a diversification strategy
* Hire a chief diversity officer

Step 1: Evaluate Customer Trends

Consider who your clients were 10–20 years ago. This historic reference is necessary to reflect on who your customers were, how their needs have changed and how you can anticipate their future wants. Take the U.S. Postal Service as an example. It has been operating at a loss for the last three years, even though it has high customer satisfaction rates, cheap prices, and compared to all other government agencies, runs like a real business. In 2009, USPS had postal rate hikes and in 2010, it eliminated 40,000 positions. But it's hard to cut your way to profit. And it's difficult to generate a profit from one to two cents amid decreasing mail volume.

At some point, there has to be an in-depth analysis on who the customers were 20 years ago when folks primarily mailed everything, and how technology and carriers such as UPS and FedEx have changed the business environment today.

Not only do companies need to know specifically who is currently purchasing their services, but how will projected demographic and economic changes affect future business. They also need to figure out how they can tap into additional, or new, revenue streams.

Trends include data such as buying patterns, attendance rates, utilization reports, and other statistics in the past, present and future. Analyzing trends should be a key aspect of strategic planning. Having a diversity component in your strategic plan allows your company to use trends to make projections about opportunities for future growth, sales and talent.

Companies can apply the same trending practice. Evaluate customer, franchisee or employee trends using lots of details to identify gaps and opportunities. Then determine the required skills and qualities for employees who will serve your new customer or franchisee base.

Remember, diversity is not about race—it is about doing business better. And from this perspective, the franchise community can look at diversity as a vehicle to analyze an organization's path and compare it to the overall direction of the market. Can you have a plan with trends and not consider diversity? Sure, if you want a lopsided plan. The big picture is globalization, and the effect of globalization locally is diversity. Diversity should be included in your long-term customer, franchisee or employee planning processes because it takes the "big picture" into account.

Step 2: Implement a Diversification Strategy

Another big picture idea is diversification. Diversification is a form of growth marketing. It increases profitability and volume by penetrating new markets.

Diversification strategies can be applied to every industry, whether for-profit, nonprofit or educational. It can even be applied to your own individual skill sets. For example, if you are a human resources professional, diversifying your skill set means that you enhance your technical abilities in finance.

In business, a U.S.-based company may consider targeting international franchisees. Or if 95 percent of a company's customer demographics indicate it primarily serves clients in the South, it may want to consider expanding to the East Coast through an acquisition. Similarly, some may want to focus on a "Green" customer demographic or on women-owned businesses.

After looking at where your current customers or franchisees are, diversification causes you to tap into additional demographics. With all of the various differences and segments of diversity (such as income, gender, education, work history, family status, age/generation and so forth), you can become a specialist, nationally and internationally, in a different market.

To achieve diversification, an organization must be open and willing to change, as well as be committed to research and innovation. It is one of the riskiest business strategies, but the most rewarding in terms of other marketing initiatives such as market penetration, market development and product development.

Diversity has everything to do with competitive advantage and customers— including new markets, global business opportunities and new organizational strategies.

Step 3: Hire a Chief Diversity Officer

Peter Drucker was an influential pioneer and one of my favorite strategic management theorists. He made many important contributions to strategic management, but two are particularly notable. First, Drucker stressed the importance of objectives. An organization without clear objectives is like a ship without a rudder. Second, Drucker foresaw the importance of what would soon be called "intellectual capita." He predicted the rise of what he called the "knowledge worker" and explained the consequences of this for management. He said that knowledge work is non-hierarchical. Work would be carried out in teams with the person most knowledgeable in the task at hand as the temporary leader.

For your organization to be successful in reaching a culturally diverse audience, it needs someone on your team who possesses knowledge of different cultures. In the business world, this person is called the chief diversity officer. This individual will not only help you enhance your strategy with a diversity component, but he or she will also be able to use his or her knowledge to integrate diversity into all organizational functions including HR, marketing, corporate contributions, franchisee relations, supplier contracts, legal, technology and customer service to name a few.

If you hire a chief diversity officer, give that person the freedom to address issues, develop proactive solutions to potential problems and offer suggestions at the table with every other strategic business unit.

Having one point of contact for diversity ensures that one person is accountable for diversity efforts within your organization. And most importantly, the chief diversity officer position ensures that your organization has a coordinated approach to, and strategic resource for, increasing your share of a culturally diverse audience.

Critical Thinking

1. Why is a culturally diverse employee base important to an organization?
2. What makes an organization culturally diverse?
3. How can organizations encourage cultural diversity?

LEAH SMILEY is the founder and president of the Society for Diversity, an international professional membership association and diversity education provider. She can be reached at leahsmiley@societyfordiversity.org or visit www.societyfordiversity.org.

From *Franchising World*, June 2011, pp. 19–21. Copyright © 2011 by International Franchise Association. Reprinted by permission.

General Mills' Global Sweet Spot

The food giant's key overseas brand isn't Cheerios. it's Häagen-Dazs. From Paris to Shanghai, it's all about prestige—and churning out growth.

DAVID A. KAPLAN

GENERAL MILLS

RANK: No. 166
REVENUE: $14.8 billion
PROFITS: $1.5 billion
HEADQUARTERS: Minneapolis
EMPLOYEES: 33,000

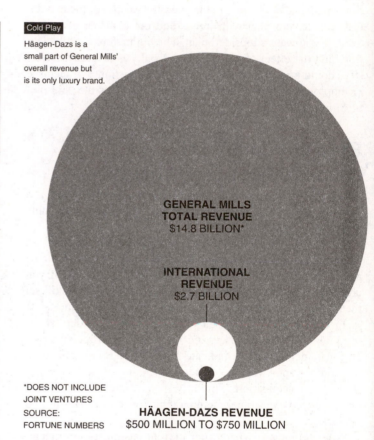

Cold Play

Häagen-Dazs is a small part of General Mills' overall revenue but is its only luxury brand.

GENERAL MILLS
TOTAL REVENUE
$14.8 BILLION*

INTERNATIONAL
REVENUE
$2.7 BILLION

*DOES NOT INCLUDE
JOINT VENTURES
SOURCE:
FORTUNE NUMBERS

HÄAGEN-DAZS REVENUE
$500 MILLION TO $750 MILLION

This twentysomething woman really loves her ice cream—or maybe she's just between boyfriends. Long brunette hair waving over her dark awaiting eyes, dressed in red chiffon, she's home alone with only a pint of vanilla. The rituals ensue. Her expectant polished lips purse, her hands caress the pint as condensation beads around the rim. With accompanying romantic strings, she speaks in alluring British not heard since Elizabeth II put the moves on Philip once upon a time: "781 heartbeats, 403 rapid breaths, 162 blinks of an eye." Oh my, please stop! No, please continue. The ice cream is "so rich it takes longer to soften into a blissful creaminess—but the waiting only makes it sweeter." Finally she squeezes the pint to push the ice cream out the top and runs her index finger through the lusciousness, as she gently puts a dollop on her tongue and encircles it with her mouth. Then comes the tag line: "Anticipated like no other—Häagen-Dazs."

Phew! This 30-second TV spot from General Mills—titled "Sensation," but described as ice cream "foreplay" by one executive—will soon be airing around the world, the first commercial for Häagen-Dazs ever to play across national boundaries. (It will have different voice-overs to match languages—including French, Portuguese, Spanish, Mandarin, and Arabic—and may be toned down in countries like China.) There'll be print advertising as well. Despite varying regional tastes and ice cream products, it's an effort to unite the brand's themes: "indulgence," "affordable luxury," and "intense sensuality," as an internal Brand Character Statement puts it. "While Häagen-Dazs can play on this sensuality in an adult, sophisticated, playful way," the statement explains, "it does so to persuade—not to

shock." Well, the Jolly Green Giant would surely be shocked. So, too, Betty Crocker—you never saw her making any double-entendres about Betty Crocker Frosting Whipped Butter Cream. The chairman and CEO of General Mills, Ken Powell, loves the sultry Häagen-Dazs ad. "It is where the brand lives," he says.

Managing the Häagen-Dazs brand, celebrating its 50th anniversary this year, is a particular challenge for General Mills, which has owned it since acquiring Pillsbury entirely in 2001. How General Mills does so is a case study in exploiting a nonpareil niche brand, especially in the burgeoning overseas market. Powell, who oversees dozens of General Mills consumer brands including iconic Cheerios, values both the Häagen-Dazs brand itself and its international significance. "It is a jewel of a brand for us," he says.

With roots dating to the 1860s, General Mills is a low-key multinational based in Minneapolis and isn't exactly known for ad campaigns equating sex and food. Moreover, rather oddly, the Midwestern company doesn't control the product in the U.S., where about 45% of all Häagen-Dazs is sold. All of the company's Häagen-Dazs revenue, in other words, comes from overseas. Nestlé, the Swiss giant, had shared U.S. rights to Häagen-Dazs in a joint venture with Pillsbury; when General Mills bought Pillsbury, Nestlé exercised its right to operate Häagen-Dazs in the U.S. (and Canada) for 99 years—paying several hundred million dollars for the privilege. (Nestlé declined to discuss financial figures for this story.) So, in the largest market for ice cream in the world—Americans per capita eat 19.8 pounds a year—General Mills is shut out from capitalizing on the Häagen-Dazs name or running the new ad. What's more, General Mills is only the fourth-largest player in the global ice cream industry. Unilever, the British-Dutch conglomerate (which owns Häagen-Dazs's main U.S. competitor, Ben & Jerry's) and Nestlé control about a third of the market, followed by Japan's Lotte. General Mills has barely a 2% share. The fact General Mills has done so well with Häagen-Dazs internationally is testament to its own corporate creativity.

High-end, sit-down Häagen-Dazs shops in spectacular locations like the Champs-Élysées in Paris or by the Bund in Shanghai have enabled the brand to have a different aspirational image than in the U.S., where scoop-and-run shops are more of an afterthought to the impersonal retail supermarket and convenience-store business. In aisle 29 you buy a pint of Rum Raisin and move on to eggs and OJ. The Häagen-Dazs shops abroad sell more than scoops. There's ice cream sushi in China, ice cream *teppanyaki* appetizers in Japan, and a handmade Limited Edition $65 Iceberg Glazed White-Chocolate Holiday Cake in Paris only. Häagen-Dazs shops introduce many locals to the product, but the shops, too, aim to lure you into a mindset, much as Starbucks says $5 buys you a lot more than coffee. It's the reason, for example, Häagen-Dazs is the official ice cream at Wimbledon and the French Open and for all performances at the Royal Albert Hall in London.

Shops bring in less than a fifth of General Mills' Häagen-Dazs revenue but nonetheless are "the physical embodiment of the brand," according to the brand statement. They "provide an ideal environment in which to experience a unique Häagen-Dazs moment." As such moments can cost $79 for a four-person ice cream fondue in France—dip your gorgeous array of multicolored ice cream balls in warm chocolate sauce, and eat before they melt!—they're also a sweet way to cash in. They represent a very different M.O. for Häagen-Dazs than Nestlé's in the U.S.

Any U.S. company knows international is where opportunity rests. General Mills, No. 166 on the *Fortune* 500 and the third-largest domestic food company (behind Kraft and PepsiCo), had revenues of $14.8 billion last year ($16 billion including revenue from joint ventures), with about 18% coming from international sales. Those sales are about five times what they were in pre-Pillsbury days and have risen an average of roughly 8% a year since 2006. The business consists chiefly of four product groups: cereals (in partnership with Nestlé); snacks (like Nature Valley bars); convenience meals (like Old El Paso and Wanchai Ferry); and Häagen-Dazs. Last quarter alone, earnings rose 18% primarily because of sales abroad. Global Häagen-Dazs sales, in 81 countries, are up 11% for the 2011 fiscal year to date, almost double the growth rate for all General Mills international brands.

Although Häagen-Dazs brings in only half to three-quarters of a billion dollars in sales (the company doesn't disclose the exact figure)—a fraction of General Mills' overall take—it's a vital part of the international business. In China alone, Häagen-Dazs last year brought in revenue of about $100 million. In the last three years there, Häagen-Dazs has grown at an annualized rate of 21%. Revenue in France was about $80 million, and in Britain about half that—both countries with single-digit rates of growth.

Yet numbers don't tell the complete story. As a "superpremium" product, Häagen-Dazs has among the highest profit margins in the company. Just as important, in both emerging and developed markets the brand is a symbol of prestige. In China, for example, Häagen-Dazs products like store-bought "mooncakes" during Mid-Autumn Festival are prized gifts. Some couples in China order Häagen-Dazs wedding cakes costing as much as $2,000.

In a global economy, in which brands now transcend cultures, Häagen-Dazs considers its competition less Ben & Jerry's than Louis Vuitton. General Mills can't claim that about Old El Paso Refried Beans. "If our mindset is competing in ice cream, we fail because we're charging two to three times what others are charging," says David Clark, the vice president and brand steward for Häagen-Dazs worldwide. His is a brand-new position at General Mills headquarters, designed to better coordinate marketing. His father used to run the old Eskimo Pie company in Richmond. While General Mills is a conservative operation with homespun principles, Clark still has to keep his freezer stash of Häagen-Dazs sampling products under double lock and key behind an unmarked door. (It's W3-34 if you're stopping by.) "What consumers value," Clark says, "is the experience we deliver—the 'for me' experience at home or the 'for us' experience at a shop."

Ice cream is a food category worth $74 billion annually worldwide. It's highly fragmented. But Häagen-Dazs stands out at the premium end. "It's highly differentiated, beautifully positioned across markets—and with lots of growth opportunities," says the 57-year-old Powell, who's worked at General Mills three decades and made his name as a top executive abroad. (He met his future wife in college when he ran Harvard Student Agencies, which puts out the venerable Let's Go travel guides; she went Europe.) "We can do green tea in Asia, we can do different versions of flavors in Europe—Häagen-Dazs works everywhere."

Its very name is an exercise in contrivance. "Häagen-Dazs" means nothing. Reuben Mattus, a 48-year-old Polish-American entrepreneur, came up with it with his wife in 1961. Having served for years in the fading ice cream business of his widowed mother—he first peddled ice cream pops from a horse-drawn wagon in the streets of the Bronx—Mattus now wanted to go his own way, with a superpremium brand targeted at adults rather than children. And he intended to charge double or more what ordinary ice cream cost. While other manufacturers battled it out at the low end of an existing industry, Mattus intended to create demand for a nonexistent category.

His dense product was made with butterfat and only real ingredients like eggs and fruit, in contrast to the artificial flavor and bulking agents found in cheaper brands of ice cream. Unlike conventional fare, Mattus's contained little air, or, in the parlance of the trade, "overrun." His pint actually weighed more. It also was intended to be kept at a lower temperature than other ice cream (–23° F), the better to make it firmer and slower to melt—and someday make TV models have to wait for it to soften into a blissful creaminess.

"Häagen-Dazs," Mattus thought, conferred foreign cachet and evoked the purity of Scandinavian milkmaids. (Never mind the ice cream there wasn't very good.) Early Häagen-Dazs cartons included a map of Denmark, even though the contents were surely made in the U.S.; the umlaut over the first "a" was his idea—even though Danish knows no such usage. When the product was introduced in France, the French couldn't pronounce it. (Twenty years later similarly faux-Scandinavian Frusen Glädjé came on the market, sold in celebrated, strange white plastic tubs. Although Häagen-Dazs sued for deceptive trade practices, a federal court laughed it off, since Häagen-Dazs was engaged in similar gamesmanship. Frusen Glädjé still disappeared after barely more than a decade.)

The Häagen-Dazs store on the Champs Élysées in Paris takes in $9.5 million annually and sells as many as 15,000 scoops in a day

Mattus started with only vanilla, chocolate, and coffee. He bought vanilla beans from Madagascar and chocolate from Belgium. The business grew slowly, with Häagen-Dazs available only at gourmet markets in Manhattan and in shops near ice-cream consumption zones like U.S. college towns. In the 1970s national distribution expanded to major supermarket chains and franchised scoop shops coast to coast. Mattus sold the company for $70 million to Pillsbury in 1983.

That year the first international shops opened—in Hong Kong and Singapore. Two years later Germany and Britain got the first European shops. Today the distinctive Häagen-Dazs logo—black letters against a white background, with gold trim—appears in 700 or so shops outside the U.S. and Canada. China has the most, with 112. Then come Spain, France, Mexico, and Japan. There are shops in Saudi Arabia, Israel, Malaysia, Morocco, Turkey, Kuwait, Brazil, and Costa Rica—and a new one in New Delhi. Says Chris O'Leary, COO of General Mills' international division: "It's our most important single brand outside the United States." Remarkably, virtually all of it for General Mills' foreign markets outside Japan is made in a single French plant—in the town of Arras. Packages say MADE IN

FRANCE, which adds status, particularly for the Chinese, who might be forgiven for wondering why a "Scandinavian" product is manufactured in the countryside outside Paris.

It is a great thoroughfare of the world. In the 8th arrondissement of Paris, from the Arc de Triomphe in the west to the Place de la Concorde in the east, the Champs-Élysées has history, energy, commerce—and, amid the stores and bistros, the biggest Häagen-Dazs shop anywhere. Only 40 shops overseas are considered flagships—in places like Leicester Square in London, Teatro Calderón in Madrid, and City Centre in Dubai. Of those highly prominent shops, the late-night Champs-Élysées is No. 1 in sales.

Opened in 1997, it takes in $9.5 million annually and on a single summer day can sell 15,000 scoops, which doesn't include cappuccinos, sodas, or any of the $16 Nutty Caramel Semi-Freddo ("layers of Dulce de Leche and Pralines & Cream, caramelized hazelnuts, and butterscotch sauce on a base of ladyfingers—for one person"; please declare your extra weight at customs). That $9.5 million is as much as 25 times that of a small Häagen-Dazs shop elsewhere in Paris. As in many countries, of Häagen-Dazs's roughly $80 million in annual revenue in France, about a third comes from shops. The rest comes from sales of pints and mini-cups in such large supermarkets as Carrefour, as well as from distribution partnerships with the likes of Air France, the National Opera of Paris, and various hotel chains ("Hello, room service?").

The *raison d'être* of the glass-fronted Champs-Élysées shop is the 200-seat sidewalk café along the avenue; from here you can watch up close as eight lanes of Parisians drive like Bostonians. There are burgundy Häagen-Dazs-logoed umbrellas and, of course, haughty *serveurs*. On a sunny spring afternoon, I'm here for *Fortune* conducting intensive research. I, of course, fail to order the correct bottled water—to go with my Banana Caramel Crêpe. *Mon Dieu!* When the weather's good, many of the shop's patrons, a million a year, will spend 45 minutes on a festive dessert—and drop $30 a head. Inside is a traditional scoop operation—with lines out the door some evenings; Macadamia Nut Brittle is most popular. On the second floor is a dining area—and above that, the "ice bäar," a fluorescent-lit purple VIP and party space, complete with booze, bouncers, and some ice cream too.

While cash flow's terrific, it's the strategic benefit of the shop that's key. It's about brand awareness and image. "We provide an indulgent experience," says Olivier Faujour, the new president of General Mills France. "But in France the competition is broad if you talk indulgence, where people are very demanding." (Faujour is a great marketing man. At one of Paris's hot new restaurants, he urged me to order the steak tartare. I did. Then he got fish, cooked.) "There is a mystique about this particular Häagen-Dazs shop," says Isabelle Moynier, the marketing director of General Mills France. It's where Rafael Nadal came in every night a few years ago during the French Open to order a triple scoop of Cookies & Cream. He won.

For all the macadamia nut brittle of Paris, though, it is in an emerging market like China where General Mills most salivates.

It is here that every Häagen-Dazs executive says the potential of the brand lies. General Mills says it expects sales in China, with its population of 1.3 billion and ascending middle class, to triple and to account for fully half its international growth over the next five years. Last year Häagen-Dazs's revenue was a third of General Mills' total in China—but half its profit there. Understanding the inimitability of Chinese culture—you're not in Paris anymore—is essential to Häagen-Dazs's mission.

The brand arrived only 15 years ago, yet China is already its No. 2 foreign market, behind only Japan. Unlike in other countries, about 80% of Häagen-Dazs revenue in China comes from shops. That's because grocery stores typically stop carrying most ice cream during winter, when demand wanes. Freezer space in Chinese homes is also limited, and refrigeration in stores isn't up to Häagen-Dazs's chilly standards—so much so that it has installed 5,000 of its own freezers, at $15,000 apiece, around the country.

So Häagen-Dazs for the moment is a shops-driven business, all the more so during the lunar year when the mooncakes come out. No less than 28% of Häagen-Dazs's China revenue is from mooncakes, according to Gary Chu, the company's Rutgers-trained president of Greater China. As the business matures, retail will grow. "You start in the shops to build a brand image," says CEO Powell. "As you get traffic and people recognize the brand, you start advertising and putting the product in retail outlets."

In Shanghai's 12 flagships, you quickly learn, thank goodness, that it's not really "sushi" ice cream. Nobody's mixing bluefin tuna in with Chocolate Chip Cookie Dough. But the popular dish is an example of how Häagen-Dazs encourages what O'Leary calls "local interpretation." Costing about $11, sushi ice cream consists of four dishes served on a square lacquer plate. It's meant to look like the Japanese cuisine called *kaiseki,* which is a series of exquisitely arranged bites of fish, meat, and vegetables. At Häagen-Dazs the dishes are a fruit plate; red-bean cake; sweet red-bean soup—and three scoops of vanilla, strawberry, and green tea. The "sushi" effect is achieved by wrapping each scoop around the edge not with seaweed but with a layer of chocolate.

One of the flagships overlooks Xintiandi, a bustling dining and retail spot in the center of Shanghai. The place to be is the café upstairs, where waitresses wear berets and claret-colored dresses. Young couples linger here. It's a place to show your love. The menu has a single word on the cover: "indulgence," naturally. Taking in all the indulgence around him a few weeks ago, Chu says the target audience for Häagen-Dazs is 25-year-old women, who come to indulge themselves or have their boyfriends indulge them. They should have their wallets at the ready: Soft-serves at the nearby McDonald's costs 45¢. Here a single scoop of vanilla is seven times that.

Chu likes to recount a local newspaper story about the young woman with a boyfriend who refused to take her to a Häagen-Dazs shop because it was too expensive. Whereupon, as she told the paper, "I dumped him." Chu's eyes widen. He beams. In her he sees the future. "Now that," he says, appreciating those who appreciate the finer things in life, "is the kind of customer we want." Maybe that's her in the new TV ad.

Critical Thinking

1. How can a premium brand work in global trade?

2. Why does the concept of a premium brand go against the idea that price needs to be driven down in the global marketplace?

3. How has Häagen-Dazs become a global brand?

Fortune editor-at-large Bill Powell contributed reporting from Shanghai. He and his daughter also ate a lot of ice cream there.

Expanding Opportunity at the Base of the Pyramid

In the last decade, C. K. Prahalad and others have argued that the 4 billion people living on less than $2 a day—a group in society that wields trillions of dollars in economic power—is a major, untapped market (Prahalad, 2006). Indeed, there is mounting evidence that the world's poorest people are not only viable producers for a host of products and services, but they also are eager consumers of the basic necessities of the developed world—from mobile phones to soap to banking and insurance products.

DAVID G. ALTMAN, LYNDON REGO, AND PEG ROSS

Recognizing this opportunity, a number of multinational companies launched initiatives to explore the untapped market potential at the base of the economic pyramid (BoP). These multinationals, however, are not focused solely on developing new markets. They are becoming aware, through the efforts of some government organizations, NGOs and philanthropic organizations, that an effective way to eliminate poverty is to provide the poor with access to markets and credit, meaningful goods and services, and opportunities to enhance their skills and business practices. By exploring BoP opportunities, these companies also can have a positive impact on the lives of the poor.

Given the global financial crisis and the ever-expanding gap between the rich and the poor, we may be at the nexus of a major societal shift. A shared view is developing across diverse constituencies that the poorest of the world are a source of abundant resources rather than a societal burden. This is an ideal time to bring diverse players together to experiment with innovative approaches to pressing challenges.

This is an ideal time to bring diverse players together to experiment with innovative approaches to pressing challenges.

By joining forces, the commercial and nonprofit sectors can work together "to enable the poor, especially the poorest, to create a world without poverty" (Grameen Foundation, 2008). From this vantage we explore five lessons learned from organizations that actively are engaged in work at the base of the pyramid and the implications for human resource leaders working in these companies.

Lesson 1: The BoP Has Consumers *and* Producers

The first shift in thinking that needs to be made is how we define people at the BoP. The consumer's goal in this space is to secure affordable food, housing, health care, economic livelihood, education and other essential products and services. In pursuit of these goals, the BoP customer has a few key concerns:

1. easy access to known, needed goods at affordable prices;
2. solutions to daily life challenges; and
3. the opportunity to participate in economically productive activities.

Organizations serving the BoP market strive to accomplish these tasks:

1. generate revenue from existing products;
2. develop new products to meet new market needs; and
3. be good global citizens by using their products and expertise to help solve fundamental social problems.

To meet the needs of the BoP market, companies will need to pursue relationships with local delivery providers, social development players, entrepreneurs, government officials and potential customers.

Beyond an enormous untapped consumer market, those at the lowest levels of the global economy can be effective and viable producers, contributing real economic value to themselves and their business partners. A stunning example is the Indian dairy cooperative, Gujarat Cooperative Milk Marketing Federation (GCMMF), which operates under the brand name Amul (GCMMF, 2009). Poor rural farmers sell the daily output of their few buffaloes to the cooperative of which they are part owners. The cooperative takes care of everything else, from picking up of milk in the village to manufacturing and marketing the end products.

The scale of the business is impressive: 2.7 million producers are responsible for a daily output of more than 10 million liters of milk that accounted for more than $1.3 billion in sales in 2008. Individually, these poor producers would not have access to efficient markets, but when their production capacity is combined they are powerful—GCMMF is India's largest food products marketing organization.

It is difficult to see a group needier or more removed from our traditional notions of producers or consumers than beggars in Bangladesh. Yet micro-lender Grameen Bank saw things differently. In his Nobel Prize acceptance speech, Grameen Bank founder, Muhammad Yunus, recounts:

"Three years ago we started an exclusive programme focusing on the beggars. Loans are interest-free; they can pay whatever amount they wish, whenever they wish. We gave them the idea to carry small merchandise, such as snacks, toys or household items, when they went from house to house for begging. The idea worked. There are now 85,000 beggars in the program. About 5,000 of them have already stopped begging completely. The typical loan to a beggar is $12." (Yunus, 2006)

Lesson No. 1 teaches us that the poor of the world should not be viewed only through the lens of charity.

Lesson 2: Public/Private Partnerships Create Opportunities at the BoP

Inspired by the work of Yunus and Grameen Bank, Grameen Foundation (GF), a U.S.-based nonprofit that has supported the global microfinance industry since the mid 1990s, provides products and services that enable microfinance institutions to use both microfinance and technology to grow and reach ever greater numbers of the world's poorest.

Sometimes called "banking for the poor," microfinance gives very poor people around the world access to credit and other financial services to empower them to pull themselves out of poverty. Relying on their traditional skills, entrepreneurial instincts and hard work, microfinance clients, mostly women, use small loans (usually less than US$200) and other financial services to run small businesses. GF has developed deep business partnerships with BoP customers and organizations serving the BoP. The foundation intends to change mindsets and challenge conventional wisdom by demonstrating to the private and public sectors that these alliances can benefit all parties involved by creating meaningful self-employment opportunities that improve lives.

Wireless Reach

One example is how Qualcomm, the large telecommunications company, works in partnership with Grameen to provide phones to poor people. The initiative started in 2006 with an initial grant from Qualcomm's Wireless Reach initiative that enabled Grameen Foundation's Technology Center to test the feasibility of expanding its successful Village Phone program to Indonesia. Based on the pioneering work of the Grameen Village Phone in Bangladesh, Village Phone and Village Phone Direct extend the benefits of affordable telecommunications access in a sustainable, profitable and empowering way.

Designed to create profitable micro-franchise telecommunications businesses owned and run by poor entrepreneurs, these Village Phone Operators (VPOs) operate their businesses in rural villages where no telecommunications services previously existed. They rent the use of the phone to their community on a per-call basis. The VPOs provide affordable rates to their patrons while earning enough to repay their loans and earn profits that allow them to make investments in their children's health, nutrition and education, and in other business ventures.

In July 2008, GF, Qualcomm's Wireless Reach initiative, a local telecommunications operator and microfinance partners launched Indonesia's first Village Phone program. This program has created more than 137 new businesses in West Java and Banten, all owned and operated by women. Going forward, the partnership will focus on developing the capacity of wireless telecommunications and microfinance institutions by expanding the program to at least 1,000 new Village Phone businesses, reaching up to 500,000 poor Indonesians who currently do not have access to telecommunications services.

This collaboration has evolved into a successful public/private alliance where Qualcomm and GF have been able to combine expertise and experience to spur innovative business solutions for the poor. It also is enabling both organizations to meet their missions.

For Qualcomm, this alliance is a good fit with its Wireless Reach initiative, which supports programs and solutions that bring the benefits of 3G connectivity to developing communities globally. For GF, the relationship with Qualcomm provides a multiplier effect for the limited resources it has to invest.

Grameen-Jameel

In 2003, GF formed a unique partnership with Abdul Latif Jameel Group, a Saudi conglomerate, to support the growth and impact of microfinance across the Arab world. Poverty is an endemic problem in the region, where an estimated 75 million people live on less than $2 a day. This alliance was consolidated in 2007 to form Grameen-Jameel Pan-Arab Microfinance Limited (Grameen-Jameel), a for-profit company headquartered in Dubai, UAE. Jointly owned by GF and Bab Rizq Jameel Limited, a subsidiary of Abdul Latif Jameel Group, Grameen-Jameel is modeled after the social business enterprise concept promoted by Yunus. It reinvests all of its profits into the business rather than distributing dividends. Grameen-Jameel's vision is to reach 1 million new active microfinance clients in the Arab world by 2011 by forming strategic partnerships with microfinance institutions (MFIs) that share its values.

The partners receive a wide range of support, including financing through its $50 million guarantee fund, technical assistance, training and access to best practices resources that have been translated into Arabic. Grameen-Jameel already has reached more than 300,000 new microfinance clients through its partners in Egypt, Jordan, Lebanon, Morocco, Tunisia and Yemen. It is the first social business in the Arab world and an example of how two very different organizations, a Western nonprofit and a for-profit, privately held Saudi company, can come together for a common social good.

As these and other examples illustrate, the challenge of the customer-organization interface at the BoP is to manage relationships between the for-profit players and local organizations that will be involved in implementing the market solutions. There are many questions at the heart of these relationships:

- What profit is enough (and too much) for the for-profit partner?
- How can the impact on alleviating poverty be measured?
- How can tradeoffs between doing well (financially) and doing good (improving the lives of those at the BoP) be managed effectively when competing interests exist?
- What unintended effects, both positive and negative, occur to organizations and BoP customers when innovations are introduced?

Lesson No. 2 teaches us that, despite these questions, non-traditional partners can come together to create new opportunities for those at the BoP.

Lesson 3: The BoP Can Drive Innovation

Some organizations have begun to recognize that the BoP can be a driver of innovation. Cosmos Ignite Innovations developed a product designed to meet the need of the poor for access to lighting. The product also addresses the health and environmental problems associated with using polluting kerosene lamps. The company started by studying the problem at the grassroots. Cosmos Ignite wanted to understand the social need and what barriers existed that its solution would have to overcome.

The company's Mighty Light product uses the latest LED technology combined with solar energy and it is waterproof and shock proof. It has multiple functions, as a room light, reading light or flashlight. The light is strong enough to illuminate an entire room, holds an hour charge and is designed to last 100,000 hours, the equivalent of 30 years of daily use.

It is not difficult to imagine how lighting will change the lives of the more than 1.6 billion people without regular lighting—children can complete their school work after agricultural chores are completed, handwork can be done into the evening providing additional sources of income and families' health is improved with the elimination of kerosene lamps. Mighty Light is used effectively in India, Afghanistan, Pakistan, Cambodia, Nigeria, Kenya, Rwanda, Panama, Guyana and Colombia (Kapur, 2007).

Consider the work of Dr. Devi Shetty, a cardiac surgeon based in Bangalore, India. Shetty has pioneered a series of innovative solutions that have placed health care within the reach of many millions of people in India, regardless of their ability to pay.

One of the vexing challenges Shetty tackled was figuring out how to get quality health care to the large populations living in remote areas of the country. India, like many developing nations, has a population that lives largely in remote, rural villages. While 70 percent of the country's population resides in villages, 70 percent of the nation's doctors live in cities. As Shetty pondered this problem, he found that solutions existed in his own backyard.

Shetty tapped Bangalore's world-class information technology prowess and enlisted India's space agency, also headquartered in the city, to establish a telemedicine network, connected by satellite, between urban hospitals and villages. Patients in rural areas of India can be "seen" by specialists, aided by local paramedical staff who operate the rural clinics. Doctors prescribe treatment administered by the local representative, or request that serious cases be brought to urban centers for treatment.

The system improves access to health care for the rural poor, creates jobs in villages for the paramedical staff that runs the clinics, and maximizes urban doctors' efficiency and reach (Rego & Bhandary, 2006).

Lesson 3 reinforces the importance of viewing the BoP as a seedbed of innovation, grounded in overcoming need and necessity. Nurturing these seeds can unleash innovation in all sectors of society.

Lesson 4: Respond to Market Needs at the BoP with Design Thinking

In the past few years, the Center for Creative Leadership (CCL) has been experimenting with a number of models to make leadership development more affordable and accessible to people around the world (**http://leadbeyond.org/**). The goal of this work is to democratize and scale leadership development. As we embarked on this work, we first began by reading and analyzing the literature, writing reports and preparing scenario documents.

While our analysis was solid, our progress was quite incremental. We hired two of the top design and innovation firms in the world (IDEO and Continuum) to help us shift gears using "design thinking." Design thinking includes ethnographic data collection, brainstorming and rapid prototyping to uncover unmet customer needs and to create innovative solutions to meet these needs.

Continuum and IDEO encouraged us to immerse ourselves in the developing countries in which we wanted to work. The immersions and subsequent product experiments spanned developing and developed countries; corporate, nonprofit and government organizations; and different approaches to product design and delivery. These immersions brought to life the needs and aspirations of underserved populations and took us in directions we could not have envisioned via analysis of the detailed data alone. The deep insights we gained gave form to a spectrum of solutions that CCL is implementing to make leadership development more affordable and accessible for social-sector organizations, youth and young professionals in developed and developing countries.

The design-driven way of working has been mastered by a number of corporations and social enterprises that see emerging markets and low-income populations as prime growth markets. Nokia is an example of a multinational that has been exceptionally successful in BoP markets. It has three R&D facilities in India that have produced innovations such as a phone that operates for more than two weeks on a single charge and comes with a flashlight for those who live without access to dependable electricity. The phone also allows families and friends to share a device by maintaining as many as five separate phone books and providing controls for how much an individual user can talk or spend (Ewing, 2007).

The design-driven way of working has been mastered by a number of corporations and social enterprises that see emerging markets and low-income populations as prime growth markets.

Similarly, companies such as P&G, which generates $20 billion from developing markets, find that localizing capacity is essential to keeping costs down and leveraging local knowledge and relationships. For example, P&G products often wound up hidden under the cashier's counter in crowded retail stores, to be sold on request. By hiring local sales agents, P&G was able to build ties to store owners and better negotiate display space (Byron, 2007).

In some cases, the solutions are inspired by bringing together disparate concepts that span developing and developed worlds. For example, Dr. Govindappa Venkataswamy (or Dr. V as he is commonly known) of Aravind Eye Care in Madurai, India, was inspired by McDonald's Hamburger University. Through studying the hamburger chain's operations, he saw that low-cost, high-quality and volume could be attained through carefully managed operations. The model he created has enabled eye doctors to conduct 2,600 surgeries each year, compared to the current prevailing average of 400 operations (Miller, 2006).

BoP solutions often set improbably lofty goals that are brought to life through iterative experimentation. The One Laptop per Child Project had a three-year gestation period through which a network of hardware and software designers experimented with a variety of features and options to address key BoP limitations. The initial product specs called for a laptop that was intuitive to children, heat-proof, dust-proof, drop-proof, spill-proof, designed to work with limited power and Internet access, and priced at a fifth the price of the cheapest laptop available. The product that made it to market, named the XO, was priced closer to $200 but has accomplished many of its seemingly unrealistic objectives (Pogue, 2007).

As these examples illustrate, success in BoP markets requires the kind of empathetic and imaginative approaches that design thinking incorporates as a best practice. It also requires leveraging local talent to acquire insights, maintain relationships and trim costs. Fortunately there is no deficit of talent at the BoP, only the need to see the abundant opportunity and unlock the vast human potential that exists within it.

Lesson 5: The BoP is a Source of Employees

For most multinational corporations, success in emerging markets necessitates identifying, hiring, developing and utilizing local talent. Pantaloon, a large Indian retail giant, has had commercial success hiring employees at the BoP. They recruit and train youth from India's slums to become clerks and baristas, some of whom go on to become managers and entrepreneurs. The head of training at Pantaloon, K.C. Kurien, reports that he built the company's leadership-training program on an insight he had at a traffic intersection in Mumbai. Watching beggars work the line of cars, he noticed that those with greater social skills were more successful. If self-confidence and social skills work for beggars, he asked himself, what could they do for motivated people from the slums? Pantaloon's program has been highly successful in driving employee engagement, customer service, innovation and growth.

Along similar lines, Mobile Metrix is an on-the-ground marketing organization that works in developing countries to help public- and private-sector organizations collect grassroots data that inform product and service development for the BoP market. To obtain these data, they hire local young people (ages 16–24), provide them with training on how to use handheld computers and then send them into their communities to collect data on community needs. After products are developed, these young people also have the opportunity to be employed in marketing and distribution, benefiting both them and the organizations that now have access to hard-to-reach communities and consumers.

Another innovative organization that is bringing essential products, jobs and empowerment to disadvantaged populations is VisionSpring (formerly Scojo Foundation). VisionSpring is working to provide reading glasses to the poor; 700 million of the world's poorest suffer from presbyopia (blurry up-close vision), which undermines their ability to do many work tasks such as sewing or sorting grain. The organization's business model is to train and engage local women as "vision entrepreneurs," which in many cases leads to a doubling of their income. The company operates in more than a dozen countries, and as of 2008 had sold nearly 90,000 pairs of reading glasses and trained more than 1,000 Vision Entrepreneurs (MacMillan, 2008).

If Grameen Bank can turn beggars into successful entrepreneurs, if Pantaloon can turn slum dwellers into confident store clerks and managers, if Mobile Metrix can successfully employ youth in hard-to-reach communities to help drive product development and sales, and if VisionSpring can employ poor women to help improve the eyesight of others, consider the societal impact if thousands of organizations were to include the BoP as a source of employees.

Relevance to HR Leaders

The vast untapped market at the BoP represents a potential opportunity for organizations that find their traditional markets are becoming saturated and their profit margins are shrinking. The IMF notes that India and China—countries made up largely of poor people—are the main engines of world growth (Callen, 2007). The World Bank reports that developing countries are responsible for 40 percent of the world's economy (World Bank, 2007).

Success at the BoP requires a new orientation however. Working at the BoP requires a rejection of the notion that the poor are passive recipients of charity, incapable of being consumers or producers. It also requires innovation to create or adapt product, services and business models. This, in turn, requires new capabilities within organizations and their people.

For senior HR leaders, these new business opportunities will require developing people (and teams) who can work successfully in BoP environments and with non-profit partners. What corporations can learn from non-profits is how to work with scarce resources, create broad alliances and build movements and tap passion and unlock potential. The head of a corporation in Chile explained that young people who join the corporate sector after completing a service learning program in rural Chile are much in demand and are deemed able to think more holistically and be more persevering and resilient.

From another lens, engaging with BoP markets provides a lever for organizational transformation, increased employee engagement and stronger community relations. Employees can gain opportunities to develop their strengths and apply them in service of social as well as business goals, enhancing organizations' effectiveness as well as corporate brands. In an era of growing demands for triple-bottom-line approaches, a company that serves the BoP can be more attractive to customers and employees.

The greatest barrier to traverse is that of mindset. Mohammed Yunus likens the untapped potential of the poor, limited by the lack of opportunity, to a seed of a tree that is planted in a tiny pot. The same seed planted in the fertile ground can grow to be a great tree (Knowledge@Wharton, 2005). The potential for companies with the BoP is much the same. If planted in a small pot of opportunity they will yield little. Nurtured in a supportive corporate culture, however, the BoP represents significant growth potential for organizations and their shareholders, employees and customers. HR leaders can lead the way by helping create cultures that enable this transformation.

References

Byron, E. (2007, July 16). P&G's global target: Shelves of tiny stores. *The Wall Street Journal*, p. A1.

Callen, T. (2007, October 17). Emerging markets main engine of growth. *IMF Survey Magazine*, p. 195.

Ewing, J. (2007, May 4). First mover in mobile. *BusinessWeek*, p. 60.

Grameen Foundation. (2008). *Mission statement*. Washington, DC: Author.

Gujarat Cooperative Milk Marketing Federation (GCMMF). (2009). Retrieved March 6, 2009, from www.amul.com.

Kapur, S. (2007, August 14). Innovating for the bottom of the pyramid. *Business Standard*. Retrieved March 6, 2009, from www.business-standard.com/india/storypage.php?autono=294343.

Knowledge@Wharton. (2005). *Muhammad Yunus, banker to the world's poorest citizens, makes his case*. Retrieved April 5, 2009, from http://knowledge.wharton.upenn.edu/article.cfm?articleid=1147.

MacMillan, G. (2008). *45 social entrepreneurs who are changing the world*. Retrieved March 13, 2009, from www.fastcompany.com/social/2008/profiles/scojo-foundation.html.

Miller, S. (2006, August 5). McSurgery: A man who saved 2.4 million eyes. *The Wall Street Journal*, p. A6.

Pogue, D. (2007, October 4). Laptop with a mission widens its audience. *The New York Times*. Retrieved from www.nytimes.com/2007/10/04/technology/circuits/04pogue.html.

Prahalad, C. K. (2006). *The fortune at the bottom of the pyramid: Eradicating poverty through profits*. Upper Saddle River, NJ: Pearson.

Rego, L., & Bhandary, A. (2006). New model: A social entrepreneur changes the landscape. *Leadership in Action*, 26(1), 8–11.

Yunus, M. (2006). Nobel Lecture, Oslo, December 10, 2006. Retrieved February 14, 2009, from http://nobelprize.org/nobel_prizes/peace/laureates/2006/yunus-lecture-en.html.

Critical Thinking

1. Why are the world's poor an attractive market?
2. How would you create a marketing plan to sell to the world's poor?
3. How big is the market for the world's poor?

DAVID G. ALTMAN, PhD, is executive vice president, Research, Innovation and Product Development at the Center for Creative Leadership (CCL), a global non-profit organization. Prior to joining CCL, he spent 20 years as a public health researcher, advocate and professor.

LYNDON REGO, MBA, is director, Innovation Incubator at the Center for Creative Leadership, where he helps steer a broad initiative to extend leadership development to underserved populations across the world.

PEG ROSS is director of the Human Capital Center at Grameen Foundation, where she helps microfinance institutions strengthen their people practices and align them with business strategy. She has held corporate HR leadership positions in a variety of industries and obtained her master's degree in Organization Development from Loyola University of Chicago.

From *HRPS People & Strategy*, vol. 32, issue 2, June 2009, pp. 47–51. Copyright © 2009 by Human Resource Planning Society. All rights reserved. Reprinted by permission. www.hrps.org.

Hailun Piano and the Quest for Quality

Hindered in the domestic Chinese market by peculiar tax laws, Hailun was forced to build a better product or perish. This tough lesson has served the company well as it expands its global presence.

On the Saturday before the opening of the Music China Fair in Shanghai, a multinational team of piano designers is crowded around a hand-carved piano at the Hailun Piano factory in Ningbo, 175 miles to the south. The special edition concert grand with its images of Chinese landscapes carved in rosewood will be the centerpiece of Hailun's exhibit at the show. Voicing specialist Sibin Zlatkovic is making his final adjustments to its exposed strings while the rest of the team looks on. "We did this kind of work at Bösendorfer," says Basilios Strmec, an Austrian who is now president of Hailun USA. "This is gorgeous, all hand-carved. It took 19 months to build."

The show piece piano represents a first step into the luxury market for Hailun, whose mid-priced pianos have taken hold throughout North America and Europe as well in as in the domestic Chinese market. Last year the brand received worldwide exposure in the form of a red lacquered grand piano built for ceremonies in the run-up to the Beijing Olympic Games.

Behind the scenes, Hailun's team of artistic and technical experts is as international as its aspirations. In China for the upcoming trade show, along with Strmec, are American Frank Emerson, who designed pianos for Baldwin and later for Mason & Hamlin, is a recipient of the Friendship Medal, the highest honor presented by the Chinese government to foreigners who have made outstanding contributions to China's economic and social progress. Veletzky, the owner of Austrian piano maker Wendl & Lung, is Hailun's senior technical advisor and directs the distribution of Hailun in the European market. Zlatkovic, also of Wendl & Lung, is Hailun's director of voicing and tuning and instructor to the company's team of voicers at the factory in Ningbo.

In about two days the whole team will make the road trip to Music China over the newly constructed Hangzhou Bay Bridge, which has reduced the travel time between Ningbo and Shanghai from a circuitous four hours to a straight shot of two-and-a-half. It's just one example of a rapid modernization that touches everything from China's infrastructure to its economy and the lifestyle of its people.

Middle aged Chinese people can remember being taught as children about the evils of capitalism, Western culture, and all of its trappings, including classical music. Today, knowledge and appreciation of classical music is regarded as a mark of sophistication. As in Western countries, ownership of a high-caliber piano—even among those who don't play—is considered a status symbol. "Twenty or 25 years ago, there probably wasn't a piano in the city of Ningbo," says Emerson. "And now we're building them by the hundreds."

The explosion of China's middle class, usually estimated between 200 and 300 million, has made China the fastest-growing market for Hailun, whose domestic sales have risen 40% in two years. Moreover, market research shows that Chinese people, particularly the younger generation, aren't just able to buy more things—they have higher expectations for the products they purchase than ever before. "There's a different turn in Chinese perceptions and values," says Strmec. "They have awakened to the idea of quality."

The history of the Hailun Piano Company will illustrate how circumstances pushed the company to market its pianos on quality rather than price. Founder Hailun Chen, who came from a background in tool manufacturing, started the company in 1987 as a parts manufacturer for other piano makers. When Hailun shifted into piano production in 2002, it built its first pianos for export only to avoid the tax penalty imposed by the Chinese government on private businesses competing with government-owned companies in the Chinese domestic market. Later the company did introduce its pianos to the domestic market, but the embedded cost of the tax would make it impossible to compete with other Chinese-made pianos on price alone. "Hailun had to build a higher-quality piano to justify the higher price," says Emerson. "This gave them even more incentive to produce the best product they could."

Once established as a piano maker, Hailun dedicated a $44 million capital outlay capital outlay toward equipping its 430,000-square-foot factory with custom-designed CNC machinery. A rigorous apprenticeship program was established, recruiting 40 engineering students per year from the Ningbo Institute of Technology. Only the top three are offered permanent jobs. All Hailun workers are trained for at least one year—four years for those involved in tuning and voicing—before being allowed to work on pianos headed for the market. They are paid 25% more than the average Chinese factory worker. "We want to ensure that what we send out is a product of integrity, that there's quality behind it," says Strmec.

Four years ago, Strmec was vice president for U.S. marketing and sales for Bösendorfer, whose exclusive reputation is built on its annual production of 400 and retail prices of $120,000 and more. Hailun, with its annual production of 8,000 and typical price points between $10,000 and $20,000, demands a different mindset, but some of the principles still apply.

"Bösendorfer continues to survive and command prices of $120,000 and $130,000 because they do not cut corners," says Strmec. "We can't compromise on little things to make our pianos two dollars cheaper. If you're trained in the mentality that people value quality, you'll have the courage to go out on the market and say, 'This is quality—try it and see for yourself,' instead of apologizing for the price."

> We can't compromise on little things to make our pianos two dollars cheaper. People value quality. You need the courage to say, 'This is quality—try it and see for yourself,' instead of apologizing for the price.

Indicating a soundboard in production on the factory floor, he says, "Do you see the grain of the wood, how the rings are close together? A good soundboard has very close-together rings—that means the wood has grown very slowly and has greater resonance." Later, in a room of finished pianos due for transport to the Music China Fair, he points out the characteristic texture of the genuine ebony keys on one of Hailun's higher-end grands. "It's a little bit rougher; it gives the pianist a better grip," he says.

On this trip to the factory in Ningbo, Hailun's design team is refining its newest high-end feature, the inclusion of a sostenuto pedal on two upright models, the HU 6 and HU 7, due to be presented at the winter NAMM show. By incorporating the sostenuto, considered a feature for the professional market, the designers aim to match the range of expression found in a fine European instrument. "It's the mark of a high-end piano," says Emerson. "If you want to be counted among that class of piano, you have to have it."

As a Chinese manufacturer, Hailun faces the preconceptions of consumers in the West, where Chinese products sometimes carry associations with product recalls and quality-control snafus. Even within the music products industry, Hailun fights the perception that the lower cost of Chinese-made products indicates shoddy workmanship more than the lower cost of doing business in China. Zlatkovic counters, "If I were to build the same piano in Boston or Vienna, it would have to cost three to four times more because of the cost of the electricity, the real estate, the insurance, etc. Everything would be more expensive. By building it in China, I can sell it as a less expensive piano, but that doesn't make it a lower-quality piano."

Strmec says, "It's a shame that the word 'Chinese' should be associated with poor quality. We want to change that perception to reflect the tremendous history of this country and the integrity behind our product."

Considering, incidentally, the range of multinational influences behind Hailun pianos, it's fair to pose the question of whether they should be considered Chinese instruments at all.

"What is the word President Obama used to describe himself during the election?" says Strmec. "Our pianos are mutts. On the Chinese side they reflect considerable ingenuity and investment in both machinery and people. But the genius behind them is also American, is Austrian, is French—it's the best ideas coming together."

> Our pianos are mutts. On the Chinese side they reflect considerable investment in machinery and people. But the genius behind them is also American, Austrian, French—it's the best ideas come together.

A Family Business

Hailun personnel say the company is very much a family business. Several members of the upper level management are related to Hailun Chen, including his cousin May Wang, who is vice president of sales to the U.S. market and also serves as primary translator among the Chinese personnel and visiting experts from the Europe and the U.S. But those who have worked there for any length of time say the sense of family extends to the entire team—even foreigners—to a degree that's unusual for China, where close friendships and casual socializing among colleagues is less common than in the U.S. For lunch at the factory, Hailun executives and visiting designers eat family style at a round table, where at least three languages are often spoken at once but communication proceeds with surprising fluency. After a round of cards with a group of Hailun factory employees, Strmec says, "At what other company would a guy who works in the factory be allowed to win money from the president of the U.S. branch of the company? Other companies try to create that camaraderie, but they keep it at arm's length. There's none of that here. There is a unique skill that Mr. Chen brings to this company that has nothing to do with building pianos and everything to do with building positive international relationships."

The Voice of the Piano

Because there's no global consensus on what a piano ought to sound like, Hailun builds and voices its various models according to the tastes of the markets they're destined for. Zlatkovic can deliver a scholarly synopsis of voicing preferences around the world, from the delicate tone favored by the Europeans to the bolder tastes of the Americans. Time, too, has altered overall norms in voicing. Zlatkovic will tell you that trends in piano voicing, which ran to the warm and mellow during the 1920s and '30s and shifted to favor a harsher, stronger sound through the latter part of the 20th century, have come full circle in the early part of the 21st century. "If you transported a pianist from 30 years ago and had him play on one of the mellower-sounding pianos we're voicing today, he wouldn't like it because he wouldn't think it sounded aggressive enough," says Zlatkovic.

More an art than a science, voicing is said to be one of the most difficult concepts to impart to students of the trade. Compounding the challenge for Zlatkovic and his trainees is the lost knowledge that comes from China's long prohibition on Western music and culture. "What I can't give my voicing students is my experience of all the other instruments I have in my mental library," says Zlatkovic. "They have the talent, but they don't have the same cultural reference point as we have in the West. That's why they welcome the expertise we can bring them from the U.S. and Europe, where the piano tradition has existed for so long."

The European Strategy

With a 300-year legacy in piano building, the European markets present special challenges for a new, foreign-made piano. Hailun's European strategy relies heavily on its association with Wendl & Lung, the century-old Viennese piano manufacturer now owned by Peter Veletzky. Veletzky, who at the age of 22 became Austria's youngest master piano builder, represents the fourth generation of his family to head the company. Since forming a partnership with Hailun in 2003, Veletzky has overseen the distribution of Hailun pianos in Europe, where they are sold under the Wendl & Lung name. "Peter's participation has created a lot of credibility for us, both in Europe and in other parts of the world," says Strmec.

In Europe, as in North America, the repercussions of the economic crisis have created an opening for a mid-priced piano modeled after the European tradition in fine piano making. "With our products that offer a lot of value at a very modest price, we are better positioned in this economic climate than many European manufacturers," says Veletzky. "I say that with both a smile and a tear: a smile, because we've done well in Europe, very well, and a tear for the European piano industry, which in large part is suffering."

The Future of Hailun Piano

After the Music China Fair, Hailun's hand-carved concert grand, called Dreams of the East, sold to a Chinese businessman for approximately $347,000. Following the blockbuster sale, Hailun plans tentatively to craft a similar piano for the 2011 winter NAMM show, and eventually to build up to 50 such instruments each year for the luxury market. But within its primary mid-priced niche, Hailun maintains its focus on building what many say is the missing piece for some of China's most promising companies: a brand that commands recognition and respect in the West. A sleek new Hailun Piano website, tailored to the U.S. market, was scheduled to launch around the first of the year. On other fronts, Hailun is pursuing artist endorsements to match faces and sounds with the Hailun name. "Ultimately, Hailun wants to serve the stages of concert halls and recording studios with instruments worthy of musicians and music connoisseurs of every musical persuasion," says Strmec. "My conviction is that a brand constitutes a promise that is consistently fulfilled to its customers. For Hailun to develop into a brand that follows through on that promise would be my greatest source of pride."

Critical Thinking

1. Why is quality important to Hailun Piano?
2. Why is it more difficult for Hailun Piano to sell in its own market than overseas?
3. Why is it that the company was originally focused on exporting rather than its domestic market?

From *Music Trades*, February 2010, pp. 126–128, 130, 132–133. Copyright © 2010 by Music Trades Corporation. Reprinted by permission.

Distant Dilemmas

Before sending executives on assignments in countries with questionable business practices, HR professionals must help prepare them for the ethical predicaments that may await them there.

MARK MCGRAW

No one is naïve enough to think that bribery, kickbacks and other corrupt business practices don't exist here in the United States. But it's also understood that such practices are, at best, unethical and, at worst, illegal—not to mention potentially costly for companies caught engaging in them.

But in some countries, bribes, illegal payments and other underhanded activities are simply an accepted part of doing business. And if recent statistics are any indication, the current recession is only compounding the problem.

According to a recent Ernst & Young survey, half of the 2,246 respondents in major countries across Europe said they felt that one or more types of unethical business behaviors was acceptable, including 25 percent who thought it fine to give a cash bribe to win work. By country, that figure rose as high as 38 percent in Spain, 43 percent in the Czech Republic and 53 percent in Turkey.

In the same survey by the New York-based business and financial advisory firm, more than half of respondents said they expected corporate fraud to increase over the next few years, with 54 percent of participants from Western Europe and 55 percent from Central and Eastern Europe expressing the same sentiment.

While questionable business practices may become more accepted by workers in some places, governments in revenue-starved countries are focusing more closely than ever on violations of international anti-corruption laws and the accompanying fines that can be doled out.

Expatriates can easily, even unwittingly, violate such laws, especially when they are relocated to a country awash in corruption. Corporate counsel may be aware of this growing concern, but experts say HR must take on an equally large role in preparing expatriates for the vastly different business environments they may find themselves in overseas.

Hard Lessons

Some companies have discovered the hard way that the cost of an expatriate's unethical behavior can be steep. Consider Lucent Technologies, for example, the former telecommunications giant that merged with Alcatel to become Alcatel-Lucent, based in Murray Hill, N.J., in 2006.

In 2004, the company fired four China-based executives for alleged violations of the Foreign Corrupt Practices Act. No arrests were made, but, as part of an intercession agreement reached with the United States Department of Justice in December 2007 the company agreed to pay $2.5 million in civil penalties and fines to settle the allegations—which included making payments to Chinese government officials to travel to the United States and elsewhere for sightseeing and entertainment between 2000 and 2003.

According to a suit filed in the United States District Court for the District of Columbia, the Securities and Exchange Commission alleged that Lucent spent upwards of $10 million in travel and entertainment expenses for about 1,000 employees of state-owned or state-controlled telecommunications businesses in China that were prospective or existing Lucent customers. The suit alleged that the foreign officials spent little or no time actually visiting Lucent facilities, and that the company improperly recorded the expenses in its corporate books.

In December of last year, Siemens paid $1.6 billion—the largest fine for bribery in modern corporate history, according to *The New York Times*—in a settlement with the Justice Department and the Securities and Exchange Commission. As part of the settlement, Siemens also pleaded guilty to violating accounting provisions of the FCPA. The agreement came two years after midlevel executive Reinhard Siekaczek was arrested for his role in overseeing "an annual bribery budget of about $40 million to $50 million" to make payments to well-placed officials in countries such as Vietnam, Venezuela, Italy and Israel, according to the *Times*.

The payments, Siekaczek told the paper, were "vital to maintaining the competitiveness of Siemens overseas."

"It was about keeping the business unit alive," he said, "and not jeopardizing thousands of jobs overnight."

Granted, Siekaczek's intentions, at least in his mind, may have simply been to keep the business afloat in trying times, by whatever means necessary. Regardless, say experts consulted for this story, it should be clear to expatriates that bribery and other corrupt practices are unacceptable, regardless of the setting or circumstances.

HR must play a key role in hammering that message home, says Stewart Black, associate dean of executive development programs at INSEAD, an international graduate business school with North American offices in New York.

"If you make the situation difficult enough, even 'ethical people' will make bad choices."

—STEWART BLACK, INSEAD

"If you make the situation difficult enough, even 'ethical people' will make bad choices," says Black, who is also an affiliate professor of organization behavior at INSEAD, and the executive director of the INSEAD Center for Human Resources in Singapore. "Part of HR's role is to highlight the human, social [and] relational side of a situation. The more demanding the situation, the more careful the selection [of the employee to handle it] and the more intensive the training needs to be."

The best companies decrease the likelihood of potential expats making "bad choices" in foreign countries by looking beyond their technical skills when evaluating them for overseas assignments, says William Sheridan, vice president of international human resource services at the New York office of the National Foreign Trade Council.

"Smarter companies," he says, "don't rely solely on an employee's performance record in [his or her] home country—or the employee's manager's recommendation alone—but are aware that working in a foreign setting is different, and that social skills are as important as accumulated business skills, perhaps even more important.

"Adaptability to new situations is critical," Sheridan says. "Often, the more adaptable employee will outperform a colleague who had higher job-performance ratings in the home country."

Training, Training, Training

Selecting an executive with a consistent moral compass and an ability to adjust is a good start to ensuring ethical behavior overseas.

Pinpointing such employees requires some legwork on HR's part, says William Devaney, co-chair of the Foreign Corrupt Practices Act and Anti-Corruption Group at Washington-based business law firm Venable.

"Look at their reviews, speak to their supervisors and speak to the employees themselves," Devaney says. "You want to try to identify the employee who will not take the expedient route over the ethical when faced with the challenge of dealing with corrupt bureaucracies."

But, moreover, HR should be heavily involved in extensive training for these employees about to go abroad, experts say.

First and foremost, HR must work closely with corporate counsel to ensure that expatriates understand the implications of the Foreign Corrupt Practices Act and other anti-corruption measures, Devaney says.

The U.S. employee needs to understand that the FCPA, which addresses accounting-transparency requirements under the Securities Exchange Act and contains anti-bribery provisions, applies to individuals specifically, even when working abroad and/or working for a non-U.S. company or a non-U.S. affiliate, he adds.

Such training should be conducted in person at least once a year, and should be overseen "by in-house counsel well-versed in the FCPA or outside counsel [with expertise on] the FCPA," Devaney says. "That way, the employees can discuss real-life [events] and walk through various situations that might present themselves [in other countries]. If live training is not possible, there are Internet training programs available that can be bolstered by training programs that management conducts."

Executives overseas should be made aware they have a responsibility beyond themselves, too.

"The [executive] also needs to understand that he, as well as the company, is responsible for the company's agents in the foreign country," Devaney says. "The employee must ensure that the local agents or contractors he is dealing with are not making corrupt payments."

"This can be difficult in areas of the world where such payments are the norm," he says. "But turning a blind eye to the issue can cost the company untold millions in fines and expose the employee to criminal prosecution."

HR, along with the general counsel's office, must also ensure "there is worldwide training, so that anti-corruption is a worldwide initiative and not something viewed internally as stopping at the U.S. border," he says.

Most companies have a code of conduct that employees must be in compliance with wherever they do business, says Achim Mossmann, managing director of global mobility advisory services in KPMG International Executive Services practice, based in New York.

However, some countries' practices may pose a dilemma to expatriates, he says.

"For example, in some countries, gift-giving is seen as an acceptable way to 'move a transaction along.' Training can help employees understand what specific business practices to expect in certain countries and what behavior is acceptable in certain situations," he says.

"Role playing, training scenarios and case studies can help employees understand acceptable gift-giving—a $30 bottle of wine, perhaps—versus what could be characterized as bribery or corruption—a $1,000 cash payment."

HR should play a sizable role in orchestrating local and global training for expatriates, Mossman says. Setting up a companywide program is typically done with help from outside vendors, he says, "to assist with the development and implementation of this type of training."

When searching for a vendor to lead expat training, HR should develop a general outline explaining the type of training they would like to provide, issue a request for proposal and select a vendor capable of developing the necessary content and materials, he adds.

The actual training can happen in two ways, Mossman says. The vendor can conduct in-person training or develop a

Web-based training module. Or, after developing the program, the vendor "trains the trainer," in many cases an HR professional, who then delivers the training.

"Many organizations like this model, because it allows them to hire someone from the outside with the expertise to develop the training content and materials, and then have an in-house HR professional who knows the organization conduct the training, which helps from a credibility standpoint."

Thoroughly documenting that expatriates have received such training will help distance the company from the unscrupulous actions of a rogue employee, says Mossman, who advises HR executives on managing international-assignment programs.

"In these scenarios, there are always two potential culprits—the employee and the employer," he says. "The employer will need to show an investigating authority that it provided the employee with sufficient information and training, as a first line of defense. Appropriate documentation can demonstrate that the employer has made sufficient efforts to ensure that the employee has received adequate training and information."

Monitoring the Situation

There are clearly questions to answer and scenarios to consider before sending an executive on assignment to a country with corrupt business practices. But the company's—and the HR executive's—job isn't over once the expatriate gets on the plane.

HR executives should stay in frequent contact with the recently transferred executive, Devaney says, and establish a support system that offers expatriates guidance in the event that ethical quandaries arise.

"The company should have a hotline, where any anti-corruption questions or issues can be openly and, if necessary, anonymously discussed," he says. "If the HR executive sees any problems in the anti-corruption area, he or she should notify the general counsel's office immediately."

"Without a sounding board," Black adds, "the expat is on his or her own. HR needs to be close enough to the employee that he or she feels comfortable enough to discuss questionable situations," he says, "without the immediate pressures of business results that are often implicitly or explicitly there in discussions of the same issue with line executives."

The careful selection and appropriate training of expatriates is lacking at many companies, but even when both are done well, HR must still help keep a close eye on operations in countries with questionable business ethics, says Black.

"To not have HR as a sounding board in a knowingly corrupt country is like deciding not to buy flood insurance when you are in an established flood plain," he says.

Ultimately, he says, that decision could cost an organization millions of dollars, not to mention destroy the good will it has worked hard to create among its customers and public.

"Trust me," Black says, "the *International Herald Tribune* does not care that the situation was almost impossible. They only care that an ethical lapse makes for a great story."

"It takes decades to build up public trust and credibility, and it can take only minutes for it to go up in a toxic cloud," he adds.

Critical Thinking

1. Why are corrupt practices in other countries a problem for American corporations?
2. Are corrupt practices on the rise?
3. Why are they on the rise?
4. How can American executives deal with this problem?

From *Human Resource Executive*, January 2010. Copyright © 2010 by Human Resource Executive. Reprinted by permission of LRP Publications.

The Impact of Globalization on Income and Employment: The Downside of Integrating Markets

Michael Spence

Globalization is the process by which markets integrate worldwide. Over the past 60 years, it has accelerated steadily as new technologies and management expertise have reduced transportation and transaction costs and as tariffs and other man-made barriers to international trade have been lowered. The impact has been stunning. More and more developing countries have been experiencing sustained growth rates of 7–10 percent; 13 countries, including China, have grown by more than 7 percent per year for 25 years or more. Although this was unclear at the outset, the world now finds itself just past the midpoint in a century-long process in which income levels in developing countries have been converging toward those in developed countries. Now, the emerging economies' impact on the global economy and the advanced economies is rising rapidly. Until about a decade ago, the effects of globalization on the distribution of wealth and jobs were largely benign. On average, advanced economies were growing at a respectable rate of 2.5 percent, and in most of them, the breadth and variety of employment opportunities at various levels of education seemed to be increasing. With external help, even the countries ravaged by World War II recovered. Imported goods became cheaper as emerging markets engaged with the global economy, benefiting consumers in both developed and developing countries.

But as the developing countries became larger and richer, their economic structures changed in response to the forces of comparative advantage: they moved up the value-added chain. Now, developing countries increasingly produce the kind of high-value-added components that 30 years ago were the exclusive purview of advanced economies. This climb is a permanent, irreversible change. With China and India—which together account for almost 40 percent of the world's population—resolutely moving up this ladder, structural economic changes in emerging countries will only have more impact on the rest of the world in the future.

By relocating some parts of international supply chains, globalization has been affecting the price of goods, job patterns, and wages almost everywhere. It is changing the structure of individual economies in ways that affect different groups within those countries differently. In the advanced economies, it is redistributing employment opportunities and incomes.

For most of the postwar period, U.S. policymakers assumed that growth and employment went hand in hand, and the U.S. economy's performance largely confirmed that assumption. But the structural evolution of the global economy today and its effects on the U.S. economy mean that, for the first time, growth and employment in the United States are starting to diverge. The major emerging economies are becoming more competitive in areas in which the U.S. economy has historically been dominant, such as the design and manufacture of semiconductors, pharmaceuticals, and information technology services. At the same time, many job opportunities in the United States are shifting away from the sectors that are experiencing the most growth and to those that are experiencing less. The result is growing disparities in income and employment across the U.S. economy, with highly educated workers enjoying more opportunities and workers with less education facing declining employment prospects and stagnant incomes. The U.S. government must urgently develop a long-term policy to address these distributional effects and their structural underpinnings and restore competitiveness and growth to the U.S. economy.

Jobless in the U.S.

Between 1990 and 2008, the number of employed workers in the United States grew from about 122 million to about 149 million. Of the roughly 27 million jobs created during that period, 98 percent were in the so-called nontradable sector of the economy, the sector that produces goods and services that must be consumed domestically. The largest employers in the U.S. nontradable sector were the government (with 22 million jobs in 2008) and the health-care industry (with 16 million jobs in 2008). Together, the two industries created ten million new jobs between 1990 and 2008, or just under 40 percent of total additions. (The retail, construction, and hotel and restaurant industries also contributed significantly to job growth.) Meanwhile, employment barely grew in the tradable sector of the U.S. economy, the sector that produces goods and services that can be consumed anywhere, such as manufactured products, engineering, and consulting services. That sector, which accounted for more than 34 million jobs in 1990, grew by a negligible 600,000 jobs between 1990 and 2008.

Dramatic, new labor-saving technologies in information services eliminated some jobs across the whole U.S. economy. But employment in the United States has been affected even more by the fact that many manufacturing activities, principally their lower-value-added components, have been moving to emerging economies. This trend is causing employment to fall in virtually all of the U.S. manufacturing sector, except at the high end of the value-added chain. Employment is growing, however, in other parts of the tradable sector—most prominently, finance, computer design and engineering, and top management at multinational enterprises. Like the top end of the manufacturing chain, these expanding industries and positions generally employ highly educated people, and they are the areas in which the U.S. economy continues to have a comparative advantage and can successfully compete in the global economy.

In other words, the employment structure of the U.S. economy has been shifting away from the tradable sector, except for the upper end of the value-added chain, and toward the nontradable sector. This is a problem, because the nontradable sector is likely to generate fewer jobs than is expected of it in the future. Moreover, the range of employment opportunities available in the tradable sector is declining, which is limiting choices for U.S. workers in the middle-income bracket. It would be unwise to assume that under present circumstances, employment in the government and health care in the United States will continue to grow as much as it had been growing before the recent economic crisis. If anything, it is remarkable that the U.S. economy did not have much of an employment problem until the recent economic crisis. If the nontradable sector continues to lose its capacity to absorb labor, as it has in recent years, and the tradable sector does not become an employment engine, the United States should brace itself for a long period of high unemployment.

For What It's Worth

One way to measure the size of a company, industry, or economy is to determine its output. But a better way is to determine its added value—namely, the difference between the value of its outputs, that is, the goods and services it produces, and the costs of its inputs, such as the raw materials and energy it consumes. (Value added comes from the capital and labor that turn the inputs into outputs.) Goods and services themselves are often purchased as intermediate inputs by other companies or industries, legal services purchased by a corporation being one example. The value added produced by all the industries in all the sectors of an economy adds up to that country's GDP. Unlike employment, value added in the tradable and nontradable parts of the U.S. economy has increased at a similar rate since 1990. In the nontradable sector, which experienced rapid employment growth, this means that value added grew slightly faster than employment: value added per employee increased modestly, by an annual average of 0.7 percent since 1990. On the tradable side of the U.S. economy, where employment levels barely increased, both value added overall and value added per employee rose very swiftly as the U.S. tradable sector moved up the value-added chain and grew in sync with the global economy. Whereas in the nontradable sector, value added per employee grew from $72,000 to over $80,000 between 1990 and 2008, in the tradable sector it grew from $79,000 to $120,000—in other words, it grew by just about 12 percent in the nontradable sector but by close to 52 percent in the tradable sector.

Most striking are the trends within the tradable sector. Value added rose across that sector, including in finance, where employment increased, and in manufacturing industries, where employment mostly declined. In fact, at the upper end of the manufacturing chain, value added increased so much that it outweighed the losses at the lower end caused by the movement of economic activity from the United States to other countries.

Value added represents income for someone. For employed people, it means personal income; for shareholders and other owners of capital, profit or returns on investment; for the government, tax revenues. Generally, the incomes of workers are closely correlated with value added per employee (this is not the case in the mining industry and utilities, however, where value added per employee is much higher than wages because these activities are very capital intensive and most value added is a return on capital). Since value added in the nontradable part of the U.S. economy did not rise much, neither did average incomes in that sector. In the tradable sector, on the other hand, incomes rose rapidly along with value added per employee thanks both to rising productivity gains in some industries and the movement of lower-income jobs to other countries. And since most new jobs were created in the nontradable part of the economy, in which wages grew little, the distribution of income in the U.S. economy became more uneven. The overall picture is clear: employment opportunities and incomes are high, and rising, for the highly educated people at the upper end of the tradable sector of the U.S. economy, but they are diminishing at the lower end. And there is every reason to believe that these trends will continue. As emerging economies continue to move up the value-added chain—and they must in order to keep growing—the tradable sectors of advanced economies will require less labor and the more labor-intensive tasks will shift to emerging economies.

Highly educated U.S. workers are already gravitating toward the high-value-added parts of the U.S. economy, particularly in the tradable sector. As labor economists have noted, the return on education is rising. The highly educated, and only them, are enjoying more job opportunities and higher incomes. Competition for highly educated workers in the tradable sector spills over to the nontradable sector, raising incomes in the high-value-added part of that sector as well. But with fewer jobs in the lower-value-added part of the tradable sector, competition for similar jobs in the nontradable sector is increasing. This, in turn, further depresses income growth in the lower-value-added part of the nontradable sector. Thus, the evolving structure of the global economy has diverse effects on different groups of people in the United States. Opportunities are expanding for the highly educated throughout the economy: they are expanding in the tradable sector because the global economy is growing and in the nontradable sector because that job market must remain competitive with the tradable sector. But opportunities are shrinking for the less well educated.

Faced with an undesirable economic outcome, economists tend to assume that its cause is a market failure. Market failures come in many forms, from inefficiencies caused by information gaps to the unpriced impacts of externalities such as the environment. But the effects on the U.S. economy of the global economy's structural evolution is not a market failure: it is not an economically inefficient outcome. (If anything, the global economy is generally becoming more efficient.) But it is nonetheless a cause for concern in that it is creating a distributional problem in the advanced economies. Not everyone is gaining in those countries, and some may be losing.

Although everyone does benefit from lower-priced goods and services, people also care greatly about the chance to be productively employed and the quality of their work. Declining employment opportunities feel real and immediate; the rise in real incomes brought by lower prices does not. For example, according to recent surveys, a substantial number of Americans believe that their children will have fewer opportunities than they have had. The slow recovery from the recent economic crisis may be affecting these perceptions, which means that they might dissipate as the situation improves and growth returns. But the long-term structural evolution of the U.S. and global economies suggests that distributional issues will remain. These must be taken seriously.

Making It Work

Analysts have been quick to point out that not all the structural changes under way in the U.S. economy should be attributed to greater openness in the global economy. Some important changes in employment patterns and income distribution are the result of labor-saving information technology and the automation of transactions. Automation has undoubtedly cut jobs in the information- and transaction-intensive parts of value-added chains throughout the U.S. economy, in both the tradable and the nontradable sectors. But if that were the only trend, why would employment decline so much more in manufacturing than in other industries?

One answer might be that information processing and automation occupy a more significant fraction of the value-added chain in manufacturing. But this is not true. Information-processing technology, for example, has eliminated jobs throughout the U.S. economy, including in finance, retail, and the government —all areas in which employment has grown. The structural trends affecting the U.S. economy cannot be explained by changes in technology alone. To think otherwise tends to yield the misleading conclusions that technology, not the global economy, is the principal cause of the United States' employment challenge and that the most important forces operating on the structure of the U.S. economy are internal, not external. In fact, all these factors are relevant, with some more significant in some sectors of the economy than in others.

If giving technology as the preferred explanation for the U.S. economy's distributional problems is a way to ignore the structural changes of the global economy, invoking multinational companies (MNCs) as the preferred explanation is a way to overstate their impact. MNCs are said to underpay and otherwise exploit poor people in developing countries, exporting jobs that should have stayed in the United States.

MNCs do, indeed, play a central role in managing the evolution of the global economy. They are the principal architects of global supply chains, and they move the production of goods and services around the world in response to supply-chain and market opportunities that are constantly changing. MNCs have generated growth and jobs in developing countries, and by moving to those countries some lower-value-added parts of their supply chains, they have increased growth and competitiveness in advanced economies such as the United States. A June 2010 report by the McKinsey Global Institute estimated that U.S.-based MNCs accounted for 31 percent of GDP growth in the United States since 1990.

With ample labor available in various skill and educational categories throughout the tradable sector globally, companies have little incentive to invest in technologies that save on labor or otherwise increase the competitiveness of the labor-intensive value-added activities in advanced economies. In short, companies' private interest (profit) and the public's interest (employment) do not align perfectly. These conditions might not last: if growth continues to be high in emerging economies, in two or three decades there will be less cheap labor available there. But two or three decades is a long time.

In the meantime, even though public and private interests are not perfectly aligned today, they are not perfectly opposed either. Relatively modest shifts at the margin could bring them back in sync. Given the enormous size of the global labor force, the dial would not need to be moved very much to restore employment growth in the tradable sector of the U.S. economy. Specifically, the right combination of productivity-enhancing technology and competitive wage levels could keep some manufacturing industries, or at least some value-added pieces of their production chains, in the United States and other advanced countries. But accomplishing this will require more than a decision from the market; it must also involve labor, business, and governments. Germany, for one, has managed to retain its advanced manufacturing activities in industrial machinery by removing rigidities in the labor market and making a conscious effort to privilege employment over rapid rises in incomes. Wages may have increased only modestly in Germany over the past decade, but income inequality is markedly flatter there than in the United States, where it is higher than in most other industrial countries and rising steadily.

Conditioning access to the domestic market on domestic production is a form of protectionism and a way to try to limit the movement out of the country of jobs and of value-added components in the supply chain. This is more common than might be supposed. It exists in the aerospace industry; and in the 1970s and 1980s, in the car industry, quotas on Japanese imports to the United States led to an expansion of the manufacture of Japanese cars in the United States. However, if the large economies—such as China, the European Union, Japan, or the United States—pursue protectionist measures on a broad front, the global economy will be undermined. Yet that may be exactly what happens if employment challenges such as the ones affecting the United States are not tackled differently. With pressure on government budgets at all levels, rapidly rising health-care costs, a fragile housing market, the post-crisis effort to curb excess consumption and boost savings, and the risk of a second economic downturn, it is highly unlikely that net employment in the nontradable sector of the U.S. economy will continue to grow as rapidly as it has been.

The drop in domestic consumption in the United States has left the country with a shortage of aggregate demand. More public-sector investment would help, but the fiscal consolidation currently under way may make expanding government investment difficult. Meanwhile, because private-sector investment responds to demand and currently there is a shortfall in demand caused by the economic crisis and increased savings by households, such investment will not return until domestic consumption or exports increase. Therefore, the United States will need to focus on increasing job growth in the tradable sector. Some growth will naturally come from the high-value-added part of that sector. The question is whether there will be enough growth and whether the educational attainment of U.S. workers will keep pace with rising job requirements at that level. There are reasons to be skeptical.

The Big Tradeoff

It is a common view that the market will solve the disparities in employment and incomes once the economic crisis recedes and growth is restored. Warren Buffett and other very smart, experienced, and influential opinion-makers say so clearly. But as this analysis suggests, they may not be right. And as long as their view dominates U.S. public policy and opinion, it will be difficult to address the issues related to structural change and employment in the United States in a systematic way.

What is needed instead of benign neglect is, first, an agreement that restoring rewarding employment opportunities for a full spectrum of Americans should be a fundamental goal. With that objective as a starting point, it will then be necessary to develop ways to increase both the competitiveness and the inclusiveness of the U.S. economy. This is largely uncharted territory: distributional issues are difficult to solve because they require correcting outcomes on the global market without doing too much damage to its efficiency and openness. But admitting that not all the answers are known is a good place to begin. With considerable uncertainty about the efficacy of various policy options, a multistakeholder, multipronged approach to addressing these distributional problems is best. The relevant knowledge about promising new technologies and market opportunities is dispersed among business, the government, labor, and universities, and it needs to be assembled and turned into initiatives. President Barack Obama has already appointed a commission, led by Jeffrey Immelt, the CEO of General Electric, to focus on competitiveness and employment issues in the U.S. economy. This is an important step forward. But it will be hugely difficult to invest in human capital, technology, and infrastructure as much as is necessary at a time of fiscal distress and declining government employment. And yet restoring opportunities for future generations requires making sacrifices in the present.

Given the structural changes under way in the U.S. economy—especially the growing premium on highly educated workers at the top end of the value-added chain—education should be boosted. As many people as possible should be able to compete in that part of the economy. But if this goal is clear, the ways to achieve it are less so. Improving the performance of the educational system has been a priority for some years, yet the results are in doubt. For example, the Organization for Economic Cooperation and Development administers a set of standardized tests, the Program for International Student Assessment, across more than 60 countries, advanced and developing, to measure the cognitive skills of teenage students. The United States ranks close to the average in reading and science and well behind most countries in math.

The problems in the quality and effectiveness of parts of the U.S. educational system have been recognized for some time. Numerous attempts to improve matters, including administering national standardized tests and providing merit-based compensation, have thus far yielded inconclusive results. And the problem extends beyond the school system. A lack of commitment to education in families and in communities makes the entire field of education seem unattractive, demoralizing dedicated teachers and turning off talented students from teaching. That, in turn, reduces the incentives of communities to value the primacy of education. To break this pattern, it will be necessary to shift communities'—and the country's—values about education through moral leadership, at both the community and the national levels. Creating attractive employment opportunities conditional on educational success is another important incentive. One comes full circle, in other words: increased educational effectiveness is needed for the United States to be competitive, and the promise of rewarding employment is a necessary incentive for committing to improving education.

As important as education is, it cannot be the whole solution; the United States will not educate its way out of its problems. Both the federal and state governments must pursue complementary lines of attack. They should invest in infrastructure, which would create jobs in the short term and raise the return on private-sector investment in the medium to longer term. They should also invest in technologies that could expand employment opportunities in the tradable sector of the U.S. economy at income levels other than the very top. The private sector will have to help guide these investments because it has much of the relevant knowledge about where these opportunities might lie. But this effort will also require the participation of the public sector. The U.S. government already invests heavily in science and technology but not with job creation as its primary focus; that has generally been viewed only as a beneficial side effect. It is time to devote public funding to developing infrastructure and the technological base of the U.S. economy with the specific goal of restoring competitiveness and expanding employment in the tradable sector. The tax structure also needs to be reformed. It should be simplified and reconfigured to promote competitiveness, investment, and employment. And both loopholes and distorting incentives should be eliminated. For example, corporate tax rates and tax rates on investment returns should be lowered in order to make the United States more attractive for business and investment. MNCs with earnings outside the United States currently have a strong incentive to keep their earnings abroad and reinvest them abroad because earnings are taxed both where they are earned and also in the United States if they are repatriated. Lower tax rates would mean a loss in revenue for the U.S. government, but that could be replaced by taxes on consumption, which would have the added benefit of helping shift the composition of demand from domestic to foreign—a necessary move if the United States wants to avoid high unemployment and an unsustainable current account deficit.

But even these measures may not be sufficient. Globalization has redefined the competition for employment and incomes in the United States. Tradeoffs will have to be made between the two. Germany clearly chose to protect employment in the industries of its tradable sector that came under competitive threat. Now, U.S. policymakers must choose, too.

Some will argue that global market forces should simply be allowed to operate without interference. Tampering with market outcomes, the argument goes, risks distorting incentives and reducing efficiency and innovation. But this is not the only approach, nor is it the best one. The distribution of income across many advanced economies (and major emerging economies) differs markedly. For example, the ratio of the average income of the top 20 percent of the population to the average income of the bottom 20 percent is four to one in Germany and eight to one in the United States. Many other advanced countries have flatter income distributions than the United States, suggesting that tradeoffs between market forces and equity are possible. The U.S. government needs to face up to them.

Experimenting the Way Forward

The massive changes in the global economy since World War II have had overwhelmingly positive effects. Hundreds of millions of people in the developing world have escaped poverty, and more will in the future. The global economy will continue to grow—probably at least threefold over the next 30 years. One person's gain is not necessarily another's loss; global growth is not even close to a zero-sum game. But globalization hurts some subgroups within some countries, including the advanced economies.

The late American economist Paul Samuelson once said, "Every good cause is worth some inefficiency." Surely, equity and social cohesion are among them. The challenge for the U.S. economy will be to find a place in the rapidly evolving global economy that retains its dynamism and openness while providing all Americans with rewarding employment opportunities and a reasonable degree of equity. This is not a problem to which there are easy answers. As the issue becomes more pressing, ideology and orthodoxy must be set aside, and creativity, flexibility, and pragmatism must be encouraged. The United States will not be able to deduce its way toward the solutions; it will have to experiment its way forward.

Source

Spence, Michael. "The impact of globalization on income and employment: the downside of integrating markets." *Foreign Affairs* 90.4 (2011): 28. *General OneFile*. Web. 20 Dec. 2011.

Critical Thinking

1. How does globalization impact the incomes of some people?
2. Are there losers in globalization?
3. What can be done about people who are not benefiting from globalization?

MICHAEL SPENCE is Distinguished Visiting Fellow at the Council on Foreign Relations and the author of *The Next Convergence: The Future of Economic Growth in a Multispeed World.* He received the Nobel Prize in Economics in 2001.

Learn the Landscape

When Managing Benefits Globally, Government-Provided Services, National Mandates and Cultural Expectations Come into Play

David Tobenkin

When managing benefits for a far-flung international workforce, global HR managers and benefits consultants say best practices converge into one master directive: Take nothing for granted.

HR managers should first establish, or help establish, a global corporate benefits strategy, consultants say. The most common strategy is to design a plan that complies with applicable laws and matches the benefits of competitors, says Richard Polak, president and chief executive officer of the Los Angeles-based HR consultancy IBIS Advisors.

"Decide who you want to be," says Carol Olsby, GPHR, a principal at the Seattle area-based HR consultancy Carol Olsby & Associates. For example, one of her clients is Helsinki-based Tieto Corp. The information technology services company focuses on having low turnover for its 17,000 "high-value" employees. "Technology people have many options for employment," so Tieto wants its benefits "to be among the top choices in the marketplace," she explains.

HR professionals at Nalco Co. take a different approach. The Naperville, Ill.-based water treatment company has more than 11,500 employees operating in 130 countries. "It's absolutely our global philosophy to be at the 50th percentile among companies for both benefits and compensation," says Judith Wierman, GPHR, a director of human resources at Nalco's Energy Services Division. "We are a pay-for-performance firm. If your performance exceeds expectations, you can expect that total compensation will be above market. Benefits to us are just the price of admission, so we do what the market is doing."

When developing a global benefits strategy, HR professionals who are knowledgeable about international benefits have much to contribute to the discussion. That's because benefits differ across the globe.

In each country where a company employs workers, the benefits package will vary because it will reflect a different combination of:

• Government-provided benefits.

• Government-mandated benefits that employers are required to provide.

• Supplemental benefits that employers make available.

Ensuring Compliance

To comply with applicable laws and regulations, HR managers and consultants say assembling the right global benefits team is essential. The team typically includes local HR professionals hired directly or under contract, local employment lawyers, international tax counsel, and international HR consultants. Clear communication is critical: "Don't take anything for granted. You need to ask what everything means," Polak says.

Governments in many countries are more involved in providing or mandating employee benefits than the U.S. government is. One positive aspect of governments' involvement: Many compliance obligations, although highly regulated, have been clarified and simplified, says Francois Choquette, senior vice president of Aon Hewitt's global benefits practice. "Thus, if you provide medical insurance as required, you most likely are in compliance," he explains.

On the other hand, sensitive issues—such as using benefits strategies to avoid taxation on compensation in the European Union and other high-taxation zones—should be carefully checked for their legality, says Stefan Corbanie, a partner in the Brussels office of law firm Eversheds International. The tax treatment of supplemental benefits also represents a factor in whether planned benefits will be attractive to employees.

In some parts of the world, government rules on benefits that are announced but not enforced are among the trickiest compliance areas for HR managers.

"Two years ago, there was a push in the United Arab Emirates for residents to register with the government authority to get single ID cards," recalls Brad Boyson, SPHR, GPHR, head of HR and corporate services for Hamptons MENA, a property company with operations throughout the Middle East. "HR departments rushed to have their staffs comply by the deadline. It was the law." But authorities weren't ready to process the applications, so the deadline kept being extended. Similar events occur in India and China, Boyson says. Despite the uncertainty, he advises that it's always better for HR professionals to "err on the side of caution."

Beyond compliance, HR professionals need to determine how much more than the required minimum they should provide. It is important to closely examine the standard benefits offered by established companies. Prudent HR professionals "benchmark on local conditions and add as needed," Boyson says. He considers it "naïve" for global companies to simply import their standard international practices. They often do not realize "the cost of doing so, over the long run, can be astronomical," he says. "You cannot be altruistic when it comes to benefits."

In addition, international HR experts say U.S. HR professionals operating globally frequently fail to realize how much harder it is in Europe and many other countries to take away a benefit once it has been given.

Customary Benefits

Then there are the benefits themselves. The most common international employee benefits are similar to those offered in the United States, but there are considerable variations.

Leave

The most widespread benefit provided around the globe relates to basic time off, including time for bereavement, illness, maternity and vacation, Boyson says. U.S. federal laws do not require employers to provide paid vacation or leave time. In contrast, many developed countries mandate several weeks or more of employer-paid leave. In the United Kingdom, for example, effective April 2010, all female employees are entitled to up to 52 weeks of paid maternity or adoption leave, with the first six weeks paid at 90 percent of full pay and the remainder at a fixed rate, says Kendal Callison, GPHR, a Seattle area-based global HR consultant.

Leave can be a significant issue in some parts of the world, Boyson notes. "Certain Muslim religious holidays are mandatory leave in many countries," he says. "It's usually in the labor code as a type of pure entitlement to which a company can't say

no. Similarly, during the holy month of Ramadan, workers have restricted hours."

Health and wellness

The second most common benefit provided internationally is health care. Most national governments, even in the developing world, are far more involved than the United States in providing or mandating health care services. In countries where government-provided benefits are extensive, HR executives may find little need to add to them.

In many countries, however, governments provide only very basic health care services, Boyson notes. Even in those with good overall health care systems, an elective procedure might not be covered or employees might be placed on waiting lists. Thus, many companies supplement nationally provided health care benefits, says Lisbeth Claus, SPHR, GPHR, a professor of global HR at Salem, Ore.-based Willamette University.

In less-developed parts of the world, quality of care is often a problem. One of Polak's clients is a religious organization that has 1,400 people on its payroll throughout Africa. "They provide health care for everyone," he says. But "they lack medicines, enough doctors, and what care there is may not be up to Western standards. The same is true in Western China and certain parts of India."

In-kind benefits

Another common benefits category provides allowances for the costs of transportation, housing or other services.

In many European Union countries, Boyson says, companies frequently reward workers through in-kind benefits to reduce taxes. The idea is that "If I gave you money, you'd be taxed. So I'll give you transportation instead," he explains.

Many companies in Northern Europe, for example, have professional events in Southern Europe during the winter that are essentially paid vacations, Claus notes. Meal vouchers are also common in some European countries.

Workers in the emerging economic powerhouses want different in-kind benefits. Education benefits, including English and leadership training, motivate many workers in China, Olsby says.

Indian workers expect companies "to offer very heavy benefits," generally more than 10 different types, she adds. Some companies even offer health insurance or other benefits to employees' parents. "Their salaries are not as high, but their total rewards package is large," Olsby says.

Retirement and severance

With respect to retirement benefits, much depends on what a government requires. Social security or pension-type benefits

Most Prevalent Supplemental Employee Benefits

Benefits large employers typically choose to provide employees in certain countries.

	Pension	Medical	Car benefit	Other cash allowances	Life and long-term disability
Brazil	√	√	√	√	√
France		√	√		√
India		√		√	
Japan	√				√
Mexico		√		√	√
United Kingdom	√		√		√
United States	√	√			√

Source: Aon Hewitt, 2011

Online Resources

For more information on international benefits, including detailed tables comparing common benefits across countries, see the online version of this article at www.shrm.org/hrmagazine/0511BenefitsAgenda.

are provided by many governments, particularly in the developed world. In France, government-provided retirement benefits replace 70 percent of pay. Where the benefits are generous, corporations often do not supplement them.

Executives typically take another approach in some of the poorest developing countries. "In Botswana, Congo and Nigeria, there is a high occurrence of AIDS and a low life expectancy," Polak says. "People there are not interested in retirement programs. They want cash and immediate benefits like medical care."

Retirement benefits are being affected by global trends, including the movement from defined benefit pensions to defined contribution plans, such as 401(k)-type plans. Companies are offering defined contribution plans in developing countries where retirement benefits previously have not been provided.

Implementing these programs may not be easy. Nalco executives are considering establishing a 401(k) plan for employees in India. "We are looking to see if that is feasible if there is a vesting requirement," says Nalco's Wierman. She notes that these employees may not stay long enough to get vested because they have so many job opportunities.

Other considerations, such as cultural norms, can also play roles in benefits selection. HR professionals must tailor benefits to different classes of workers, including employees in the local market; expatriate workers from other countries; and contract workers, who may or may not be required to receive benefits under the laws of the country.

Critical Thinking

1. What are some of the differences in benefits when there are employees in different countries?

2. What are some of the different expectations when their employees from different countries?

3. How can this be reconciled?

DAVID TOBENKIN is an attorney and freelance writer in Chevy Chase, Md.

From *HR Magazine*, 56(5), May 5, 2011, pp. 51–52, 54. Copyright © 2011 by Society for Human Resource Management (SHRM), Alexandria, VA. Reprinted by permission via the Copyright Clearance Center.

Explaining High Oil Prices

The U.S. economy is no longer what's driving the market.

CHRISTIAN BERTHELSEN

The U.S. economy is limping along, unemployment is still high, and gasoline demand for this time of year is at its lowest since the 1990s.

So why does a barrel of domestic crude cost around $100?

Nymex crude futures have been on a tear lately, soaring 35% from the beginning of October to their recent peak in mid-November, and have crossed the $100-a-barrel threshold a handful of times. Various causes have been cited, including optimism that Europe's debt crisis would be resolved soon and a tightening supply picture. Fears have also surfaced that global supplies could be disrupted because of geopolitical fallout over Iran's alleged nuclear ambitions.

What Next?

That helps explain where prices have been. As for where they are headed from here, the big-picture consensus is that despite weakness in the U.S., economic growth and energy demand are strong enough in the rest of the world, particularly in emerging markets, for traders to continue bidding up prices.

"The U.S. is no longer in the driver's seat as far as oil prices," says James D. Hamilton, an economics professor at the University of California, San Diego, who has researched the relationship between energy prices and the economy.

Growth in demand in emerging markets as a whole is expected to slow from the torrid pace seen in recent years. But forecasts say it will still outpace demand in the U.S. and Europe and will still be strong enough to push oil prices higher. In the major emerging markets that oil investors focus on, such as China, India and Brazil, demand is still expected to grow 4.6% this year and 4.4% in 2012, according to data from the U.S. Energy Information Administration.

"Emerging markets will probably continue to grow faster than advanced economies," José Sérgio Gabrielli de Azevedo, chief executive of Brazilian oil giant Petroleo Brasileiro SA, or Petrobras, said earlier this month at the Platts Global Energy Outlook Forum in New York. "The growth pattern of those economies is more energy-intensive than [first-world] growth." He added: "The era of cheap oil is over."

Tight global supplies are expected to keep prices high as well, even with the resumption of flows from Libya, where for months the revolution halted prewar exports of 1.6 million barrels a day. As much as one-half of Libya's former oil exports are expected to be restored by year-end, but there is still little slack in the global system.

Says Mr. Hamilton, "As long as growth from the emerging economies continues, as long as world production fails to keep up with that, we're going to see upward pressure on prices."

Rising prices are leading to changes in the direction of flows in the global marketplace for oil products. One big example: Surging foreign demand for fuel products refined from crude—particularly for distillates such as diesel—has turned the U.S. into a net exporter of fuels.

"I think there's been a trend over the last few years toward a more global [oil] product market," says Antoine Halff, senior economist at the U.S. Energy Information Administration. "It used to be the crude market was fairly global, but the product markets were regional. But that's changed. We've seen more international trading of products, more long-haul trading and new players. New exporters, new importers, new trade flows."

This trend got a boost from the announcement last month that a U.S. pipeline reversal will allow crude to be pumped out of storage facilities in Cushing, Okla., and down to refineries on the Gulf Coast. The move is expected to bring the cost of West Texas Intermediate oil closer to parity with the more expensive global Brent benchmark and make U.S. crude more competitive with international supplies.

Speculation and Recovery

Debate continues over how big a role financial speculation plays in driving recent price increases. No definitive conclusions have been drawn. But money managers from hedge funds, pension funds and other large private interests have been pouring money into Nymex crude contracts. The net long position of money managers surged 48% during the October to mid-November run-up, and the notional value of their positions increased $10.4 billion, to $21.5 billion over that period, according to calculations based on data from the Commodity Futures Trading Commission.

In a recent speech, Abdulla Salem El-Badri, secretary general of the Organization of Petroleum Exporting Countries, blamed the recent jump in prices on speculators, noting that the number of financial oil contracts being traded is 35 times greater than the actual physical supply. (OPEC often blames high prices on market speculation.)

Whether it's emerging-market demand or speculation that's boosting prices, the end result doesn't bode well for a U.S. economic recovery. Generally, high oil prices—particularly at $100 a barrel and above—are thought to be a drag on a weak economy, either directly, by siphoning off consumer spending, or indirectly, by making people unwilling to spend. Every $10 increase in the barrel price is believed to shave a few tenths of a percent off the growth of gross domestic product. Fuel prices were cited as a factor in the bankruptcy filing of AMR Corp., the parent of American Airlines, whose 78,000 employees face the possibility of contract renegotiations and lower pension payments.

"We did see slower growth [in 2011] than many people expected, and oil prices were one factor," says Mr. Hamilton, the San Diego professor. But, he adds, "I do not expect that current prices of Brent or West Texas Intermediate [crude] would be, in and of themselves, reason to anticipate another downturn in the U.S."

Critical Thinking

1. Why is the price of oil going up in the United States when demand is going down?
2. Would more production of oil drive the price down?
3. What is the role of the economic growth of other nations in the price of oil?

MR. BERTHELSEN is a reporter for *Dow Jones Newswires* in New York. He can be reached at christian.berthelsen@dowjones.com.

Keynote Panel Session 1: Whose Income Is It? How Business Is Caught in the Global Competition and Controversy for Tax Revenues

This panel set the tone for the entire Symposium with a strategic discussion on the global race among countries to attract and retain business operations in their jurisdictions. In this increasingly competitive global environment, tax controversy across multiple jurisdictions is becoming a frequent occurrence in both developed and developing countries as well as in the 50 U.S. states.

TIMOTHY M. McDONALD ET AL.

Introduction

MS. OLSON: Thank you. We have a great group for this opening discussion which we have titled, *Whose Income Is It?* First, to my immediate left is Michael Mundaca. Mike is the Deputy Assistant Treasury Secretary for International Tax Affairs. At this point, he is the most senior person in tax policy at the Treasury Department, and he is wearing a lot of different hats. Clearly, he is the Acting Assistant Secretary *de facto* if not *de jure*. We are really pleased, Mike, that you could take the time this morning to come over to be with us. Mike has been at Treasury for about a year and a half. This is his second stint at Treasury. In between those stints, he was with Ernst & Young in Washington, D.C. In his previous stint at Treasury, he served as the Deputy International Tax Counsel. I had the pleasure of working with him during that period of time, which spanned the late 1990s and early part of this decade. Mike's biography also includes his service as the Treasury senior advisor on electronic commerce.

Next to Michael is Tim McDonald. Tim is the Vice President for Finance and Accounting, Global Taxes, at the Procter & Gamble Company. Tim has been with Procter & Gamble since 2003. He is responsible for all matters pertaining to corporate income taxes globally including the tax policy positions that the company takes involving legislation, planning, compliance and audit defense. He has a staff of 200 people to keep up with P&G's global tax function, which is located in 32 different countries.

Next to Tim is Joel Walters, who is the Corporate Finance Director at Vodafone in London. Joel is a graduate of the University of Minnesota Law School, and also has an LLM from Georgetown. Before joining Vodafone, Joel worked for Diageo and Grand Met.

So, three great panelists. We are happy to have all three of them with us this morning.

We are going to start with some slides that will set the backdrop for our discussion. They help to illustrate the kinds of things that Grant Aldonas spoke about in the opening session that are important for us to bear in mind as we consider the question—whose income is it?

- Slide 1, *Growth in U.S. Exports and Imports, 1992–2007,* is a graphic depiction of the change in U.S. exports and imports from 1992 to 2007. The yellow bars on the left are 1992, and the gray bars on the right are 2007. What you see in the graph is a remarkable increase in the quantity of exports and imports on the part of the U.S. You can see over the course of the last 15 years how much more globally interconnected we have become, and the graph illustrates the importance of being globally interconnected.

- Slide 2, *Foreign Direct Investment Inflows,* is a graphic depiction of foreign direct investment flows from 1990 to 2000 to 2006. The yellow segments at the top of each of those bars are foreign direct investment flows into developing countries. The gray segments are flows into developed countries. You can see that there is a shift occurring with more foreign direct investment flows to the developing world relative to the developed world over the period from 1990 to 2006.

- Slide 3, *Top 20 Countries Ranked by GDP 1992 & 2007,* shows the top 20 countries ranked by GDP in 1992 and 2007. Focusing on the changes in the chart, China moved from number eight on this list in 1992 to number four in 2007. India moved from number 15 in 1992 to number 12 by 2007. Russia, which was not on the list at all in 1992, moved to number 11 in 2007. Perhaps with what is going on with petroleum markets, Russia will fall on the list

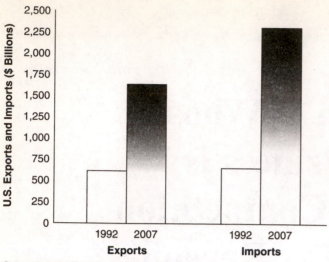

Growth in U.S. Exports and Imports, 1992–2007

Source: U.S. BEA International Economics Accounts.

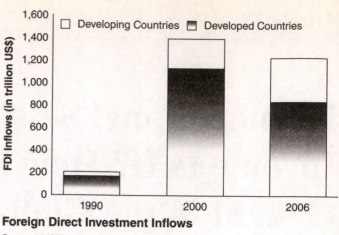

Foreign Direct Investment Inflows

Source: UNCTAD, World Investment Report 2007.

again in coming years. There are countries that were on the list in 1992 that have dropped off entirely by 2007. These represent remarkable shifts. What the changes illustrate is the importance of participation in the emerging world, as well as in the developed world because there is a lot of growth occurring in the developing world.

- Slide 4, *Relative Rates of Growth and Contributions to GDP between 1992 and 2007,* illustrates relative rates of growth and contributions to global gross domestic product between 1992 and 2007. The top part of the chart, which includes developed countries, has growth rates much less significant than the emerging market and developing countries in the bottom half of the chart, where the average growth rate was 287 percent during that period of time—three times as much as the growth rate among the advanced countries. We still see a significant contribution, 62 percent, to world growth on the part of the developed countries, but that is because of the size of the United States and European economies relative to the size of the economies of emerging market and developing countries. The key point is that emerging market and developing countries are becoming rapidly more important for economic growth.

The key point is that emerging market and developing countries are becoming rapidly more important for economic growth.

- Slide 5, *Future Population,* shows future projected population by mid-2050. Population growth is projected to be high in the developing world. India is at the top with one and three-quarter billion people, China is next with nearly a billion and a half, and the U.S. is in third place with 438 million. So, what we see is a rapidly growing population outside of the U.S. and the developed world. It is important to understand in considering why

there is so much investment outside the U.S. that we are only five percent of the world's population. So there are literally billions of reasons for businesses to invest in places other than the U.S.

- Slide 6, *Penetration Rates of New Technologies in Selected Countries, 2006,* is an interesting depiction of the penetration rates for new technologies. What the chart indicates is that there is a lot of room for growth in PC usage, in Internet usage, and in cellular subscription in the developing world.

Top 20 Countries Ranked by GDP 1992 & 2007

GDP Rank	1992	2007
1	United States	United States
2	Japan	Japan
3	Germany	Germany
4	France	China
5	Italy	United Kingdom
6	United Kingdom	France
7	Spain	Italy
8	Canada	Spain
9	China	Canada
10	Brazil	Brazil
11	Mexico	Russia
12	Netherlands	India
13	Korea	Mexico
14	Australia	Korea
15	India	Australia
16	Sweden	Netherlands
17	Switzerland	Turkey
18	Argentina	Sweden
19	Belgium	Belgium
20	Taiwan	Indonesia

Source: International Monetary Fund.

Relative Rates of Growth and Contributions to GDP between 1992 and 2007

	1992	2007	1992–2007	
	GDP	**GDP**	**GDP Growth**	**Contribution to World Growth**
United States	6,038	13,808	118%	25%
EU-15	2,990	15,728	97%	25%
Japan	3,770	4,382	16%	2%
Other	2,190	5,271	148%	10%
Advanced Countries	**20,227**	**39,188**	**94%**	**62%**
China	488	3,280	672%	9%
India	281	1,101	292%	3%
Other developing Asia	608	1,402	176%	3%
Western hemisphere	1,329	3,609	172%	7%
Middle East	448	1,400	212%	3%
Africa	410	1,107	170%	2%
Central & Eastern Europe	412	1,890	358%	5%
Other	123	1,696	1281%	5%
Emerging Market and Developing Countries	**3,998**	**15,484**	**287%**	**38%**
World	**24,226**	**54,673**	**125%**	**100%**

Source: International Monetary Fund.

Projected Population Mid–2050 (Millions)

Range : 0 – 1,755 Billion

India	1,755
China	1,437
United States	438
Indonesia	343
Pakistan	295
Nigeria	282
Brazil	260
Bangladesh	215
Congo De Rep of	189
Phillippines	150
Ethiopia	148
Mexico	132
Egypt	118
Vietnam	113
Russia	110

Future Population

Source: Population Reference Bureau.

- Slide 7, *Economic Growth,* is a comparison of real growth and capital flows in the emerging world. Note that growth is headed off the charts in the emerging markets and developing world.
- Slide 8, *Corporate Tax Rates,* has two charts illustrating corporate tax rates. The chart on the left depicts the combined U.S. rate relative to non-U.S. OECD (Organisation for Economic Co-operation and Development) countries. Relative to the rest of the

OECD, we see the U.S. tax rate dropped in 1986 with the enactment of the Tax Reform Act of 1986, which was fully implemented by 1989. Then the rest of the world began to follow U.S. corporate rates down. Other countries have continued to cut their corporate rates, while we have stayed at about the same point for the last 20 years, resulting in a significant wedge between U.S. corporate tax rates and those of the rest of the OECD.

Penetration Rates of New Technologies in Selected Countries, 2006

	PC Usage	Internet Usage	Cellular Subscriptions
United States	80%	70%	80%
EU 15	60%	52%	108%
Brazil	20%	23%	53%
Russia	13%	18%	106%
India	3%	11%	15%
China	6%	10%	35%

Source: UN Stats, Millennium Development Goals Indicators.

Corporate Tax Rates

MR. MUNDACA: Thanks, Pam. These numbers are very interesting. I think what we are going to try to do here is link together some of what Grant Aldonas was talking about and what Pam was talking about to what is happening in globalization, what is happening in trade, what is happening in the international tax space, what is happening with corporate tax rates, with corporate tax audits, what is happening to multinationals and how they are treated around the world by the various tax authorities. The corporate tax rates I think are a good place to start. As Pam's slides indicate, only the U.S., Brazil and Sweden (countries in the top 20 by GDP) have not lowered their corporate tax statutory rates since 2000, and only the U.S. rate has gone up, because of some State tax changes. That is a stark statistic. Looking just at OECD countries, the U.S. statutory rate is now about 50 percent higher than the average OECD rate. The average OECD rate now is about 25 percent. So even amongst the 30 countries of the OECD, the U.S. is an outlier.

A couple of other facts to keep in mind, though. The U.S. marginal corporate tax rate, the tax rate applied to the last dollar earned by a corporation, is about average amongst other large economies due to the fact that we have a narrower corporate tax base (because of accelerated depreciation and treatment of interest payments) relative to other countries. And that is again a trend that the U.S. has not yet taken up—broadening the corporate tax base and lowering the corporate tax rate. That is, the U.S. still has a fairly narrow corporate tax base.

Another thing to keep in mind is that the U.S. collects less revenue as a share of GDP from its corporate tax than other major trading partners do.

So how do you pull all this together, how do you make sense of all this? How do we have a high corporate tax rate and yet collect less corporate tax than our major trading partners as a percentage of GDP.

A couple of facts make us unique: The amount of business income earned by corporations in the U.S. is less than 50 percent of the total business income earned, which is an important factor to keep in mind as we talk about what we are doing on corporate taxes. For us, corporate tax reform is only half or even less than half of the story of business tax reform, and that has to be taken into account especially as we consider the effects on competitiveness both domestically and internationally. Changes we make to the corporate tax system don't necessarily spread across business income evenly.

We must keep all these facts in mind as we talk about the future of the corporate tax system in this country. And as Pam alluded to, there is going to be a lot of pressure in the United States to do some reform.

Now, a lot of the talk has been about health care, and that is going to be the legislative focus, I think, for the rest of this year. Some tax reform may be part of that, but I think, in the short term—potentially not this year, but certainly early in this administration—tax reform is going to be a focus, and corporate tax reform in particular. We are going to see soon the release of an outline of the President's first budget, and there will be, as you have seen in the press and as was alluded to last night in the President's address to Congress, some corporate tax matters addressed in that budget.

Taxation of Foreign Source Income

Another trend I think we need to keep in mind. What about the taxation of a foreign source income? We have talked about how the U.S. is an outlier on corporate tax rates generally. What about the taxation of foreign source income?

Most of our major trading partners have moved over the last couple of years—while they have moved to lower their corporate tax rates and broaden their corporate tax base, by eliminating preferences, such as accelerated depreciation, for example—they have moved to narrow the base by excluding large chunks of foreign source income, especially dividends from controlled foreign corporations.

We, the U.K. and Japan are the primary large economies with worldwide systems at this point, but as you all know, Japan and the U.K. appear now to be moving toward significant territorial reforms, which will leave us, of the large economies, with Ireland, Mexico and Korea, as the last standing that have a worldwide tax system.

Again, I think as we look at what reform is coming down and what we need to do, we have to be cognizant of our place in the global community and how our tax rules may be out of sync at this point with those of some of our major trading partners.

A larger question to consider as you look at this is, if the trend is to drop corporate tax rates, and narrow the corporate tax base to domestic income by excluding foreign income, is the corporate tax a dying animal, is it something that countries are moving away from entirely?

Enforcement

Having said that, looking at enforcement, we see the real oddity of what is developing. While countries have been lowering their rates and in essence foregoing their tax on foreign source income, they have upped their enforcement of the laws that remain in place. They have been—and I think we will hear about this from Tim and Joel—more aggressive in trying to collect the revenues under these new systems that they have put in place. Again, it's a tension I think we are going to see very starkly over the next couple of years: the need for countries to continue to create jobs and grow countered by the need for revenue. There is also obviously a political element to this, that the loss of jobs to countries overseas and the shrinking of corporate tax base are very hot political issues, and countries have to

126

address that. But again, as I see it from where I sit, there are these tensions countries are going to have to resolve. Every country recognizes, especially now, the need to grow, the need to create jobs, but they also recognize that the revenue needs of their countries are growing and they need sources of revenue for those revenue needs.

While countries have been lowering their rates and in essence foregoing their tax on foreign source income, they have upped their enforcement of the laws that remain in place.

With that, I will turn to the business colleagues to see if they are seeing the same sort of trends that I am seeing, that even as corporate tax rules are changing and potentially becoming more favorable to corporations, the enforcement of those rules is becoming quite tight.

Business Perspective

MR. WALTERS: I will kick off on the business perspective. There will be lot of consistencies in the things I say, to previous comments. There is a lot of overlap from my perspective. I think my role in this panel is to set the stage and begin the business aspect of the view of where we are today and what we are seeing out there.

I had an interesting conversation last night with someone. We were talking about the tension that is out there that was just being described. The comment was correctly made that it is always going to be the case, isn't it, that you are always going to have business moving at a dramatic speed and government always a bit chasing behind trying to sort out how to deal with the new world and how to tax and protect their revenue base. But I think this is more than that now. I think that it is probably indeed fair to say that this is always true. But in my view, and what I see day to day, the acceleration and the dramatic pace is a seismic change in how business operates in a global way and how governments need to deal with this. When you come to sessions like this people are always saying we are at a crossroads. Today is the day it has become dramatic. But I do honestly believe at this moment the changes are seismic, we are in a very different world, and that is what we are dealing with.

Tim is going to get more into the detail of what we are seeing out there and what's happening in the governments as they are trying to deal with some of this. So I will just kind of set the stage in a general way.

I guess the first thing I would say is that my perspective isn't as somebody who spends a lot of time thinking about capital import or export neutrality. I am not a policy guy, so I don't spend as much time thinking about how rates or basis of taxation compare to other governments from a policy perspective. I am just a guy who, on a day-to-day basis, makes decisions about where Vodafone is going to operate its business. We are out making choices on a daily basis. What is the environment in which we want to operate? That's the perspective I come from. I do care about the policy and administration in the countries that we operate, so these questions are of interest to me, and I do think about them. But the bigger policy questions are not what I do. We make decisions. Where should we put this business activity? That is the perspective I come at it from.

Seismic Change

In terms of the pace of change, let me just give you a little bit of background, because I think it is important. When you think about Vodafone in particular, you can really see what I mean by seismic change. The first mobile phone call made by a Vodafone executive in the U.K. was in 1985, so 24 years ago was the start of our business. This year we will produce about $70 billion of revenue, and that is in a market that some people estimate to be $1 trillion in terms of telecommunications globally. So that is what has changed in our business in just 24 years.

We started out in Newbury, England, and we began as a U.K.-based business. This year about four percent of our global profits will be generated in the U.K., so 96 percent of our business is in countries outside of the U.K. where we are competing with a whole variety of competitors. Everybody from 02 to T Mobile in terms of global competitors, local mobile virtual network operators (MVNOs) who are buying and selling air time locally, traditional government-owned telecommunications companies, and, increasingly, the Googles and the Microsofts of the world who are all trying to get into the space.

So, we are out dealing with a very global environment, very fast-changing business, spending 96 percent of our time competing in a true global marketplace, and that is our business. I think that it is very important to have that in mind. We are not a domestic U.S. company or U.K. company who is interested in global taxation. We are a global company that competes all around the world.

While that is happening, the attention and focus on business performance, as most of the people in the room know, has dramatically increased as well. One example I can give of that. Last June we released some of our KPIs (Key Performance Indicators), which we do, because we only do half-year and full-year results in the U.K., so the other two quarters we do KPI results with some broad indicators of how we are performing. We came out and basically said that we were performing well all across our sectors, but we said we are starting to see some softness in specific places. We got really punished for that in terms of the analyst's view and the market reaction. I think the moral of that is that in the world we live in, where it used to be the case if you could perform on a portfolio basis, or perform in 96 out of 100 markets, the markets would give you credit for that.

Tax in the Boardroom

Today there is just no sympathy for failing to deliver on every line, in every market, every day, and there is no opportunity to err in that. And what does that mean? That means on every line of the Profit and Loss Statement, cash flow, balance sheet, everything we do, we are looking for a competitive advantage and complete certainty. That is our objective as a business. That is what we are out pursuing, and the tax lines are no different in that.

That means, on every line of the Profit and Loss Statement, cash flow, balance sheet, everything we do, we are looking for a competitive advantage and complete certainty.

I am usually surprised when I get the reaction, yes, but, you know, people shouldn't be out competing on the tax line, should they, they shouldn't be trying to drive down their tax burden on a global basis. But tax is no different in business—trying to drive that down when living in a very difficult global competitive environment.

There was some discussion a few years back in the U.K. about bringing tax into the board room, and I was always skeptical that tax wasn't already in the board room and that the boards of big companies weren't considering tax on a detailed basis. Even if I am wrong and there was a gap here, there no longer is a gap because tax is front and center, certainly in our board room. I think I could safely say that the boards of other big companies are focused on this as well. I have to deliver every year an effective tax rate for the market. I have to deliver every year the cash flow. We have committed to the market that we are going to produce between five and six billion pounds of free cash flow on an annual basis, and tax is a big contributor to that. I also have to deliver as much certainty as I can in a very uncertain world and what the next couple of days are going to be talking about on the tax controversy. For example, you can see by looking at our annual report, we have about two billion pounds of tax at stake in some litigation in the U.K.

Most everybody, because they always come up and talk to me about it when they see me, know that we are in litigation in India on a $2 billion issue. We have to try to manage that kind of controversy, that kind of difficulty and again be creating a competitive advantage and certainty. I don't think it's just in the board room where we perceive that this is important. It is really important,

I will give you a couple of examples. In November of 2005, when we did our results, one of the things that we announced was that we had five billion pounds of provisions for tax disputes on the balance sheet that would be rolling out over the next three years, and our share price just got punished for that over the next couple of days. All the newspapers in the U.K. jumped on it. One of the headlines I can remember was "Vodafone reveals 5 billion pound tax hole." So they were paying attention and tax was important.

Another story. I was on a bus at the Milan airport going out to get on a plane, and somebody walked up to me and said, "I know who you are. I am an analyst, and we just took the Vodafone outlook up on the back of your outlook on tax, and I just wanted to come up and tell you that we are going to be announcing that today."

So this has a real impact. People are paying attention to tax, so it is not just the board that is telling me we need to produce certainty and competitiveness in the tax lines. It is real and it's getting reflected in the share price, and you can see that. So, therefore, it is simply a fact that business is going to look to seek those things out and it is going to locate its business activities and it is going to operate in a way in which it can achieve them.

Again, I mention that sometimes I am surprised that people act like, why should you be doing that with tax? I can understand that with labor costs, transportation costs, energy costs, but tax isn't a cost that you should be pursuing opportunities to maximize efficiency. In my view, it is absolutely what we should be doing.

The reason I feel like we can be doing that is at Vodafone we have a code of conduct in tax, which dictates the decisions we make and how we operate. We have worked out with many tax authorities—including HMRC (Her Majesty's Revenue and Customs) in the U.K.—principles of working, which are about openness and transparency. And Vodafone has values, and with the Tax Department that I lead, we talk about being proud of what we do. In my view, as long as we do all of those things, and we operate in that way, it is perfectly legitimate for us to seek competitiveness and certainty on all the tax lines and drive performance to the bottom line. So, we are out doing that even if some people may be surprised or even uncomfortable.

With that said, then, we are therefore seeing businesses really pushing to try to create maximum performance.

As was mentioned, that is coming at the exact same time governments are seeing unprecedented need for cash, unprecedented need for revenue, and tremendous tension on their bottom line. And we are absolutely seeing that, and this is the topic for the next couple of days. We are absolutely seeing that in debates over who gets to tax what in this global environment. Ninety-six percent of my profits are outside the U.K. The discussion is very much front and center. Who gets to tax that, and everyone is focused on trying to do that.

Who Gets to Tax It Today and Tomorrow?

First, is what I call who gets it today. This is the operational tax aspect, transfer pricing, VAT (Value Added Tax), those kinds of things. As I said, we have got lots of litigation, we have got lots of controversy, we have got lots of issues with virtually every tax authority in every country we operate, all focused on who gets to tax it today, because of these operational issues.

We are also seeing it on the policy side. Who gets to tax it tomorrow. The U.K., as was mentioned, had a lot of discussion last year about how it would tax foreign profits. In my view, the U.K. did the right thing and stepped back from the direction it was going about a year or so ago in terms of taxing worldwide income on certain kinds of businesses, instead, looking to develop a more focused territorial structure with anti-avoidance rules. Again I think this is right, but a lot of debate and discussion around that is yet to come.

I think all that says is that as we continue to pursue performance, governments are seeking who can tax it today and who can tax it tomorrow strategies. The level of controversy, the level of difficulty is absolutely growing and I think fundamentally changing, and not just as a natural evolution but something more dramatic and important.

Again, Tim is going to go into that a little bit more fully in terms of administration and policy. I think the one thing I would say, which I have heard I think a couple of times already this morning, and as long as I have got the microphone I will take the opportunity to throw it out, because I may not have it again for a while. For me, this comment is fundamentally focused on emerged economies. Having an approach of tax administration and development of their policies which is designed principally to track down and drag back income generating activities when they leave is out dated. It's a very defensive strategy that focuses on when a company or a business sets up operations somewhere for a whole variety of reasons, what are the rules we need to go out and claw back, so we can tax it?

The fundamental change in my mind, which will deal with the seismic shift with global companies and trying to deal with government's appetite and need for revenues in this kind of environment, is when those emerged economies start saying instead

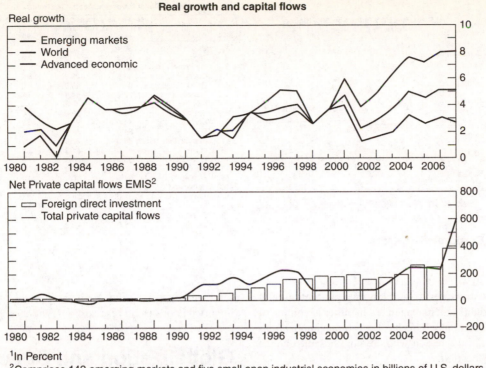

Real growth and capital flows

Real growth

- Emerging markets
- World
- Advanced economic

Net Private capital flows EMIS²

- Foreign direct investment
- Total private capital flows

¹In Percent
²Comprises 142 emerging markets and five small open industrial economies in billions of U.S. dollars.

Source: IMF World Economic Outlook Database, October 2008

Economic Growth

Source: Bank for International Settlements, CGFS Paper No 33/ at 23.

how do I create a policy of administration that plays offense and invites those businesses to put their operations in my country and attracts and retains those businesses. That will fundamentally change this. Then these governments will go to companies and businesses and say you are looking for competitiveness, you are looking for certainty, we are going to provide that to you. Operate here. That will change the dynamic, and I think that's really where we need to go with all of this. Tim?

Cash Flow Matters

MR. McDONALD: Thanks. I am from Procter & Gamble and I guess Joel and I have a lot of similarities and some differences. My company is much older than Vodafone. P&G is now 172 years old. And yet we are both very global. P&G now has over 60 percent of its sales outside the U.S., and we are focused on making that percentage more significant, because over 95 percent of the world's consumers do not live in the U.S.

We do see a lot of the same things that Joel describes, and I think the one difference I would emphasize probably more is the cash flow aspects of tax policy. I think what has been externally validated as more important than perhaps most believed in the last 12 months is that cash flow truly matters. The current global financial crisis painfully proves the point. Cash flow is how companies survive, it is how they fund growth, it is how they pay their workers, and whether they can pay their workers more, and tax policies directly affect not only a company's P&L performance but also its competitiveness due to the cash flow impacts of tax policy.

So, as much as I care about the P&L, and I care about my company's stock price, it is the cash flow that determines a business

decision's true economics. We at P&G have a very robust culture talking about building the company for the next generation of management, the next generation of shareholders and how does the company prosper for an additional 100 years. In that longer run horizon, cash flow is everything. It's whether your company survives or not, and so to that extent, our tax policy choices in the context of a global economy may be about something much bigger than their narrowly conceived tax technical point or about any one company and whether their stock is up or not. These policy choices may be much more about the U.S. economy's long-term level of prosperity. So, I think the tax policies being discussed today are critically important so that we get the potentially big policy choices correct. I think we are at an inflection point in the U.S. of either becoming more similar and competitive with the other economies of the world or more isolationists, dissimilar and noncompetitive with the rest of the globe, ultimately, our choices will dramatically affect our children's standard of living.

Global Multinationals

This panel is charged to set up the entire conference to discuss globalization, international tax policies and their effect on competitiveness. The title to our panel "Whose income is it?" is kind of interesting. It has two prongs. Superficially, this is just a question about transfer pricing. There is however a much more basic issue being discussed at the root cause. The tax audit challenges are now much more contentious and occurring even where the transfer pricing has clearly been correctly done. Fundamentally, there is often an unstated question about why the company operates in a different and more global manner than in the past? The modern

129

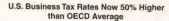

U.S. Business Tax Rates Now 50% Higher
than OECD Average

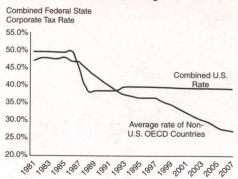

Corporate Tax Rates

2009 International Corporate Income Tax Rates

GOP Rank	Country	2000 Statutory Corporate Tax Rate	2009 Statutory Corporate Tax Rate	Change from 2000 to 2009
1	United States	39.4	39.5	0.1
2	Japan	43.3	41.3	2.0
3	Germany	52.0	33.0	10.1
4	China	33.0	25.0	8.0
5	United Kingdom	30.0	28.0	2.0
6	France	32.0	34.4	3.3
7	Italy	39.5	30.3	0.2
8	Spain	35.0	30.0	5.0
9	Canada	44.0	35.0	0.0
10	Brazil	34.0	34.0	0.0
11	Russian Ferderation	35.0	22.0	13.0
12	India	45.0	41.8	3.2
13	Korea Rep	30.0	25.0	5.8
14	Mexico	35.0	28.0	7.0
15	Australia	34.0	30.0	4.0
16	Netherland	35.0	25.5	9.5
17	Turkey	33.0	20.0	13.0
18	Belgium	40.2	34.0	6.2
19	Sweden	28.0	28.0	0.0
20	Indonesia	30.0	28.0	2.0

business management structures often focus on a concentration of intellectual property rights and management in either a regional or global entrepreneurial company. This has tax revenue implications to the other countries in the region who are not chosen to be the regional entrepreneur location.

The audit question is often, is this business description real and substantive from a business perspective or an artificial tax gimmick? Why did the tax revenue drop and apparently should we attempt to stop the tax base from moving out of that tax authority's country? To understand these tax questions, I think you have to step back and understand that business, as Grant Aldonas described in our opening Keynote speech, is operating very differently, in irreversible ways, as compared to even 15 or 20 years ago. Most companies operated in many countries (*i.e.,* as multinationals) 20 years ago, but they weren't operating as integrated global multinationals. They operated like, as we at P&G did, as small copies of the global parent company in each of their foreign countries. They had fully staffed corporate functions and a largely autonomous management structure in every country. So, in most countries, the byproduct was a tax audit environment that was stable. The tax authorities in each country got their shot at taxing all of the manufacturing and sales activity in their country on a full local entrepreneurial basis as less probably as a royalty back to the country of the parent company.

There might have been a controversy if you had sustained losses in a country, which maybe was explainable. You might have had some contested discussion, if you predominantly imported goods to their country at resale minus, or predominantly sourced out of that country as a manufacturing source at cost plus.

But an interesting dynamic occurred when all the multinational companies were on the locally autonomous "country by country" management structure, what I will hereafter call the "same country" structure. The tax authorities were constrained and couldn't get too aggressive on a transfer pricing theory or method selection because often they would be defending the opposite side of the argument in their next unrelated Competent authority case. Using aggressive transfer pricing theory would actually hinder their revenue collection efforts somewhere else because they had to be theoretically consistent. So, for example, if they wanted to aggressively go after manufacturing income and over emphasize a manufacturer's appropriate return, they may be creating a problem

for themselves auditing a taxpayer whose transactions involve imported goods using resale minus, and *vice versa.*

Globalization and Specialization

What has really changed is that businesses are now global, and they have to be global. Those that are not operating globally are probably not long for this world if their competitors become effective global multinationals, at least for most business models.

What has really changed is that businesses are now global, and they have to be global, and, in fact, those that are not operating globally are probably not long for this world if their competitors become effective global multinationals, at least for most business models.

The globalization point is worth developing. In Grant's keynote speech, he talked about the reduction of various barriers to global trade. I think the reduction in many barriers, customs duties, the currency control restrictions, the WTO trade barrier rules, have all promoted globalization and to some extent tax competition.

P&G is a consumer products company, for us globalization is also about the consumer tastes. What we observe is a homogenization of consumer base beyond country borders. Basically, our consumers are looking more and more the same by region and even globally, and, in fact, we tell the street, for the last eight or nine years that we are focused on our 23 global billion dollar brands. We have moved away from regional brands, and for the most part we have divested or are questioning local-only brands, because they are not as relevant to us, and they are not part of our strategic advantage. So, these regional and globalizing trends take us away from a geographic country focus. That change leads P&G and companies like us to a different management structure and different way of doing business. This is not a fad. Thinking and acting globally is actually a survival issue. If you can achieve a more efficient business model, you must, because others will. For many companies, like P&G, globalization is closely linked to specialization and scale. Achieving scale and specialization whenever you can becomes an imperative. Purchasing for example is no longer done on a country-by-country basis; it has to be done strategically with global price, quality and replenishment standards under competitive volume-based bidding.

Specialization for my company also impacted our main expertise: marketing. Under our prior "same country" local model the country president had very high levels of authority in deciding how her country was managed. The country president would commit to annual sales, net income and cash flow growth objectives and as a result were given wide range of authority in how to deliver these commitments. Our "same country" management structure produced some crazy behavior from a marketing perspective. Sometimes a country president would position a premium tiered product as mid-tier to generate more country sales. In places in Europe where advertisement and image/product placement spills over into neighboring countries this level of lack of coordination is destructive to the greater marketing strategy. It created confusion in branding and image and wasted advertising. We had to evolve away from that type of decentralized marketing. We also had brand-new innovative products launched in our home country. It took us three or four years to launch it in other countries, because the country structure left local management the prerogative to say when they were going to go forward with that large and expensive new product launch campaign, and if they couldn't meet their numbers that year, they held back, they delayed the new product launch. What happened? Our competitors did copy-cat products and they launched their imitator product in other markets ahead of us. In those markets, the copy cat competitor was viewed as the innovator. As a branded company, we can't let that happen, so we had to become more global.

Tax Auditor Expectation Gap

The globalization trend and the evolution of modern global business models are creating a new tax audit paradigm which appears to have drastically reduced the constraint on aggressive audit theory consistency previously described. Now, places that previously were more reasonable and balanced in their audit approach are becoming extremely aggressive and revenue result orientated. These same locations tend to be high-tax countries that are rarely selected as regional entrepreneurial locations. So, what does that mean for the tax revenues? Well, the authorities have a revenue expectation, and this business dynamic has drastically disrupted that historic revenue expectation that they had. They don't have the same entrepreneurial business activity and as a result the same type of revenue sources. Instead they have generally a reduced but more stable tax revenue stream. So, their first reaction is that they don't like it. They don't like the lost revenue, they don't believe the business model works of that real business risk and management activity have been transferred out of their country. They really don't want to ordinarily be a routine low-risk country (unless losses are involved). Unfortunately, we can't have every country as an entrepreneur. The model is, at a minimum, a regional model or possibly global model, but it can't be a per-country model.

So, that leads us to expectation gaps. Interestingly, the theoretical acceptance of the regional entrepreneurial model has recently been accepted in the U.S. After a long discussion on the contract manufacturing regulations, I think, more or less, the U.S. got it right. I think there are some people that are disappointed. There is perhaps a heavy dependence on personal activity on individuals and whether they do substantial contribution, but I think there is at least some overall recognition, for the first time, that this model actually can work without triggering a likely Subpart F inclusion. I think the foreign tax audit environments are catching up with this acceptance of these new business models, but our experience is that it is expensive and somewhat painful. Our experience is all over the map. We have some countries that have actually readily accepted the explanation, audit it aggressively, but the audit produced no change in audit results. We often followed up with an APA (Advance Pricing Agreements) request which was granted and some have expired and been actually renewed without difficulty. In contrast, we have had one country where we went in, got a pre-ruling before the business converted to the regional entrepreneurial structure. They were all fine with it. Administrations changed. The next administration wholly repudiates the rulings. They sued themselves (the government) in court to invalidate the ruling.

They said that the former administration was incompetent, immoral and whatever else they could come up with. They actually asserted a PE (Permanent Establishment) and 100-percent attribution of profits without a profit or return for the 3,000-person headquarters that actually managed that country. In fact, they said it was impossible for us to run our business outside that country. The government official talked in terms of the business as theirs, possessive plural, and I actually said to them, this income is not yours, in fact, the last time I checked your government doesn't own a single share of my parent company or our subsidiaries.

But there was an assertion that they had a stake in our business and its historic income levels, and they weren't willing to let it change. Their theory overrode their treaty obligations with the country where the regional entrepreneur was located as well as our understanding of their domestic law. They also had an alternative theory that there was a deemed sale of the entire business at its "fair market value" *based on its historic cash flows*. This local affiliate was a licensee who had no local intangibles in that country to speak of and yet they said they want to tax in perpetuity the income stream of the former business model, and they want it as an upfront cash payment. Fortunately, things did settle down. Two administrations later, five years of audits, an additional year and a half of competent authority and a bilateral APA application, and we finally got an acceptance of routine returns and a transition payment that was modest and that recognized our transfer pricing view of the business. This was an extremely difficult audit and it was an OECD country.

MS. OLSON: But not an OECD country that is here today.

MR. McDONALD: That's true; it was a different country. In another country, I will call this audit "a theory in search of facts," the auditors constantly were trying to find facts that would disprove our description of the business and prove their hypothesis. At one point they actually visited our regional headquarters, and as they walked away said, "I wish my boss was here. He doesn't believe this place exists." After a total of five years of audit, two additional years of competent authority negotiations, we finally resolved 12 years once again with routine profits and a respecting of the conversion and obtained a five-year bilateral APA. Smaller countries are a little less predictable. We have got one that is espousing a Philip Morris-Italian PE theory that we are still working, but overall, we have been making pretty good progress. We have got eight OECD countries with APAs and four non-OECD jurisdiction APAs. We are trying to expand our ruling coverage and have more APA rulings pending. But what we do see is there is a tremendous amount of cost, energy and hostility to the idea that the world changed. P&G is regularly audited in probably at least 40 countries. Fortunately for P&G, we operate a similar business model around the world. Our goal is therefore to continue to expand our APA footprint. We are probably going to head towards obtaining and then maintaining rulings in 30 countries. Our intention is to use the moral authority of 30 governments all accepting the transfer pricing theory and results to convince the 31st, the 32nd, and 33rd country that they need to be relatively similar.

The World Is a Single Market

So, what does this mean beyond P&G? Well, as I stated initially, the bigger policy implications of not embracing a company's need to evolve and to effectively compete globally are stark. This is related to the larger debate about maintaining deferral in the U.S. international tax rules. In both cases, there are asserted challenges about whether the business rationale and competitiveness policy claims are real. In the deferral debate, we risk being labeled unfairly as unpatriotic for developing our foreign market potential. There is a confusion that assumes that if you investing in the foreign markets it is to the detriment of domestic investment, as if it is an "either-or choice." The truth is we invest everywhere we have a return. We are not capital constrained, so if there are opportunities to invest in the U.S., and there are, we are investing and we are expanding in the U.S., but we are also investing and expanding abroad. Ninety-five percent of the world's consumers live outside the U.S.A lot of our future growth is outside the U.S. because our market share and household penetration rates are much lower there. If we don't grow outside the U.S., and our non-U.S. competitors prosper there, we will eventually die here. Some believe that the arm's-length transfer pricing rules are flawed or dead, as I think some have said, and that businesses as a conclusion should not be allowed to evolve or restructure without tax.

I think these beliefs are misplaced. I think, number one, the business reality is the world is a single market or will evolve into a single market. You need to be efficient, and you need to be competitive with all the global players not just those from the U.S. The reason is not an esoteric P&L reason. It is because if you don't have competitive cash flows; you will not be competitive long term, and you will lose the survival race. The old business model designs need to evolve. You cannot have policy that freezes a business structure, and the reason is simple. New companies will not be constrained by a historic inefficient design pre-tax. They will be allowed to optimize from a clean slate unencumbered by history in a much more rational way that globally runs a global enterprise more efficiently on a pre-tax basis. If you don't let existing/historic competing companies have the same type of opportunity to evolve globally in an efficient pre-tax structure, then you have pre-ordained all existing/historic businesses to slowly die or be acquired. And by the way, those global designs also have an opportunity to be more efficient on a tax basis as well.

The U.S. should not make our U.S.-based multinational any more noncompetitive given our existing worldwide system with its difficult foreign tax credit methodology, and a tax rate that is almost 15 percentage points above the norm. The pressure is acute. If you have 15 to 20 percent cash flow disadvantage as compared to your non-U.S. competitors, the outcome is known, it is just a question of how long it will take for them to win the race. Those that have that kind of structural cash flow disadvantage cannot win. To say otherwise is to think that you are immune from these market realities. It is implicitly an arrogant belief to think that there are to be no competitiveness consequences, Americans would need to be uniquely brilliant versus the rest of the world. They implicitly would have to out-think the foreign competitor on every other line of P&L to compensate for this cash flow disadvantage on tax policy. I do not think that anyone informed in tax policy actually believes that Americans have a unique monopoly on great ideas to win the race despite an uncompetitive tax policy.

It is important to note that a unilateral uncompetitive tax policy precludes a level playing field for U.S. multinationals as compared to their foreign competitors, because the U.S. is the only major economy with global multinationals that still has a worldwide taxation system. The U.S. does not have jurisdiction to impose our policies globally on non-U.S. multinationals. The same is true for any country as compared to the foreign multinationals of that country. The U.S. also does not have unique insight to dictate policy either by edict or by moral persuasion.

We have jurisdictional constraints on whether we can impose the theory. First, for almost 100 years, income tax treaties have allocated taxation rights for corporate income taxation based on source and residency principles. Even where you don't have a treaty, we have a national interest in trying to preserve treaty-like policies and respect that same type of allocation rights. It also probably often overlooked, the trade rules have drastically curtailed the ability to equalize the playing field for U.S. multinationals because it is impermissible under trade rules to have a border adjustment for income tax or any other direct tax. Ironically, probably not thought of at the time, indirect taxes like VAT are permissibly adjusted at the border, and as a result they are probably our future.

So, if we cannot compel consistent global tax policies on the foreign multinational, where does that take us? Well, I think some are arguing we just need to get the rest of the world back on the right page and this tax policy "crisis" of harmful tax competition and global multinationals unpatriotic behavior of "shipping jobs offshore" is solved. Essentially it is a belief that even if we cannot compel the other governments to adopt tax policies strongly similar to ours, they will be convinced to do so once they understand that all governments will be better off and, what some economists call "global welfare" will be achieved, if we end tax competition. Everyone should therefore adopt a pure worldwide system without deferral, or maybe just a U.S. hybrid system and possibly with the same rates we have, or a territorial system, but in a theoretically pure design that raises more revenue than repeal of deferral. The truth is, these options are all theoretically possible, but practically, they are *not at all realistic,* because no government will actually pursue policies that are not in its national interest. They don't actually pursue global welfare as the theory might suggest.

This is not just assertion or hypothesis, the experiment has been run. For the last 20 years, governments have been cutting their tax rates, meanwhile encouraging discussions about stopping harmful tax competition. It is kind of ironic that they have lulled the U.S. to sleep with their rhetoric while they cut their home country tax rates. Their behavior speaks louder than their words. We just haven't followed suit. I think if you look at the EU experience in particular, it is fascinating. The larger countries of the EU for 15 years tried to discuss, threaten and attempted to cajole Ireland and more recently the new entrants to not have a low tax rate for corporations. They even threatened to curtail their infrastructure expenditures to the new EU entrants, but what did the governments there do? They politely listened but didn't change their policies. It was because they viewed it was in their national self-interest to help promote the growth of their multinationals and the foreign multinationals that operate in their country, and they exploited their competitive advantages including tax competition, because their job is to promote the national welfare of their citizens.

Ironically, across the EU now, the idea of stopping tax competition in practice has waned. Even the countries that were the most vocal against tax competition such as Germany and France have cut their rates rather dramatically over the last couple of years.

So, where do we go broadly from a corporate income tax policy? We have two choices. We can almost unilaterally continue our historic worldwide tax policy with high rates. It has implicit assumptions that there are no competitiveness consequences for U.S. multinationals because there are no real foreign competitors' effects to worry about. There is an implicit belief that the U.S.-centric leadership role, both economically and as a policy matter, will carry the day and that others will follow. I think behavior suggests not. The world has in effect moved away from our international tax policies and theory.

We, in effect, can choose to just maintain or modify slightly our current system despite the rest of the world having a very competitive corporate tax landscape, or we pursue an alternative described below, which in my personal view is a more appealing new policy choice. I think we should pursue the predominant international norm on tax policies and design. We would need to adopt a competitive definition of a tax base, a competitive tax rate at or below the OECD average, and we need to maintain the competitiveness of rate. So if other countries cut their rates further, as I predict they will, we cut our rate appropriately to remain competitive as part of the norm of international design. The U.S. would also adopt a territorial system like all of our major trading partners that is realistic, and does not have wholesale disallowance of domestic expenses. It also follows that we do what other countries have done to address the revenue shortfall that these first two policies create by also adopting a legally permissible indirect tax such as a VAT. The advantage of a VAT is that equitably, taxes identical domestic and nondomestic goods equally and therefore it eliminates a dramatic distortion in competitiveness and trade. If you do these three things, you will also politically need to address progressive concerns, and there are tools to deal with that.

We probably have to think about a more progressive income tax, we probably have to deal with our payroll tax system, and we probably have to think about a VAT rebate mechanism for at least poverty level and below household income levels, so that we don't inadvertently shift the tax burden to those that can't afford it. But the advantage of the cluster of these three or four policies is that we probably have a system that is much more immune from distortions of globalization and yet still raises revenue and, if designed right, probably can do it on a quite progressive basis.

I think the second choice gives us stronger long-term GDP growth, at least according to Treasury, implicitly, that would also give us more tax revenue if there is more growth. It would probably produce higher real wage growth. There is plenty of academic research that analyzes corporate tax rates and real wages which suggests, if corporate income tax rates are above the norm, real wage growth is suppressed. In fact, separately, there is robust research that shows that global multinationals in the U.S. pay their employees significantly higher salaries for similar jobs compared to domestic-only companies. Part of that is because they are more successful enterprises. I think that is a desirable thing. If we, instead of cursing the global multinationals, embrace them and try to help them grow, we actually have a strategy that probably promotes greater job growth and retention of the most valuable jobs in the economy. Our historic policy choices unfortunately probably cannot achieve these same objectives as efficiently.

Another Look at Corporate Tax Rates

MS. OLSON: Thank you, Tim. Slide 8 shows the OECD average corporate tax rate being slightly above 25 percent. Senator Grassley said we ought to get our corporate rate down to 25 percent. Chairman Rangel's bill from the last session of Congress took rates down to 30 1/2 percent with some fairly significant base broadening—though Mr. Rangel's staff has said that they got to a 30 1/2-percent rate without breaking a sweat—and Mr. Rangel has said that he wants to bring that rate down a little bit further. I am not sure whether Mr. Rangel plans to go quite as far as Senator Grassley's 25 percent. We are looking at a large need for revenue based on the projected budget deficit, including the enactment of the stimulus bill last week. So we face a need for more revenue.

Other countries around the globe face a need for more revenue, as well. Mike, we would be interested in your thoughts about whether we can get the additional revenue we need out of the income tax base or whether we have to turn to a VAT as Tim suggests. The press pool comments from the fiscal responsibility summit on Monday indicated that there was some discussion about a VAT in the tax session. Mike, we are also interested in your observations, based on your engagement with international organizations and other countries during the year and a half that you have been back at Treasury, on what other countries are thinking about taxes, trying to tax income on a global basis or on a local basis, and where things are going.

MR. MUNDACA: I think what Tim talked about is not only what companies are facing, but what governments are facing as well, which is they both are recognizing that the business landscape has shifted, which is why you have seen such developments as the dropping of the corporate tax rate and the move toward a territorial system. On the other hand, our governments know, as Joel mentioned, that companies are competing on taxes as well, that they are looking to drive down their tax costs just like they are looking to drive down all sorts of other costs, and therefore, governments, because of the need for revenue, because of their knowledge of company behavior, and because of their experience of looking at their tax collections over the last couple of years from multinational corporations, have started to increase their enforcement and have started to come up with some new and novel theories of how to tax under current law. So, even as they are driving down rates, and even as they are in essence giving up taxing a big chunk of foreign source income, we have seen international organizations and other countries, posit expanded theories of jurisdiction to tax, thus expanding the tax base even as they give up on taxing foreign source income, that is by considering a narrower slice of income as foreign. So, therefore, we are seeing countries expand what they consider to be domestic source income. We have seen countries as well try to mold the treaties and transfer pricing rules that they have agreed to implement in a way that looks at business restructuring as an opportunity to either continue to tax what has left, or to impose an exit task on what is leaving. Again, countries are realizing that business is mobile, but many have not yet come to the realization that when they leave, the country loses their rights to tax if they have moved toward a territorial system.

So, we have seen in the OECD and elsewhere again some novel theories on how countries that do see operations leaving, that do see so-called supply chain management structures coming in with respect to their multinationals may hold on to more of the tax base than perhaps their domestic rules would otherwise allow without these overlays of some more novel theories of jurisdiction to tax. I think that is going to continue. I don't think it is an overstatement, as Ed Kleinbard's article on territoriality[1] points out, that territoriality increases to an extraordinary degree the pressure on transfer pricing rules, and that is already an area that already is under a good deal of pressure. So we have seen countries again moving toward more enforcement, more again novel theories of tax jurisdiction and transfer pricing to try to keep some of the tax base they see leaving because of their move to territoriality and because of business' moves of personnel, investment, etc., to other jurisdictions. As Tim mentioned, and this is I think something else to consider, back in the 1960s when our international tax rules were formed, many of the assumptions underlying those rules was that income was being deflected to jurisdictions in which there was no economic activity, and that what we really had to do was try to match the economics with the tax, and that is a lot of what Subpart F was about. But again, as Tim mentioned, investment is what is shifting now, it is not a mere income shift; it is an investment shift. And that creates a new problem: You don't want your tax rules to say, in essence, well, what we would like you to do is not shift investment and assets overseas, but if you do, you are outside our tax net, and if you don't, then, you will be, because we know what the response is going to be. Investment and assets will be shifted overseas, and jobs are going to follow. And the tax rules, pushed them offshore. So again I think that is part of what countries are struggling with, that they have made these changes to their tax rules and are now having to live with the consequences. We will see, especially as countries like Japan and the U.K. and others get more experience with territoriality and its implications, what the next generation of tax changes is going to be. I think for the U.S., and if we have this conference on Friday as opposed to today, there might be a little bit more to tell on what some of the President's plans might be, after the budget outline is released tomorrow, but I don't think it will be any surprise to anyone who listened to the President's address last night, that he will not be proposing a territorial system, that when he talked about closing the loopholes that allow corporations to send jobs overseas, he wasn't previewing a move toward a territorial system. We will have, as we move forward, two different world views. We will have the U.S. worldwide tax system and then we will have all of our major trading partners having moved toward a territorial system, and we will see how the tensions between those views play out.

Question & Answer

MS. OLSON: We have a few questions here from the audience. The first one says, "It is interesting to look at the differences between the way other countries have gone and the way the U.S. is going. Is there anything that you have seen in the discussions with other countries that is pointing them in a different direction than the direction it appears we may be taking in the budget?"

MR. MUNDACA: It would be interesting if you have a chance to ask anyone from the U.K., their experience, and the Japanese, the ones moving the most recently toward a territorial system, what motivated them. But we have seen in discussions with other countries that the motivation is twofold. It is their experience in trying to tax foreign source income and their economic analysis of the effects of moving toward a territorial system. I think many of these countries have become convinced that it is the best way for them to maintain the investment that comes into their countries and maintain the health of their multinationals.

Again, we will see if that is the right choice or not. The counter to that is that a lot of these countries are now seeing, that having moved to a territorial system, their multinationals are seeking to lower their local corporate taxes by moving investment and jobs outside of that country. Again, there are two ways to respond to that. You can (1) move back to a worldwide system or increase enforcement and come up with broader views of your jurisdiction to tax, or (2) you can drive your rates down further. I think a lot of countries are having to face that now, that having moved to a territorial system, what their next move is going to be. It seems the initial response is this enforcement response, this moving toward a broader view of jurisdiction. We have seen coming out of Europe this week a lot of noise from France and from Germany and others on anti-tax haven initiatives, because they think tax havens are sucking out their, not just individual, but corporate tax base, as well. So, I think the initial response has been on that front, the enforcement and broadening of jurisdiction front. We will see if that is successful and if countries may then have to move toward either rethinking the move to territoriality or perhaps to further drive down rates.

MS. OLSON: How do we define "tax haven" for purposes of the exercise that is underway? If you have rates under 20 percent, are you a tax haven?

MR. MUNDACA: A couple of bills use a list, and I think there are a couple of important co-sponsors on some of those bills, but—not speaking for the administration—in forming any list, you have to be very careful as a general, so-called "tax haven" list probably isn't going to be much help to anybody. You need to know why you are forming this list: The list of countries that may be used by individuals, for example, to hide money in banks is very different from a list where corporations might use low tax rates in order to generate better returns on their investments, and no one list is going to serve all the different purposes people want to put these lists to.

It might be better if we were going to go this route to have different sorts of initiatives that focus on individuals, that focus on evasion as opposed to avoidance, that focus on the different uses to which tax havens are put. But at least in the rhetoric coming out of Europe, I haven't seen that subtlety in the analysis. I think they are looking to a very broad definition, that is, a country that has any one of the criteria that were set way back in the late 1990s, the low tax rate, the lack of transparency, the so-called ring fencing—giving special rates for foreign investment. Again, a list that includes all countries that do all of those things, it is going to be, not only quite long, but I think quite unwieldy and ineffective in addressing the problems tax havens present.

MS. OLSON: We have a question from the audience for Joel. The question is whether you can provide some more details about the arrangements with HMRC regarding openness and transparency.

MR. WALTERS: I am happy to do that. I see Dave Hartnett (Permanent Secretary for Tax, Her Majesty's Revenue & Customs) is here, and he can comment if he would like to, as well. The history is actually quite simple. There have been discussions in the U.K. for quite a while as to whether should there be a contract between business and HMRC in terms of how we operate together.

I didn't think that there could be such a thing as a contract, because I am not in a position to bind my shareholders to do anything that I am not required to do by law or regulation, and therefore, it felt to me like that was going too far. But what did feel to me was right is I want an organization that operates in an open and transparent way.

We only do tax planning if we think (1) the law supports us; (2) we think the law is intended to support us, we are not just slipping through a hole in the law; (3) that it is consistent with our values and we are satisfied that it is something we would want to do. If all those things are true, then, there is no reason we shouldn't be open and transparent and deal with tax authorities in a respectful way and communicate in the right way with each other.

So, we sat down with HMRC and we said, let's put together some principles on how we act, how we operate with each other, and on a quarterly basis we will give each other 360° feedback as to how we are doing. And we do that, and I think it has been a great thing, because I think it has moved the level of trust up. I think it has moved the level of communication up. And I think that in my view it reinforces the values that I want in the team, because the team knows whatever it is we do from a planning perspective or however we act today, we are going to openly discuss that with HMRC someday in the future. It reinforces the ways of working that I want from the team. So, it is really just a set of principles that we sat down and we agreed we would operate under and we would test each other on how we are doing. I think it has been a really positive thing from my perspective.

MS. OLSON: Terrific. Any closing comments from any of the three of you? Thanks everyone.

Notes

1. This panel discussion took place at the 10th Annual Tax Policy and Practice Symposium, *Certainty in an Uncertain World? Revolving Cross-Border Tax Controversies,* held on February 25–26, 2009. The panelists' comments were edited, annotated and augmented prior to publication.

2. Edward D. Kleinbard, *Throw Territorial Taxation From the Train,* Tax Notes, Feb. 5, 2007.

Critical Thinking

1. How do tax rates impact on business decisions?
2. Why are they important?
3. What would be the result of high tax rates for a country?
4. What would be the result of low tax rates for a country?

TIMOTHY M. MCDONALD, Vice President—Finance & Accounting, Global Taxes, Procter & Gamble MICHAEL MUNDACA, Deputy Assistant Secretary (International Tax Affairs), U.S. Department of the Treasury JOEL WALTERS, Corporate Finance Director, Vodafone PAMELA F. OLSON, Partner, Skadden, Arps, Slate, Meagher & Flom LLP (Moderator)

Building the Supply Chain of the Future

YOGESH MALIK, ALEX NIEMEYER, AND BRIAN RUWADI

Getting there means ditching today's monolithic model in favor of splintered supply chains that dismantle complexity, and using manufacturing networks to hedge uncertainty.

Many global supply chains are not equipped to cope with the world we are entering. Most were engineered, some brilliantly, to manage stable, high-volume production by capitalizing on labor-arbitrage opportunities available in China and other low-cost countries. But in a future when the relative attractiveness of manufacturing locations changes quickly—along with the ability to produce large volumes economically—such standard approaches can leave companies dangerously exposed.

That future, spurred by a rising tide of global uncertainty and business complexity, is coming sooner than many companies expect. Some of the challenges (turbulent trade and capital flows, for example) represent perennial supply chain worries turbocharged by the recent downturn. Yet other shifts, such as those associated with the developing world's rising wealth and the emergence of credible suppliers from these markets, will have supply chain implications for decades to come. The bottom line for would-be architects of manufacturing and supply chain strategies is a greater risk of making key decisions that become uneconomic as a result of forces beyond your control.

Against this backdrop, a few pioneering supply chain organizations are preparing themselves in two ways. First, they are "splintering" their traditional supply chains into smaller, nimbler ones better prepared to manage higher levels of complexity. Second, they are treating their supply chains as hedges against uncertainty by reconfiguring their manufacturing footprints to weather a range of potential outcomes. A look at how the leaders are preparing today offers insights for other companies hoping to get more from their supply chains in the years to come.

Twin Challenges

The stakes couldn't be higher. "In our industry," says Jim Owens, the former chairman and CEO of construction-equipment maker Caterpillar, "the competitor that's best at managing the supply chain is probably going be the most successful competitor over time. It's a condition of success."[1] Yet the legacy supply chains of many global companies are ill-prepared for the new environment's growing uncertainty and complexity.

A More Uncertain World

Fully 68 percent of global executives responding to a recent McKinsey survey said that supply chain risk will increase in the coming five years.[2] And no wonder: the financial crisis of 2008 dramatically amplified perennial sources of supply chain uncertainty—notably the trajectory of trade and capital flows, as well as currency values—even as the crisis sparked broader worries about the stability of the financial system and the depth and duration of the resulting recession. While many of these sources of uncertainty persist, it's important to recognize that new, long-term shifts in the global economy will continue to pressure supply chains long after more robust growth returns.

The increasing importance of emerging markets tops the list of these uncertainties. Economic growth there will boost global energy consumption in the coming decade by about one-third. Meanwhile, the voracious appetite of China and other developing countries for such resources as iron ore and agricultural commodities is boosting global prices and making it trickier to configure supply chain assets. Worries about the environment are growing, too, along with uncertainty over the scope and direction of environmental regulation.

These long-term trends have knock-on effects that reinforce still other sources of uncertainty. Growth in developing countries contributes to volatility in global currency markets and to protectionist sentiment in the developed world, for example. What's more, different growth rates across various emerging markets mean that rising labor costs can quickly change the relative attractiveness of manufacturing locations. This past summer in China, for example, labor disputes—and a spate of worker suicides—contributed to overnight wage increases of 20 percent or more in some Chinese cities. Bangladesh, Cambodia, and Vietnam experienced similar wage-related strikes and walkouts.[3] Finally, as companies in developing markets increasingly become credible suppliers, deciding which low-cost market to source from becomes more difficult.

Rising Complexity

Manufacturing and supply chain planners must also deal with rising complexity. For many companies, this need means working harder to meet their customers' increasingly diverse requirements. Mobile-phone makers, for example, introduced 900 more varieties of handsets in 2009 than they did in 2000. Proliferation also affects mature product categories: the number of variants in baked goods, beverages, cereal, and confectionery, for instance, all rose more than 25 percent a year between 2004 and 2006, and the number of SKUs[4] at some large North American grocers exceeded 100,000 in 2009.

Meanwhile, globalization brings complexities as rising incomes in developing countries make them extremely desirable as markets, not just manufacturing hubs. Efficient distribution in emerging markets requires creativity, since retail formats typically range from modern hypermarkets to subscale mom-and-pop stores. In Brazil, for example, Nestlé is experimenting with the use of supermarket barges to sell directly to low-income customers along two tributaries of the Amazon River.[5]

Meeting the Challenge

In such a world, the idea that companies can optimize their supply chains once—and for all circumstances and customers—is a fantasy. Recognizing this, a few forward-looking companies are preparing in two ways. First, they are splintering their traditional monolithic supply chains into smaller and more flexible ones. While these new supply chains may rely on the same assets and network resources as the old, they use information very differently—helping companies to embrace complexity while better serving customers.

Second, leading companies treat their supply chains as dynamic hedges against uncertainty by actively and regularly examining—even reconfiguring—their broader supply networks with an eye toward economic conditions five or ten years ahead. In doing so, these companies are building diverse and more resilient portfolios of supply chain assets that will be better suited to thrive in a more uncertain world.

From One to Many

Splintering monolithic supply chains into smaller, nimbler ones can help tame complexity, save money, and serve customers better. Let's look at an example.

Splintering Supply Chains: A Case Study

A US-based consumer durables manufacturer was losing ground to competitors because of problems with its legacy supply chain. Years before, the company—like many global manufacturers—had sent the lion's share of its production to China while maintaining a much smaller presence in North America to stay close to the majority of its customers. One legacy of the move: all of its plants, relying on a unified production-planning process, essentially manufactured the full range of its thousands of products and their many components.

Now, however, increasingly volatile patterns of customer demand, coupled with product proliferation in the form of hundreds of new SKUs each year, were straining the company's supply chain to the point where forecasting- and service-related problems were dissatisfying key customers.

In response, the company examined its portfolio of products and components along two dimensions: the volatility of

demand for each SKU it sold and the overall volume of SKUs produced per week. Armed with the resulting matrix, the company began rethinking its supply chain configuration.

Ultimately, the company decided to split its one-size-fits-all supply chain into four distinct splinters. For high-volume products with relatively stable demand (less than 10 percent of SKUs but representing the majority of revenues), the company kept the sourcing and production in China. Meanwhile, the facilities in North America became responsible for producing the rest of the company's SKUs, including high- and low-volume ones with volatile demand (assigned to the United States) and low-volume, low-demand-volatility SKUs (divided between the United States and Mexico). Ramping up production in a higher-cost country such as the United States made economic sense even for the low-volume products because the company could get them to market much faster, minimize lost sales, and keep inventories down for many low-volume SKUs. Moreover, the products tended to require more specialized manufacturing processes (in which the highly skilled US workforce excelled) and thus gave the company a chance to differentiate itself in a crowded market.

However, the company didn't just reallocate production resources. In tandem, it changed its information and planning processes significantly. For the portfolio's most volatile SKUs (the ones now produced in the United States), the company no longer tried to predict customer demand at all, choosing instead to manufacture directly to customer orders. Meanwhile, managers at these US plants created a radically simplified forecasting process to account for the remaining products—those with low production runs but more stable demand.

For overseas operations, the company continued to have its Chinese plants produce finished goods on the basis of long-run forecasts, as they had done before. The forecasts were now better, though, because planners were no longer trying to account in their models for the "noise" caused by the products with highly volatile demand.

Together, the changes helped the company reduce its sourcing and manufacturing complexity and to lower its cost of goods sold by about 15 percent. Meanwhile, it improved its service levels and shortened lead times to three days, from an average of ten. Quality also improved across the company's full range of products.

How Many Splinters?

The first question for organizations exploring multiple supply chains is how many are needed?. Answering it requires a close look at the way the supply chain assets that a company uses to manufacture and distribute its products matches up against the strategic aspirations it has for those products and their customers.

This requirement seems obvious, but in practice most companies examine only the second half of the equation in a sophisticated way; they can, for example, readily identify which products they see as leaders on cost, service, innovation, or (most likely) some combination of these. Fewer companies seriously examine the operational tradeoffs implicit in such choices, let alone make network decisions based on those trade-offs.

Oftentimes, a good place to start is to analyze the volatility of customer demand for a given product line against historical production volumes and to compare the results against the total landed cost for different production locations. This information provides a rough sense of the speed-versus-cost trade-offs and can even suggest locations where supply chain splinters might ultimately be located. A global consumer-packaged-goods maker, for example, quickly saw that two-thirds of the demand associated with a key product line (about 40 percent of the company's product portfolio) could be moved from a higher-cost country to a lower-cost one without hurting customer service.

Of course, companies must carefully check these broad-brush analyses against customer needs. The consumer goods company, for instance, found that packaging innovation was a differentiator for some of its products and thus configured a single production line in the new, lower-cost location to make packaging for several markets quickly. By contrast, in automotive and other assembly-based industries, we find that the customers' responsiveness and the complexity of individual products are important inputs that help determine where supply chains might be splintered.

Second-Order Benefits

While dividing a supply chain into splinters may seem complicated, in fact this approach allows companies to reduce complexity and manage it better because operational assets can be focused on tasks they're best equipped to handle. At the same time, the added visibility that a splintered approach offers into the guts of a supply chain helps senior managers more effectively employ traditional improvement tools that would have been too overwhelming to tackle before.

After the consumer durables maker divided its supply chain into smaller ones, for example, it was able to use formerly impractical postponement approaches (producing closer in time to demand to keep holding costs low). The company's US plants now combined various SKUs into semifinished components that could quickly be assembled into products to meet customer orders. Indeed, the lower inventory costs this move generated partially offset the higher labor costs of the US factories.

Likewise, the global consumer-packaged-goods maker found that after splintering its supply chain, it was more successful at applying lean-management techniques in its plants. Among the benefits: much faster changeover times in higher-cost production locations, enabling them to handle product-related complexity more effectively.

Use Your Network as a Hedge

The advantages that multiple supply chains confer are most valuable if companies view them dynamically, with an eye toward the resiliency of the overall supply chain under a variety of circumstances. Will the various strands of a particular global supply network, for example, still make sense if China's currency appreciates by 20 percent, oil costs $90 a barrel, and shipping lanes have 25 percent excess capacity? It's critical for organizations to determine which of the many questions

like these are right to ask and to invest energy in understanding the global trends underpinning them. Some companies are already thinking in this way. Nike, for example, long a leader in emerging-market production, manufactured more shoes in Vietnam than in China for the first time in 2010.[6]

In fact, we believe that the ability of supply chains to withstand a variety of different scenarios could influence the profitability and even the viability of organizations in the not-too-distant future. In light of this, companies should design their portfolios of manufacturing and supplier networks to minimize the total landed-cost risk under different scenarios. The goal should be identifying a resilient manufacturing and sourcing footprint—even when it's not necessarily the lowest-cost one today. This approach calls for a significant mind-set shift not just from operations leaders but also from CEOs and executives across the C-suite.

At the consumer durables manufacturer, for example, senior executives worried that its reliance on China as a hub could become a liability if conditions changed quickly. Consequently, the company's senior team looked at its cost structure and how that might change over the next five to ten years under a range of global wage- and currency-rate conditions. They also considered how the company could be affected by factors such as swinging commodity prices and logistics costs.

The company determined that while China remained the most attractive manufacturing option in the short term, the risks associated with wage inflation and currency-rate changes were real enough to make Mexico a preferable alternative under several plausible scenarios. Consequently, the company has begun quietly building its supplier base there in anticipation of ramping up its manufacturing presence so that it can quickly flex production between China and Mexico should conditions so dictate.

Similarly, the global consumer-packaged-goods manufacturer is examining where dormant capacity in alternative low-cost countries might help it hedge against a range of labor cost, tariff, tax, and exchange-rate scenarios. The company is also factoring in unexpected supply disruptions, including fires, earthquakes, and labor-related strife.

A North American industrial manufacturer chose to broaden its footprint in Brazil and Mexico to hedge against swings in foreign-exchange rates. In particular, the company invested in spare capacity to make several innovative, high-end components that it had formerly produced only in Europe and the United States because of the advanced machining and engineering required. The investment is helping the company hedge against currency swings by quickly transferring production of the components across its global network to match economic conditions. Moreover, the arrangement helps it better support its supply partners as they serve important growth markets.

Making these kinds of moves isn't easy, of course, since any alterations to a company's supply chain have far-ranging implications throughout the organization. For starters, such changes require much more cooperation and information sharing across business units than many companies are accustomed to. Indeed, the organizational challenges are so significant that for many companies, a hands-on effort by the CEO and others across the C-suite is needed for success.

Nonetheless, the rewards are worthwhile. By creating more resilient and focused supply chains that can thrive amid heightened uncertainty and complexity, companies will gain significant advantages in the coming years.

Another Uncertainty

Protectionism could change the economics of a supply chain at the stroke of a pen. Our research suggests, for example, that the total landed cost of making assembled mechanical products such as washing machines in a given low-cost country could plausibly swing up to 20 percent given different tariff scenarios.

For more on how to develop scenarios in light of demographic, technological, macroeconomic, and other global trends, see "Applying global trends: A look at China's auto industry," on mckinseyquarterly.com.

Notes

1. Jim Owens made this remark in an interview conducted by Hans-Werner Kaas on September 20, 2010. For more from that interview, read "My last 100 days," on page 104.

2. For more, see "The challenges ahead for supply chains: McKinsey Global Survey results," mckinseyquarterly.com, November 2010.

3. Tim Johnston, "Striking Cambodian workers reflect Asia trend," Financial Times, September 13, 2010.

4. Stock-keeping units.

5. Tom Muiler and Iuri Dantas, "Nestlé to sail Amazon Rivers to reach emerging-market consumers," Bloomberg News, June 17, 2010.

6. Fiscal year.

Critical Thinking

1. Why is the supply chain important?

2. What are some of the considerations for establishing the supply chain?

3. How can the supply chain be maintained and improved for the future?

YOGESH MALIK is principal in McKinsey's Cleveland office; ALEX NIEMEYER, is a director in the Miami office, BRIAN RUWADI is principal in McKinsey's Cleveland office.

Acknowledgment—The authors wish to acknowledge Sebastien Katch for his valuable contributions to this article.

UNIT 4

Issues in International Business

Unit Selections

Learning Outcomes

After reading this Unit, you will be able to:

- Describe some key points of direct foreign aid.

- Explain what emerging markets can do to build on their successes.

- Explain why corporate social responsibility is important.

- Describe what happens to countries where graft becomes widespread.

- Explain whether corporations should be ethical in their global dealings, and who should define what is ethical for corporations when they conduct business with different cultures and societies.

Student Website

www.mhhe.com/cls

Internet References

China.org
   www.china.org.cn
CIVICUS
   http://civicus.org
Downsizing of America
   www.nytimes.com/specials/downsize/glance.html
Green Peace
   www.greenpeace.org/usa
The Development Gateway
   www.developmentgateway.org
The Economic Times
   www.theeconomictimes.com

One half of the world's population lives in the developing world. Three of the four largest countries in terms of population are among the developing world countries: China, India, and Indonesia. China and India alone account for 2.4 billion people, more than twice the entire population of Europe, Canada, Japan, Australia, New Zealand, and the United States combined. The fate of what happens in the developing world will be the fate of what happens in the global economy. India and China, as well as many of the other developing countries, are the ones that are coming out of the global recession much faster than the developed countries, and the game in international trade and development would appear to be changing.

Companies from China and India seem to be investing in some of the lesser developed parts of the world and especially Africa. For years, both Chinese and Indian companies have been off-shoring highly labor-intensive, low-skilled work to lower-cost venues. The "flip-flop" business was off-shored long ago. Today, much of that investment is focused on countries in Africa where economic development has not occurred on the scale that it has in Asia. There are many opportunities in Africa for investment, and Chinese and Indian organizations are aggressively pursuing those opportunities. Today, African trade with China and India roughly equals that of Africa's traditional trading partners in Europe and the United States.

Foreign aid has been a way for developed countries to attempt to assist lesser and least developed countries. But, that foreign aid has often come with strings attached to it. Often the money must be used to purchase items from the donating country, often specific items. This is not the best use for the foreign aid money. The receiving country's main need may be for farm equipment, but the foreign aid money may require them to purchase military equipment. The countries will take the money and buy the equipment, but what they really needed were tractors, not tanks.

The way organizations are operated outside the developed world can, at times, be very ethically challenging. Many countries outside the developed world have no rules or regulations on how the employees of corporations should be treated. If they do have rules, those rules are either loosely enforced or not enforced at all. The safety of the workers is sometimes compromised in an effort to squeeze the last nickel of profit out of the operation without regard for the safety of the workers. Long-term health considerations are tossed aside in the knowledge that the workers will have little recourse against their employer when they become ill. Developed countries have a responsibility to address these issues as discussed in "How Civil Society Can Help: Sweatshop Workers as Globalization's Consequences."

Global corporate citizenship goes beyond just being a good neighbor. Global corporate citizenship means taking an active role in the important issues facing the international environment, including climate change, water shortage, infectious diseases, and terrorism. Global corporate citizenship means being an active player in the development of the future of the world's international environment. It goes beyond the traditional concept of simply writing a check for a good cause and walking away from the problem for someone else to spend the money. It means getting involved, and the company actively spending

© Flying Colours Ltd/Getty Images

the money itself to see that it is appropriately utilized and that the firm gets it money's worth. Companies will be criticized for taking this approach, for taking too active a role in how their resources are spent. But, history has shown that too much of corporate philanthropy has been wasted, especially in the developing world, so organizations owe it to themselves, the recipients, and their stockholders to make certain that the money and investments they make are utilized more effectively.

The greening of the economy has been a major factor in both the domestic and the international agenda. President Obama has made the green economy a major part of the agenda of his administration. The same can be said in the international environment. Everywhere, organizations are seeking to become more "green" in the way they do business. This benefits the company from several perspectives. First, from the perspective of costs, becoming green generally means using less carbon-based energy, and as the price of carbon-based energy is almost certain to climb in the long-run, going green will help to keep costs down. The second is from a marketing perspective. Greener products are generally viewed more favorably by consumers, giving the company a better image overall. Finally, the third reason is that more and more countries are demanding that companies produce products that are green as opposed to the old formulas for producing those products. This includes automobiles that get better gas mileage to laundry products that produce less environmental pollutants. Going green simply makes sense for any corporation.

There is, however, one aspect of the green economy that green organizations need to be careful of. Corporate sponsorship can be very dangerous for green organizations to either seek or accept. While these corporate organizations may want to affiliate themselves with particular environmental groups as a part of their corporate strategy of becoming green, it may not be in the best interests of the green organization to accept the affiliation. Accepting money from a large corporation generally means that the large corporation will list the fact that they support

"X" group on its website and in its corporate literature. It has, after all, donated money to the organization, usually on an annual basis. The money the corporation has donated is probably relatively small in terms of the corporation's coffers, but likely to be large in terms of the green organization. Money, it should be remembered, can be like a drug—after a few years the green organization can become dependent on that money from the corporate source. The removal of those funds, or even the threat of removal of those funds, can place the mission of the organization in jeopardy. Green organizations would do well to be cautious in dealing with large corporations and keep them at arms length.

There are many issues in the international business environment. More issues will be coming to the forefront every day. Terrorism, another oil crisis, war, ethnic cleansing, another economic crisis may all be on the horizon. But good news can also be there too. Wars eventually do end, tyrants are eventually toppled, and economic crisês are eventually resolved. Since the start of the industrial revolution, about 250 years ago, technology has found a way to resolve many of the problems that have plagued the human race for centuries. There have been much darker times than the ones we live in today. There is hope. Whatever the crisis, this too, shall pass.

Foreign Aid, Capitalist Style

Poor countries that want money from the Millennium Challenge Corp. pledge to end corruption and embrace democracy. Can this little-known agency change the model for global aid?

NINA EASTON

Dole Food Co. has been knocking on his door, but Tony Botchway wasn't sure he wanted to cut a deal. Five years ago, this Ghanaian farmer could only dream of becoming a supplier to the world's largest producer of fruits and vegetables. Now he's producing 4,500 hectares of sweet pineapples and mangoes, and selling them for juicy profits (profits he wasn't sure he wanted to share) to Spain and Switzerland. His Bomarts Farm has expansion plans that local banks are happy to finance. And he can afford to pay his nearly 750 workers above minimum wage, while providing lunch and free medical care. "We're ready to compete with Costa Rican producers," he told me as we stood in front of his new processing plant in central Ghana's Nsorbi, just weeks before he ultimately decided to ink a deal with Dole.

Botchway and his workers have U.S. taxpayers to thank for all this, specifically, a little-known foreign-aid program called the Millennium Challenge Corp., which has poured more than half-a-billion dollars into Ghana alone since 2006. Since its founding in 2004 the agency, which enjoys bipartisan support, has committed some $8 billion to projects in developing countries such as the Philippines, Georgia, and El Salvador.

Some of you are surely rolling your eyes at the thought of more American dollars flowing into foreign lands—taxpayers already provide some $34 billion a year in economic aid through agencies such as USAID. But the MCC program is international aid that capitalists can embrace: The agency's founding principle is that economic growth is the best antidote to poverty, and so while some money is funneled to schools and hospitals, MCC's biggest grants, or "compacts," are aimed at kick-starting private enterprise. In Ghana, for example, the MCC money has been used to train 65,000 farmers, build storage facilities, and pave gutted dirt roads so that they can get fresh produce to markets.

MCC itself takes a businesslike approach to its disbursements. Countries that apply for funds must meet a rigorous checklist. An MCC grant isn't a blank check—and unlike other foreign aid it is designed to end. "My goal is to replace our money with private sector money," says Daniel Yohannes, an Ethiopian-born banker from Colorado who was tapped by

President Obama in 2009 to run the agency. When I visited Ghana, a digital clock in the local agency office was counting down the days till the end of its five-year compact. After that, it's pencils down. If Ghana wants more money, it must compete against other countries with a new proposal addressing a new industrial sector. No country has yet received a second compact, though a handful—including Ghana—are in the running.

In contrast to most other foreign-aid programs, MCC grants come with tough strings attached: Only democratic countries with a commitment to economic freedom can compete for the money. Fall down on that and you're booted—as Nicaragua learned in 2008, when suppressing political opposition in local elections cost the country a $62 million grant. When the Malawi government used violence to quell demonstrators, MCC threatened to halt its $350 million grant.

MCC was the brainchild of former Secretary of State Condoleezza Rice. She says that, going back to her days as national security adviser, she was dismayed by the way agencies such as USAID, the World Bank, and other bloated bureaucracies administered aid, letting corruption and fat overhead siphon off money, or wasting dollars on regimes that suppressed private markets and political opposition, keeping poverty rates high. "I couldn't defend a lot of foreign aid over the past years, much of which disappeared into the pockets of corrupt foreign leaders," Rice tells me. In 2002, President George W. Bush, flanked by U2 star Bono, proposed increasing development aid by 50% through what he called a "millennium challenge account." (Bono later told Rice that he was initially skeptical about the Bush White House's plans; MCC has since become a program supported by both sides of the aisle, and venture capitalist Alan Patricof, a longtime Democrat, sits on the MCC board of directors.)

The Bush administration also hoped MCC would help it achieve its foreign policy goals. In her forthcoming book *No Higher Honor*, Rice describes the MCC as a pillar of a broader post-9/11 national security strategy to promote American values abroad. "We were looking at how to build well-governed states that take care of their people. And to do that, foreign aid had to be a two-way street," she says in an interview. "It had to be transparent."

MCC COMPACTS

TRANSPORTATION, FARMING AND IRRIGATION
Honduras
Funded Projects Completed (Ended 2010)
The $215 million compact targeted the productivity of small farms, training more than 7,000 farmers, and improved access to major markets. MCC dispensed all of that funding, except $10 million discontinued after political upheaval in 2009.

FARMING AND IRRIGATION, ROADS
Armenia
Partially Defunded (Ended 2011)
MCC paid out $177 million of its original $235 million grant, bolstering the agricultural sector and making major improvements to irrigation. The remaining funding for roads was cut amid concern over unrest following the country's disputed 2008 elections.

EDUCATION, ROADS, HEALTH CARE, ENERGY, AND MORE
Mongolia
In Progress (End Date 2013)
The $285 million grant aims to boost economic activity by supporting vocational training, strengthening property rights, increasing adoption of energy-efficient products, and doing major roadwork in the country's north-south economic corridor.

GOVERNANCE, FINANCE AND BANKING, TRANSPORTATION
Benin
Successfully Completed (Ended 2011)
The $307 million grant is aimed at expanding the country's port to triple capacity. It jump-started small business with property title and registration systems, streamlined a clogged court system, and cut corruption.

HEALTH CARE, WATER, EDUCATION, GOVERNANCE
Lesotho
In Progress (End Date 2013)
The $363 million grant is extending the water system for industrial and domestic use, improving health outcomes, and removing barriers to foreign and local private sector development.

Compact Commitments, BY SECTOR, IN BILLIONS

WATER SUPPLY AND SANITATION $0.8 ENERGY $0.6

TRANSPORT $2.9   AGRICULTURE $1.6   BANKING AND FINANCIAL SERVICES $0.5   OTHER $0.9

MCC's philosophy is that local ownership ensures that countries have a stake in success. Bush described it as "partnership, not paternalism." Projects are designed and administered by a coalition of government officials and business, labor leaders, and environmentalists—in an often hotly debated process that acts as its own exercise in democracy, Rice says.

Early results suggest the model is working: Honduran farmers linked to MCC projects have seen their incomes rise nearly 90% in two years; in Armenia, projections say, it's 150%. Former Ghanaian President John Kufuor, recent winner of the 2011 World Food Prize, gives MCC a big piece of the credit for a decade where per capita income tripled and hunger was dramatically reduced. MCC's $547 million five-year plan to home-grow a Ghanaian agribusiness industry has enabled farmers to move away from subsistence toward a modern business approach that ensures revenue, not just family supper, Kufuor explains.

MCC recognizes that capitalism needs more than money to thrive, and so it forces grant winners to maintain standards on everything from immunization to education of girls to a strict rule of law—all keys to an egalitarian society where free markets can thrive. In turn, qualifying for an MCC grant has a financial halo effect on countries, or "a kind of a Good Housekeeping seal of approval" for would-be foreign investors, says Patricof, the MCC board member. After MCC made a grant to the African nation of Benin, Bolloré, a French conglomerate, followed with a $256 million investment of its own.

With big American bucks on the line, countries like Benin found the motivation to finally clean up tangled property title systems, giving landowners the collateral they needed to access credit. MCC-sponsored business registration centers offer entrepreneurs an incentive to quickly open legitimate, taxpaying companies.

MCC money gives political leaders the backbone to get tough on corruption and reform court systems, two notorious problems that keep foreign investors at bay. When I toured Benin and Ghana, government ministers praised MCC for helping "correct certain behaviors." (Translation: MCC provided air cover for government efforts to weed out corruption.)

Despite the leverage that money buys, deploying billions of U.S. taxpayer dollars to fight global poverty through economic growth hasn't been easy—as I learned in Benin.

Other african nations have minerals or diamonds or oil. Tiny Benin, a former French colony of 9 million people, has its port—a gateway for imports traveling to landlocked West African countries. More than half of MCC's $307 million grant to Benin was aimed at expanding the Port of Cotonou to accommodate today's supertankers. The construction came in on time and on budget. Ending corruption is a bigger project.

Intolerance for corruption is the sine qua non of MCC dealmaking. Bribery, kickbacks, and other illicit activities can do serious damage to a country's reputation, erode government treasuries, and scare off investors. In Benin, customs fees have been an easy source of pocket money for customs agents. And the deal with MCC requires that to end. (Benin qualified for a grant because of a better-than-average corruption problem.) Automated systems installed as part of the port expansion are helping. In August, Benin's newly reelected President Thomas Yayi Boni gave a speech declaring that bribe-takers will be punished.

I arrive in the capital city of Cotonou in September, two weeks after that speech, and it quickly becomes clear that the heat is on him. Customs agents are threatening a strike in retaliation. Yayi, meanwhile, doesn't want to lose his U.S. grant—nor the opportunity to compete for a second one. He is also, by all accounts, sincerely committed to his anticorruption campaign; lost revenue is pinching his government.

Yayi and his government have taken notice of *Fortune*'s presence, with ministers opening their doors to make the case for U.S. investment in their country. They've also taken note of the arrival of Jonathan Bloom, who oversees MCC's West Africa grants. Bloom is a soft-spoken Harvard Business School graduate who nonetheless describes himself as a "straightforward, effective hard-ass"—qualities Yayi witnesses firsthand.

During our visit Yayi calls a meeting with his port minister and Bloom to make the case for more MCC money. Bloom has a rigid counteroffer: Benin must complete unfinished business from the first compact, including the meeting of deadlines and ending corruption. Benin can pursue a second compact, but the competition is fierce. "It's far from automatic," Bloom says.

The next morning, over breakfast, the port minister, Jean-Michel Abimbola—who also chairs the local MCC board—argues that Benin needs more than MCC's money; its anticorruption demands "provided a kind of magic potion for the way forward." Adds Abimbola: "I wish it would not stop at this step, but it has changed laws and behaviors."

In mid-September, a few weeks after Bloom departs, customs agents respond to Yayi's anticorruption campaign with two short strikes. But Yayi refuses to back down; the Benin legislature passes—and courts uphold—a ban on customs agents strikes. Anticorruption measures move forward. Officials from the Danish shipping giant Maersk and Bolloré tell me they are optimistic that import traffic through Benin will triple in the coming years.

N

o one at MCC kids himself that Benin's battle against corruption is anything but an ongoing operation. But it's one worth fighting because of its link to job creation—and, thereby, poverty reduction. MCC field workers like to think of themselves as a sort of special ops force of donor aid—a lean, mobile machine that intervenes and then, just as

important, leaves. Only two MCC staffers work full-time on the ground in each country, backed by a team of engineers and auditors in Washington. USAID and the World Bank, by contrast, maintain big, stationary units in the countries where they provide aid.

To be sure, MCC doesn't engage in all the laudable humanitarian efforts that consume much of the USAID budget—coming to the rescue after floods, earthquakes, famine. It doesn't have a mission to, say, end a killer like malaria, as the Gates Foundation does. Nor are MCC's architects alone in recognizing the merits of capitalism in combating poverty. The World Bank has long had a private sector arm called the IFC—which partnered with MCC on Benin's port, among many other projects. The bank's current president, Robert Zoellick, has convinced pension and sovereign wealth funds to invest in poor developing nations, while promoting innovations like J.P. Morgan-designed hedging tools to help emerging agribusinesses manage risks like weather and pricing. "We see our job as creating conditions for markets to flourish, to draw more capital in," Zoellick tells *Fortune*.

But MCC dares to promote a view—economic growth as the best antipoverty tool—that is often at odds with much of the donor community, which remains suspicious of capitalism. Economic growth is mentioned only twice in a recent 44-page United Nations report, Paul Farmer, UN deputy special envoy for Haiti, has pointed out. Yet as Farmer noted in a recent *Foreign Policy* article on Haiti relief efforts, "All humans need money—they need it to buy food and water every day. And no matter how hard the government or the aid industry tries, people will want for all three things until they are employed."

Helping the world's poor consumes less than 1% of the U.S. budget. Still, why should strapped American taxpayers continue to pour billions of development aid into poor countries?

Condi Rice, now a professor at Stanford University, is blunt: "Foreign aid is one of the most important parts of diplomacy. We need countries that are responsible. A stable society is not going to become a failed state." But, she adds pointedly, "every taxpayer ought to be asking, Is it working?" It may be too early to declare MCC's approach a success, but the tiny agency certainly gives the taxpayer real bang for the buck.

Critical Thinking

1. What kind of foreign aid is effective? Why?
2. Is government stability an important consideration when giving foreign aid?
3. What role does corruption play in the effectiveness of foreign aid?

Emerging Challenges

Emerging Markets Must Adapt to the New Global Reality by Building on Their Economic Success

MIN ZHU

In the wake of the recent crisis, a two-speed recovery shifted global economic growth from advanced to emerging and developing economies.

While gross domestic product (GDP) in advanced economies grew on average 3 percent in 2010, emerging and developing economies grew 7.2 percent. The IMF forecasts that the two-speed trend will continue this year. Advanced economies are projected to grow 2.5 percent and emerging and developing economies 6.5 percent, their consumption surging too. In absolute terms, emerging and developing economies will consume $1.7 trillion more in goods and services this year than last year.

Naturally, the rapid growth in emerging markets is swiftly lifting their importance in the global economy. They account for nearly two-thirds of the total growth in global output in the past two years, compared with one-third in the 1960s. Their contribution to foreign trade is also large and increasing, even though advanced economies trade almost twice as much.

The growing heft of emerging market economies is part of a long-term trend. In each of the past five decades, the growth rate of emerging and developing economies exceeded that of advanced economies—at times by a large margin. As a result, at the end of last year emerging and developing economies accounted for 48 percent of global output (measured in terms of purchasing power parity—using the exchange rate at which the currency of one country must be converted into that of another country to buy the same amount of goods and services in each country).

The trend may well continue for a while (see chart). The overall economic conditions in emerging economies are quite favorable: relatively small fiscal deficits, manageable public debt, stable banking systems, low cyclical unemployment, and strong growth momentum. In contrast, many advanced economies are facing serious challenges that stem from big government deficits, large public debt, problems in their banking systems, high unemployment rates, and weak growth. In addition, recent structural changes in emerging economies support the three key drivers of growth: the labor force is growing at a rapid pace and populations are urbanizing, investment is growing with support from ample foreign capital, and productivity is

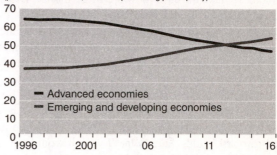

Crossing paths
Emerging and developing economies' share of world gross domestic product (GDP) will exceed that of advanced economies starting in 2013.

(percent of world GDP, based on purchasing power parity)

— Advanced economies
— Emerging and developing economies

Source: IMF, World Economic Outlook database.

increasing as production moves up the value-added chain. If current trends continue, in two decades annual global output will more than double, from $78 trillion to $176 trillion (in today's money), of which $61 trillion in additional output will come from emerging and developing economies, while advanced economies' contribution will be about $37 trillion.

Major Shifts in Global Economy

Strong demand and supply growth are taking place in economies whose populations are much bigger than those of advanced economies. Three billion people live in Brazil, Russia, India, and China—the so-called BRICs—alone, compared with 1 billion in advanced economies. When all emerging and developing economies are combined, they account for 85 percent of the world's population. Incomes of large numbers of people are rising rapidly and causing tectonic shifts in major aspects of the global economy:

- *Food:* Global demand for food is rapidly rising as large numbers of people enjoy higher per capita incomes, allowing them to buy more nutritious foods. Demand is rising for basic foodstuffs and for food products with higher value added.

- *Nonfood commodities:* The need for better housing and transportation and more energy is placing tremendous upward demand pressure on nonrenewable resources, such as petroleum and metals. The numbers are staggering. During the past 10 years, while global oil consumption increased by 13.5 percent, oil consumption in emerging markets increased by 39 percent—and their share of global consumption grew from one-third to one-half. And almost all the additional global demand for copper, lead, nickel, tin, and zinc came from major emerging market economies. During the next five years, for example, emerging markets' share of global copper consumption is projected to jump to three-quarters from only one-third a decade ago.

- *Capital flows:* Although emerging and developing economies account for almost half of world GDP, they hold only 19 percent of world financial assets. As money chases growth and opportunity, global financial and capital flows are shifting toward emerging market economies. The movement of only 1 percent of financial assets in advanced economies into emerging markets is equivalent to the current flow of foreign direct investment from advanced economies into emerging markets. Indeed, capital flows from the United States to emerging markets increased from an annualized $300 billion during 2006–07 to an estimated $550 billion in 2010, while flows to advanced economies declined from $900 billion during 2006–07 to $600 billion in 2010. Strong capital inflows are putting upward pressure on consumption and asset prices in emerging markets, and risk is building in the financial sector.

- *Patterns of production:* Global manufacturing production patterns are shifting. Emerging market economies are producing more high-technology machinery and equipment, and low-technology manufacturing is increasingly moving to lower-income countries.

- *Trade:* Global trade patterns will gravitate toward emerging markets. Emerging market economies' strong growth both in production and in domestic consumption will lead to more trade with advanced economies and, notably, among themselves.

- *Environment:* The toll on the environment is growing. Pollution is visible in the air and water, and the potential consequences will be devastating if the world does not reduce its carbon footprint.

Broad Changes Needed

Only with deep structural changes in growth models, policies, and lifestyles can emerging market economies address the long-term challenges they face.

A growth model that depends on demand from advanced economies will no longer serve emerging markets well. Emerging markets should shift their focus from growth led by external demand to internally generated, supply-driven growth. Policies should follow and pay particular attention to the supply side. Emerging markets should take the following steps:

- Make every effort to continue increasing their agricultural output to cope with the surge in demand for food. This will require not only supporting investment in agriculture, but also encouraging research and development to promote innovation and productivity growth in the agricultural sector.

- Pay particular attention to their service sector, because it creates employment at a sustainable pace. Policies should be geared toward opening, not closing, markets to competition, as has been customary in many economies. In particular, governments should refrain from excessively protecting small businesses, at the expense of consumers. In particular, governments should actively dismantle monopolies so that anyone who wants to enter a market can do so, which would boost efficiency and reduce price pressures.

- Invest heavily to eliminate bottlenecks. For the government this means investing in infrastructure, especially in transportation and energy, and ensuring entry and exit to all markets so that firms can take advantage of business opportunities. This also means educating and training workers to increase efficient use of capital and to boost household incomes. Investing in the application of established and new technologies will also help boost productivity.

Macroeconomic stability is paramount for other policies to work effectively. So *emerging markets need to maintain strong fiscal, financial, and external buffers and implement good macrofinancial policies.* Emerging markets must also continually improve institutions with a view to designing and implementing better policies.

There are two areas I think are critical for the future of emerging markets: building viable pension and health care systems and reforming financial systems. As populations grow, pension systems in most emerging markets will put an undue burden on the next generation or, if benefits are reduced, risk pushing large pockets of the population back into poverty. Similarly, major reforms are needed to broaden access to higher-quality health care. There are both successful and unsuccessful examples of pension and medical care reform in advanced economies, and emerging markets should learn from these examples and design systems to fit their own circumstances.

Emerging markets should also reform their financial systems, which are at the center of economic activity—channeling countries' savings into investment, which is the key component of growth. Financial institutions also play an important role in facilitating capital flows from abroad, which are expected to remain strong in the medium term in response to favorable growth opportunities in emerging markets. Reforms are needed to ensure that the financial sector serves the economy rather than the other way around and that losses are not socialized while gains are privatized.

Finally, and perhaps most fundamentally, *there is a need to foster a lifestyle that is more respectful of the earth and its finite resources*. For example, most of us need to use less energy, use it more efficiently, and produce it more cleanly. We also need to be much more mindful of what we consume and how we consume it. It is very difficult to change such behavior, but governments can create the right incentives by pricing carbon correctly, including the environmental cost of our activities in the system of national accounts, and adding the true value of ecosystems into our national wealth calculations.

For most emerging and developing economies the past two years were great, and the future looks rosy. But there is no guarantee that the good times will last. In fact, that bright future will probably not materialize if the challenges I have outlined are

not given priority and addressed satisfactorily. Modern history is replete with sobering cases of policy paralysis and ensuing lost years and decades.

Critical Thinking

1. Why are developing economies becoming more important?
2. How have they emerged faster from the global economic recession?
3. What does this mean for the future of the global economy?

MIN ZHU is Special Advisor to the IMF's Managing Director.

From *Finance & Development*, 48(2), June 2011, pp. 48–49. Copyright © 2011 by The International Monetary Fund and the World Bank. Reprinted by permission of The International Monetary Fund and the World Bank via the Copyright Clearance Center.

How Civil Society Can Help
Sweatshop Workers as Globalization's Consequence

JEFF BALLINGER

Italy's idyllic region of Tuscany is known as a top-tier tourist destination. Less well known is that it is also one of Europe's frontiers of human trafficking and a case-study in the effects of globalization. The garment and textile factories of Prato figured prominently in Italy's "miracle" economic performance of the 1950s and 1960s, with more than 4,500 small shops producing many of the world's most sought-after brands. Garment production is buoyant there again, but "economia sommersa" (submerged economy) sweatshops account for more than a third of the goods produced, and many of the Chinese workers are working long hours for little or no pay, due to huge debts to trafficking gangs. Now that the new anti-immigration mayor is closing illegal operators, hundreds of workers without legal working papers are in limbo as the Chinese government has refused the Italian government's attempts at repatriation.

Immigrant-bashing media in Italy decry the rise of sweatshops, but NYU's Andrew Ross points out that they had their place in Prato decades ago, when there was a high-wage "core" fed by peripheral sweatshops. Hence, the current situation is not a "Chinese import." This mobile workforce has been a hallmark of globalization, spawning a hugely contentious debate and ugly—if understandable—resentment.

Aside from the worker migration topic, there are other key globalization questions as well. Has globalization turned good companies bad? Has the outsource model forced the buyers to accept the often brutal practices of supplier-factory managers in some of the world's most corrupt and lawless environments? Is the current wage allocation truly fair and efficient? Several myths occlude helpful discussion of these questions and the solutions to their larger underlying issues.

There is one myth that has served the most vulnerable industries (electronics, toys, garments, and footwear) well over the last decade: a global brand will meticulously monitor its supply chain because conscientious consumers, informed by the latest technologies, will punish the company at the retail level for any transgression. Rather, according to Jeffrey Swartz, the CEO of Timberland, consumers do not think too much about workers' rights in the supplier factories. "Don't do anything horrible or despicable" and the company will be safe, he opined in late-2009. His remarks are supported by a striking example: the complete lack of media attention when the toy-maker Mattel scrapped all factory monitoring in 2010.

> ## Has the outsource model forced the buyers to accept the often brutal practices of supplier-factory managers in some of the world's most corrupt and lawless environments?

Another misperception—shared by "free trade" critics and proponents alike—is the race-to-the-bottom discourse, which posits that any improvement in wages or conditions will send factory managers off in search of more vulnerable workers. In 2000, shortly after the anti-WTO protests in Seattle, over 200 economists sent an open letter to college presidents in the United States that chastised them for too easily acceding to the students' demand to clean sweatshop-stained apparel out of university bookstores. The message was simple: they will hurt the very workers that they are trying to help because of this outsourcing imperative to seek lower standards.

In practice, there appears to be much room for wage improvement. Indonesia's "real" wage nearly tripled in the early 1990s, while foreign investment continued to flow. China and Vietnam have pushed up minimum wages several times in the last five years while maintaining double-digit growth rates. The incontrovertible and simplest proof that there is ample room for wage growth may be seen in the cost breakdown for a typical university-logo "hoodie"—the labor cost of the US$38 garment is less than 20 cents, while the university's licensing fee is over two dollars.

One of the most refreshingly honest voices in the global workers-rights field, Dr. Prakash Sethi, has addressed what is perhaps the most pernicious myth: Northern-based "buyers" have an arm's-length relationship with their Korean, Taiwanese, or Chinese suppliers and therefore are not responsible for their well-documented records of contumacy. For years he was the architect of Mattel's efforts to track compliance with supplier "codes of conduct"—pushing outsource factories to observe local laws, prohibit child labor, etc.—and he has done consulting work in this field for several other Fortune 500 firms. He says that the major global players, including the World Bank, the OECD countries, and the International Labor Organization, have failed to apply pressure on low-cost producing

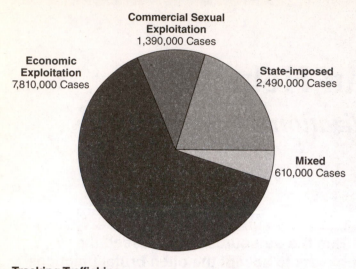

Forced Labor Worldwide
Considering Categories of Trafficking

Commercial Sexual
Exploitation
1,390,000 Cases

Economic
Exploitation
7,810,000 Cases

State-imposed
2,490,000 Cases

Mixed
610,000 Cases

Tracking Trafficking
International Labor Organization; 2005

countries that do not protect workers' health, safety, or human rights. Boldly, he has also called on corporations to pay restitution to developing-world workers for "years of expropriation" enabled by corrupt, repressive regimes. Particularly poignant is his brusque assertion that "bigotry" was at the root of most companies' refusal even to try to grapple with some of these issues. Lending weight to Sethi's call for restitution is a pair of recent capitulations by Nike in claims against contract factories in Honduras and Malaysia, wherein Nike paid several millions of dollars to harmed workers.

For almost two decades, policy-makers have suffered the deleterious effects of these myths, resulting in inefficient allocations of time and effort. The child labor controversy offers a concise example. Although there were never more than a negligible percentage of 10- to 13-year-olds in factories, hundreds of millions of dollars have been directed at this perceived problem since the early 1990s. A focus on raising adult wages and thereby eliminating the need for the children to help support the family, by contrast, might have resulted in hundreds of thousands of poor families being able to keep those same children in school. What then is the current situation? How has globalization affected the production sector, wages, and working conditions?

Globalization and Supply-chains

Before globalization, most consumer-product companies were vertically-integrated—design, production, and marketing all occurred in one country. Then, a boom in out-sourcing created the global "supply-chain," an interesting twist to the familiar sweat-shop narrative.

The result may be seen in sub-Saharan Africa, Southeast Asia, and the Middle East. In the last, for example, a reader unfamiliar with the current practices of global garment producers may well ask why Jordanian factories are filled with Asians,

when Jordan's unemployment rate lies between 13.4 percent to 30 percent (official/unofficial figures). The answer, of course, is that the supplier factories can pay foreign workers less and being "guests" they are less likely to make trouble.

An observer with more knowledge about global supply chains and garment production after the formation of the World Trade Organization would perhaps point to the remedy in the 2001 US-Jordan Free Trade Agreement, which contains "labor rights" requirements. Unsurprisingly, Jordanian officials aver that all workplaces are inspected and workers, of every nationality, in the 100+ factories are protected. In an altogether too common oversight, the reporters who noted this pledge presented no enforcement statistics to support the claim, and one can only conclude that the agreement's requirements remain empty' promises.

New Abuse, Intriguing Opportunity

Sending workers abroad to the newly rich Gulf countries in the 1970s was perhaps the first meaningful benefit of globalization for states such as Egypt, the Philippines, Bangladesh, Pakistan, and India, since workers' remittances meant billions of dollars. After the outsourcing boom of the 1980s, filling factories with foreign workers became a familiar practice in Taiwan and South Korea, where shoe and apparel brands "nudged" long-time suppliers towards cheaper labor in China and Indonesia. As democratization in the late-1980s began to push up wages in the factories that have churned out millions of pairs of sneakers each month since the mid-1970s, they were soon filled with cheaper immigrant workers from the Philippines, Thailand, and later, Vietnam.

The issue remained below the radar for over a decade, despite Fortune magazine's searing portrayal of factories in Taiwan in 2003, which dubbed it "indentured servitude." With the lack of attention, brands sourcing from the factories suffered no sustained criticism for their contractors' abusive practices, nor for those of labor suppliers or "brokers," who often become prone to corruption on both ends: supply and delivery. Over the last decade, a "perfect storm" has developed: lucrative contract-labor fees (often triple what laws allow); growing demand for workers, coupled with relative impunity for brokers; bigger profits; malleable "host" governments for contract-factories; and finally, complacence on the part of buyers. Most striking about the last is the surprising ease with which Corporate Social Responsibility (CSR) tactics such as simple codes of conduct for supplier factories with cheap (and easily manipulated) "social audits" refuted "sweatshop" allegations.

The Role of Civil Society

There is, however, hope for consumer power: globalization's fallen barriers have made it possible for small civil society organizations to punch above their weight in trans-border solidarity campaigns. One such group is the Committee to Protect Viet Workers (CPVW) which, as the name makes clear, has a narrow focus, with a global reach and membership, as it draws volunteers from Europe, North America, and Australia. One of the clear positives of globalization is the access to news media

Minimum Estimate of Forced Labor in the World

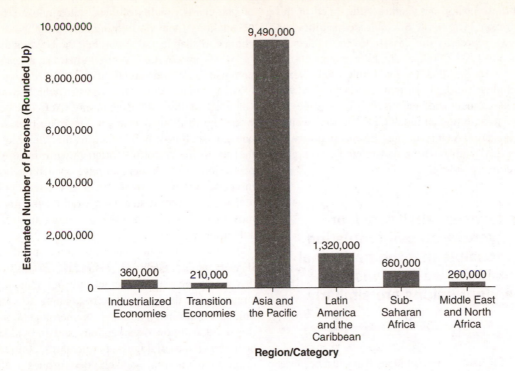

Work without Consent
International Labor Organization; 2005

outlets enabled by hundreds of these new citizen-watchdog nongovernmental organizations, who are joining the more-established legal aid and independent trade union movements.

Being based outside of Vietnam, the CPVW is free to advocate on behalf of several independent union activists now jailed in Vietnam. Although many grievances had come to the fore since foreign investment began to transform the country in the mid-1990s, the powerful 2006–7 wave of wildcat strikes—protests generally spontaneous in nature with ad-hoc leaders preferring anonymity—focused on wages. Inflation had hit double digits in 2006, but Vietnamese workers' wages in exports-factories had been fixed at US$42 per month for over a decade. An assessment of the protests yields some interesting findings: more than 70 percent of the 580 strikes took place at foreign-investment factories, with Nike—the country's largest "buyer" with over 200,000 contract-factory employees—suffering wage-related protests in more than a third of its 35 source factories. These huge shoe and apparel factories are also plagued by extraordinarily high turnover rates, mainly due to forced overtime and pressures to boost production.

The CPVW began observing "destination" countries when Vietnamese authorities dramatically increased the number of workers sent abroad in the period from 2006 to 2008. Workers returning from Malaysia informed CPVW's correspondents about cheating and horrendous living conditions at a t-shirt factory producing for Nike. The nongovernmental organization then turned the controversy into a minor scandal in Australia, and Nike immediately put the issue on the "fast track" for settlement, which contrasts sharply with the contemporaneous case in Honduras, which dragged on for two years. One possible

explanation for the disparate treatment is the media, since the Vietnamese migrants' story was presented as a case of "human trafficking on a massive scale." Nike's contract-workforce in Malaysia numbered around 10,000 at the time; 1,100 foreign workers at the t-shirt factory are receiving about $2,000 each as restitution (paid in installments over nearly three years). The company will not reveal settlement deals at the other workplaces. The investigation itself earned the Best TV award at 2009's Every Human Has Rights ceremony in Paris.

Forcing a Re-examination of CSR?

A CPVW activist recently expressed frustration that Nike has for years had "independent" inspectors inspect its contract factories in Malaysia. How could it be, then, that workers worked under "indentured servitude" conditions which were clear for all to see, but inspections never disclosed this fact? The CPVW merely brought to public view what inspectors should have brought to the fore years ago. Perhaps the answer lay in the circumstance of Nike's "independent" inspectors, which number over 70, in an in-house CSR team of 215. The methodology deployed by most of these "responsibility" operations places great emphasis on the cultivation and maintenance of "stakeholder" relationships—predominantly, civil society organizations in both producer- and consumer-nations. Standard-setting and analysis of supplier-factory performance is certainly a part of their work, but the company's buyers operate with a wholly different set of metrics.

To return to the beginnings of CSR in the mid-1990s would show a very strong link to the sweatshop controversy. In other words, the current proliferation of CSR artifice and funding started with anti-sweatshop activism, as illustrated in the huge jump in mentions of "Corporate Social Responsibility" or "CSR" in major news sources, from 28 articles in the decade 1988–98, to 561 from 1998–2003, to 2,643 between 2003–2008. The means of gathering this data, a simple Lexis-Nexis search, points to another issue. Given that this explosion was driven by worker mistreatment and below-subsistence wages, it would be reasonable to assume that much CSR "action" would be concentrated in this area. As it turns out, the vast majority of CSR press releases deal with environment-related issues and less than 1 percent concern workplace issues.

> **If workers are deceived, distracted, or dispirited by buyer-driven self-regulation schemes, it is possible that the traditional strategies available to workers wishing to form independent unions are similarly affected.**

Just to reiterate, CSR had an incredible growth spurt because of workers' exploitation related to outsourcing, but the industry relies almost exclusively on environmental initiatives to demonstrate some kind of "responsibility" progress. Recently, in recognition of this fact, more CSR officers have simply replaced "responsibility" with "sustainability" in their titles and work-product.

Refreshing the Anti-Sweatshop Struggle

The corporate self-regulation "solution" which consisted of codes of conduct for supplier factories and spot-checking by social auditors has been a chimera. Since the early Clinton years, global labor rights received scattershot support; grants would go abroad through the Department of Labor or the State Department's Bureau for Democracy, Labor, and Human Rights. Many of these focused on "capacity-building" for workplace inspectors, but paid little attention to the lack of political will to actually do the enforcement work in any given country. Several millions more are funded more effectively each year through the AFL-CIO, though this has declined precipitously since the 1980s.

Addressing the rule of law as applied to the workplace ought to be a key priority for President Obama's State Department, even given the chance that such a worker-advocacy platform may discomfit countries such as China (a big holder of US Treasury bonds), Turkey (where the Pentagon's needs often drive U.S. policy), and Bangladesh (which has a host of stability concerns), to name a few. For far too long, autocratic regimes have received conflicting advice from American policy makers. The boiler-plate nostrums involving multiparty democracy and clean government made little practical sense when China, pre-reform Indonesia, and Vietnam were experiencing

growth rates which were the envy of most poor nations. The off-the-charts venality of these states mocked the World Bank's decade-long focus on fighting corruption. Now is the time and climate to change and strengthen the US signals.

At an appropriate venue—such as a gathering of trade unionists and labor rights activists in Mexico or Thailand—Obama should outline the ways in which workers are disadvantaged in the global economy. Activists across the globe would be thrilled to hear an American president calling into question such neoliberal tenets as the "flexible" workforce and the necessary "reform" (often downward-leveling of worker protections), which together have opened the door to a noxious insecurity of employment. As an exercise in public diplomacy, a clear and forceful statement would bring hope to opposition movements fighting entrenched economic elites allied with autocratic regimes.

Policy and program energies simply need to be redirected. If workers are deceived, distracted, or dispirited by buyer-driven self-regulation schemes, it is possible that the traditional strategies available to workers wishing to form independent unions are similarly affected. Numerous national and international trade union organizations and individual leaders have been drawn into dialogues, partnerships, conferences, and pilot programs with "multi-stakeholder" groups or the corporations directly. Many of these activities lent an undeserved patina of respectability to corporate self-regulation, often under the rubric of CSR. In addition, the long tweaking, critiquing, and field assessing of code-of-conduct "social audits," sometimes undertaken directly by unions and labor rights NGOs, diverted precious resources from the challenging task of devising realistic worker-empowerment strategies.

Further research is desperately needed on the actual labor law enforcement performance in countries where most low-skill assembly takes place. While living in Indonesia twenty years ago, I asked the US Embassy's labor attaché to get labor law enforcement numbers from the Ministry of Manpower in Jakarta. We learned that there were over 700 inspectors who found a total of 12,640 violations that year, but only 60 cases made it to the first adjudicative step; of these, only nine verdicts were reported. Ten years later, the Ministry again provided enforcement statistics: This time 700 inspectors only managed to do 243 factory visits for the entire year. Presumably, government officials—pressured by foreign investors to reduce the amount of bribe-seeking from various departments—restrained inspectors from making factory visits.

It is clear that a new architecture of rights must be erected, beginning with a no-nonsense survey of current practices. Every labor attaché or labor reporting officer at an American embassy should compile the following facts: Has the country signed International Labor Organization Convention 81 (Labor Inspection)? If so, when is the last time a report was sent to Geneva? How many labor inspectors are there? How many factory inspections were done last year? What is the number of violations found? How many prosecutions started? How many back pay awards were made? Our attachés should also map out the bureaucratic chain of command, with names of responsible local officials and an account of who-reports-to-whom—beginning in huge export-processing zones. This is information about dysfunctional governance unavailable to local journalists, legal aid, and worker-assistance organizations. US-based companies importing more than US$50 million worth of goods should have to post these findings on their corporate websites—in both English and the local language—for every country in which they have more than three contract factories.

This data should be folded into a matrix maintained by a nongovernmental organization working under a several-year grant from the State Department's Bureau of Human Rights, Democracy, and Labor. Alongside the raw numbers, wiki-style narratives should be included on such issues as freedom for nongovernmental organizations operating in the labor sector, labor history, recent strikes, opinions on the adequacy of the minimum wage, academic papers on all these issues, and contact information for unions and activist groups. Such an interactive website would make possible a global dialogue about key issues.

The world's workers need this dialogue both to build resilient movements and to challenge globalized production practices now ruled by top-down declamations, such as those issued in the World Bank's "competitive index," which ranks countries higher for ease of hiring and firing, reduced severance benefits, and other employer-friendly policies, or its recent study which concludes that workers have to sacrifice even more than they have already, in the name of economic growth. These overweening influences—that are keeping the workers' share of a US$38 hoodie frozen at 20 cents—are being challenged by brave activists every day. The Hoover Institution's Larry Diamond sums up the tool-kit succinctly as "struggle, personal risk-taking, mobilization, and sustained imaginative organization." The path to meaningful change may debut some attention-grabbing tactics (perhaps young workers in Vietnam will tweet-up wages using their incredibly cheap mobile phones), but the "struggle" piece of this is age-old.

Leaders in rich countries need to rethink policies that have been foisted upon them by free-market fundamentalists over the past three decades of globalization. Enforcement need not be a cudgel used by politicians pandering to the fearful; lovely Prato should be a model of fair governance over a diverse landscape

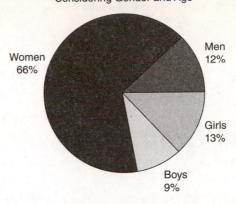

Profiling the Victims*
Considering Gender and Age

*Profile of victims indentified by State authorities in 61 countries where was collected, aggregated for 2006.

Assessing the Abused
International Labor Organization; 2005

of small shops, where consumers need not pay more and the bel paese receives tax revenue. It is possible with some of the steps outlined above. Countries wishing to attract foreign investment would feel pressure from rich-nation governments to protect their workers. This modest push may not offset the global business community's antipathy toward regulation, but it may begin to redress the balance.

Critical Thinking

1. What is the ethical responsibility of the developed world toward manufacturing practices in the developing world?
2. How important are cheap products to the developed world?
3. Are sweatshops a logical consequence of manufacturing in the developing world?

JEFF BALLINGER is Director of Press for Change, a human rights organization with a focus on worker rights in the developing world. He has just finished three years as a Research Associate at the Harvard Kennedy School.

Map Room

Global Graft

Last November, Transparency International released its fifteenth annual Corruption Perceptions Index (CPI), ranking 180 countries and territories on a scale of zero to ten—with zero the most corrupt, ten the purest. Only 49 nations scored five or above. New Zealand ranked highest with a grade of 9.4; Somalia, not surprisingly, ranked lowest with 1.1—both filling the same slots they had a year earlier. But other nations bounced up and down the scale from 2008 to 2009, earning points for reforms, crackdowns, and rhetoric, or losing points amid new scandals. Here are nine of the biggest movers and shakers of the past year.

MEXICO, 72 to 89 (−17)

When Felipe Calderon became president in December 2006, he

CORRUPTION INDEX

0–1.9
2.0–3.9
4.0–5.9
6.0–7.9
8.0–10

made it a priority to crack down on the explosion of drug violence in Mexico—rooting out politicians and local law enforcement officers believed to be on the payrolls of the nation's drug cartels. In 2009, Mexicans witnessed standoffs between local and federal officers, and the arrest of 10 of the country's mayors charged with links to local crime syndicates. The result was a heightened awareness by Mexicans of the shocking extent to which corruption has pervaded their government.

BOLIVIA, 102 to 120 (−18)

President Evo Morales lost credibility last year in a bribery scandal. Santos Ramirez, president of the state oil company and a close Morales aide, was caught taking bribes worth more than $1 million in exchange for oil contracts. The deals became public after bandits killed a Bolivian oil executive carrying a $450,000 bribe for Ramirez's brother-in-law. As the scam unraveled publicly, Morales fired Ramirez—after initially defending him—placing the company under tighter scrutiny. Eventually, Hugo Morales, Evo's brother, was linked to the thieves who killed the executive. The widely publicized scandal saw Bolivians lose faith in key institutions of the state.

THE GAMBIA, 158 to 106 (+52)

The Gambia's president, Yahya Jammeh, seized power in a military coup in 1994. His slogan: "transparency, accountability, and probity." Since then, Gambia has been on a rollercoaster ride up and down the CPI ranks: 90th in 2004, 158th in 2008, back up to 106th in 2009. Jammeh has been involved in a host of scandals, including using millions of dollars of Gambian tax receipts as "gifts" at the naming ceremony of his son. By the end of 2008, Jammeh returned to his sermon of transparency, lining up cabinet ministers for scrutiny by an anti-corruption commission, though it is understood that the president's personal wealth is still growing.

LEBANON, 102 to 130 (−28)

In last year's parliamentary elections, candidates railed against bribe-taking by incumbents and praised new electoral laws, including a ceiling on campaign spending. But candidates themselves hid funds in multiple accounts and tapped streams of cash from throughout the region to pay rivals to withdraw, buy positive TV coverage, and offer free plane tickets for expatriates to come home and vote.

MOLDOVA, 109 to 89 (+20)

Corruption has always been a pressing issue, but it's recently become a top priority for the nation's reformers. Five years ago, one study observed a mentality of acceptance and fatalism about the hold corruption had on society. Then the Moldovan government installed the sweeping Anti-Corruption Alliance, playing host to 29 non-governmental organizations that work to reduce systemic corruption through national and local initiatives. Prime Minister Vladimir Filat has taken a more active role in combating corruption by raising his involvement with a new body that works to eliminate money laundering and the financing of terrorism.

KAZAKHSTAN, 145 to 120 (+25)

Kazakhstan's jump up the rankings came after the government embraced a series of anti-corruption measures, including ratifying the UN conventions against corruption and transnational organized crime, and forming a special body to fight corruption and economic crimes. New legislation also redistributed power between law enforcement bodies in the investigation of corruption crimes. Despite these developments, the level of corruption in Kazakhstan is still estimated by some experts to be very high, with the judicial system, law enforcement, and the bureaucracy governing property rights particularly vulnerable.

INDONESIA, 126 to 111 (+15)

In 2009, Indonesia made big strides in reducing corruption after 32 years of President Suharto's "kleptocracy"—jumping 15 places on the CPI. Its Corruption Eradication Commission prosecuted graft and bribery in government budgets and procurements, with a 100 percent conviction rate, even indicting the father-in-law of the president's son. But in November, just after the 2009 CPI was released, the anti-corruption commission got caught up in its own scandal. Two commissioners were arrested for accepting bribes to let a businessman flee the country before trial. Nobody's perfect.

IRAN, 141 to 168 (−27)

The election of President Mahmoud Ahmadinejad ushered in an era of mounting corruption. In 2004, Iran was a near-respectable 87 on the CPI; five years later, it sits at 168, just behind Haiti. Why? In part, because Ahmadinejad promoted many of his former cronies from the Islamic Revolutionary Guard to government positions, handing over control of a large chunk of the nation's economy. Construction firms and developers linked to the Guards receive massive contracts, presenting opportunities for corruption. In November, the Telecommunication Company of Iran was sold for $7.8 billion to a company run by the Guards, with the contesting bidder later shown to be a fake.

TANZANIA, 102 to 126 (−24)

Despite the recent establishments of three ethics bodies, Tanzania's political and administrative system is still rife with all levels of corruption. The auditor general says 20 percent of the government budget is lost to corruption, while a World Bank survey says 50 percent of companies have made "informal payments" to win contracts. Not a single large-scale case has been prosecuted. In 2008, Prime Minister Edward Lowassa resigned amid charges he had awarded the untested Texas-based Richmond Development Company a $179 million emergency power contract in 2006, which it never fulfilled.

Critical Thinking

1. What, in your opinion, is a common thread running across the countries listed here?
2. Do you think graft will always be with us? Explain.
3. What steps do you believe should be taken to address the problem?

Deadly Business in Moscow

An American lawyer's experience underscores the lawlessness outsiders operating in Russia can face.

Tom Cahill

Jamison Firestone was at his desk when the commotion began. On the morning of June 4, 2007, the American attorney heard loud voices coming from the reception area of his law firm, Firestone Duncan, on Krasnoproletarskaya Street in Moscow. He went out to investigate and was greeted by two dozen officers from the Russian Interior Ministry.

Over the next seven hours, he says, the security forces corralled Firestone and his staff in a conference room, ransacked the offices, and confiscated computers and documents. When one of Firestone's employees objected, he was beaten so severely he required hospitalization for three weeks.

On the same day, Russian police raided the Moscow headquarters of one of Firestone's clients, the prominent foreign investment firm Hermitage Capital Management. Its founder, the American-born financier William Browder, had become a strong critic of the state-controlled energy conglomerate Gazprom and has been barred from reentering Russia since 2005. The searches of the offices marked a major escalation in Hermitage's conflict with the Russian government. And Firestone, 44, who had spent 18 years helping Western companies navigate the murky waters of Russia's legal system, knew what it could mean. "Corrupt law enforcement is the single biggest risk to business in Russia," he says. He braced for the worst.

His fears came true within months, when records confiscated during the June 2007 raids allegedly were used in an elaborate $230 million fraud that exploited three Hermitage funds to extract phony tax refunds from the Russian government. In 2008 an attorney from Firestone's firm who helped represent Hermitage was imprisoned on tax charges; he died behind bars last November after being denied medical treatment, creating a furor in Moscow. Finally, last year two unsuccessful attempts were made to steal $21 million in taxes paid to the Russian government by a company for which Firestone served as general director, he says. The people behind these attempts used his forged signature to seek rebates, a method similar to that used in the Hermitage case, he adds.

"Stealing the Country"

Now Firestone, a former board member of the American Chamber of Commerce in Russia, has fled to London, fearing that he, too, could end up in jail. "Police [in Russia] have to stop being the Mafia," he says. "These people are stealing the country."

The alleged victimization of Browder and Hermitage is well known. In interviews with Bloomberg News, however, Firestone for the first time is alleging government-sponsored fraud aimed at him personally. His account underscores the arm-twisting and lawlessness that can afflict outsiders doing business in Russia. As widely reported, oil giants British Petroleum and Royal Dutch Shell have suffered politically backed attempts to wrest control of aspects of their Russian operations. The French carmaker Renault likewise has come under government pressure to assist a Russian manufacturer in which it had invested.

The risk of being targeted for abuse by government officials—sometimes operating in league with Russian businesses—is a central reason the country has attracted less than one-fifth the foreign investment in China and Brazil and half of what's invested in India, according to three years of data compiled by fund tracker EPFR Global.

Corruption is a central reason Russia has attracted far less investment than China or Brazil.

In the wake of the death of Firestone's colleague, Sergei Magnitsky, the heads of the Moscow police's tax crimes department and the city's prison division were both fired. That's not enough, says Browder, 45, who has been based in London for the past five years. "We've written well-documented complaints to the top law enforcement officers in the country that a number of police officers, judges, organized criminals, and businessmen have been involved in the theft of almost $500 million from the state and were involved in imprisoning Sergei Magnitsky," he says.

In October 2008, Magnitsky complained about the Hermitage case to Russia's State Investigative Committee, the equivalent of the U.S. Federal Bureau of Investigation. He said the officers involved in the raid on the law firm may have been linked to the Hermitage fraud, according to a transcript of his testimony.

A little more than a month later, on Nov. 24, 2008, five officers arrived at Magnitsky's home at 7 A.M. and took him in for questioning. He was accused of involvement in an alleged tax fraud perpetrated by Hermitage and was pressured to withdraw his complaint and implicate Browder, according to petitions Magnitsky filed with the Interior Ministry's Investigative Committee. "When I repeatedly rejected these propositions by the investigators pushing me to commit such a base act, the conditions of my detention become worse and worse," Magnitsky wrote in a Sept. 11, 2009, filing. Two months later, on Nov. 17, the 37-year-old father of two died from toxic shock and heart failure after being held in pretrial detention for 358 days.

Some of the records taken from Firestone's office in the 2007 raid involved an investing company called OOO Anrider. The documents showed that Anrider had paid $21.6 million in taxes in 2006, according to Firestone. A filing with Russian tax authorities dated Apr. 24, 2009, claimed that Anrider overpaid taxes by $21 million and deserved a refund. Firestone says he learned of the filing after the claim was rejected and copies of the papers were sent to him. The documents included what Firestone alleges were forgeries of his signature and Anrider's corporate seal. Someone, he says, was trying to use his identity to steal tax revenue and, in the process, possibly implicate him.

The lawyer, a native New Yorker who began studying Russian in high school and speaks it fluently, alerted tax authorities last August that the claim was bogus, documents show. The tax office didn't respond, and the police declined to open an investigation.

The Russian Interior Ministry's Investigative Committee declined to comment about Firestone or Magnitsky; it would only confirm that it is investigating Browder for alleged tax fraud. "He's screaming that they stole his companies, but he's not talking about the tax he didn't pay," spokeswoman Irina Dudukina says. "If he thinks he's innocent, then he should give evidence."

Browder, who has been placed on the Interior Ministry's wanted list, says his companies were all audited and that no tax claims have been filed against them. "They're trying to cover an enormous crime against the budget with fabricated allegations," he says.

Firestone agrees. "When you see corruption on this scale at the same time as the President is demanding investigations and cracking down, it's brazen," he says. He left his apartment in Moscow before Christmas, as if going away for the holiday, and hasn't been back.

Critical Thinking

1. Do you think there is corruption in Moscow?
2. What do you think this means when attempting to do business in Russia?
3. Do you think this is holding back the Russian economy?

Current Mission Statement Emphasis: Be Ethical and Go Global

Darwin L. King, Carl J. Case, and Kathleen M. Premo

Introduction

Mission statements are vital communications used by corporations to define themselves to their various stakeholders including customers, employees, creditors, and stockholders. Mission statements can be as short as one sentence or expand to one or two paragraphs. These statements attempt to communicate the organization's values, purpose, identity, and primary business goals. Mission statements are often longer than a vision statement which provides a broader statement reflecting the future aspirations of the company.

Fred David argues that a mission statement is a declaration of an organization's "reason for being" (David, 2009). A clear mission statement is necessary for the firm to effectively establish objectives and formulate long-term strategies. David also states that every organization has a reason for being and any organization that fails to develop a comprehensive and inspiring mission statement loses the opportunity to present itself favorably to existing and potential stakeholders. According to David, a good mission statement reveals an organization's customers, products or services, markets, technology, concern for survival, growth, and profitability, philosophy, self-concept, concern for public image, and concern for employees. These factors, he believes, serve as a practical framework for evaluating and writing mission statements.

Peter Drucker believes that firms need to develop a mission statement that answers the questions "What do we want to become?" and "What is our business?" when the firm has been successful (Drucker, 1974). This proactive approach attempts to define how the firm can continue to excel and improve operations. Many authors feel that organizations develop mission and vision statements only when the company is in trouble (David, 2009). This reactive approach is far less effective and David feels that development of mission statements in times of crisis is a gamble that "characterizes irresponsible management."

Rebecca Leet believes that developing a mission statement is especially important for non-profit organizations and charities (Leet, 2008). Leet feels that just as strategic planning taught groups how to organize and focus their functions internally to achieve their missions, developing a strategic message teaches them how to organize and focus externally by recognizing who their supporters are and linking the organization's goals to what drives people to take the action it seeks. This basic philosophy applies to for-profit organizations since these firms want customers to continue purchasing their goods and services and also hope that stockholders and employees will continue to support the organization.

According to King and Cleland, a carefully constructed mission statement must, among other things, ensure unanimity of purpose within the organization, provide a basis, or standard, for allocating organizational resources, establish a general tone or organizational climate, serve as a focal point for individuals to identify with the organization's purpose and direction, and specify organizational purposes and translate them into objectives for the firm (King and Cleland, 1979). It is clear that a mission statement is expected to serve many purposes as it includes goals and objectives that affect both internal and external stakeholders.

Steiner feels that a mission statement should be expressed at high levels of abstraction (Steiner, 1979). He feels that mission statements are not designed to express concrete ends but instead should promote "motivation, general direction, an image, a tone, and a philosophy to guide the enterprise." Steiner feels that excess detail in the statement could be counterproductive. A certain amount of vagueness provides more flexibility in adapting to changing environments and internal operations (Steiner, 1979).

Vern McGinnis believes that a good mission statement must accomplish a number of important objectives (McGinnis, 1981). First, the statement must define what the organization is and what it expects to be in the future. Next, the mission must distinguish the organization from all others. In addition, it must be limited enough to exclude some ventures but broad enough to allow for creative growth. The mission statement must also serve as a framework for evaluating both current and prospective activities. Finally, it must be stated in terms that are clear enough to be understood throughout the entire organization.

This certainly shows that much is expected from one short communication that affects both internal and external stakeholders.

Many authors report that an increasing number of organizations are developing and issuing mission statements (David, 2009). David states that some firms issue mission statements simply because they are fashionable and the "thing to do." He argues that proactive organizations systematically revisit and revise both their mission and vision statements and treat them as living documents. This is certainly a logical approach since the internal operations of the firm and the external environment are constantly changing. A mission statement must be revised as the goals and objectives of the firm are updated.

The first author of this article previously published a review of Fortune 100 mission statements in the Academy of Managerial Communications Journal (King, 2001). It is the authors' intent in this paper to compare the 2001 mission statement content with the current 2008 versions. The appendix includes a listing of mission statements from the top 50 companies found in the 2008 Fortune 100 summary. The authors' analysis includes a review of the stakeholders and the goals and objectives of the firm. Significant changes in both of these areas are reviewed in this paper.

Review of Previous Literature and Related Findings

A significant amount of research has been conducted concerning mission statements in recent years. Firms realize that this brief communication is critically important to both internal and external stakeholders. The management and employees of the organization look to the mission statement in an attempt to determine if their daily decisions support the mission of the firm. External stakeholders including creditors and stockholders look to the mission statement in an attempt to understand the primary goals and objectives of the company. An effective mission statement is also necessary for colleges and universities as faculty and administration formulate strategic plans based on their effect on the school's mission.

In recent years, mission statements can generally be found on company websites. In a previous 2005 study by Jones, Little, and Lovett, the authors found that only 327 or 65% of the Fortune 500 companies included a mission statement on their website (Jones, Little, and Lovett, 2005). The mission statements were located predominantly (60%) under the "About the Company" caption on the website. The remaining 40% of the firms listed the mission statement under other corporate information, investor relations, or a variety of other places on the site. In many cases the mission statement was not readily accessible by an interested party.

A later study in 2007 by some of the same authors found that the number of Fortune 500 firms that posted a mission statement on their website had increased to 415 or 83% of the firms (Jones, Lovett, and Blankenship, 2007). Surprisingly, 85 organizations did not place their mission statement on their webpage. A survey of these firms by these authors found that of the 25 firms that responded only six supplied a mission statement.

The other 19 businesses stated that they had no mission statement, replied with auto-response and gave no further help, or stated other reasons why the mission statement was not available such as it was being revised.

Historically, mission statements have included a listing of primary stakeholders and the basic goals and objectives of the organization. The first author's study in 2001 involved a review of both of these areas. King based his study on the 2000 Fortune 100 list and found that customers, stockholders, and employees were the three most mentioned stakeholders (King, 2001). The most commonly mentioned goals or objectives of the firm included quality, general core values, leadership, global emphasis, technology, profits, and ethics. This was in the pre-9/11 and Sarbanes-Oxley period. The authors hope to compare and contrast these mission statements with those in the 2008 Fortune list. A summary of the 2000 Fortune 100 mission statements is provided in Table 1.

Table 1 2000 Fortune 100—Mission Statements That Included:

Customers 61	Quality 25
Stockholders 34	Core Values 25
Employees 21	Leadership 17
Competitors 9	Global 15
Suppliers 6	Technology 14
Government 2	Environmental 9
Profits 6	Ethics 3

The mission statements of 2000 showed very little emphasis on ethics since only three firms (3%) from the top 100 companies included this concept. Also, at this time, only nine firms (9%) included the importance of protecting the environment. In recent years, ethical practices and "going green" to protect the environment have been extremely important goals for all business organizations. The importance of being a global business was only emphasized in 15% of the top 100 firms in 2000. It was logical that the two top stakeholders mentioned in mission reports were customers and stockholders with customers mentioned twice as often as stockholders. Finally, employees were also commonly mentioned with 21% of the companies including them in the mission.

The authors, in their study of 2008 Fortune top 50 firms, were interested in the revisions and modifications that firms have made in the last eight years in their mission statements. Did the 9/11 tragedy and the passage of the Sarbanes-Oxley Act in 2002 have a significant effect on the published mission statements of the largest firms? If so, these firms should emphasize ethical behavior and social responsibility (and protection of the environment) in their 2008 mission statements. Also, with the rapid development of technology and the ability to market goods internationally, these mission statements should also show increased emphasis on becoming a global company. The following section of this paper provides a mission statement content summary of the 2008 statements.

2008 Top 50 Fortune Company Mission Statements

The appendix includes the details of the top Fortune 50 company's mission statements. Only two firms (4%), Berkshire Hathaway and Lehman Brothers Holdings, did not provide a mission or vision statement, a corporate credo, or a list of core values. The appendix includes the other 48 company's communication in the form of one of the previously mentioned documents. In the previous 2000 study of the Fortune 100 firms, a total of 13 (13%) companies did not have a mission statement available for public review. It appears that most organizations in 2008 realize the importance of providing a thoughtfully developed mission statement to all stakeholders. Table 2 summarizes the mission statement content of the 2008 Fortune top 50 firms.

Table 2 2008 Fortune Top 50—Mission Statements That Included:

Customers 31	Quality 26
Employees 17	Global 17
Communities 15	Ethics 15
Stockholders 14	Environmental 8
Core Values 7	Leadership 7
Suppliers 5	Profits 6
Government/Laws 2	Technology 1

Table 2 shows that for the top 50 Fortune firms' customers and employees continue to be the most mentioned stakeholders. From a goals and objectives point of view, the importance of producing and selling a quality product was most often included in the mission statement. The next two most common goals included being a global provider of goods and services and a firm that considers ethics and ethical behavior to be of primary importance. In an effort to better present the results from the 2000 study that included the top 100 firms and the 2008 study that included the top 50 companies, a table is presented below that utilizes a percentage format. Table 3 summarizes the percentage of firms whose mission statements included the following stakeholders and goals from the Fortune listing of firms from 2000 and 2008.

It appears that the largest organizations have embraced the term "communities" in their mission statements. In 2000, only 6% of mission statements included the concept of communities. Only eight years later, 30% of the top businesses have chosen to include this term. Examples of the "communities" concept include:

- Chevron: Our Company's foundation is built on our Values, which distinguish us and guide our actions. We conduct our business in a socially responsible and ethical manner. We respect the law, support universal human rights, protect the environment, and benefit the communities where we work.
- Valero Energy: Commitment *to* our Communities— We are committed to taking a leadership role in the

Table 3 Percentages of Mission Statements Containing the Following Words:

Stakeholder	2000 Study	2008 Study
Communities	6%	30%
Competitors	9%	0%
Customers	61%	62%
Employees	21%	34%
Govt./Law	2%	4%
Stockholders	34%	28%
Suppliers	6%	10%
Goal/Objective		
Core Values	25%	14%
Environmental	9%	16%
Ethics	3%	30%
Global	15%	34%
Leadership	17%	14%
Profits	6%	12%
Quality/Value	25%	52%
Technology	14%	2%

communities in which we live and work by providing company support and encouraging employee involvement.
- Cardinal Health: We consider the highest standards of personal and professional ethics as the cornerstone of trust among our customers and ourselves; We deliver on the commitments we make; We recognize our obligation to the communities where we live and work; We hold ourselves accountable not only for what we achieve but how we achieve it.

It also appears that firms have considered the importance of the Sarbanes-Oxley Act and its emphasis on ethical behavior. In the 2000 mission statements only 3% included the important goal of emphasizing ethics and ethical behavior. That figure increased ten-fold in 2008 with 30% of the firms including this critically important concept in their current statement. Examples of an emphasis on ethics include:

- Exxon Mobil: Is committed to being the world's premier petroleum and petrochemical company. To that end, we must continuously achieve superior financial and operating results while adhering to the highest standards of business conduct.
- Chevron: See above with communities.
- AT&T: We operate with unyielding integrity, obeying all laws and adhering to a stringent code of business conduct. We will not tolerate unethical business conduct by our team members.
- General Electric: Always With Unyielding Integrity.

The comparison of the 2000 and 2008 mission statements also shows a significant increase in the percent of mission statements that include employees (21% in 2000 and 34% in 2008).

This is not surprising as organizations realize that their most precious asset is their employees. The number of mission statements naming stockholder decreased from 34% in 2000 to 28% in 2008. Those firms that listed "core values" in the place of a traditional mission statement decreased from 25% to 14% probably due to the firm actually preparing a more traditional mission statement.

The percentage of firms stating the goal or objective of being a global company increased significantly from 15% to 34%. This is logical since current technology allows even small firms to construct a homepage on the Worldwide Web and sell goods and services internationally. Some typical examples included:

- Ford: We are a global family with a proud heritage passionately committed to providing personal mobility for people around the world.
- ConocoPhillips: Use our pioneering spirit to responsibly deliver energy to the world.
- Procter & Gamble: We will provide branded products and services of superior quality and value that improve the lives of the world's consumers.

Finally, a major change in these large company mission statements is the number that includes the goal of producing a high quality good or service or one that is of exceptional value to the firm's customers. The percent of statements that included this concept increased from 25% in 2000 to 52% in 2008. Examples of these firms included:

- Procter & Gamble: See statement above.
- State Farm Insurance: Our success is built on a foundation of shared values—quality service and relationships, mutual trust, integrity and financial strength.
- Costco Wholesale: We will realize this mission by setting the highest standards in service, reliability, safety, and cost containment in our industry.

The following sections of this paper provide examples of mission statements that emphasize several stakeholders or goals and objectives. These are illustrative of the information that large firms are attempting to communicate to all interested parties. These mission statements clarify the purpose and direction of the company and discuss what goals and stakeholders are most important to the firm.

Stakeholder Examples

Certain mission statements include multiple stakeholders which show the concern of the company for a number of diverse groups. The following three examples clearly show the firm is concerned with a variety of external parties. The first statement listed below from Kroger company is a clear and concise mission that includes all major stakeholders. The next mission statement for Marathon Oil includes the popular term "communities" and mentions the importance of the firm's business partners. The third example for Wachovia Corporation not only mentions a number of important stakeholders but also emphasizes ethical behavior in the process of "doing what is right."

Kroger
Our mission is to be a leader in the distribution and merchandising of food, health, personal care, and related consumable products and services. By achieving this objective, we will satisfy our responsibilities to shareowners, associates, customers, suppliers, and the communities we serve.

Marathon Oil
Marathon is a company that strives to bring value and values together. We create value for our shareholders and provide quality products and services for our customers. In doing so, we act responsibly toward those who work for us, the communities in which we operate and our business partners.

Wachovia Corporation
Vision Statement: We believe Wachovia's depth of expertise, breadth of products, multiple delivery choices, and financial strength create long-term value. Our goal is to be regarded as the nation's premier financial services company by doing what's right for shareholders, customers, communities, and employees.

Goals or Objectives Examples
The first example from Caterpillar Corporation is very comprehensive. It not only names a variety of stakeholders but also reviews the firm's goals of leadership, quality and value, profits, ethics, and social responsibility. The second example is the mission statement for American International Group. The effects of the Sarbanes-Oxley Act (SOX) are visible as the firm uses the term "corporate culture" in their mission. SOX emphasizes the fact that every firm must maintain an ethical corporate culture in all of their daily operations. The final example is from Merrill Lynch. This mission statement clearly emphasizes ethical behavior and responsible citizenship. Since SOX, large corporations realize that they must establish a corporate culture that emphasizes ethical behavior and social responsibility.

Caterpillar
Caterpillar will be the leader in providing the best value in machines, engines, and support services for customers dedicated to building the world's infrastructure and developing and transporting its resources. We provide the best value to customers.

Caterpillar people will increase shareholder value by aggressively pursuing growth and profit opportunities that leverage our engineering, manufacturing, distribution, information management, and financial services expertise. We grow profitably.

Caterpillar will provide its worldwide workforce with an environment that stimulates diversity, innovation, teamwork, continuous learning and improvement and rewards individual performance. We develop and reward people.

Caterpillar is dedicated to improving the quality of life while sustaining the quality of our earth. We encourage social responsibility.

American International Group
As a global financial services organization, we have committed our resources to developing products and services that address

the needs of our clients as well as promote a corporate culture that values integrity, diversity, innovation, and excellence.

Merrill Lynch

At Merrill Lynch, Responsible Citizenship is more than a principle. It is a way of life. Through our global philanthropic efforts, we combine our financial resources and expertise with our greatest asset, our people, to build brighter futures in the communities throughout the world in which our employees and clients live and work. To achieve that goal, our charitable giving targets innovative and effective programs for children and youth that provide direct services, have potential for broad impact, and offer significant volunteer opportunities for Merrill Lynch employees.

Conclusion

This paper has compared mission statement content from 2000 with current Fortune 500 listings in 2008. It appears that SOX has had an effect on the content of the mission statements as 30% of the 2008 statements reviewed included wording related to ethics or ethical behavior. This was a ten-fold increase from 2000 when only 3% included this topic. Emphasizing the fact that the firm markets internationally is also very common with 34% of the mission statements including this practice. Another goal that is commonly stated in 2008 missions is the providing of a quality product or service that is of exceptional value to the customers. Quality and value were mentioned in 52% of the statements reviewed which was more than twice the percentage in 2000. The concept of being a global provider of a good or service also increased significantly from 15% in 2000 to 34% in 2008. Customers continue to be the most common stakeholder discussed in a mission statement with 62% of 2008 statements including this group.

The term "communities" has become a very popular word in current mission statements. In 2008, 30% of the mission statements reviewed included this term compared to only 6% in 2000. This emphasis on community demonstrates a broadening of company focus beyond those parties with whom they directly interact. It is a more universal term which could be tied to the increased emphasis on ethical behavior. No longer concerned with only their customers, employees, and business partners, these companies have extended their responsibilities to include the larger global "community" to which they belong.

The authors believe many of these trends will continue in the future. Corporate mission statements will increasingly discuss ethics and ethical practices, concern for global "communities," the importance of customers and employees, the desire for effective international operations, the importance of social responsibility and care of our planet, and the constant striving for a quality product that provides value to the customers. Without a doubt, much is expected from one brief corporate communication called a mission statement.

Final Note: A site that the authors found to be very beneficial when performing mission statement research is located at www.company-statements-slogans.info/index.htm. This site summarizes many mission, vision, and core value statements of large corporations on an annual basis.

Appendix

Mission Statements

1. Wal-Mart:	Our mission is to help people save money so they can live better.
	Mission of Wal-mart.com (online-specific):
	Walmart.com is passionate about combining the best of two great worlds—technology and world-class retailing—to give customers a wide assortment of their favorite products, Every Day Low Prices, guaranteed satisfaction, friendly service, convenient hours (24 hours, 7 days a week) and a great online shopping experience.
2. Exxon Mobil:	Is committed to being the world's premier petroleum and petrochemical company. To that end, we must continuously achieve superior financial and operating results while adhering to the highest standards of business conduct. These unwavering expectations provide the foundation for our commitments to those with whom we interact.
3. Chevron:	Our Company's foundation is built on our Values, which distinguish us and guide our actions. We conduct our business in a socially responsible and ethical manner. We respect the law, support universal human rights, protect the environment, and benefit the communities where we work.
4. GM:	GM is a multinational corporation engaged in socially responsible operations, worldwide. It is dedicated to provide products and services of such quality that our customers will receive superior value while our employees and business partners will share in our success and our stock-holders will receive a sustained superior return on their investment.
5. ConocoPhillips:	Use our pioneering spirit to responsibly deliver energy to the world.
6. General Electric:	Core Values: Passionate—Curious— Resourceful—Accountable—Teamwork—Committed—Open—Energizing, Always With Unyielding Integrity.
7. Ford Motor:	We are a global family with a proud heritage passionately committed to providing personal mobility for people around the world.

(continued)

Mission Statements

8. Citigroup:	Our goal for Citigroup is to be the most respected global financial services company. Like any other public company, we're obligated to deliver profits and growth to our shareholders. Of equal importance is to deliver those profits and generate growth responsibly.
9. Bank of America:	Our Philosophy: We believe, very simply, that it is the actions of individuals working together that build strong communities . . . and that business has an obligation to support those actions in the communities it serves.
	Core Values: Doing the right thing, Trusting and teamwork, Inclusive meritocracy, Winning, Leadership.
10. AT&T:	Mission/Vision: We aspire to be the most admired and valuable company in the world. Our goal is to enrich our customers' personal lives and to make their businesses more successful by bringing to market exciting and useful communications services, building shareowner value in the process.
	Values: Customers—We value our customers and treat them with respect, providing friendly, courteous, knowledgeable, and prompt service at all touch points. We seek and are driven by our customers' feedback.
	Integrity—We operate with unyielding integrity, obeying all laws and adhering to a stringent code of business conduct. We will not tolerate unethical business conduct by our team members.
	Performance—We continually raise our performance to exceed customer and shareholder expectations. We strive to be the best wireless company in the world.
	Teamwork—We partner with one another—respecting new viewpoints, building trust, enhancing communications, and sharing best practices to deliver world-class products and services.
	People—We value our team members and treat them with respect, providing an environment where diverse individuals can develop and are expected to perform to their full potential.
11. Berkshire Hathaway:	No mission statement found
12. J.P. Morgan Chase & Co:	Vision Statement: At JPMorgan Chase, we want to be the best financial services company in the world. Because of our great heritage and excellent platform, we believe this is within our reach.
13. American International Group:	As a global financial services organization, we have committed our resources to developing products and services that address the needs of our clients as well as promote a corporate culture that values integrity, diversity, innovation and excellence.
14. Hewlett Packard:	To provide products, services and solutions of the highest quality and deliver more value to our customers that earns their respect and loyalty.
15. International Business Machines:	At IBM, we strive to lead in the invention, development and manufacture of the industry's most advanced information technologies, including computer systems, software, storage systems and microelectronics.
	We translate these advanced technologies into value for our customers through our professional solutions, services and consulting businesses worldwide.
16. Valero Energy:	As a leading refiner and marketer, we are committed to following these guiding principles to achieve excellence in our business, our industry, and our relationships with our employees and communities.
	Commitment to Safety—The safety of our employees, our operations, and our communities is our highest priority.
	Commitment to Our Stakeholders—We are committed to delivering long-term value to all stakeholders—our employees, investors, and customers—by pursuing profitable, value-enhancing strategies with a focus on world-class operations.
	Commitment to Our Employees—Our employees are our No. 1 asset. We are committed to providing a challenging, enjoyable and rewarding work environment, which fosters creative thinking, teamwork, open communication, respect and opportunity for individual professional growth and development.
	Commitment to the Environment—We are committed to producing environmentally clean products, while striving to improve and enhance the environmental quality of our operations within our local communities.
	Commitment to our Communities—We are committed to taking a leadership role in the communities in which we live and work by providing company support and encouraging employee involvement.

(continued)

Mission Statements

17. Verizon:

As a leader in communications, Verizon's mission is to enable people and businesses to communicate with each other. We are also committed to providing full and open communication with our customers, employees and investors.

Core Purpose: We bring the benefits of communications to everybody.

Commitment to Service and Vision Statement: Verizon's commitment to top quality service is well known. Verizon is the pre-eminent service provider in the industry. Our legacy of customer service—bolstered by the nation's largest and most reliable network—is unparalleled. And, we continue to make strong progress in delivering on our promise to be the nation's best provider of quality local, data and long distance services.

18. McKesson

Our mission is to provide comprehensive pharmacy solutions that improve productivity, profitability and result in superior patient care and satisfaction.

19. Cardinal Health

Ethical Values: We consider the highest standards of personal and professional ethics as the cornerstone of trust among our customers and ourselves; We deliver on the commitments we make; We recognize our obligation to the communities where we live and work; We hold ourselves accountable not only for what we achieve but how we achieve it.

20. Goldman Sachs Group

To promote innovation and excellence in education and youth development worldwide.

Business Principles: Our clients' interests always come first. Our experience shows that if we serve our clients well, our own success will follow.

Our assets are our people, capital and reputation. If any of these is ever diminished, the last is the most difficult to restore. We are dedicated to complying fully with the letter and spirit of the laws, rules and ethical principles that govern us. Our continued success depends upon unswerving adherence to this standard.

21. Morgan Stanley

Vision Statement: The talent and passion of our people are critical to our success. Together, we share a common set of values rooted in integrity and excellence.

Core Values: Excellence—Integrity—Entrepreneurial Spirit—Teamwork—Respect for Individuals & Cultures.

22. Home Depot

Mission: The Home Depot is in the home improvement business and our goal is to provide the highest level of service, the broadest selection of products and the most competitive prices.

Core Values: Excellent customer service, Taking care of our people, Giving back, Doing the "right" thing, Creating shareholder value, Respect for all people, Entrepreneurial spirit, Building strong relationships

23. Procter & Gamble

Purpose: We will provide branded products and services of superior quality and value that improve the lives of the world's consumers. As a result, consumers will reward us with leadership sales, profit, and value creation, allowing our people, our shareholders, and the communities in which we live and work to prosper.

24. CVS Caremark

Our Mission: Above all else . . . our mission is to improve the lives of those we serve by making innovative and high-quality health and pharmacy services safe, affordable, and easy to access.

Our Values: Our Customers—We are passionate and relentless in our goal to continuously innovate and improve service to our customers . . . every day, everywhere, and every customer.

Our Colleagues—We work as a team. We are committed and act with integrity. We all deserve respect as well as a supportive work environment that recognizes and rewards our contributions . . . we accept nothing less.

Our Contributions—In the end, it's all about results—achieving our financial goals as well as giving back to the communities we serve. We hold each other accountable for all aspects of our performance . . . without exception.

(continued)

Mission Statements

25. United Health Group	Our mission is to help people live healthier lives. We seek to enhance the performance of the health system and improve the overall health and well-being of the people we serve and their communities.

We work with health care professionals and other key partners to expand access to high quality health care so people get the care they need at an affordable price.

We support the physician/patient relationship and empower people with the information, guidance and tools they need to make personal health choices and decisions. |
26. Kroger	Our mission is to be a leader in the distribution and merchandising of food, health, personal care, and related consumable products and services. By achieving this objective, we will satisfy our responsibilities to shareowners, associates, customers, suppliers, and the communities we serve.
27. Boeing	Our mission is to be a leader in the distribution and merchandising of food, health, personal care, and related consumable products and services. By achieving this objective, we will satisfy our responsibilities to shareowners, associates, customers, suppliers, and the communities we serve.
28. Amerisource-Bergen	Strategies: Run healthy core businesses; Leverage strengths into new products and service; Open new frontiers; People working together as a global enterprise for aerospace leadership.
29. Costco Wholesale	To build shareholder value by delivering pharmaceutical and healthcare products, services and solutions in innovative and cost effective ways. We will realize this mission by setting the highest standards in service, reliability, safety and cost containment in our industry.
30. Merrill Lynch	At Merrill Lynch, Responsible Citizenship is more than a principle. It is a way of life.

Through our global philanthropic efforts, we combine our financial resources and expertise with our greatest asset—our people—to build brighter futures in the communities throughout the world in which our employees and clients live and work. To achieve that goal, our charitable giving targets innovative and effective programs for children and youth that provide direct services, have potential for broad impact, and offer significant volunteer opportunities for Merrill Lynch employees. |
| 31. Target | Our mission is to make Target the preferred shopping destination for our guests by delivering outstanding value, continuous innovation and an exceptional guest experience by consistently fulfilling our Expect More. Pay Less.® brand promise. |
| 32. State Farm Insurance Company | State Farm's mission is to help people manage the risks of everyday life, recover from the unexpected and realize their dreams.

We are people who make it our business to be like a good neighbor; who built a premier company by selling and keeping promises through our marketing partnership; who bring diverse talents and experiences to our work of serving the State Farm customer.

Our success is built on a foundation of shared values—quality service and relationships, mutual trust, integrity and financial strength.

Our vision for the future is to be the customer's first and best choice in the products and services we provide. We will continue to be the leader in the insurance industry and we will become a leader in the financial services arena. Our customers' needs will determine our path.

Our values will guide us. |
| 33. WellPoint | Mission: WellPoint's objective is to improve the health of the people we serve. The WellPoint Companies provide health security by offering a choice of quality branded health and related financial services designed to meet the changing expectations of individuals, families and their sponsors throughout a lifelong relationship.

Vision: WellPoint will transform our industry, becoming the most valued health plan through a new generation of consumer-friendly products that put individuals back in control of their health and financial future. |

(continued)

Mission Statements

34. Dell

Dell Values—Vision Statement: Dell is committed to being a good neighbor in the communities we call home. We must continue to grow responsibly—protecting our natural resources and practicing sustainability in all its forms—and improve the communities where we live and work through our financial and volunteer efforts.

35. Johnson & Johnson

No mission statement; credo instead:

We believe our first responsibility is to the doctors, nurses and patients, to mothers and fathers and all others who use our products and services. In meeting their needs everything we do must be of high quality. We must constantly strive to reduce our costs in order to maintain reasonable prices. Customers' orders must be serviced promptly and accurately. Our suppliers and distributors must have an opportunity to make a fair profit.

We are responsible to our employees, the men and women who work with us throughout the world. Everyone must be considered as an individual. We must respect their dignity and recognize their merit. They must have a sense of security in their jobs. Compensation must be fair and adequate, and working conditions clean, orderly and safe. We must be mindful of ways to help our employees fulfill their family responsibilities. Employees must feel free to make suggestions and complaints. There must be equal opportunity for employment, development and advancement for those qualified. We must provide competent management, and their actions must be just and ethical.

Our final responsibility is to our stockholders. Business must make a sound profit. We must experiment with new ideas. Research must be carried on, innovative programs developed and mistakes paid for. New equipment must be purchased, new facilities provided and new products launched. Reserves must be created to provide for adverse times. When we operate according to these principles, the stockholders should realize a fair return.

We are responsible to the communities in which we live and work and to the world community as well. We must be good citizens—support good works and charities and bear our fair share of taxes. We must encourage civic improvements and better health and education. We must maintain in good order the property we are privileged to use, protecting the environment and natural resources.

36. Marathon Oil

Marathon is a company that strives to bring value and values together. We create value for our shareholders and provide quality products and services for our customers. In doing so, we act responsibly toward those who work for us, the communities in which we operate and our business partners.

37. Lehman Brothers Holdings

No mission statement found

38. Wachovia Corporation

Vision Statement: We believe Wachovia's depth of expertise, breadth of products, multiple delivery choices, and financial strength create long-term value. Our goal is to be regarded as the nation's premier financial services company by doing what's right for shareholders, customers, communities, and employees.

39. United Technologies

Quality Statement: UTC is committed to continuous improvement. We operate an extensive research program to identify innovations and technologies to enable us to relentlessly improve the quality of our product.

40. Walgreens

No mission statement; Creed instead.

We believe in the goods we merchandise, in ourselves and in our ability to render satisfaction.

We believe that honest goods can be sold to honest people by honest methods.

We believe in working, not waiting; in laughing, not weeping; in boosting, not knocking; and in the pleasure of selling our products.

We believe that we can get what we go after, and that we are not down and out until we have lost faith in ourselves.

We believe in today and the work we are doing, in tomorrow and the work we hope to do, and in the sure reward the future holds.

Mission Statements

41. Wells Fargo	Our product: SERVICE. Our value-added: FINANCIAL ADVICE. Our competitive advantage: OUR PEOPLE.
42. Dow Chemical	To constantly improve what is essential to human progress by mastering science and technology.
43. MetLife	All customers are "Met for Life." By balancing the efficiencies of new technologies with the personal touch of highly trained and motivated professionals, we are able to deliver solutions and services that exceed our customers' expectations. We thereby earn their loyalty.
44. Microsoft	To enable people and businesses throughout the world to realize their full potential.
45. Sears Holdings	To grow our business by providing quality products and services at great value when and where our customers want them, and by building positive, lasting relationships with our customers.
46. United Parcel Service	As the world's largest package delivery company and a leading global provider of specialized transportation and logistics services, UPS continues to develop the frontiers of logistics, supply chain management, and e-Commerce . . . combining the flows of goods, information, and funds.
47. Pfizer	Mission Statement: We will become the world's most valued company to patients, customers, colleagues, investors, business partners, and the communities where we work and live.
	Our Purpose: We dedicate ourselves to humanity's quest for longer, healthier, happier lives through innovation in pharmaceutical, consumer, and animal health products.
48. Lowe's	Vision Statement: "We will provide customer-valued solutions with the best prices, products and services to make Lowe's the first choice for home improvement.
49. Time Warner	Creativity—We thrive on innovation and originality encouraging risk-taking and divergent voices.
	Customer Focus—We value our customers putting their needs and interests at the center of everything we do.
	Agility—We move quickly embracing change and seizing new opportunities.
	Teamwork—We treat one another with respect—creating value by working together within and across our businesses.
	Integrity—We rigorously uphold editorial independence and artistic expression earning the trust of our readers, viewers, listeners, members and subscribers.
	Diversity—We attract and develop the world's best talent seeking to include the broadest range of people and perspectives.
	Responsibility—We work to improve our communities taking pride in serving the public interest as well as the interests of our shareholders.
50. Caterpillar	Caterpillar will be the leader in providing the best value in machines, engines, and support services for customers dedicated to building the world's infrastructure and developing and transporting its resources. We provide the best value to customers.
	Caterpillar people will increase shareholder value by aggressively pursuing growth and profit opportunities that leverage our engineering, manufacturing, distribution, information management and financial services expertise. We grow profitably.
	Caterpillar will provide its worldwide workforce with an environment that stimulates diversity, innovation, teamwork, continuous learning and improvement and rewards individual performance. We develop and reward people.
	Caterpillar is dedicated to improving the quality of life while sustaining the quality of our earth. We encourage social responsibility.

References

David, F.R. (2009). *Strategic Management: Concepts and Cases (Twelfth Edition).* Upper Saddle River, NJ: Pearson Prentice Hall.

Drucker, P. (1974). *Management: Tasks, Responsibilities, and Practices.* New York, NY: Harper & Roe.

Jones, I.S., D.L. Little & D. Blankenship (2006). Mission Statements on Fortune 500 Web Sites: A Descriptive Analysis. *Journal of Business and Behavioral Sciences,* Fall 2006, 74–84.

Jones, I.S., M.G. Lovett & D. Blankenship (2006). Mission Statements on Fortune 500 Web Sites: A Descriptive Analysis. *Journal of Business and Behavioral Sciences,* Fall 2006, 74–84.

King, D.L. (2001). Mission Statement Content Analysis. *Academy of Managerial Communications Journal,* 5(1–2), 75–100.

King, W.R. & D.I. Cleland (1979). *Strategic Planning and Policy.* New York, NY: Reinhold Publishing.

Leet, R.K. (2008). Strong Messages Mean Strong Leaders. *Chronicle of Philanthropy,* 20(13), 36.

McGinnis, V. (1981). The Mission Statement: A Key Step in Strategic Planning. *Business,* 31(6), 41.

Steiner, G. (1979). Strategic Planning: What Every Manager Must Know. New York, NY: The Free Press.

Critical Thinking

1. Why would major corporations focus on the global economy?

2. Why would major corporations focus on being ethical in the global economy?

3. Why would this be focused on in the mission statement?

From *Academy of Strategic Management*, November 2010, pp. 71–87. Copyright © 2010 by Bloomberg Allied Academies. Reprinted by permission.

Corporate Social Responsibility: Pros and Cons

Ashiq Hussain

Corporate social responsibility has become a global phenomenon and an interesting topic which continues to grab the attraction of audiences across the world including writers, analysts, governments, think tanks, non-governmental organizations and corporations.

It is known by different terms: corporate sustainability, corporate conscience, corporate citizenship, corporate social investment, socially responsible investment, business sustainability, and corporate governance.

Stephanie Maier, Strategic Research Development Manager at The Ethical Investment Research Services has given a much broader definition of CSR:

Corporate governance defines a set of relationships between a company's management, its board, its shareholders and its stakeholders. It is the process by which directors and auditors manage their responsibilities towards shareholders and wider company stakeholders. For shareholders it can provide increased confidence of an equitable return on their investment. For company's stakeholders it can provide an assurance that the company manages its impact on society and the environment in a responsible manner.

CSR is the continuing commitment by business to behave ethically and contribute to economic development while improving the quality of life of the workforce and their families as well as of the local community and society at large. Furthermore, it is about how companies manage the business processes to produce an overall positive impact on the society.

According to Mallen Baker, strategic advisor and founding director of Business Respect, CSR is perceived in different ways in different societies. In US, it is defined in terms of a philanthropic model. In Philippines, "it is about business giving back to the society". The European model of CSR is more sustainable as it focuses on operating in a socially responsible way complemented by investment in communities.

According to my viewpoint, in developing economies like Pakistan it is perceived as "rescuing the society from natural calamities" because these countries usually encounter with natural catastrophes that cause irreparable financial,

infrastructural, and human losses primarily because of lack of contingency plans. In such a scenario local and multinational organizations cultivate rescue plans to help the local community in order to pull her out of such crisis. Pakistan encountered a major earthquake on 8th October, 2005. Shell Pakistan contributed around US$0.5 million for relief activities and these funds were channeled through different relief programs (e.g. Sarhad Rural Support Program, SUNGI, Marie Adelaide Leprosy Center and other reputable NGOs that were working diligently to provide assistance to the affected people especially in remote areas).

Moreover, medical team of doctors and paramedics in ambulances equipped with medicines were mobilized to provide medical assistance in the affected region on urgent basis. Furthermore, Pfizer Pakistan also joined hands with Shell Pakistan and actively supported "Join hands with Shell" program, and donated medicines to the relief camps.

Organizations are getting benefit from CSR concept in one way or the other, but this is not single reason why they are dealing with this idea.

The essence of this concept is achieved when organizations have a strong faith in the act of doing well, not just for themselves and their immediate intermediaries but also for all the stakeholders.

Over the period of years, many of the organizations have realized the importance of corporate conscience and it becomes an integral part of their corporate philosophy. It is not treated as a side function, but firms are trying to make it an integral part of their business model. For example, Pakistan Tobacco Company (a member of British American Tobacco Group) established afforestation program in collaboration with Australian Aid International to provide potable water, sanitation facilities and hygiene education to over 65,000 people in Thatta, Sindh and distributed over four million saplings across the country in capital Islamabad, Khyber-Pakhtunkhwa and Punjab. Pakistan Tobacco Company also collaborated with the National Highway Authority planting over 300,000 saplings along the M1 Motorway from Islamabad to Peshawar during 2010.

In the same year when Pakistan encountered historic flood, that affected around 20 million people in the region the company provided food packages and water purification tablets to the affectees. Mobile medical units mobilized to administer typhoid vaccination. They also provided support to rehabilitate a number of houses damaged by the floods. More than 10,000 entrepreneurs got support from the company to rebuild their livelihoods after flood. According to the company publications, in the year 2010 the company invested around US$1.9 million in CSR activities.

CSR was introduced around 50 years back but it got momentum in the late nineties but in the first decade of this century, it became the integral part of strategy of a number of national, multinational and global organizations. In the current scenario, two schools of thoughts influence CSR: one favors this concept while the other opposes it.

One, who favors, argues that companies may be exposed to a variety of legal and standing risks if they do not have adequate social compliance or corporate social responsibility programs in place. CSR program can be an aid to recruitment and retention, particularly within the competitive graduate student market and can also help to improve the perception of a company among its staff, particularly when staff is also involved in CSR activities.

They also argue that global market has become so competitive that it has never been earlier and organizations are striving for unique selling proposition that can separate them from the competition in the minds of consumers. CSR can play a role in building customer loyalty based on distinctive ethical values.

Organizations are pursuing global expansion and developing global markets through merger/acquisition strategy. They encountered with a number of challenges e.g. rituals, believes, customs, government legislation, environmental laws etc to penetrate in the foreign markets and need to understand these issues first before they go for expansion. In such situations, CSR can be used as a strategic tool to gain public support for their presence in the global markets, helping them sustain a competitive advantage by using their social contributions to provide a subconscious level of advertising.

Dame Anita Roddick, founder of The Body Shop said, "The business of business should not just be about money, it should be about responsibility. It should be about public good, not private greed." She based her business on five values: support community trade, defend human rights, oppose animal testing, active self-esteem, and protect our planet. Body shop is growing and getting popularity globally not only because of its product but also for commitment on these values and CSR.

Supporters of CSR also believe that corporations are motivated to become more socially responsible because their most important stakeholders expect them to understand and address the social and community issues that are relevant to them. Now organizations are trying to understand what causes are important to internal stakeholders e.g. employees; because of the many interrelated business benefits that can be derived from increased employee engagement and key external stakeholders e.g. customers, consumers, investors, communities in the areas where the corporation operates. People who favor CSR feel uncomfortable when one asks for ROI (Return on Investment) on CSR expenditures and they view it as an inadequate

question because they believe it would help the organizations in other ways e.g. protecting tangible and intangibles. A company's brands, intellectual property, and goodwill may represent a significant amount of its present and future economic value.

They claim that some organizations have also faced economic damages when their corporate reputations and brands were assailed, and possible lost sales through consumer boycotts. Firms can lend help from CSR to manage such risks and to ensure legal compliance.

For example, Pakistani mobile phone consumers started boycotting the service of Norwegian cellular company Telenor to protest against the publication of blasphemous caricatures of Prophet Muhammad (PBUH) by Danish newspapers and other European dailies in 2006. Telenor users got messages on their mobile phones to stop using the service of the company as a protest against the publication of derogatory cartoons by Western media. Telenor started losing consumer base rapidly and as a result faced mega losses. The company embarked a number of projects under the umbrella of CSR to get its position back. Emergency response program was established to address unforeseen circumstance e.g. flood, earthquake etc. and program is led by Telenor employees. They also initiated other programs e.g. Khuddar Pakistan, Naya Qadam, Blood Donation, DUA etc. to take stakeholders in confidence and to protect its tangible and intangible assets.

The other group who denies the importance of CSR concept is of the view that the reason, why companies exist, is profit and if companies will invest in anything that does not create obvious financial gain then it will impact on its profitability. One of the most common arguments companies make when indicating reluctance to CSR policies is the disadvantage it causes against companies that do not. Without strict adherence industry wide, some companies argue that they cannot fall behind by putting money into CSR programs.

Some critics believe that CSR programs are undertaken by companies such as to distract the public from ethical questions posed by their core operations. They argue that some corporations start CSR programs for the commercial benefit they enjoy through raising their reputation with the public or with government. They suggest that corporations which exist solely to maximize profits are unable to advance the interests of society as a whole.

They also comment that from commercial perspective a company supposes to full fill its consumer needs and wants and design its products/brands accordingly. But when CSR is included in company policy it would detract and put focus on other dimensions that are least concerned with consumer needs and wants, thus putting resources instead of R and D on marketing side.

How long CSR will remain a prominent business concern? According to the My Efficient Planet website, CSR has existed for more than 50 years. However, its prominence as a major business consideration has certainly increased in the 21st century due to heightened awareness of ethical issues in business and environmental preservation standards. Detractors argue that CSR emphasis is a short-term fad in response to prominent scandals.

Like every concept, CSR has merits and demerits, some people favor and some oppose it. I believe that companies, irrespective their size, should go with CSR because they have to pay back to the communities where they are operating, utilizing resources and generating sales and profits. Employees should be involved in such projects because it gives sense of inspiration and motivation to the employees who are engaged and these projects make them feel proud that they are able to do something for their own communities with the help of the organization. Furthermore, CSR provides an opportunity to an organization to be different from other organizations in the industry and provide a subconscious level of advertising to stakeholders. CSR also helps organizations to protect their tangible and intangible assets and to build desired image in the community, as a result it will ensure their business sustainability and expansion in the global market.

Source

"CORPORATE SOCIAL RESPONSIBILITY: PROS and CONS."
Pakistan & Gulf Economist 10 July 2011. *General OneFile*.
Web. 29 May 2012.

Critical Thinking

1. Do you think companies should engage in corporate social responsibility (CSR)?

2. Why do you think CSR is defined differently in different societies? Could it be that different societies have different needs?

3. What are some of the ways that a global corporation could address CSR in different countries, say the United States versus China versus Kenya?

From *Pakistan and Gulf Economist*, July 10, 2011, pp. 1–4. Copyright © 2011 by Pakistan and Gulf Economist. Reprinted by permission.

UNIT 5
The Future and International Business

Unit Selections

Learning Outcomes

After reading this Unit, you will be able to:

- Explain how you think the evolving global demographics will change world trade; how you think these changes will affect society; and what is likely to be the impact on the developing world as well as the developed world.

- Describe the concept of the BRIC countries, whether you think Russia should be included, and explain the N-11.

- Explain what you think is likely to happen as the middle class declines in the developed world. Discuss the rise of the middle class in the developing world and why that is that important. Also explain what it will take to be a part of the middle class in the future.

- Discuss what is happening in Europe. Explain how Europe can keep up with the United States and the rest of the world. Describe some of the demographic changes that are happening in Europe that will make this more difficult.

- Describe what kind of job you think you will be doing and where you think you will be working in the future; what you think the chances are that you will be working outside your home country during your career; and whether you would be willing to work in another country if the pay was lower, but your standard of living was about equal because of price purchase parity.

Student Website
www.mhhe.com/cls

Internet References

Commission on the Future of the Worker-Management Relations
www.dol.gov
The Economist
www.theeconomist.com
The Futurist
www.wfs.org/futurist.htm.

The world has changed. But, the question is, where does the world go from here and how is that going to impact world trade? There are certainly trends that can be identified for the future. The first is the ascendancy of countries from the third world. People have identified the BRIC (Brazil, Russia, India, and China) countries as the ones to watch in the future, but it would seem that one of the countries, Russia, may not belong in that list. Russia is losing population at the rate of about 1 million people per year and male life expectancy is on a par with many third-world countries. Rather than being on the ascent, Russia's fate would seem to be tied to the price of oil, and the political situation in the country remains unclear.

There are, however, countries that do bear watching in addition to Brazil, India, and China, sometimes referred to as the N-11 (Bangladesh, Egypt, Indonesia, Iran, Korea, Mexico, Nigeria, Pakistan, the Philippines, Turkey, and Vietnam). Indonesia, the largest Muslim country in the world and the fourth largest country in terms of population, seems to have overcome decades of political corruption and strife and would now seem to be on the path to economic prosperity. Vietnam is now one of the fastest growing economies in the world, although from a very small base. In South America, Chile, while not a member of the N-11, has reconciled a recent history of political turmoil and appears to be on the way toward economic prosperity. All three of these countries have one thing in common in that they recently overcame periods of turmoil whether political, military, or both. They are now coming out of that period and are on their way to developing mixed capitalist economies where individual effort is rewarded and economic growth is being experienced.

A defining trend in society that will certainly affect international business is "The New Population Bomb: The Four Megatrends That Will Change the World." World demographics are certain to change over the next 50 years. In the developed world of the United States, Europe, and Japan, the percentage of the world's population is almost certain to decline and the actual number of people in many of the countries may also decline.

Probably the most obvious example is Japan, which has the highest life expectancy of almost any country in the world. It also has one of the lowest birth rates of any of the developed countries. This causes what demographers call an inverted pyramid where there are more people in the more senior age brackets than in the younger age brackets. Seniors require more in the way of services, such as medical and social, than do healthy younger people. Unfortunately, it is the healthy younger people who have to pay for the services because the seniors have retired and are now living off their pensions and whatever Social Security–like programs the government has in place. This is a problem faced to varying degrees by every developed country.

Conversely, in the developing world, while life expectancy is increasing, it still does not match that of the developed world, and the fertility rate (number of live births per woman of child-bearing age) in some instances is as high as five, while in the developed world, in some countries it is as low as 1.1. It means that, in some countries, in the developing world, the population will triple in the next fifty years, while in the developed world, in some countries the population could drop by half.

© Chad Baker/Getty Images

The population bomb will create problems for both the developed world and the developing world. For the developed world, the question is how will the promises that have been made to all of the citizens be kept? How will Social Security–like programs and medical care be paid for as more and more people require more and more services that will have to be paid for by fewer and fewer people? As these programs start to take a larger share of the gross domestic product of the society, how much will be left over from the rest of the economy? How much will productivity in the society have to increase to cover these increases just to stay even or expand the economy?

In the developing world, population explosion means that attempting to spread resources over a population pool that is expanding faster than the available resources is only going to lead to poverty and unrest. It means that these countries may never catch up with the developed world. The only way that the developed world and the developing world can possibly deal with their respective problems is for people from the developing world to immigrate to the developed world. This will solve the problem of not having enough people to support the aging populations of the developed world, and it will relieve the stress in the developing world of too many people attempting to live off too few resources. But, it also means that there will be significant changes in the developed world. Significant minorities will exist in societies that were once extremely homogeneous. Learning to deal with these new citizens is certain to stress the developed world.

Companies that are able to deal with this new developing future are the ones that will be investing in that future. Industries that will survive will be the ones that invest in research and development. Countries and societies that do not invest in the future, that do not have the flexibility that will be needed for the future will be the ones that will fall behind the rest of the world. Some may say that there is a "Crisis That You Don't Know" in Europe that reflects this situation. Many of Europe's countries have found it difficult to have the flexibility to deal with the rapid changes in the global economy and are finding themselves being left in the dust by other more elastic economies. Some of the difficulties in places like Greece, Portugal, Spain, and Italy are examples of this problem.

Finally, learning to deal with the future global economy means learning. Education and training are not a once and done experience anymore and flexibility is the key to career success. It is a global economy and it is a global workforce. That means to be successful, individuals must learn to be mobile and to be able to go where the work is, and where the work is may not necessarily be in their hometown, their home state, or even their home country. For the past several hundred years people have come to North America in search of work. In the not too distant future, people may be leaving North America in search of work as discussed in "Finding a Job in the 21st Century."

The world has certainly changed. Dealing with these changes will be the challenge that will face everyone in the 21st century. It is a new world, one with many challenges, many opportunities, and many changes yet to come.

The New Population Bomb: The Four Megatrends That Will Change the World

JACK A. GOLDSTONE

Forty-two years ago, the biologist Paul Ehrlich warned in The Population Bomb that mass starvation would strike in the 1970s and 1980s, with the world's population growth outpacing the production of food and other critical resources. Thanks to innovations and efforts such as the "green revolution" in farming and the widespread adoption of family planning, Ehrlich's worst fears did not come to pass. In fact, since the 1970s, global economic output has increased and fertility has fallen dramatically, especially in developing countries.

The United Nations Population Division now projects that global population growth will nearly halt by 2050. By that date, the world's population will have stabilized at 9.15 billion people, according to the "medium growth" variant of the UN's authoritative population database World Population Prospects: The 2008 Revision. (Today's global population is 6.83 billion.) Barring a cataclysmic climate crisis or a complete failure to recover from the current economic malaise, global economic output is expected to increase by two to three percent per year, meaning that global income will increase far more than population over the next four decades.

But twenty-first-century international security will depend less on how many people inhabit the world than on how the global population is composed and distributed: where populations are declining and where they are growing, which countries are relatively older and which are more youthful, and how demographics will influence population movements across regions.

These elements are not well recognized or widely understood. A recent article in The Economist, for example, cheered the decline in global fertility without noting other vital demographic developments. Indeed, the same UN data cited by The Economist reveal four historic shifts that will fundamentally alter the world's population over the next four decades: the relative demographic weight of the world's developed countries will drop by nearly 25 percent, shifting economic power to the developing nations; the developed countries' labor forces will substantially age and decline, constraining economic growth in the developed world and raising the demand for immigrant workers; most of the world's expected population growth will increasingly be concentrated in today's poorest, youngest, and most heavily Muslim countries, which have a dangerous lack of quality education, capital, and employment opportunities; and, for the first time in history, most of the world's population will become urbanized, with the largest urban centers being in the world's poorest countries, where policing, sanitation, and health care are often scarce. Taken together, these trends will pose challenges every bit as alarming as those noted by Ehrlich. Coping with them will require nothing less than a major reconsideration of the world's basic global governance structures.

Europe's Reversal of Fortunes

At the beginning of the eighteenth century, approximately 20 percent of the world's inhabitants lived in Europe (including Russia). Then, with the Industrial Revolution, Europe's population boomed, and streams of European emigrants set off for the Americas. By the eve of World War I, Europe's population had more than quadrupled. In 1913, Europe had more people than China, and the proportion of the world's population living in Europe and the former European colonies of North America had risen to over 33 percent. But this trend reversed after World War I, as basic health care and sanitation began to spread to poorer countries. In Asia, Africa, and Latin America, people began to live longer, and birthrates remained high or fell only slowly. By 2003, the combined populations of Europe, the United States, and Canada accounted for just 17 percent of the global population. In 2050, this figure is expected to be just 12 percent—far less than it was in 1700. (These projections, moreover, might even understate the reality because they reflect the "medium growth" projection of the UN forecasts, which assumes that the fertility rates of developing countries will decline while those of developed countries will increase. In fact, many developed countries show no evidence of increasing fertility rates.) The West's relative decline is even more dramatic if one also considers changes in income. The Industrial Revolution made Europeans not only more numerous than they had been but also considerably richer per capita than others worldwide. According to the economic historian Angus Maddison, Europe, the United States, and Canada together produced about 32 percent of the world's GDP at the beginning of the nineteenth century. By 1950, that proportion had increased to a remarkable 68 percent of the world's total output (adjusted to reflect purchasing power parity).

This trend, too, is headed for a sharp reversal. The proportion of global GDP produced by Europe, the United States, and Canada fell from 68 percent in 1950 to 47 percent in 2003 and will decline even more steeply in the future. If the growth rate of per capita income (again, adjusted for purchasing power parity) between 2003 and 2050 remains as it was between 1973 and 2003—averaging 1.68 percent annually in Europe, the United States, and Canada and 2.47 percent annually in the rest of the world—then the combined GDP of Europe, the United States, and Canada will roughly double by 2050, whereas the GDP of the rest of the world will grow by a factor of five. The portion of global GDP produced by Europe, the United States, and Canada in 2050 will then be less than 30 percent—smaller than it was in 1820.

These figures also imply that an overwhelming proportion of the world's GDP growth between 2003 and 2050—nearly 80 percent—will occur outside of Europe, the United States, and Canada. By the middle of this century, the global middle class—those capable of purchasing durable consumer products, such as cars, appliances, and electronics—will increasingly be found in what is now considered the developing world. The World Bank has predicted that by 2030 the number of middle-class people in the developing world will be 1.2 billion—a rise of 200 percent since 2005. This means that the developing world's middle class alone will be larger than the total populations of Europe, Japan, and the United States combined. From now on, therefore, the main driver of global economic expansion will be the economic growth of newly industrialized countries, such as Brazil, China, India, Indonesia, Mexico, and Turkey.

Aging Pains

Part of the reason developed countries will be less economically dynamic in the coming decades is that their populations will become substantially older. The European countries, Canada, the United States, Japan, South Korea, and even China are aging at unprecedented rates. Today, the proportion of people aged 60 or older in China and South Korea is 12–15 percent. It is 15–22 percent in the European Union, Canada, and the United States and 30 percent in Japan. With baby boomers aging and life expectancy increasing, these numbers will increase dramatically. In 2050, approximately 30 percent of Americans, Canadians, Chinese, and Europeans will be over 60, as will more than 40 percent of Japanese and South Koreans.

Over the next decades, therefore, these countries will have increasingly large proportions of retirees and increasingly small proportions of workers. As workers born during the baby boom of 1945–65 are retiring, they are not being replaced by a new cohort of citizens of prime working age (15–59 years old).

Industrialized countries are experiencing a drop in their working-age populations that is even more severe than the overall slowdown in their population growth. South Korea represents the most extreme example. Even as its total population is projected to decline by almost 9 percent by 2050

(from 48.3 million to 44.1 million), the population of working-age South Koreans is expected to drop by 36 percent (from 32.9 million to 21.1 million), and the number of South Koreans aged 60 and older will increase by almost 150 percent (from 7.3 million to 18 million). By 2050, in other words, the entire working-age population will barely exceed the 60-and-older population. Although South Korea's case is extreme, it represents an increasingly common fate for developed countries. Europe is expected to lose 24 percent of its prime working-age population (about 120 million workers) by 2050, and its 60-and-older population is expected to increase by 47 percent. In the United States, where higher fertility and more immigration are expected than in Europe, the working-age population will grow by 15 percent over the next four decades—a steep decline from its growth of 62 percent between 1950 and 2010. And by 2050, the United States' 60-and-older population is expected to double.

All this will have a dramatic impact on economic growth, health care, and military strength in the developed world. The forces that fueled economic growth in industrialized countries during the second half of the twentieth century—increased productivity due to better education, the movement of women into the labor force, and innovations in technology—will all likely weaken in the coming decades. College enrollment boomed after World War II, a trend that is not likely to recur in the twenty-first century; the extensive movement of women into the labor force also was a one-time social change; and the technological change of the time resulted from innovators who created new products and leading-edge consumers who were willing to try them out—two groups that are thinning out as the industrialized world's population ages.

Overall economic growth will also be hampered by a decline in the number of new consumers and new households. When developed countries' labor forces were growing by 0.5–1.0 percent per year, as they did until 2005, even annual increases in real output per worker of just 1.7 percent meant that annual economic growth totaled 2.2–2.7 percent per year. But with the labor forces of many developed countries (such as Germany, Hungary, Japan, Russia, and the Baltic states) now shrinking by 0.2 percent per year and those of other countries (including Austria, the Czech Republic, Denmark, Greece, and Italy) growing by less than 0.2 percent per year, the same 1.7 percent increase in real output per worker yields only 1.5–1.9 percent annual overall growth. Moreover, developed countries will be lucky to keep productivity growth at even that level; in many developed countries, productivity is more likely to decline as the population ages.

A further strain on industrialized economies will be rising medical costs: as populations age, they will demand more health care for longer periods of time. Public pension schemes for aging populations are already being reformed in various industrialized countries—often prompting heated debate. In theory, at least, pensions might be kept solvent by increasing the retirement age, raising taxes modestly, and phasing out benefits for the wealthy. Regardless, the number of 80- and 90-year-olds—who are unlikely to work and highly likely to require nursing-home and other expensive care—will rise dramatically. And even if 60- and 70-year-olds remain active and employed, they will require procedures and medications—hip replacements, kidney transplants, blood-pressure treatments—to sustain their health in old age.

All this means that just as aging developed countries will have proportionally fewer workers, innovators, and consumerist young households, a large portion of those countries' remaining economic growth will have to be diverted to pay for the medical bills and pensions of their growing elderly populations. Basic services, meanwhile, will be increasingly costly because fewer young workers will be available for strenuous and labor-intensive jobs. Unfortunately, policymakers seldom reckon with these potentially disruptive effects of otherwise welcome developments, such as higher life expectancy.

Youth and Islam in the Developing World

Even as the industrialized countries of Europe, North America, and Northeast Asia will experience unprecedented aging this century, fast-growing countries in Africa, Latin America, the Middle East, and Southeast Asia will have exceptionally youthful populations. Today, roughly nine out of ten children under the age of 15 live in developing countries. And these are the countries that will continue to have the world's highest birthrates. Indeed, over 70 percent of the world's population growth between now and 2050 will occur in 24 countries, all of which are classified by the World Bank as low income or lower-middle income, with an average per capita income of under $3,855 in 2008.

Many developing countries have few ways of providing employment to their young, fast-growing populations. Would-be laborers, therefore, will be increasingly attracted to the labor markets of the aging developed countries of Europe, North America, and Northeast Asia. Youthful immigrants from nearby regions with high unemployment—Central America, North Africa, and Southeast Asia, for example—will be drawn to those vital entry-level and manual-labor jobs that sustain advanced economies: janitors, nursing-home aides, bus drivers, plumbers, security guards, farm workers, and the like. Current levels of immigration from developing to developed countries are paltry compared to those that the forces of supply and demand might soon create across the world.

These forces will act strongly on the Muslim world, where many economically weak countries will continue to experience dramatic population growth in the decades ahead. In 1950, Bangladesh, Egypt, Indonesia, Nigeria, Pakistan, and Turkey had a combined population of 242 million. By 2009, those six countries were the world's most populous Muslim-majority countries and had a combined population of 886 million. Their populations are continuing to grow and indeed are expected to increase by 475 million between now and 2050—during which time, by comparison, the six most populous developed countries are projected to gain only 44 million inhabitants. Worldwide, of the 48 fastest-growing countries today—those with annual population growth of two percent or more—28 are majority Muslim or have Muslim minorities of 33 percent or more.

It is therefore imperative to improve relations between Muslim and Western societies. This will be difficult given that many Muslims live in poor communities vulnerable to radical appeals and many see the West as antagonistic and militaristic. In the 2009 Pew Global Attitudes Project survey, for example, whereas 69 percent of those Indonesians and Nigerians surveyed reported viewing the United States favorably, just 18 percent of those polled in Egypt, Jordan, Pakistan, and Turkey (all U.S. allies) did. And in 2006, when the Pew survey last asked detailed questions about Muslim-Western relations, more than half of the respondents in Muslim countries characterized those relations as bad and blamed the West for this state of affairs.

But improving relations is all the more important because of the growing demographic weight of poor Muslim countries and the attendant increase in Muslim immigration, especially to Europe from North Africa and the Middle East. (To be sure, forecasts that Muslims will soon dominate Europe are outlandish: Muslims compose just three to ten percent of the population in the major European countries today, and this proportion will at most double by midcentury.) Strategists worldwide must consider that the world's young are becoming concentrated in those countries least prepared to educate and employ them, including some Muslim states. Any resulting poverty, social tension, or ideological radicalization could have disruptive effects in many corners of the world. But this need not be the case; the healthy immigration of workers to the developed world and the movement of capital to the developing world, among other things, could lead to better results.

Urban Sprawl

Exacerbating twenty-first-century risks will be the fact that the world is urbanizing to an unprecedented degree. The year 2010 will likely be the first time in history that a majority of the world's people live in cities rather than in the countryside. Whereas less than 30 percent of the world's population was urban in 1950, according to UN projections, more than 70 percent will be by 2050.

Lower-income countries in Asia and Africa are urbanizing especially rapidly, as agriculture becomes less labor intensive and as employment opportunities shift to the industrial and service sectors. Already, most of the world's urban agglomerations—Mumbai (population 20.1 million), Mexico City (19.5 million), New Delhi (17 million), Shanghai (15.8 million), Calcutta (15.6 million), Karachi (13.1 million), Cairo (12.5 million), Manila (11.7 million), Lagos (10.6 million), Jakarta (9.7 million)—are found in low-income countries. Many of these countries have multiple cities with over one million residents each: Pakistan has eight, Mexico 12, and China more than 100. The UN projects that the urbanized proportion of sub-Saharan Africa will nearly double between 2005 and 2050, from 35 percent (300 million people) to over 67 percent (1 billion). China, which is roughly 40 percent urbanized today, is expected to be 73 percent urbanized by 2050; India, which is less than 30 percent urbanized today, is expected to be 55 percent urbanized by 2050. Overall, the world's urban population is expected to grow by 3 billion people by 2050.

This urbanization may prove destabilizing. Developing countries that urbanize in the twenty-first century will have far lower per capita incomes than did many industrial countries when they first urbanized. The United States, for example, did not reach 65 percent urbanization until 1950, when per capita income was nearly $13,000 (in 2005 dollars). By contrast, Nigeria, Pakistan, and the Philippines, which are approaching similar levels of urbanization, currently have per capita incomes of just $1,800–$4,000 (in 2005 dollars).

According to the research of Richard Cincotta and other political demographers, countries with younger populations are especially prone to civil unrest and are less able to create or sustain democratic institutions. And the more heavily urbanized, the more such countries are likely to experience Dickensian poverty and anarchic violence. In good times, a thriving economy might keep urban residents employed and governments flush with sufficient resources to meet their needs. More often, however, sprawling and impoverished cities are vulnerable to crime lords, gangs, and petty rebellions. Thus, the rapid urbanization of the developing world in the decades ahead might bring, in exaggerated form, problems similar to those that urbanization brought to nineteenth-century Europe. Back then, cyclical employment, inadequate policing, and limited sanitation and education often spawned widespread labor strife, periodic violence, and sometimes—as in the 1820s, the 1830s, and 1848—even revolutions.

International terrorism might also originate in fast-urbanizing developing countries (even more than it already does). With their neighborhood networks, access to the Internet and digital communications technology, and concentration of valuable targets, sprawling cities offer excellent opportunities for recruiting, maintaining, and hiding terrorist networks.

Defusing the Bomb

Averting this century's potential dangers will require sweeping measures. Three major global efforts defused the population bomb of Ehrlich's day: a commitment by governments and nongovernmental organizations to control reproduction rates; agricultural advances, such as the green revolution and the spread of new technology; and a vast increase in international trade, which globalized markets and thus allowed developing countries to export foodstuffs in exchange for seeds, fertilizers, and machinery, which in turn helped them boost production. But today's population bomb is the product less of absolute growth in the world's population than of changes in its age and distribution. Policymakers must therefore adapt today's global governance institutions to the new realities of the aging of the industrialized world, the concentration of the world's economic and population growth in developing countries, and the increase in international immigration.

During the Cold War, Western strategists divided the world into a "First World," of democratic industrialized countries; a "Second World," of communist industrialized countries; and a "Third World," of developing countries. These strategists focused chiefly on deterring or managing conflict between the First and the Second Worlds and on launching proxy wars and diplomatic initiatives to attract Third World countries into the First World's camp. Since the end of the Cold War, strategists have largely abandoned this three-group division and have tended to believe either that the United States, as the sole superpower, would maintain a Pax Americana or that the world would become multipolar, with the United States, Europe, and China playing major roles.

Unfortunately, because they ignore current global demographic trends, these views will be obsolete within a few decades. A better approach would be to consider a different three-world order, with a new First World of the aging industrialized nations of North America, Europe, and Asia's Pacific Rim (including Japan, Singapore, South Korea, and Taiwan, as well as China after 2030, by which point the one-child policy will have produced significant aging); a Second World comprising fast-growing and economically dynamic countries with a healthy mix of young and old inhabitants (such as Brazil, Iran, Mexico, Thailand, Turkey, and Vietnam, as well as China until 2030); and a Third World of fast-growing, very young, and increasingly urbanized countries with poorer economies and often weak governments. To cope with the instability that will likely arise from the new Third World's urbanization, economic strife, lawlessness, and potential terrorist activity, the aging industrialized nations of the new First World must build effective alliances with the growing powers of the new Second World and together reach out to Third World nations. Second World powers will be pivotal in the twenty-first century not just because they will drive economic growth and consume technologies and other products engineered in the First World; they will also be central to international security and cooperation. The realities of religion, culture, and geographic proximity mean that any peaceful and productive engagement by the First World of Third World countries will have to include the open cooperation of Second World countries.

Strategists, therefore, must fundamentally reconsider the structure of various current global institutions. The G-8, for example, will likely become obsolete as a body for making global economic policy. The G-20 is already becoming increasingly important, and this is less a short-term consequence of the ongoing global financial crisis than the beginning of the necessary recognition that Brazil, China, India, Indonesia, Mexico, Turkey, and others are becoming global economic powers. International institutions will not retain their legitimacy if they exclude the world's fastest-growing and most economically dynamic countries. It is essential, therefore, despite European concerns about the potential effects on immigration, to take steps such as admitting Turkey into the European Union. This would add youth and economic dynamism to the EU—and would prove that Muslims are welcome to join Europeans as equals in shaping a free and prosperous future. On the other hand, excluding Turkey from the EU could lead to hostility not only on the part of Turkish citizens, who are expected to number 100 million by 2050, but also on the part of Muslim populations worldwide.

NATO must also adapt. The alliance today is composed almost entirely of countries with aging, shrinking populations and relatively slow-growing economies. It is oriented toward the Northern Hemisphere and holds on to a Cold War structure that cannot adequately respond to contemporary threats. The young and increasingly populous countries of Africa, the Middle East, Central Asia, and South Asia could mobilize insurgents much more easily than NATO could mobilize the troops it would need if it were called on to stabilize those countries. Long-standing NATO members should, therefore—although it would require atypical creativity and flexibility—consider the logistical and demographic advantages of inviting into the alliance countries such as Brazil and Morocco, rather than countries such as Albania. That this seems far-fetched does not minimize the imperative that First World countries begin including large and strategic Second and Third World powers in formal international alliances.

The case of Afghanistan—a country whose population is growing fast and where NATO is currently engaged—illustrates the importance of building effective global institutions. Today, there are 28 million Afghans; by 2025, there will be 45 million; and by 2050, there will be close to 75 million. As nearly 20 million additional Afghans are born over the next 15 years, NATO will have an opportunity to help Afghanistan become reasonably stable, self-governing, and prosperous. If NATO's efforts fail and the Afghans judge that NATO intervention harmed their interests, tens of millions of young Afghans will become more hostile to the West. But if they come to think that NATO's involvement benefited their society, the West will have tens of millions of new friends. The example might then motivate the approximately one billion other young Muslims growing up in low-income countries over the next four decades to look more kindly on relations between their countries and the countries of the industrialized West.

Creative Reforms at Home

The aging industrialized countries can also take various steps at home to promote stability in light of the coming demographic trends. First, they should encourage families to have more children. France and Sweden have had success providing child care, generous leave time, and financial allowances to families with young children. Yet there is no consensus among policymakers—and certainly not among demographers—about what policies best encourage fertility.

More important than unproven tactics for increasing family size is immigration. Correctly managed, population movement can benefit developed and developing countries alike. Given the dangers of young, underemployed, and unstable populations in developing countries, immigration to developed countries can provide economic opportunities for the ambitious and serve as a safety valve for all. Countries that embrace immigrants, such as the United States, gain economically by having willing laborers and greater entrepreneurial spirit. And countries with high levels of emigration (but not so much that they experience so-called brain drains) also benefit because emigrants often send remittances home or return to their native countries with valuable education and work experience.

One somewhat daring approach to immigration would be to encourage a reverse flow of older immigrants from developed to developing countries. If older residents of developed countries took their retirements along the southern coast of the Mediterranean or in Latin America or Africa, it would greatly reduce the strain on their home countries' public entitlement systems. The developing countries involved, meanwhile, would benefit because caring for the elderly and providing retirement and leisure services is highly labor intensive. Relocating a portion of these activities to developing countries would provide employment and valuable training to the young, growing populations of the Second and Third Worlds.

This would require developing residential and medical facilities of First World quality in Second and Third World countries. Yet even this difficult task would be preferable to the status quo, by which low wages and poor facilities lead to a steady drain of medical and nursing talent from developing to developed countries. Many residents of developed countries who desire cheaper medical procedures already practice medical tourism today, with India, Singapore, and Thailand being the most common destinations. (For example, the international consulting firm Deloitte estimated that 750,000 Americans traveled abroad for care in 2008.)

Never since 1800 has a majority of the world's economic growth occurred outside of Europe, the United States, and Canada. Never have so many people in those regions been over 60 years old. And never have low-income countries' populations been so young and so urbanized. But such will be the world's demography in the twenty-first century. The strategic and economic policies of the twentieth century are obsolete, and it is time to find new ones.

References

Goldstone, Jack A. "The new population bomb: the four megatrends that will change the world." *Foreign Affairs* 89.1 (2010): 31. *General OneFile.* Web. 23 Jan. 2010. <http://0-find.galegroup.com.www.consuls.org/gps/start.do?proId=IPS&userGroupName=a30wc>.

Critical Thinking

1. Why is the decline in the population of Europe important?
2. Why is the aging population in the developed world important?
3. Why is the growing population in the developing world important?
4. Do you think that moving the population of the world to the cities is a good thing? Explain.

From *Foreign Affairs*, vol. 89, no. 1, January/February 2010, pp. 31–43. Copyright © 2010 by Council on Foreign Relations, Inc. Reprinted by permission of Foreign Affairs. www.ForeignAffairs.org.

The Man Who Named the Future

GILLIAN TETT

On the desk of Jim O'Neill, chief economist for Goldman Sachs, stand four filmsy flags. They look out of place among the expensive computer terminals of the investment bank's plush London office, like leftovers of a child's geography homework or cheap mementos from backpacking trips to exotic parts of the world. But these flags hint at a more interesting story—of the latest way in which money and ideas are reshaping the world. The small scraps of fabric are pennants for big countries: Brazil, Russia, India and China. And a decade ago, O'Neill decided to start thinking of them as a group—which he gave the acronym Bric.

It was a simple mental prop. The bolder move was to predict– publicly, and in Goldman's name—that by 2041 (later revised to 2039, then 2032) the Brics would overtake the six largest western economies in terms of economic might. The four flags would come to represent the pillars of the 21st-century economy.

At the time, many scoffed at this idea. The predictions turned conventional western wisdom on its head; and O'Neill hardly seemed an obvious champion of the concept. A large man with working-class Manchester roots, he does not exude the aura of any globetrotting elite. His office is decorated with splashes of cherry red memorabilia from Manchester United Football Club, and he still speaks with the thick, flattened vowels of his childhood. Indeed, when O'Neill coined the term Bric in 2001, he had never properly visited three of the four countries (the exception was China), and spoke none of their languages. Yet, notwithstanding those unlikely beginnings, in the past decade, Bric has become a near ubiquitous financial term, shaping how a generation of investors, financiers and policymakers view the emerging markets: companies ranging from Nissan to media group WPP have developed Brics business strategies; several dozen financial institutions now run Brics funds; business schools have launched Brics courses; and this April Phillips de Pury will be holding a Brics-themed auction. "The Brics concept . . . that O'Neill created . . . has become such a strong brand," says Felipe Goes, adviser to the mayor of Rio de Janeiro, who is organising the first Brics think-tank.

O'Neill speaks in smaller spheres for a moment: "It has transformed my life," he says.

To some critics, the fuss about Brics is overblown. The term is hype, spin, from a bank and banking industry accustomed to

disguising such guff as genuinely new ideas and concepts—the better to profit from them. "Brics is really just marketing—it's nonsense!" says Charles Dumas, a London-based economist who disputes many elements of the Brics concept, such as the idea that these countries will keep growing inexorably into the future. Others are more cynical still, arguing that Goldmans Sachs has used the concept to extend its global power, and thus turbo-charge its formidable profit-making machine. O'Neill denies this latter accusation. "I really believe in this idea of Brics, that this idea can make the world a better place—it's what drives me," he says.

But even if Brics is self-interested spin, such spin—an idea in itself, really—can sometimes take on a life of its own, beyond what its creators expect or even hope for. By creating the word Brics, O'Neill has redrawn powerbrokers' cognitive map, helping them to articulate a fundamental shift of influence away from the western world. And if you believe that the way humans think and speak not only reflects reality, but can shape its future path too, then this Brics tag has itself come both to reflect and drive the change—albeit from some unlikely beginnings.

The way O'Neill, 52, tells the tale of how he developed the Brics—and he is a born raconteur—starts, a touch melodramatically, on the day terrorists flew aircraft into the World Trade Centre and Pentagon, killing thousands of people.

The son of a postman, O'Neill grew up in south Manchester, where he studied at the local comprehensive (Oasis's Noel and Liam Gallagher were pupils there too, albeit later) and spent much of his time playing football. After school, he decided to study at Sheffield University, partly because it offered easy access to watch Manchester United. (Today, he has season tickets at Old Trafford, and leaves spare tickets behind the bar at a local pub, for childhood friends to use.) During his time there, between "getting drunk and playing football", O'Neill discovered a passion for economics. And after completing a doctorate in the subject, he worked as a foreign exchange analyst at a series of City banks, eventually joining Goldman in 1995 as co-head of economics. In the summer of 2001, Gavyn Davies, O'Neill's highly respected co-chief, announced his departure– leaving O'Neill the sole leader, and under huge pressure to perform. "I thought: 'Oh my god, I have got to put my imprint on this department,' he recalls. 'I was searching for a theme and a new idea.'"

Inspiration came—a bittersweet gift. On September 11, as the first aircraft approached the Twin Towers, where he had delivered a lecture a few days earlier, O'Neill was hosting a global video conference call. Halfway through, the New York faces vanished from the screen. O'Neill later learnt the staff had been safely evacuated from their offices, but he still reeled in shock at the events. In the days that followed, his mind began to whir. As a foreign exchange analyst, O'Neill had always been a passionate advocate of globalisation, and was fascinated by the rising power of Asia. And to him, the horror in Manhattan was a powerful demonstration of exactly why the non-western world was starting to matter more and more—albeit in a negative way. However, O'Neill also believed—or hoped—that this shift in power could be seen in a more positive sense, too. "What 9/11 told me was that there was no way that globalisation was going to be Americanisation in the future—nor should it be," he says. "In order for globalisation to advance, it had to be accepted by more people . . . but not by imposing the dominant American social and philosophical beliefs and structures."

In practical terms, O'Neill decided, that meant economists had to look more closely at how non-western economies could wield more power in the future. As he scoured the globe, he became increasingly fascinated by four countries: Brazil, India, Russia and China. In one sense, the four seemed disparate, separated geographically and culturally; they had never acted as a bloc in any way, never conceived of themselves as a unit. Yet what they all shared in 2001 were large populations, underdeveloped economies and governments that appeared willing to embrace global markets and some elements of globalisation. To O'Neill, these characteristics made them natural sisters: they all had the potential for rapid future growth.

Excited, he tried to work out how to label this bunch. Since China was easily the largest, it made sense to put its name first. "Lloyd Blankfein [Goldman Sachs's chief executive] always teases me about it—he says I should have called the group the Cribs," O'Neill recalls. But O'Neill thought that a word linked to babies would seem patronising. So on November 30 2001, he launched his Big Idea: Goldman Sachs's Global Economic Paper?#66, "Building Better Global Economic Brics". He predicted, soberly, that "over the next 10 years, the weight of the Brics and especially China in world GDP will grow"—and warned, perhaps a little less soberly, that "in line with these prospects, world policymaking forums should be reorganised" to give more power to the group he had now dubbed Brics.

The paper immediately sparked interest among Goldman Sachs's corporate clients, particularly those already selling—or trying to sell—consumer products to the emerging markets. "I found the Bric thing fascinating right from the start," says Martin Sorrell, chief executive of WPP. "It tapped into what we had been already discussing." But to many investors and bankers—including some inside Goldman Sachs—it all seemed rather fanciful, particularly given that countries such as Brazil had recently experienced hyperinflation. "When I first spoke at a big group in Rio [after the paper was published], it was to around 1,000 investors from all of Latin America," recalls

O'Neill. "The guy who was introducing me whispered in my ear as he went to the podium, 'we all know that the only reason the B is there is because without it there is no acronym.'"

But O'Neill kept discussing the concept with colleagues and in 2003 his team produced the next offering: a paper called "Dreaming with Brics: The Path to 2050". It boldly declared that by 2039 the Brics group could overtake the largest western economies in scale. "The list of the world's 10 largest economies may look quite different in 2050," it said. That prediction launched O'Neill's team into what he calls Briclife. Within days, Goldman economists were flooded with e-mails from executives at companies ranging from mobile telecoms group Vodafone to miner BHP Billiton to Ikea and Nissan. By luck—or insight—O'Neill had produced this tag just as many western businesses were trying to hone their strategies to sell products to the non-western world, or to use regions such as China as a manufacturing base. And in a world where corporate boards face information overload, Brics suddenly provided executives with a snappy way of discussing strategy. Better still, unlike phrases such as "emerging markets" or "developing world", Brics did not sound patronising, or unpromising; it was neutral, strong, politically correct.

Soon rivals, such as HSBC and Deutsche Bank fund unit DWS, were launching dedicated investment funds marketed under the label of Brics. "We asked our lawyers if we could trademark the word Brics, but they said not—apparently it's not a product," O'Neill recalls. Steadily, the brand spread, taking on a life beyond Goldman. Initially, most hedge funds ignored the concept as marketing hype. But as investors began to purchase assets specifically linked to the rise of Brics, the hedgefunders recognised that the way that China, say, was making cars could affect demand for Brazilian copper. New correlations were developing in asset prices, amid strong investment flows (since 2003, the Brics stock markets have risen from 2 to 9 per cent of global market capitalisation, and O'Neill forecasts they will represent almost 50 per cent of global market capitalisation in 2050).

Unsurprisingly, O'Neill's rivals started to snipe. Some economists said it was ridiculous to make forecasts as far out as 2050, particularly since many of O'Neill's projections seemed to involve extrapolating current growth on a straight line. Others took issue with the idea that the four Bric countries could–or should–be described as a group. "Economically, financially and politically, China overshadows and will continue to overshadow the other Brics," analysts at Deutsche Bank argued. Some banks tried to ban their employees from using the B word. "Why the hell should we do Goldman's marketing for it?" says the chief executive of one of the world's biggest investment banks. Meanwhile, out in the market, some investors suggested it would be better to talk about Bricks (with Korea included), or Brimck (with Mexico as well) or even Abrimcks (chucking in the Arab region and South Africa). One market wag joked that somebody should start trading the Cement bloc (Countries Excluded from the Emerging New Terminology).

O'Neill fought back. The Goldman team started to crank out Bric research, looking at everything from the future size of the Indian middle class to car use in Brazil. In an effort to soothe some ruffled feathers, in 2005 O'Neill tried to explain why Korea and Mexico had not been included in his big idea (the rather arbitrary-sounding reason was that they were members of the Organisation for Economic Co-operation and Development). He also tried to placate some of the non-Brics by offering a new term: the "N-11", or Next Eleven nations on the list to emerge as powers. This was a confusingly broad club, encompassing Bangladesh, Egypt, Indonesia, Iran, Korea, Mexico, Nigeria, Pakistan, the Philippines, Turkey and Vietnam, but within months companies such as Nissan and WPP were bandying "N-11" around their boardrooms. Another marketing tag—or boundary on a cognitive map—had been born.

Nor was it just the corporate world getting excited. O'Neill heard that politicians in Nigeria were slapping the term on their internal propaganda campaigns, redefining some of the slogans for their own ends; it was uncannily reminiscent of how 19th-century Nigerians once transposed the language of the Anglican Church to their own cultural traditions.

Perhaps the most remarkable aspect of O'Neill's golden child is what it didn't do: collapse under scrutiny as the credit crisis hit. Over the past two years, many of Wall Street's big ideas have been exposed as woefully ill-conceived at best, utterly fallacious at worst. However, during the great re-reckoning, the Brics concept has flourished. Most of the Brics and N-11 emerged from the crisis well, relative to the economies of the western world. Their banking systems are intact, and their economies are growing at breakneck speed. "As a result," wrote O'Neill in a recent paper, "we think our long-term 2050 Bric 'dream' projections are more, rather than less, likely to materialise." More specifically, Goldman now predicts that China's economy will become as big as the US's by 2027, while the total Brics group will eclipse the big western economies by 2032—almost a decade sooner than first thought.

That, O'Neill argues, will overturn many western assumptions about how the world works. These days, Goldman aggressively recommends that investors decide which western companies to invest in based on whether they are selling to the Brics and N11, rather than just western consumers. (In another piece of neat cultural transposition, Goldman recently dubbed this strategy "investment in the Brics Nifty 50" [companies which sell to the Brics region]—a reference to the "nifty 50" of big western companies that were beloved by investors back in the 1970s, when it was presumed that the US and Europe would provide the engines of growth.) "We estimate that two billion people could join the global middle-class by 2030, mainly from Brics," Goldman's latest research note trills.

The argument is beloved by some investors. "Had you heeded O'Neill's work and gotten invested in the stock markets of those four nations [back in 2001], you'd have made more money this past decade than by doing virtually anything else conceivable," declared Joshua Brown, an influential investment commentator, on his Wall Street blog last month. (O'Neill brushes off the praise as "somewhat embarrassing".) Others fear it is the next big bubble. To some, the exclusion of countries such as South Africa—or even Indonesia—looks increasingly odd. And the inclusion of Russia is presenting an ever-greater headache, given that the Russian economy was the one Bric to take a real fall in the credit crisis—so severe, in fact, that some investors (and even a few bankers inside Goldman) suspect it is now time to kick Russia out of the group.

Unsurprisingly, O'Neill is reluctant to undermine Goldman's relations with Moscow by doing that. Although he admits that Russia has "disappointed", he also insists that if the country "recovers strongly and quickly in 2010 and 2011, as we expect, we believe it will deserve its Bric status."

But now another Brics-related phenomenon is emerging. In the early years of Bric-dom, the four countries chosen by O'Neill had different reactions to the designation. There was delight in Russia, bafflement in China, cynicism in Brazil and indifference in India. Now, the countries are using the idea to forge tentative links in reality—not just the world of investment ideas. In May 2008, Russia hosted the first formal Bric summit, a meeting of Bric foreign ministers in Yekaterinburg. In July 2009, it followed this with a formal gathering of all four Bric heads of state.

As meetings go, these were symbolic, not substantive. Although the four countries discussed how they could better co-ordinate their affairs to gain greater influence—and seek alternatives to the dollar—they did not agree on any tangible steps. But this year in the early summer, the four countries will meet again, this time in Brazil. In anticipation, the Brazilian authorities are establishing a group of academics and a formal think-tank to brainstorm how to develop the Brics agenda. As part of that, they plan to host a conference next month in Rio—with the participation of O'Neill himself. McKinsey, which has used a version of the Brics concept in its consulting strategy, will also be involved.

It might seem ironic that the four countries would choose a term created by an American bank to define themselves but it is not unprecedented. When countries such as India first developed their sense of national identity and rebelled against the British—or when Soviet republics such as Uzbekistan developed a similar nationalism–they did so using the borders that had also been imposed, artificially and arbitrarily, by an outside power. When the cognitive map is redrawn by a dominant power—even in the world of marketing and investment bank "spin"—it tends not to be erased so much as appropriated.

"Is there much evidence that the Brics countries are collaborating today in practical terms?" O'Neill asks. "Not really, no. But that could change in the future—you look at how Brazil supplies commodities which China needs . . . or the fact that they all have quite similar ideas about how to manage their economies."

Or as Felipe Goes, the Brazilian official in Rio charged with setting up the world's first Brics think-tank, says: "It is somewhat ironic [that we use the word Brics] . . . but that reflects the fact that in the modern world it is people like Goldman Sachs and McKinsey who have the resources and minds to develop ideas." Indeed, what makes a large institution such as Goldman so influential these days is not simply its trading acumen and political connections, but also its ability to invest heavily in what bankers sometimes call "thought-leadership", by funding analysis and ensuring it is read around the world.

Back in New York, some of Goldman's older managers are aware of the cultural ironies of the Brics boom. During the first 120 years of its history, Goldman made most of its profits from American markets, and today the firm is often viewed as the most politically well-connected of the US banks. If you step into the office of its headquarters at 85 Broad Street, in downtown Manhattan, the first thing that you see is a vast American flag, looming over the dull brown marble lobby. Yet appearances can deceive. While O'Neill has spent the past decade trying to carve out his own intellectual niche by promoting the Brics, so too—far more discreetly—Goldman has been remaking itself, building activities outside the American heartland to capture the growth that O'Neill forecasts. In the past decade, the bank has opened more offices across the world than in the whole of its previous history, and while revenues from the Americas accounted for 60 per cent of its earnings 10 years ago, they now represent about half (and far less if Latin America is excluded). Indeed, senior Goldman executives expect that within a few years, profits that are "made in America" will be a minority of total earnings.

That pattern is certainly not unique to Goldman Sachs: most other western banks have also been expanding across the globe in the past few years. Deutsche Bank, for example, has been deftly building an emerging markets derivatives franchise, while HSBC is now so convinced that its future lies in Asia that Michael Geoghegan, chief executive, recently relocated to Hong Kong from London.

Still, the swing is particularly striking at Goldman, given its all-American past. These days, one of the buzzwords at 85 Broad Street is "domestification", or the idea that the bank must build businesses around the world that provide local clients not simply with international services, but also with services in their local markets. Rather than treating non-western countries as far-flung frontiers or pawns in a trading game, the new corporate rhetoric insists that the Brics (and other non-western countries) are markets in their own rights. Thus in Brazil, Goldman recently started selling Brazilian investment funds to Brazilians. In Japan, there are staff who barely speak a word of English. And in China—where Goldman Sachs most certainly does not fly a big US flag—the bank is sponsoring a Chinese business school, to ensure access to a stream of authentically local Chinese students.

This drive is going hand in hand with a complex process of cultural engineering. As the bank acquires more non-western staff, it is devising programmes to rotate its locally hired employees through headquarters, to ensure that they learn "Goldman values". It also takes care to send staff from New York and London out to the regions, and to shuffle different ethnic groups between different regions.

As its sponsorship of Chinese business schools shows, Goldman is trying to raise a new generation of local leaders. "If you look at the history of the London office of Goldman, you can see how over a decade or two, you can have locals rise to the top," says one top executive. "That is our goal across the world. The idea is to get embedded, to show that we are there for the long term . . . but also to ensure that our Goldman values are everywhere in the world."

It all might sound reminiscent of the way the British empire operated in the 19th century—or the way the Russian Communist party once tried to knit the diverse peoples of the Soviet Union into a single ideologically based nation. Only this time, it is MBA programmes and Goldman training courses, rather than British public schools or communist training camps, that provide the cultural glue. And—perhaps most important of all—Goldman Sachs (unlike earlier empires) is not overtly acting with a nationalist or political agenda; insofar as it has a real loyalty, it is to its own bottom line and its ability to make profits.

Put it another way: Goldman will keep flying Old Glory only as long as it believes that there is profit to be made under that banner. No wonder a senior member of the US government remarked a couple of years ago, partly in jest, that sooner or later, Goldman "is going to have to choose whether it wants to really be American or not". If O'Neill is even half-right in his predictions, it may not be a straightforward choice.

Gillian Tett is the FT's capital markets editor. Her last piece for the magazine was about the JP Morgan bankers who invented the "credit derivative"—and their reactions to the derivatives-induced financial crisis. Read it at www.ft.com/foolsgold.

On Monday, the FT begins a five-part series on Bric consumers—who they are, what they buy, who is selling to them and what their rise means for the global economy.

Critical Thinking

1. Brazil, Russia, India, and China are referred to as the "BRIC" countries and are considered to be high-growth countries. Do you think these countries represent the top growth countries?

2. Is this list up to date?

3. Are there other countries that should be considered?

The Future of History: Can Liberal Democracy Survive the Decline of the Middle Class?

FRANCIS FUKUYAMA

Something strange is going on in the world today. The global financial crisis that began in 2008 and the ongoing crisis of the euro are both products of the model of lightly regulated financial capitalism that emerged over the past three decades. Yet despite widespread anger at Wall Street bailouts, there has been no great upsurge of left-wing American populism in response. It is conceivable that the Occupy Wall Street movement will gain traction, but the most dynamic recent populist movement to date has been the right-wing Tea Party, whose main target is the regulatory state that seeks to protect ordinary people from financial speculators. Something similar is true in Europe as well, where the left is anemic and right-wing populist parties are on the move.

There are several reasons for this lack of left-wing mobilization, but chief among them is a failure in the realm of ideas. For the past generation, the ideological high ground on economic issues has been held by a libertarian right. The left has not been able to make a plausible case for an agenda other than a return to an unaffordable form of old-fashioned social democracy. This absence of a plausible progressive counter-narrative is unhealthy, because competition is good for intellectual—debate just as it is for economic activity. And serious intellectual debate is urgently needed, since the current form of globalized capitalism is eroding the middle-class social base on which liberal democracy rests.

The Democratic Wave

Social forces and conditions do not simply "determine" ideologies, as Karl Marx once maintained, but ideas do not become powerful unless they speak to the concerns of large numbers of ordinary people. Liberal democracy is the default ideology around much of the world today in part because it responds to and is facilitated by certain socioeconomic structures. Changes in those structures may have ideological consequences, just as ideological changes may have socioeconomic consequences.

Almost all the powerful ideas that shaped human societies up until the past 300 years were religious in nature, with the important exception of Confucianism in China. The first major secular ideology to have a lasting worldwide effect was liberalism, a doctrine associated with the rise of first a commercial and then an industrial middle class in certain parts of Europe in the seventeenth century. (By "middle class," I mean people who are neither at the top nor at the bottom of their societies in terms of income, who have received at least a secondary education, and who own either real property, durable goods, or their own businesses.)

As enunciated by classic thinkers such as Locke, Montesquieu, and Mill, liberalism holds that the legitimacy of state authority derives from the state's ability to protect the individual rights of its citizens and that state power needs to be limited by the adherence to law. One of the fundamental rights to be protected is that of private property; England's Glorious Revolution of 1688–89 was critical to the development of modern liberalism because it first established the constitutional principle that the state could not legitimately tax its citizens without their consent.

At first, liberalism did not necessarily imply democracy. The Whigs who supported the constitutional settlement of 1689 tended to be the wealthiest property owners in England; the parliament of that period represented less than ten percent of the whole population. Many classic liberals, including Mill, were highly skeptical of the virtues of democracy: they believed that responsible political participation required education and a stake in society—that is, property ownership. Up through the end of the nineteenth century, the franchise was limited by property and educational requirements in virtually all parts of Europe. Andrew

Jackson's election as U.S. president in 1828 and his subsequent abolition of property requirements for voting, at least for white males, thus marked an important early victory for a more robust democratic principle. In Europe, the exclusion of the vast majority of the population from political power and the rise of an industrial working class paved the way for Marxism. The Communist Manifesto was published in 1848, the same year that revolutions spread to all the major European countries save the United Kingdom. And so began a century of competition for the leadership of the democratic movement between communists, who were willing to jettison procedural democracy (multiparty elections) in favor of what they believed was substantive democracy (economic redistribution), and liberal democrats, who believed in expanding political participation while maintaining a rule of law protecting individual rights, including property rights.

At stake was the allegiance of the new industrial working class. Early Marxists believed they would win by sheer force of numbers: as the franchise was expanded in the late nineteenth century, parties such as the United Kingdom's Labour and Germany's Social Democrats grew by leaps and bounds and threatened the hegemony of both conservatives and traditional liberals. The rise of the working class was fiercely resisted, often by nondemocratic means; the communists and many socialists, in turn, abandoned formal democracy in favor of a direct seizure of power.

Throughout the first half of the twentieth century, there was a strong consensus on the progressive left that some form of socialism—government control of the commanding heights of the economy in order to ensure an egalitarian distribution of wealth—was unavoidable for all advanced countries. Even a conservative economist such as Joseph Schumpeter could write in his 1942 book, *Capitalism, Socialism, and Democracy*, that socialism would emerge victorious because capitalist society was culturally self-undermining. Socialism was believed to represent the will and interests of the vast majority of people in modern societies. Yet even as the great ideological conflicts of the twentieth century played themselves out on a political and military level, critical changes were happening on a social level that undermined the Marxist scenario. First, the real living standards of the industrial working class kept rising, to the point where many workers or their children were able to join the middle class. Second, the relative size of the working class stopped growing and actually began to decline, particularly in the second half of the twentieth century, when services began to displace manufacturing in what were labeled "postindustrial" economies. Finally, a new group of poor or disadvantaged people emerged below the industrial working class—a heterogeneous mixture of racial and ethnic minorities, recent immigrants, and socially excluded groups, such as women, gays, and the disabled. As a result of these changes, in most industrialized societies, the old working class has become just another domestic interest group, one using the political power of trade unions to protect the hard-won gains of an earlier era. Economic class, moreover, turned out not to be a great banner under which to mobilize populations in advanced industrial countries for political action. The Second International got a rude wake-up call in 1914, when the working classes of Europe abandoned calls for class warfare and lined up behind conservative leaders preaching nationalist slogans, a pattern that persists to the present day. Many Marxists tried to explain this, according to the scholar Ernest Gellner, by what he dubbed the "wrong address theory":

> Just as extreme Shi'ite Muslims hold that Archangel Gabriel made a mistake, delivering the Message to Mohamed when it was intended for Ali, so Marxists basically like to think that the spirit of history or human consciousness made a terrible boob. The awakening message was intended for classes, but by some terrible postal error was delivered to nations.

Gellner went on to argue that religion serves a function similar to nationalism in the contemporary Middle East: it mobilizes people effectively because it has a spiritual and emotional content that class consciousness does not. Just as European nationalism was driven by the shift of Europeans from the countryside to cities in the late nineteenth century, so, too, Islamism is a reaction to the urbanization and displacement taking place in contemporary Middle Eastern societies. Marx's letter will never be delivered to the address marked "class." Marx believed that the middle class, or at least the capital-owning slice of it that he called the bourgeoisie, would always remain a small and privileged minority in modern societies. What happened instead was that the bourgeoisie and the middle class more generally ended up constituting the vast majority of the populations of most advanced countries, posing problems for socialism. From the days of Aristotle, thinkers have believed that stable democracy rests on a broad middle class and that societies with extremes of wealth and poverty are susceptible either to oligarchic domination or populist revolution. When much of the developed world succeeded in creating middle-class societies, the appeal of Marxism vanished. The only places where leftist radicalism persists as a powerful force are in highly unequal areas of the world, such as parts of Latin America, Nepal, and the impoverished regions of eastern India.

What the political scientist Samuel Huntington labeled the "third wave" of global democratization, which began in southern Europe in the 1970s and culminated in the fall of communism in Eastern Europe in 1989, increased the number of electoral democracies around the world from around 45 in 1970 to more than 120 by the late 1990s. Economic growth has led to the emergence of new middle classes in countries such as Brazil, India, Indonesia, South Africa, and Turkey. As the economist Moises Naim has pointed out, these middle classes are relatively well educated, own property, and are technologically connected to the outside world. They are demanding of their governments and mobilize easily as a result of their access to technology. It should not be surprising that the chief instigators of the Arab Spring uprisings were well-educated Tunisians and Egyptians whose expectations for jobs and political participation were stymied by the dictatorships under which they lived.

Middle-class people do not necessarily support democracy in principle: like everyone else, they are self-interested actors who want to protect their property and position. In countries such as China and Thailand, many middle-class people feel threatened by the redistributive demands of the poor and hence have lined up in support of authoritarian governments that protect their class interests. Nor is it the case that democracies necessarily meet the expectations of their own middle classes, and when they do not, the middle classes can become restive.

The Least Bad Alternative?

There is today a broad global consensus about the legitimacy, at least in principle, of liberal democracy. In the words of the economist Amartya Sen, "While democracy is not yet universally practiced, nor indeed uniformly accepted, in the general climate of world opinion, democratic governance has now achieved the status of being taken to be generally right." It is most broadly accepted in countries that have reached a level of material prosperity sufficient to allow a majority of their citizens to think of themselves as middle class, which is why there tends to be a correlation between high levels of—development and stable democracy.

Some societies, such as Iran and Saudi Arabia, reject liberal democracy in favor of a form of Islamic theocracy. Yet these regimes are developmental dead ends, kept alive only because they sit atop vast pools of oil. There was at one time a large Arab exception to the third wave, but the Arab Spring has shown that Arab publics can be mobilized against dictatorship just as readily as those in Eastern Europe and Latin America were. This does not of course mean that the path to a well-functioning democracy will be easy or straightforward in Tunisia, Egypt, or Libya, but it does suggest that the desire for—political freedom and participation is not a cultural peculiarity of Europeans and Americans.

The single most serious challenge to liberal democracy in the world today comes from China, which has combined authoritarian government with a partially marketized economy. China is heir to a long and proud tradition of high-quality bureaucratic government, one that stretches back over two millennia. Its leaders have managed a hugely complex transition from a centralized, Soviet-style planned economy to a dynamic open one and have done so with remarkable competence—more competence, frankly, than U.S. leaders have shown in the management of their own macroeconomic policy recently. Many people currently admire the Chinese system not just for its economic record but also because it can make large, complex decisions quickly, compared with the agonizing policy paralysis that has struck both the United States and Europe in the past few years. Especially since the recent financial crisis, the Chinese themselves have begun touting the "China model" as an alternative to liberal democracy.

This model is unlikely to ever become a serious alternative to liberal democracy in regions outside East Asia, however. In the first place, the model is culturally specific: the Chinese government is built around a long tradition of meritocratic recruitment, civil service examinations, a high emphasis on education, and deference to technocratic authority. Few developing countries can hope to emulate this model; those that have, such as Singapore and South Korea (at least in an earlier period), were already within the Chinese cultural zone. The Chinese themselves are skeptical about whether their model can be exported; the so-called Beijing consensus is a Western invention, not a Chinese one. It is also unclear whether the model can be sustained. Neither export-driven growth nor the top-down approach to decision-making will continue to yield good results forever. The fact that the Chinese government would not permit open discussion of the disastrous high-speed rail accident last summer and could not bring the Railway Ministry responsible for it to heel suggests that there are other time bombs hidden behind the facade of efficient decision-making.

Finally, China faces a great moral vulnerability down the road. The Chinese government does not force its officials to respect the basic dignity of its citizens. Every week, there are new protests about land seizures, environmental violations, or gross corruption on the part of some official. While the country is growing rapidly, these abuses can be swept under the carpet. But rapid growth will not continue forever, and the government will have to pay a price in pent-up anger. The regime no longer has any guiding ideal around which it is organized; it is run by a Communist Party supposedly committed to equality that presides over a society marked by dramatic and growing inequality.

So the stability of the Chinese system can in no way be taken for granted. The Chinese government argues that its citizens are culturally different and will always prefer benevolent, growth-promoting dictatorship to a messy democracy that threatens social stability. But it is unlikely that a spreading middle class will behave all that differently in China from the way it has behaved in other parts of the world. Other authoritarian regimes may be trying to emulate China's success, but there is little chance that much of the world will look like today's China 50 years down the road.

Democracy's Future

There is a broad correlation among economic growth, social change, and the hegemony of liberal democratic ideology in the world today. And at the moment, no plausible rival ideology looms. But some very troubling economic and social trends, if they continue, will both threaten the stability of contemporary liberal democracies and dethrone democratic ideology as it is now understood. The sociologist Barrington Moore once flatly asserted, "No bourgeois, no democracy." The Marxists didn't get their communist Utopia because mature capitalism generated middle-class societies, not working-class ones. But what if the further development of technology and globalization undermines the middle class and makes it impossible for more than a minority of citizens in an advanced society to achieve middle-class status?

There are already abundant signs that such a phase of development has begun. Median incomes in the United States have been stagnating in real terms since the 1970s. The economic impact of this stagnation has been softened to some extent by the fact that most U.S. households have shifted to two income earners in the past generation. Moreover, as the economist Raghuram Rajan has persuasively argued, since Americans are reluctant to engage in straightforward redistribution, the United States has instead attempted a highly dangerous and inefficient form of redistribution over the past generation by subsidizing mortgages for low-income households. This trend, facilitated by a flood of liquidity pouring in from China and other countries, gave many ordinary Americans the illusion that their standards of living were rising steadily during the past decade. In this respect, the bursting of the housing bubble in 2008–9 was nothing more than a cruel reversion to the mean. Americans may today benefit from cheap cell phones, inexpensive clothing, and Facebook, but they increasingly cannot afford their own homes, or health insurance, or comfortable pensions when they retire.

A more troubling phenomenon, identified by the venture capitalist Peter Thiel and the economist Tyler Cowen, is that the benefits of the most recent waves of technological innovation have accrued disproportionately to the most talented and well-educated members of society. This phenomenon helped cause the massive growth of inequality in the United States over the past generation. In 1974, the top one percent of families took home nine percent of GDP; by 2007, that share had increased to 23.5 percent.

Trade and tax policies may have accelerated this trend, but the real villain here is technology. In earlier phases of industrialization—the ages of textiles, coal, steel, and the internal combustion engine—the benefits of technological changes almost always flowed down in significant ways to the rest of society in terms of employment. But this is not a law of nature. We are today living in what the scholar Shoshana Zuboff has labeled "the age of the smart machine," in which technology is increasingly able to substitute for more and higher human functions. Every great advance for Silicon Valley likely means a loss of low-skill jobs elsewhere in the economy, a trend that is unlikely to end anytime soon. Inequality has always existed, as a result of natural differences in talent and character. But today's technological world vastly magnifies those differences. In a nineteenth-century agrarian society, people with strong math skills did not have that many opportunities to capitalize on their talent. Today,

they can become financial wizards or software engineers and take home ever-larger proportions of the national wealth.

The other factor undermining middle-class incomes in developed countries is globalization. With the lowering of transportation and communications costs and the entry into the global work force of hundreds of millions of new workers in developing countries, the kind of work done by the old middle class in the developed world can now be performed much more cheaply elsewhere. Under an economic model that prioritizes the maximization of aggregate income, it is inevitable that jobs will be outsourced.

Smarter ideas and policies could have contained the damage. Germany has succeeded in protecting a significant part of its manufacturing base and industrial labor force even as its companies have remained globally competitive. The United States and the United Kingdom, on the other hand, happily embraced the transition to the postindustrial service economy. Free trade became less a theory than an ideology: when members of the U.S. Congress tried to retaliate with trade sanctions against China for keeping its currency undervalued, they were indignantly charged with protectionism, as if the playing field were already level. There was a lot of happy talk about the wonders of the knowledge economy, and how dirty, dangerous manufacturing jobs would inevitably be replaced by highly educated workers doing creative and interesting things. This was a gauzy veil placed over the hard facts of deindustrialization. It overlooked the fact that the benefits of the new order accrued disproportionately to a very small number of people in finance and high technology, interests that dominated the media and the general political conversation.

The Absent Left

One of the most puzzling features of the world in the aftermath of the financial crisis is that so far, populism has taken primarily a right-wing form, not a left-wing one.

In the United States, for example, although the Tea Party is anti-elitist in its rhetoric, its members vote for conservative politicians who serve the interests of precisely those financiers and corporate elites they claim to despise. There are many explanations for this phenomenon. They include a deeply embedded belief in equality of opportunity rather than equality of outcome and the fact that cultural issues, such as abortion and gun rights, crosscut economic ones.

But the deeper reason a broad-based populist left has failed to materialize is an intellectual one. It has been several decades since anyone on the left has been able to articulate, first, a coherent analysis of what happens to the structure of advanced societies as they undergo economic change and, second, a realistic agenda that has any hope of protecting a middle-class society.

The main trends in left-wing thought in the last two generations have been, frankly, disastrous as either conceptual frameworks or tools for mobilization. Marxism died many years ago, and the few old believers still around are ready for nursing homes. The academic left replaced it with postmodernism, multiculturalism, feminism, critical theory, and a host of other fragmented intellectual trends that are more cultural than economic in focus. Postmodernism begins with a denial of the possibility of any master narrative of history or society, undercutting its own authority as a voice for the majority of citizens who feel betrayed by their elites. Multiculturalism validates the victimhood of virtually every out-group. It is impossible to generate a mass progressive movement on the basis of such a motley coalition: most of the working- and lower-middle-class citizens victimized by the system are culturally conservative and would be embarrassed to be seen in the presence of allies like this.

Whatever the theoretical justifications underlying the left's agenda, its biggest problem is a lack of credibility. Over the past two generations, the mainstream left has followed a social democratic program that centers on the state provision of a variety of services, such as pensions, health care, and education. That model is now exhausted: welfare states have become big, bureaucratic, and inflexible; they are often captured by the very organizations that administer them, through public-sector unions; and, most important, they are fiscally unsustainable given the aging of populations virtually everywhere in the developed world. Thus, when existing social democratic parties come to power, they no longer aspire to be more than custodians of a welfare state that was created decades ago; none has a new, exciting agenda around which to rally the masses.

An Ideology of the Future

Imagine, for a moment, an obscure scribbler today in a garret somewhere trying to outline an ideology of the future that could provide a realistic path toward a world with healthy middle-class societies and robust democracies. What would that ideology look like?

It would have to have at least two components, political and economic. Politically, the new ideology would need to reassert the supremacy of democratic politics over economics and legitimate a new government as an expression of the public interest. But the agenda it put forward to protect middle-class life could not simply rely on the existing mechanisms of the welfare state. The ideology would need to somehow redesign the public sector, freeing it from its dependence on existing stakeholders and using new, technology-empowered approaches to delivering services. It would have to argue forth-rightly for more redistribution and present a realistic route to ending interest groups' domination of politics.

Economically, the ideology could not begin with a denunciation of capitalism as such, as if old-fashioned socialism were still a viable alternative. It is more the variety of capitalism that is at stake and the degree to which governments should help societies adjust to change. Globalization need

be seen not as an inexorable fact of life but rather as a challenge and an opportunity that must be carefully controlled politically. The new ideology would not see markets as an end in themselves; instead, it would value global trade and investment to the extent that they contributed to a flourishing middle class, not just to greater aggregate national wealth.

It is not possible to get to that point, however, without providing a serious and sustained critique of much of the edifice of modern neoclassical economics, beginning with fundamental assumptions such as the sovereignty of individual preferences and that aggregate income is an accurate measure of national well-being. This critique would have to note that people's incomes do not necessarily represent their true contributions to society. It would have to go further, however, and recognize that even if labor markets were efficient, the natural distribution of talents is not necessarily fair and that individuals are not sovereign entities but beings heavily shaped by their surrounding societies.

Most of these ideas have been around in bits and pieces for some time; the scribbler would have to put them into a coherent package. He or she would also have to avoid the "wrong address" problem. The critique of globalization, that is, would have to be tied to nationalism as a strategy for mobilization in a way that defined national interest in a more sophisticated way than, for example, the "Buy American" campaigns of unions in the United States. The product would be a synthesis of ideas from both the left and the right, detached from the agenda of the marginalized groups that constitute the existing progressive movement. The ideology would be populist; the message would begin with a critique of the elites that allowed the benefit of the many to be sacrificed to that of the few and a critique of the money politics, especially in Washington, that overwhelmingly benefits the wealthy.

The dangers inherent in such a movement are obvious: a pullback by the United States, in particular, from its advocacy of a more open global system could set off protectionist responses elsewhere. In many respects, the Reagan-Thatcher revolution succeeded just as its proponents hoped, bringing about an increasingly competitive, globalized, friction-free world. Along the way, it generated tremendous wealth and created rising middle classes all over the developing world, and the spread of democracy in their wake. It is possible that the developed world is on the cusp of a series of technological breakthroughs that will not only increase productivity but also provide meaningful employment to large numbers of middle-class people.

But that is more a matter of faith than a reflection of the empirical reality of the last 30 years, which points in the opposite direction. Indeed, there are a lot of reasons to think that inequality will continue to worsen. The current concentration of wealth in the United States has already become self-reinforcing: as the economist Simon Johnson has argued, the financial sector has used its lobbying clout to avoid more onerous forms of regulation. Schools for the well-off are better than ever; those for everyone else continue to deteriorate. Elites in all societies use their superior access to the political system to protect their interests, absent a countervailing democratic mobilization to rectify the situation. American elites are no exception to the rule.

That mobilization will not happen, however, as long as the middle classes of the developed world remain enthralled by the narrative of the past generation: that their interests will be best served by ever-freer markets and smaller states. The alternative narrative is out there, waiting to be born.

Source

Fukuyama, Francis. "The future of history: can liberal democracy survive the decline of the middle class?" *Foreign Affairs* 91.1 (2012). *General Reference Center GOLD*. Web. 25 Jan. 2012.

Critical Thinking

1. Is the Chinese model of economic development better than liberal democracy?

2. In a hyper-competitive global economy, can the middle class survive?

3. Is it possible that most of the population be driven to the lowest common denominator?

FRANCIS FUKUYAMA is a Senior Fellow at the Center on Democracy, Development, and the Rule of Law at Stanford University and the author, most recently, of *The Origins of Political Order: From Prehuman Times to the French Revolution*.

Article 40

The Crisis You Don't Know

Forget Austerity, sovereign debt and the euro. The roots of Europe's problems are much deeper.

ADAM DAVIDSON

One great way to start a bar fight during an American Economic Association conference is to claim that the U.S. economy is preferable to Europe's. Someone will undoubtedly start quarreling about how G.D.P. per capita doesn't measure a person's happiness. Someone else may point out that if you look at income inequality and entitlements, the average European is doing much better.

But G.D.P. per capita (an insufficient indicator, but one most economists use) in the U.S. is nearly 50 percent higher than it is in Europe. Even Europe's best-performing large country, Germany, is about 20 percent poorer than the U.S. on a per-person basis (and both countries have roughly 15 percent of their populations living below the poverty line). While Norway and Sweden are richer than the U.S., on average, they are more comparable to wealthy American microeconomies like Washington, D.C., or parts of Connecticut—both of which are actually considerably wealthier. A reporter in Greece once complained after I compared her country to Mississippi, America's poorest state. She's right: the comparison isn't fair. The average Mississippian is richer than the average Greek.

Europe is undergoing not one but two simultaneous economic crises. The first is a rapid, obvious one—all about sovereign debt, a collapsing currency and austerity measures—that we hear about all the time. The second is insidious but more important. After decades of trying, Europe as a whole still can't quite figure out how to be flexible enough to compete in the global economy.

The story of how Europe lost its flexibility can be told in three stages. First came rapid growth that economists called "convergence." With a lot of help from the U.S., Europe developed massive industrial capacity in the postwar years. Many of Western Europe's economies grew so fast that governments could easily afford health and unemployment insurance and other benefits that, by U.S. standards, were remarkably generous. Most observers expected that its wealth would soon "converge" upon that of the U.S.

But the European economy did not recover from the worldwide oil shock of 1973 nearly as quickly as its American counterpart. For more than 25 years (phase two), as its population aged, Europe's economy grew more slowly than the United States'. Its active capitals belied bloated businesses that were losing contracts to U.S. competitors or growing suburban ghettos filled with a permanently unemployed underclass.

Even its major successes—like Germany's impressive machine-tool and automotive-industrial sectors—were refinements of old ways of making money rather than innovations in new industries. Western Europe played a remarkably small role in the computer and Internet revolutions. (On the other hand, Estonia, with less than two million people, gave the world Skype.) When the economic forecasts were written during Europe's doldrums, the Continent looked destined to become a decrepit old-age home with too few young people around to pay the bills.

Enter phase three: what might be called the Principled Compromise. Increasingly since the mid-1990s, European leaders have been trying to figure out how to keep up with this new globalized digital economy. To compete with the U.S., China, India and Brazil, Europe focused more intently on broadening its internal market. It's easier for businesses to stay competitive when there are a few hundred million potential customers using the same currency and not requiring customs forms.

To many American eyes, however, Europe's creation of a common market and currency was only half the battle—and probably the less important half. It's a core view of U.S. business that success requires a degree of destruction. If workers can't be fired, companies can't drop unproductive businesses and invest in more promising new ones. If workers know they'll get generous government benefits no matter what, so the theory goes, they'll get lazy.

But just as the U.S. was dismantling much of its welfare system—replacing it with the welfare-to-work reforms of the mid-1990s—Europe was (somewhat nobly) trying to show that an economy can be humane *and* competitive. In 1994, Denmark modernized a system, which came to be known as "flexicurity," that offered American-style flexibility (layoffs, transitions into new lines of business) coupled with traditional European security. Laid-off workers were offered generous benefits, like 90 percent of their last salary for two years and opportunities to be retrained.

And it worked incredibly well. After Denmark's unemployment rate sank to among the lowest in the world, the flexicurity model spread throughout Europe. It has been successfully implemented, in locally appropriate ways, in Norway, Sweden and Finland. But in other countries—like Germany, France and Spain—similar reforms faced stiff resistance from workers who preferred the old way. Several countries applied the measures in a two-tier system: people who already had jobs were protected by pretty much the same old rules, while the unemployed—who were often younger—were offered less secure work at lower pay. Greek unions insisted on so much security and so little flexibility that now the country has neither. Flexibility has done little to help Italy, which remains effectively two countries. There is a rich nation in the north where workers earn great salaries in highly productive and competitive industries; many people south of Rome are living in a broken, developing economy that's considerably poorer than Greece.

Many now believe that Europe's decision to create a common currency ended up pushing much of the Continent further behind. Greece, Italy, Spain, Ireland and Portugal would arguably be much better off if they could simply devalue their old currencies and sell exports at a relative discount. Instead, they're stuck with a euro whose value is largely based on their more successful neighbors. The U.S. is in no position to gloat, but our basic mechanisms of competitiveness are still in place.

We'll grow again. We just need to figure out how to distribute the spoils. And Europe, we once thought, was supposed to teach us how to do this.

European leaders like to mock the U.S. for its inequality and lack of social safety net. Though, for now, it looks as if Europe is headed for a two-tier society without any plan for improving the lot of the lower tier. How can Brussels excite a generation of ambitious young people—the ones who will determine Europe's future success—when too many of them are offered low-wage, short-term work in stagnant industries to pay for the far more generous benefits their elders receive? How can Europe compete if its youth experience the flexibility while the old get the security?

Critical Thinking

1. Why is Europe becoming less competitive?

2. What is happening to the population of the countries of Europe?

3. Why is the average European not as wealthy as the average American?

ADAM DAVIDSON is a founder of NPR's "Planet Money," a podcast, blog and radio series heard on *Morning Edition, All Things Considered,* and *This American Life.*

Finding a Job in the 21st Century

Seek training, be flexible, and get hired in the fast-moving working world of the future.

JOHN A. CHALLENGER

The current recession, expected to be the worst economic crisis since the Great Depression, will surely put to rest those old concerns about looming labor shortages, right? Probably not. In fact, immigration, globalization, outsourcing, and other trends affecting employment and the workplace will evolve over the next five, 10, and 20 years to change the workplace completely, and well-trained and flexible workers will be at a premium.

More than 5 million layoffs have been announced in the United States since the beginning of 2008. Economists are projecting that U.S. unemployment may top out at 10.5% or over 11% by the middle of 2010.

At Challenger, Gray & Christmas, we look at official unemployment, but we also track job-cut announcements. These provide an indication of where the job market is going in the short term.

We observed in April that the rate of layoffs, while still high, was slowing. The global economy was not entering a roaring recovery, but we were hearing faint signals that the worst of the worst was over. On the one hand, manufacturing jobs in the United States continued to vanish. On the other hand, the layoff rate in the financial sector seemed to have stabilized.

At our firm, we talk to human-resources people around the country on a casual, anecdotal basis; the people we're speaking with are taking whatever measures they can to avoid making further layoffs. They don't want to be short-staffed in the event of a turnaround. The current cycle will surely go down in history as the worst in most people's memory. Fortunately, the future of work looks completely different.

Key Piece of Advice for Job Seekers

As unemployment continues to rise, more people are seeking help to improve their employability. My key piece of advice for job seekers is to get a fast start. Don't let your résumé gather dust. If you've been laid off, use contacts as quickly as possible to uncover new positions and opportunities.

The second piece of advice I offer is to consider changing industries. Look outside your normal boundaries, but look within your job function. You'll want to pursue jobs that correspond to your core competency and that lets you do what you do best. Your skills are your best asset; they're what you're selling. Be ready to make the potential customer list for those skills as long as possible. What many people don't realize is the variety of jobs in different fields that may be open in a single industry, requiring people with all sorts of talents and abilities.

Let me give an example: Health care is commonly touted as an industry forever in need of workers. Conversely, the personal computer (PC) market in the United States has been weak of late. Our firm counted layoffs in the computer industry up 75% in 2008 from the year before, and analysts expect PC sales to fall an additional 10% by the end of 2009.

For a qualified IT worker or computer programmer seeking employment, one strategy is to wait for the global PC market to recover. Another strategy is to sell your technical skills to a growing industry like health care.

Most of us assume that growth in health care translates into more competition among employers to find qualified nurses and doctors. Surely, the doctor and nurse shortage will continue and favor qualified candidates for those jobs in the future. But in the years ahead, as baby boomers and the United States spend more money on medical care, the industry will need more computer scientists and database technicians to streamline operations and create new systems.

The coming innovation leap that will sweep the health-care field will extend well beyond simply digitizing medical records. If the industry is to meet rising demands for service from an aging population and contain costs, it will become

U.S. Employment Ups and Downs, 2006–2016

The Five Largest Employment increases

Job	Employees, 2006	Employees, 2016	Percentage Change
Network Systems and Data Communications Analyst	262,000	402,000	53.4%
Personal and Home Care Aide	767,000	1.16 million	50.6%
Home Health Aide	787,000	1.17 million	48.7%
Computer Software Engineer	507,000	733,000	44.6%
Veterinary Technologist/Technician	71,000	100,000	41.0%

The Five Largest Employment Declines

Job	Employees, 2006	Employees, 2016	Percentage Change
Photographic Processing Machine Operator	49,000	25,000	− 49.8%
File Clerk	234,000	137,000	− 41.3%
Sewing Machine Operator	233,000	170,000	− 27.2%
Electrical and Electronic Equipment Assembler	213,000	156,000	− 26.8%
Computer Operator	130,000	98,000	− 24.7%

Source: "Employment Projections: 2006–2016." U.S. Bureau of Labor Statistics. Website, www.bls.gov

much more reliant on information technology. The industry will need to reach and train qualified workers wherever they may be through e-learning technologies. Health-care providers will want to automate the delivery of health care as much as possible; they'll want to detect symptoms and diagnose patients remotely through advanced sensing technologies.

This is only one example among many. The health-care industry also needs therapists of all types, business managers, human resource professionals, and even journalists and communications workers to track new developments and medical breakthroughs and publicize good work or medical research to the public (and to potential hospital donors). The world still needs journalists, but the information gathering and refinement process that is journalism will, more and more, happen at communications offices or niche-specific publications as opposed to regional or local newspapers. Finding opportunity in the future may mean sacrificing the dream of working for a particular cherished employer or even for a particular type of company. Many industrial titans of the twentieth century won't exist five years from now. That doesn't mean skills won't still be in demand.

The Globalized Workforce

Another question I'm asked frequently is, where are the jobs *going?* Many American workers fret about their jobs moving overseas to China and India. Outsourcing and even immigration have become convenient punching bags for pundits looking to blame someone or something for rising unemployment. But the argument that we can protect jobs by "keeping them at home" or "not hiring immigrant labor" doesn't reflect the realities of globalization or labor in the twenty-first century.

The global labor market is not a zero-sum game. If U.S. firms are going to reach new customers in China and India—and they will have to in order to grow and be relevant in the twentyfirst century—then they will have to hire workers in those countries. More people in these countries finding work will create bigger markets for U.S. goods. China will continue to build factories and operations in order to put its large population to work; India will grow as a mathematics and engineering center. In the Philippines, a great accounting and health-care center exists; in South Korea, a manufacturing base is flourishing and will continue to do so.

All of these countries will experience employment growth, and yes, some of the growth will be from American firms hiring in those countries partly to better secure access to the Chinese and Indian consumers. There's no getting around it: U.S. companies need to be able to compete in these international markets if they are to expand in the United States.

However, companies from around the world will also have plenty of reasons to hire in the United States, which has a highly skilled labor force and the most diverse population of any country. The United States is uniquely suited to reach out to a global population.

The strength of the U.S. economy lies in its ability to capture global growth and to collaborate with economies around the planet. In the years ahead, the way that growth occurs will be very different from the past. From the middle of the twentieth century onward, U.S. companies began expanding aggressively into other countries; the pursuit of global growth translated into large U.S. firms cajoling foreign officials for special treatment or special contracts to set up shop. For U.S. employees overseas, a corporate expansion meant higher salaries and more money to live apart from the local community. I call this the colonial corporate expansion model.

IBM is one of the first big companies to transition out of that mode of overseas expansion and into a more community-focused strategy. In February 2009, IBM gave 4,000 laid-off workers the opportunity to move to other countries where the company had positions open (India and Brazil, for example) through a program called Project Match. IBM was willing to pay for the move and help with visa procurement. The catch? The company told the employees that they would be paid local wages; the employees would live among the population.

Naturally, not every IBMer took to the idea. As originally reported in *Information Week,* one employee group called the Alliance@IBM was furious, complaining that the company was asking employees to "offshore themselves." They had a point; wages in India even for highly skilled IT workers are often a quarter of what they are in the United States.

But many of the employees—those with fewer commitments, who didn't have to worry about paying down a mortgage because they were young and just starting out, or who were looking to do something other than play shuffleboard in retirement—were intrigued by the idea and took the company up on the offer. Arrangements like Project Match may be a wave of the future, exciting and increasingly *de rigueur.* It reminds me of something I heard Larry Summers remark at a Harvard alumni event not long ago. When he was a student, he said, the final requirement to graduate was to swim a lap around the pool. In the future, it will be having spent a semester overseas.

Mobility, Flexibility, and the Workforce of the Future

IBM's Perfect Match program showcases one of the biggest trends to affect the future of work: increased mobility and flexibility. The information-technology revolution, which began with widespread adoption of PCs in the workplace in the 1980s, has changed virtually every aspect of doing business. In the next decade, that trend will accelerate and obliterate many long-held notions of work.

For many, the office of the future will not be an office at all. The mobile workforce will carry their office in their pocket; they'll work when it's most convenient for them or for the client. The U.S. Bureau of Labor Statistics reports that the number of Americans who worked from home or remotely at least one day per month for their employer rose from 12.4 million in 2006 to 17.2 million in 2008. (The trend may slow slightly in 2009.) Telecommuting is an easy way for employers facing tight budgets to give employees something that more and more of them say they want: time. Enhanced mobile flexibility will be a boon to the employers that take advantage of it as well. This will better enable smart companies to place employees where they can be most useful—namely, where customers and clients are located.

Contrary to a lot of popular opinion, face time is still important, but it may be less important within companies than between companies and customers.

Imagine, for instance, a customer walking into a car dealership and being greeted not by a salesperson but by an actual car designer, available to answer any and every technical query a consumer might have, or even design specifications on the spot (for a premium, of course). Many Ferrari buyers already get something like this royal treatment when they buy a new car directly from the factory in Maranello, Italy. For about $3.1 million, wealthy car enthusiasts can, in essence, design their own F430, 612 Scaglietti, or Enzo. What does the famously hobbled U.S. car industry look like when Chevrolet buyers can have the same personalized car-buying experience as someone buying a Ferrari Enzo?

Getting to that future from where we are now doesn't require a tremendous amount of technical IT innovation. What's needed is a little imagination and, again, flexibility. The twenty-somethings will lead this change. Today's younger workers will be the ones who help U.S. companies succeed abroad in the new era of globalization and mobility.

Hopefully, we'll continue to see more examples of the Project Match phenomenon playing with more people from more countries, coming to the United States to work as elements of the economy and to take advantage of U.S. educational opportunities. America's ability to attract these people is one of its key assets.

The U.S. economy will need these highly skilled workers desperately, a fact that underscores why immigration reform is so vital to the future of U.S. business. If the United States cannot remain an attractive destination for talented and well-trained workers from around the world, the country won't grow economically as it did in the past. Also, the U.S. government must find ways to support lifelong education. As new fields grow, education must become a permanent part of every worker's career.

Immigration reform and lifelong learning are critical if the United States is to overcome the looming talent shortage. In the years ahead, it will pay dividends not just economically, but also in terms of more-effective foreign policy.

The more people from more places who feel they have a connection to America—either because someone they know has gone to America on a work or student visa or because they had a positive experience with a U.S. worker locally—the more effective the U.S. government will be in marketing its policies abroad. My hope is that people from around the world still want to take part in the U.S. educational experience. But American educational institutions will also expand as global brands with campuses in China, India, Europe, Africa, and Latin America.

The opportunities of the future will go to the best-trained, most-flexible candidates, and they will be spread globally. But opportunity exists and will increase; of that you can be certain.

Critical Thinking

1. How is the job market different in the 21st century from the 20th? century?
2. Why is it important to keep one's skills up to date?
3. Will immigration from one country to another in search of work become more common in the 21st century?

JOHN A. CHALLENGER, chief executive officer of Challenger, Gray & Christmas, is one of the most quoted labor and employment experts in America. He's become a regular fixture on CNN, CBS, and a host of other networks and is a featured speaker at WorldFuture 2009, the annual conference of the World Future Society. Website www.challengergray.com.

Originally published in the September/October 2009, vol. 43, no.5, pp. 29–33 issue of *The Futurist*. Copyright © No. 5 by World Future Society, 7910 Woodmont Avenue, Suite 450, Bethesda, MD 20814. Telephone: 301/656-8274; Fax: 301/951-0394; www.wfs.org. Used with permission from the World Future Society.

Test-Your-Knowledge Form

We encourage you to photocopy and use this page as a tool to assess how the articles in *Annual Editions* expand on the information in your textbook. By reflecting on the articles you will gain enhanced text information. You can also access this useful form on a product's book support website at www.mhhe.com/cls

NAME: DATE:

TITLE AND NUMBER OF ARTICLE:

BRIEFLY STATE THE MAIN IDEA OF THIS ARTICLE:

LIST THREE IMPORTANT FACTS THAT THE AUTHOR USES TO SUPPORT THE MAIN IDEA:

WHAT INFORMATION OR IDEAS DISCUSSED IN THIS ARTICLE ARE ALSO DISCUSSED IN YOUR TEXTBOOK OR OTHER READINGS THAT YOU HAVE DONE? LIST THE TEXTBOOK CHAPTERS AND PAGE NUMBERS:

LIST ANY EXAMPLES OF BIAS OR FAULTY REASONING THAT YOU FOUND IN THE ARTICLE:

LIST ANY NEW TERMS/CONCEPTS THAT WERE DISCUSSED IN THE ARTICLE, AND WRITE A SHORT DEFINITION:

NOTES

NOTES

NOTES

NOTES

NOTES

NOTES

NOTES

NOTES